Keeping Warm

in

Hard Times

The Art of Saving Money on Home Heating Costs

William Scott Anderson

The Reader's Responsibility

This book will explain how to do many things yourself or that you can hire someone to do for you. However, if this book states how to wire a switch, reading it does not make you an electrician. As the reader, it is your responsibility to determine if you have the skills and knowledge necessary to perform the projects described.

Dedication

This book is dedicated to the joy of my life, my beautiful wife Karin, who is my sunshine that even if the sun doesn't shine, keeps my heart warm in hard times. I love you now and forever.

Table of Contents

Chapter 1

Heat is not a Luxury

My Mother-in-law is from Germany and as a child lived through the Second World War and experienced starvation and cold. Of the two, she states that being cold was worse than being hungry. To those of us who have grown up in a world where heat is taken for granted, preferring warmth over food is probably inconceivable, but then most of us have never experienced what she did. If we were, we would probably come to agree with my Mother-in-law; for it takes far less time to die of hypothermia then it does to starve.

In a cold climate like here in Wisconsin in the wintertime, if the heat is turned off, the temperature inside a home drops rapidly. For a typical home on a cold winter day, the temperature can easily fall ten degrees or more each hour. In just a few hours, it can drop to the outside temperature. In winter here, when a home furnace fails and needs repair, the call is termed an "emergency call" and the heating service company gives the call first priority. Service people are called off other jobs and rush to fix the broken furnace as quickly as possible. At night and weekends, service personnel are called on pagers or cell phones for these jobs. They have to respond quickly to restore the heat before the pipes freeze and do extensive damage. For in a cold winter without heat, it only takes a few hours to turn a cozy home into an uninhabitable freezer. Having heat in a cold climate is not the same as having cable TV, losing your cable is irritating; losing your heat is losing your home. Heat here is not an option, it is a necessity and losing it can endanger your life and your family's.

There is more to keeping the heat on then just remembering to pay the gas company and keeping your furnace in good repair. For example, a car going off the road can clip an electric pole, resulting in a local power outage. Weather can also cause wide spread outages as well. Ice storms can cause power outages over large areas that can last for days and sometimes even weeks. I still remember the ice storm we had here in 1976; a family we knew had to move in with us for about a week until their power was restored. The possibility of various events of one sort or another disrupting your electric power or your fuel supply highlights the wisdom of having a backup heating method. The fear of ice storms causing power outages, sells more wood stoves here than the slickest salesmen. The Ice storm of 76' we had here and the oil embargo in the 70's saw a rush of people installing wood stoves, for a time it seemed that nearly every one had one or was getting one. Homeowners who had never burned wood before and had little or no knowledge of how to do what they were trying to do, hastily installed Wood stoves. Many of the installations were unsafe and caused quite a number of house fires. As a result of this debacle, insurance companies came to view wood stoves as major fire risks and homeowners often found their home insurance rates rose sharply if their insurance company discovered that they had one, or they were given the choice of removing the wood stove or losing their insurance. Due to this perceived insurance problem and risk of fire, a new type of wood heating system was created, the outdoor boiler, which today is a large part of the market and yet probably never would have come to be otherwise. Viewed as fire and insurance safe, many see the oddly conceived outdoor boiler as the best choice, despite having a number of large drawbacks. This shows the importance of considering insurance costs and fire risks early on in the selection process so that these factors can be weighed realistically against the conveniences and inconveniences associated with using different heating options.

Many of the homeowners here that installed wood stoves in the late 70's, no longer have them today for another surprising reason. Most people installed wood stoves without having a source of firewood. Once they burned up what little wood they had laying around or could scrounge, they found the cost of buying firewood was more expensive than simply paying the gas bill. You need to consider the cost of the fuel you plan on using and if it is even available in your area.

In reading this book, you will need to consider your situation and whether a particular heating method will, or will not, work for you. Such as how cold are your winters, local fuel availability and costs, how much time and effort you are willing to devote to heating your house, what would be involved in changing or adding a second heating system and how much you can afford to spend on doing so.

Speaking of how much you can afford to spend, the oil embargo also created a temporary surge in another type of heating system; solar heating. The large tax credits at the time, 50% federal plus state tax credits like Wisconsin's 25% resulted in homeowners only having to pay for 25% of the cost of the solar heating system. The surge here in solar systems was unbelievable; it went from nothing, to several in every neighborhood. Contractors working for the solar companies installed nearly all the systems, so most were correctly installed. The performance of these solar systems however for the most part was dismal. I worked for a time as a repairman on those solar systems, and while many of their owners probably still think they worked great, I can tell you that most really did not provide much heat and few were cost effective. Nearly all the solar systems had repair and operating costs that exceeding the cost of the energy they saved. The old 70's solar systems were not ready for use in a northern climate, while they probably worked better down south. Today, however, the available solar systems are much better in many ways and some now work well in cold climates far surpassing the performance of the old 70's solar systems.

The 1970s were a turning point for energy use and has effected the development of what we have today. Our more recent experience of high oil prices and their possible return in the near future has caused many to look once again for alternates for keeping warm, causing us to reenact some of the events of the 70's. The difference this time, aside from the hopeful absence of disco music, is that the energy shortage then was caused by the oil embargo, a political action, while today the reason for high prices is greed and demand exceeding supply. The world economy grew to the point that it was consuming oil as fast as it could be pumped, which resulted in the suppliers being able to raise prices, which in turn opened the door for speculation in oil prices. While speculators added to the high cost of oil, they did not create it, for one cannot speculate on a surging increase in the cost of dirt. Speculation only works for things that are at least perceived to be in short supply and in the case of oil, even large oil companies were willing to pay very high prices for oil, which they only would have done if they knew it was in short supply. The reason for this is that the earth is only so large and they have been looking for oil for a long time. All of the "elephants", the very large fields of oil were found and drilled long ago. The search for oil has pushed into more and more remote areas and deeper underground and farther out into deep water in the oceans. If there were any huge amounts of cheap easy to drill oil out there, we would already be using it.

What happened with the high oil prices in 2008 was that the high cost of energy slowed the economy, which in turn caused a debit collapse, because borrowing depends on more money being available in the future. That the borrower will be able to continue to earn money over time in the future at a higher rate than the payments on the sum he borrowed in the past. If the average earnings shrink, then increasing numbers of borrowers find their dept payments over taking their incomes. Then as increasing numbers of borrowers are unable to make their payments, banks suffer losses, the number of foreclosed homes increases which brings down home prices, which in turn causes bigger bank losses. This increases the down turn and slows the economy more as there is less money available for spending on other things. It is a positive feed back loop, this collapse of the huge dept bubble that so much of the world financial system has been built on. This down turn will feed on itself for a time resulting in a reduction in the amount oil consumed by the world economy, which means we have reductions in the price of oil. The drop in oil price is only due to the drop in demand; it is not due to an increase in supply. What this means is that when, or rather if, the world economy recovers and oil demand increases, oil prices will rise once again. I believed that we have already passed the oil peak, that we have used half of the oil that exists on earth and that we saw the maximum peak of oil production in the middle of 2008. Since all the big easy oil has already been drilled, the oil of tomorrow will be harder to get and there will be less of it, in the future the global maxim amount we can pump in a month will shrink. The oil situation is like being in a room with a ceiling, which is the maximum rate at which we can pump oil, in 2008 our economy hit the ceiling and bounced back down toward the floor. The problem is that the ceiling is now slowly moving down. If our global economy goes up in the future, it will hit the ceiling at a lower level than it did before, and bounce back downward again. As the ceiling continues to move downward and oil reserves shrink, the maximum size that the future world economy can have, will shrink over time. This means that while oil prices may fall at times, the overall trend is upward. The only way for oil prices to stay low is for the world oil consumption to stay below the falling ceiling of supply. Eventually however the ceiling will drop low enough to squeeze even a world economy in a deep recession/depression. This would be a particularly bad economic situation with sky-high heating costs in the midst of a global depression. Many people could very well end up repeating the history my mother-in-law lived through. It would be wise to take practical steps now to reduce your heating costs while you can afford to, so that your energy costs will be much smaller in the future than they would be otherwise. That way if heating costs go through the roof in future, you should still be able to afford to heat your home. There is also the wisdom of having a backup heating system for an emergency for when your normal heating system is not useable due to power outage or other problems. There are many options in heating your home, making wise choices now could save you a lot of money later, and keep you warm in a time of cold and uncertainty.

Chapter 2

The Magic Furnace

The logic is simple, how would you like a new furnace that will cut your fuel bills in half? In addition, this new furnace lasts forever and never needs any maintenance or fuel. Sounds too good to be true, but it is very true. However, most people do not want to bother with it, this "miracle furnace" is insulation. For if, you were to double your home's overall insulation and cut your heat loss in half, your existing furnace would only need to run half as much and your fuel use would be cut in half. Now I probably had your interest until I said insulation, once you say insulation, people's eyes glaze over with disinterest. New over priced furnaces with lots of expensive parts that will need constant servicing, are "sexy" and exciting, while insulation is boring. Practical things that really work are often considered boring, but they are the real money savers.

Another "boring" item is your thermostat. Back in the 70's the rage was the digital setback thermostats that automatically lowered the heat setting in your house at night. These then technological wonders sold for upwards of two hundred dollars and that is in 70's dollars in the middle of an energy crisis. The reason people were willing to shell out so much money for a setback thermostat was because they were worth it. That and they were "new" and exciting. Lately I have seen some for less than thirty dollars at the hardware store so setback thermostats are no longer expensive. Today if you do not have a setback thermostat, you might as well open the windows and let the winter wind blow through, since you would have to be someone unfazed by high fuel bills. At a cost of less than thirty dollars, the thermostat could in theory save enough money in the winter to pay for itself in as little as one month. The percentage of savings is in the range of 5-15%, about a savings of 1% for each degree of setback for eight hours used daily. So dropping the temperature at night 10 degrees from 68 to 58 for eight hours would result in a 10% savings. Personally, I do not believe in going lower than 65 at night if you have infants, or very young children or the very elderly. The more expensive setback thermostats can have a number of different temperature settings for each day. You can set the temperature lower at night when you are sleeping, and during the day when you are gone at work, increasing your savings even more. However, setback thermostats do not work well on systems that are slow to heat up like some boiler systems or radiant floor heat in concrete that has a large thermal mass, since it would take too long to warm the house up again.

Another boring key item that works particularly well with a setback thermostat is to put a heavy sleeping bag on each bed. For here in Wisconsin, I bought sleeping bags rated for zero degrees, that in theory you could sleep comfortably outdoors in zero degree temperatures. A cheap synthetic rectangular sleeping bag that can be zipped open and laid flat, works well as a blanket on a queen size bed or can hang like a large spread on a twin bed. We like them so well in our house that we would not do without them. We keep them on the beds even in the summer; I just turn the blanket down if it is too warm. The kids stay warmer and so do Mom and Dad. My wife on cold nights used to roll in the blankets like a window shade and I would wake up in the middle of the night wondering where all the blankets had gone. Now my wife is warm in bed and does not roll up in the blankets any more, which has brought us closer together. So for energy savings and true togetherness, dial down that setback thermostat and snuggle up underneath really a warm sleeping bag blanket. I find a good deal of security knowing that we have these warm blankets on the beds, that even if it did get cold in the house, the kids are warm in bed.

The biggest heating loss in most homes is drafts. Just think of a well-insulated house with the windows open. It does not matter how well a home is insulated, if the wind is blowing right through it. Window replacements are normally a waste of money, since the cost is high and the difference in energy savings is small, but the difference between a drafty window and tight one is big. Drafty windows need to replaced or sealed. At your local hardware store you will find a nearly an endless selection of removable caulks, tapes and plastic covers to seal windows. Such weather stripping products have the fastest payback rates of all energy saving products on the market and are far cheaper than replacing the windows.

Doors certainly need to be weather stripped as well. Since doors are opened and closed far more than windows, the weather stripping is exposed to far more wear and tear. Many types of weather stripping tend to be too hard to compress easily, making it hard to latch the door close. Personally, I like the brass weather stripping because it lasts for years and since it is on the side of the door frame rather than on the closing edge, it does not interfere with latching. Even still, just the friction of the brass pressing on the edges of the doors can make them hard to close, so I put some furniture wax on the door edge, which makes it easier. A good sweep on the inside of the door that closes on a threshold is also necessary. If your doors do not have a raised threshold, add one, trim the door bottom edge if needed to fit over one.

Other possible draft locations are wherever there is a hole in the drywall and there are far more than you might think. Outlets, switches and light fixtures, all have a hole cut through the drywall. If you remove a switch or outlet cover, in the gap between the electrical box and the drywall, you can see your wall insulation. You can probe it with a pencil to get an ideal of type and thickness of your insulation. It was common for homes as late as the early seventies to have only two inches of insulation in the walls and some older homes have none. For sealing these gaps, Manco's "Insulating Socket Sealers" works well and is inexpensive. The bag of 12 I have lying here on the desk has a price tag of $1.49. Manco also claims on the package, that outlets and switches is where 25% of a home's drafts occur and that is more than the doors and windows combined. I think they are trying to sell a product, but for a few bucks, you can seal a lot of leaks. To install them, all you have to do is unscrew the switch and outlet covers, place a "Socket Sealer" and screw the cover back in place.

The door with the biggest heat loss in your whole house is probably your attic door. Most are located in the ceiling where the hottest air is, and since the warm air is going up and out, you do not even feel the draft. Check the fit and seal on your hatch door and weather strip it with foam or felt type weather stripping that the door can rest on. The attic insulation is best glued or tacked to the back of the door so it stays in place when the door is closed. Attic pull down stairs need to have a box build over them in the attic with a lid that opens, with insulation attached to the outside of the box. While you are in the attic, check your attic insulation, this is one case where more is better. I had only two inches in my home, which was built in 1957, when I bought it in 1987. Adding attic insulation is one of the easiest insulation jobs around, only two steps. You place a vent duct in each space between rafters, and then you blow lose fill attic insulation into the attic.   Here in southern Wisconsin, they recommend ceiling insulation of R-33, which is 10 inches of fiberglass. I brought mine up to about 30 inches, which I guess would be about R-99.

I also only had 2 inches of insulation in my house walls as well, so I bought bales of cellulose insulation at a local building supply store, which included a free or discounted rental of the blower. I drilled two, two inch sized holes for every space between the studs and blew the insulation into the walls filling the gap between the two inches of insulation I had and the nearly 4 inch space it was installed in.

The biggest improvement I have had with adding insulating to my house was when I removed the old siding and applied two-inch thick pink foam board insulation, which has an R-10 rating. Then I installed house wrap and resided the house. The difference this made was huge, my heating needs dropped by half or maybe two thirds. The reason for this huge drop in the need for heat is in part due to blocking nearly all the drafts and that the foam covered the studs, which have an insulating value of only about half of what a fully insulated wall has. Therefore, I highly recommend this insulation project. For anyone considering doing this, I will outline the steps for doing it yourself or for having a contractor do it.

This project was also the biggest I ever did and took a whole summer and most of the fall; at the end, I was racing the frost to finish painting the new siding. The first step is to remove the molding along the outside edge of the eave and pry the soffit boards down like hinges, so an eight-inch thick batt of fiberglass insulation can be installed horizontally across the top of the wall, this part of the wall near the ceiling is where the hottest air is. The width of the batt needs to be sized for the distance between the soffit and the top edge of the wall. In my case and for most houses with a standard overhang and a low slope roof, a 14 and one half inch wide batt will work nice. I used Insulation Support Wires, the type normally used between floor joists to hold insulation up in crawl spaces, between the rafters to hold the insulation down to keep it from blocking the air flow between the rafters. The air needs to be able to enter the eave vents and rise between the rafters and exit through the attic vents to dry the roof boards if they become damp and to prevent the roof from being warmed by the wall where it touches the roof. If the roof is covered with ice, and it is warmed at this point above the wall, the ice melts on the bottom side, but has nowhere to drain since the ice is still frozen on the top and on the cold eave below. The trapped water ends up flowing up underneath the shingles and leaking down inside through the ceiling near the outside wall, this is called ice damming. For an emergency fix if this happens, salt the roof in the area of the leak, so the water can drain out from under the ice.

Once the insulation is installed, nail the soffit boards back into place and replace the outside trim molding. The next step is to remove the siding, you may be able to reuse your existing siding, but my 50-year-old cedar siding splintered into so many tiny pieces that I had to replace it. If the sheathing underneath isn't good for holding nails or if you don't have any, I would suggest applying half inch thick plywood, so that you will have something to nail the foam and siding to, for it is very difficult to accurately hit the studs nailing through the siding and two inches of foam. Since the foam will move the siding out two inches, it will probably be necessary to nail cedar trim boards around the windows and doors to bring them out above level of the new siding. The foam is run tight up against the cedar trim boards, and is nailed with three-inch long plastic cap nails, which have a large plastic disk under the nail head to hold the foam. Once the foam is all up, fill any gaps with cans of spray foam and tape the joints. Next install the house wrap also using the three-inch plastic cap nails and tape the house wrap to the soffit and the cedar trim around the doors and windows. Just keep the tape back enough so the sidling and moldings will cover it. At the bottom edge, adhesive caulk and tape the house wrap to the basement wall. Then later if you put foam on the basement wall as I am doing now, it will lock the house wrap behind it, providing a very good seal. Next, you put the siding on the house. If you are reusing the old siding, you will need to shorten it to allow for the cedar trim boards around the doors and windows, and you will need to add cedar corner boards to make up for the fact that your house is now four inches longer and four inches wider. Remember to caulk and seal every opening as needed. Well, that is in a nutshell, how I spent nearly every waking minute last year, but it was well worth it. In my project, I ran fiberglass in the eave and foam below, but you can remove the soffit entirely and run foam sheets all the way up to the top of the wall. Of course then you will have to trim and reinstall the soffit boards which is more work, but you will be able to run the house wrap and foam to the top of the wall and have better draft sealing.

You will need to examine your house for where you are losing heat, or where the cold is coming in, and seal and insulate as needed. The rewards for doing so are great; I probably can now heat my house with about 10-20% of the heat that was needed when I bought it. Currently I can hopefully make it through a winter here burning three cords of firewood; if I had not added any insulation, I would have needed 15 to 30 cords. Therefore, if I had insulated years ago, if I had been burning wood all those years, I could have been saving myself as much as 27 cords a year. That is a lot of cutting, sawing and hauling I do not have to do. Insulation is by far your best investment, stocks can go up and down, furnaces can break, fuel prices can go through the roof, but insulation is there day after day keeping out the cold and reducing the amount of heat it takes to keep your house warm.

It is possible to have a home so well insulated that it almost does not need any heat, that the "waste heat" from lights, appliances and the heat from the people inside the home is enough to keep the house heated. This type of insulation is called super insulation. Although probably only the best of the super insulated homes are that well done.   It is the best way to go; and there are ways to retro fit an existing home, which will be covered in chapter 18. If I were ever to have a new house built, I would most certainly have it super insulated.   The idea of reducing my heating needs down to something that would only require an occasional small heat input is very appealing.

Insulating the ceiling, walls and floors does more than just slow the escape of your precious heat; it can make you feel warmer in your house at lower temperature settings. How this works is that one of the ways heat is transmitted is radiant in the form of rays, like the heat you feel from the sun or when in front of a warm fire. The heat is striking you in the form of rays of infrared light. When you are in a room, you feel the temperature of the air around you, and feel the exchange or level of infrared light in the room. Your body in a room at normal room temperatures is at a higher temperature than the surrounding room, and you are giving off heat. You are giving off heat in three ways; convention, the rising plume of warm air you create in a cold room. To feel this rising current of air, in a cold room just hold the collar of your shirt out a few inches for a few minutes and you will soon feel a rising flow of warm. Another way you lose heat is through conduction, like the cold you feel coming up through your shoes when you stand on cold concrete in the wintertime. Which is why metal chairs are not popular, they are such good conductors of heat that by conducting away your heat they feel so cold. Radiant heat flow is part of the way you gain and lose heat, even in a warm room surrounded by warm air and standing on a warm floor, you can still feel cold when standing in front of a large glass window in the wintertime. The reason is that the heat that you are radiating out is not being bounced back to you by the cold window, rather the window is absorbing most of it, like a black hole sucking away your body heat. Just as the radiant heat of a fireplace can warm you, cold surfaces can chill you. If you are surrounded by cold walls, you will still feel cold even at normal room temperatures, and this is why so many people feel compelled to turn up the thermostat in cold weather. However, if you add insulation, you reduce the flow of heat and the inside house surfaces are warmer and reflect more of the heat back to you and you feel warmer.

Not to be overlooked in sealing drafts and in effective use of insulation is your heating system. Duct tape is called duct tape for a reason, it was originally made for sealing ductwork and it still does that job well. Many duct systems leak hot air like politicians on Election Day, taping the loose joints and open gaps will keep the hot air in the ducts and prevent it from being wasted in the basement or crawl space. The amount of heat lost through leaky ductwork can be huge, for here, you have the hottest air in the house under the air pressure created by the furnace fan moving through thin sheet metal ducts, any open seam will allow the air to rush out. The ducts can certainly be insulated which will improve your systems performance even more.   If you have a basement, your uninsulated ductwork probably heats it for you, which sounds nice until you remember that while the upstairs walls have insulation, the basement walls are probably uninsulated concrete block. You can save a good amount of heat by closing any open duct vents in the basement and insulating the ductwork and allowing the basement temperature to drop to perhaps 55 degrees or even colder. This way your basement will be closer to the temperature of the deep soil in your location and this will greatly reduce the heat flow out through the basement walls. Despite what you may hear; earth is a lousy insulator with an insulation value of only R-2 per foot of earth, which is equal to the insulation value of about half an inch of fiberglass. To equal the insulation of three and half inches of fiberglass you would need 6 and half feet of earth. With the basement block wall having only an R value of a bit above 1, or about a quarter of an inch of fiberglass, the upper portion of the typical basement wall is very poorly insulated and loses a great deal of heat. This is why the ground does not freeze next to many basements and why the tulips by the house come up sooner in the spring. The average homeowner is using his furnace to keep the ground unfrozen next to his basement walls all winter long, which of course is a very poor investment. This waste can be avoided by wasting less heat in the basement by keeping it at a lower temperature or by insulating the basement walls.

Hydronic systems also often have minimal pipe insulation and lose a lot of heat due to this, if you do not believe me, why is the area where your pipes run so warm? Hydronic heating systems often have water temperatures of 120 to 190 degrees or even higher, and yet have far less insulation on the piping then is found in the building walls. Particularly if the piping runs through unheated spaces, the heat loss can be quite large and often goes unnoticed. Such systems can easily lose half of their heat due to such loses. Insulation can be added to the pipes by using larger pipe insulation that will fit right over the insulation already on the pipes, giving you a double layer. Fiberglass insulation can also be wrapped around the pipes in a spiraling candy cane pattern, the foil backed insulation in a narrow width works best. You may have to cut the insulation into strips narrow enough so you can wrap it around the pipes in tight places.   Do not wrap it too tight, fiberglass insulation works by the trapped air space between the glass fibers, so you do not want to squeeze the air out by crushing the insulation tight. Then tape in place with foil tap or duct tape.

On older boilers, it is possible to increase the efficiency by adding a modulating aquastat. An aquastat is a water thermostat that measures the temperature of the boiler water and has a second temperature-sensing bulb that is located outside and measures the outside air temperature. The two bulbs are filled with a refrigerant that through a long tube presses on a relay that turns the boiler on and off, with an adjustment for "hotter" and "colder". What this old time wonder does, is, as it gets colder, it raises the boiler temperature. It saves fuel by reducing the boiler temperature in warmer weather, and works even better with a warm weather shut off switch that turns the boiler off when the outside temperature is above a temperature where you would normally turn the heat off. A modulating aquastat can improve efficiency by 10%.

The other trick for hot water boilers, is to install a time delay relay that when the thermostat turns on the circulating pump (and yes, you should have a thermostat that turns the pump on so it runs only when heat is needed), delays the burner from firing to allow the hot water to circulate first for a time. This moves the hottest water out of the boiler and moves the colder water from the far ends of the heating system, that way when the boiler fires, it is heating colder water that will absorb more of the heat and less heat will go up the chimney. A delay relay can improve efficiency by 10%.

Back in the 1970's to save energy many people installed a product called Magic Heat Reclaimer which was a box like device with a tube type heat exchanger that replaced a section of stove pipe between the furnace and the chimney, that reclaimed heat that otherwise would have gone up the chimney. The unit also has a fan that was turned on by a heat sensitive switch that blows the reclaimed heat out into the area near where your stovepipe is located. This product worked great in the 1970's and is still sold and used by many today. The problem is that unless you are still using a furnace from the 1970's this is probably not a good idea. The furnaces used in the 1970 were rather inefficient and sent a lot of wasted heat up the chimney. Since 1992 oil and gas, furnaces are required by law to be at least 78% efficient, which means a lot less heat is wasted up the chimney. An 80% efficient furnace is still wasting 20% of the heat up the chimney, but if you use a heat reclaimer, you increase the efficiency, which sounds great, but if you increase it above 82% on a natural gas or oil furnace, you now have a condensing furnace. Condensing furnaces remove enough heat from the exhaust gases that the water vapor in the exhaust condenses and the water condensate is acidic and corrosive, this is why condensing furnaces have stainless steel heat exchangers and are vented with PVC pipe with a condensate trap. An 80% efficient gas furnace does not have a stainless steel heat exchanger, and gas condensate if it runs back down in the furnace will corrode it. The stovepipe will also corrode and the condensate may drip out on whatever is below, but the biggest problems will occur in the chimney. Natural gas or oil condensate will attack clay tile liners, brick and concrete, and greatly shorten the life of the chimney. The condensate may also run down inside the chimney and leak out onto the floor or even run back down inside the furnace. The condensate through its corrosive action may also create other exits from the chimney by dissolving the mortar and leaking out higher up in the house and possibly causing structural damage to the home. So before you consider using a heat reclaimer on gas or oil, furnace or boiler, check the efficiency rating so see if there is enough wasted heat to reclaim without water vapor condensing before the hot gases exit the top of the chimney. If the efficiency is unknown, look for a standing pilot light, which are not found on newer more efficient furnaces and boilers, or a stamped date well before 1992, or measure the flue stack temperature. Efficiency is revealed by the flue temperature, high efficiency units are vented in PVC pipe and have low temperatures of about 120 degrees, mid efficiency units are too hot for PVC with temperatures about 180-240 degrees, and the old low efficiency units have much higher temperatures of about 250-450 degrees. The quick old time test to for checking flue stovepipe temperature is the quick touch method. If you quickly touch the hot stove pipe very briefly and are not burned it is in the mid efficiency range, if you are burned it is quite hot and is in the low efficiency range or you are not very quick after all, well not everyone in the old days was quick either. Seriously, just use a stovepipe thermometer and only use a heat reclaimer on vent pipes that are above 300 degrees so that by the time the exhaust exits the top of the chimney it is still above 212 degrees so that no steam condensate condenses in the chimney.

A leading cause of furnaces operating inefficiently is a dirty air filter. Seriously, many people fail to check or change the furnace air filter; a plugged filter reduces airflow through the furnace and will raise the temperature in the heat exchanger sending more heat up the flue. If the filter is really plugged with dirt, it can reduce the airflow so much that the furnace will over heat and the temperature high limit switch will shut down the furnace until it cools off. If your house is cold and the furnace keeps cycling on and off, check your air filter, it could be the problem. If you are using cheap air filters that look like a piece of fiberglass insulation, they need to be changed every month that the furnace is used regularly. The cheap filters are really lousy and they let a lot of the finer dust blow right through to coat the heat exchanger, the inside of the ductwork and the inside of your house. Always use the more expensive pleated air filters, they cost more, but they remove much more of the dust and can last a few months instead of only one month. There are also extended life pleated filters that can last as long as a year. The trick for checking if a filter needs to be changed is to take it out, hold it up in front of a bright light, and see how much the light is blocked by the dust in the filter. With pleated filters, if you can clearly see the light source, the filter is still good, if the light source is harder to make out or if you see dark bands of dirt in the pleats, change the filter. A pleated filter is overdue for changing if you can see dust bunnies in the pleats or any bowing in the filter, which is due to the air pressure from the fan starting to suck in the filters because they are plugged with dirt.

The other popular place for dust to block your furnace's airflow is the cold air return register. All of your heating registers are normally located on the outside walls below windows, while cold air returns are in centrally located interior walls like the hallway. To clean, unscrew the grill and vacuum with a brush attachment on both sides. While you have the grill off, vacuum out the ductwork as far as you can reach. If you do not have a vacuum, take the grill outside and brush on both sides to remove the dust.

The simplest way of all of saving money on home heating is to turn down the thermostat, there is about a 3% savings for each degree you reduce the temperature by. Of course, this idea had all the appeal of spoiled mayonnaise when President Carter recommended turning down thermostats to 68 degrees in 1979 to save energy. A big part of the reason that Carter's recommendation flopped, is that it failed to consider humidity. The air around you contains moisture in the form of water vapor, which makes itself very apparent on hot steamy summer days and can be just as noticeable on cool winter days by its absence. Just as high humidity on a hot day makes it feel hotter than it really is, cool bone-dry air makes you feel colder than it really is. The trick is that 68 degrees is only comfortable IF the humidity is at a reasonable level (about 40% or higher). Turning down the thermostat to 68 without adding humidity is down right chilly. Carter failed to mention that to be comfortable at 68, you need a humidifier. If you have a forced air heating system, a central humidifier on the ductwork just after the furnace can maintain a proper humidity level. The problem with humidity is a little is a good thing, but too much is bad. The reason that the air is dry in your home in the winter is that as air is warmed, it can hold more water vapor than cold air. Therefore, unless you add moisture to air as you warm it, it will be come dryer. The reverse is true too, that as air is cooled, it can hold less moisture and becomes damp, if air is cooled below the level, at which it can hold the moisture it has, the excess moisture condenses. This is where dew comes from, and why as the sun warms the morning air, it disappears. While you want to add moisture to the air in your house in the wintertime to feel more comfortable, you need to keep the level of humidity below the dew point of the outside air. Otherwise, what happens is as the air leaves the house, a dew or condensate will form, that is why your windows steam up in cold weather as the air next to the glass is cooled to its dew point. The reason for concern is that houses are not air tight, and some air will leak through the walls, and if the air has too much moisture, water will collect inside the walls on the insulation and other parts of the wall. Just as water on the window glass, can lead to black moldy window frames, water in the walls can lead to black mold forming inside the walls. Some black molds are quite toxic and some houses have become so unhealthy to live in due to mold that they have had to be torn down. Therefore, it is very important not to allow the humidity level in the house to reach the dew point. This is accomplished by having a humidistat on the humidifier that senses the amount of humidity in the air and turns the humidifier off once the correct level is reached. The level is set by a dial that is set to 10 degrees F below the lowest temperature expected for the coming month. Some portable humidifiers also have a dew point setting dial, without having that kind of control; it can be difficult to control the humidity level to keep it safely below the dew point. I do not recommend using any humidifier for whole house humidification without one. You will however know then you have too much humidity in your house, because your windows will fog. From time to time, you will have foggy windows, like when you step out of the shower. This is why you run the bathroom exhaust fan, to clear out the excess moisture to keep it from condensing in the walls. Just as you control the temperature in your house, you need to control the humidity level as well. With some humidity in the air, you will find that you can turn the temperature down a bit, perhaps even down to 68 like Carter wanted, and still be comfortable while saving money on your heating costs.

For some homes, maintaining a proper humidity level will involve reducing the water vapor in the air rather than adding it. In well-insulated homes with little air leakage, little moisture is lost or absorbed by through the warming of cold air only to be later leaked out of the house taking the moisture with it. Without this normal large drain of moisture, the moisture that is normally released in the house tends to build up. Your lungs moisturize every breath you exhale, just having too many people in a tight space can easily fog the windows as so often happens in cars in cold weather. Then there are also the many other sources of water vapor such as cooking, washing dishes, showering, cleaning and laundry. In some homes, steps will need to be taken to keep the humidity level down by doing such things as putting a lid on the pot when cooking and/or running the kitchen fan, remembering to run the bathroom fan when showering, and venting the dryer exhaust outside which should be done anyway. If these steps are not enough to keep the humidity under control, you should consider using a heat recovery ventilator system. These systems exhaust air from the house through a heat exchanger used to heat the incoming outside air. These make up air systems serve three purposes, they get rid of excess humidity and carbon dioxide and they bring in fresh dry air with more oxygen. In airtight homes, the air can get stuffy, as breathing and combustion such as gas stoves, use up the oxygen and produce carbon dioxide. It is the build up of carbon dioxide that causes the stuffy sensation, just as the build up of it in your lungs is what triggers the urge to breath or in the case of your home, the urge to open a window "to get some air in". Very few homes however are so air tight that they need a heat recovery ventilator. For ventilating to get rid of humidity, be sure to get a heat recovery ventilator and not an energy recovery ventilator, which has a core designed to maintain humidity rather than to reduce it. Heat recovery ventilators are used when heating while energy recovery ventilators are used when air conditioning to keep the air from becoming too dry.

Now for Some Ways How not to Save Money

A number of different types of electric plug in "Miracle Heaters" are sold by means of various misleading claims; such as, they will reduce your home heating costs by 50%. These small 1500 watt electric heaters are ridiculously over priced, $400- $700 and produce the same amount and type of heat produced by electric heaters that sell for less than $100. The only miracle about these products is that any one is dumb enough to buy them. The Heat Surge Company that makes the Miracle Heater, Edenpure heater and the Roll-n-Glow Electric Fireplace makes all sorts of deceptive, misleading and absurdly false statements to sell their products to the unwary. Like;

"the EdenPURE uses less energy to create heat than other sources"

All electric heaters of the same wattage use the exact same amount of power and electric heaters are one of the most expensive ways of heating.

"The BTU s are basically irrelevant as a unit of measure since the patented heating process of the EdenPURE® INTENTIONALLY

does not operate using old inefficient methods of heat combustion, which is rated by using the BTU rule. Our heating method is far superior for efficiency, safety, comfort, and is providing a natural healthy indoor environment."

"BTU" is a measurement of heat, it does not matter how that heat was produced. This type of talk that their product cannot properly be measured by "irrelevant" standards, is a red flag that you are dealing with a crank, a con man, or both.

"heater can cut your heating bill up to 50% and pay for itself in a matter of weeks!"

Considering that, their heaters cost $400 or more, just how many weeks are they thinking of that you would normally use $800 worth of heating fuel? If you read the small type (if it even appears in the ad), the way you are suppose to save 50% on your heating bill, is by turning your existing home heat down to a low temperature like 50 degrees and then using their portable heater to just heat whatever room you are in. There is no savings in using their heater over any other similar electric heater; the "savings" is in drastically turning down the heat in your house. If you wish to follow this method to save money, you can save an extra $300 right off the bat by buying one of the heaters that work just as well and sell for less than $100 instead of theirs for $400.

I bought my house from a 70-year-old widower, who did this and had the heat set very low if he had it on at all. He had an electric space heater in each room and turned on only the one he was by to keep himself warm. When I moved in, the shower was dusty, probably in part because he found it too cold to shower and just using the bathroom must have been quite chilly. What I did was insulate the house and I now probably use far less energy than he did, and I heat the whole house. If you have a poorly insulated house, the answer is to insulate it. Otherwise, you might as well skip the electric space heater and get an electric hot pad and sit on it, that way you only heat yourself and not a whole room, even more "savings". The very intent of this book is that you take steps now so you do not have to resort to such desperate measures in the future. While you can save money by reducing the temperature that you heat your house to, using an electric space heater for zone heating, which is just heating the room or part of the house you are in, is expensive. The only way you get ahead financially is if the cost of the electricity for the space heater is less than the cost of using your furnace to provide rest of the heat would have been used. For each degree that you turn down your thermostat, there is about a 3% savings. So if you reduce the setting from 68 to 58 that would be about a 30% reduction in your fuel bill. To save 50% while using a space heater for zone heating, you would probably have to reduce your heat by at least 20 degrees, which could be a 60% reduction in fuel use, to allow 10% for the cost of using the electric space heater. Now heating with electrical resistance heaters, is about twice as expensive as heating with gas or oil, so you have only about 5% of the heat you normally have to make up for the 60% that you gave up to get the 50% savings. Obviously, since we are talking about a 10 to 1 reduction in available heat, this only works if you heat less than one tenth of the house with the space heater, and you have to allow for heat loss through open doorways, which can be very considerable. Therefore, in the end, to have the large savings that is claimed, you have to let most of your home become very cold and only space heat a very small part of it. If you use the space heater to heat several rooms as the apparently dimwitted ad writers say that you can do, you completely wipe out any potential savings and since electric space heaters are far more expensive to heat with than oil or gas, you will increase your energy costs instead of decreasing them. A much simpler solution is to turn off the heat in unused rooms by blocking heat vents or turning down radiators. Just do not block the one where the thermostat is or you will overheat the rest of the house. That way you can zone heat with your existing furnace without even having to buy anything and since you are not increasing your electric bill, you would save more money than using an electric heater.

I am not totally against the concept of electric zone heating, since if you only heat a small area, you can save money doing it. Probably the best use of electric space heaters is for elderly people who feel cold and have a need for a warmer temperature than it is economical to heat the house to, so rather than over heating the entire house, it makes more sense to use a space heater in one location for them. Another option is to redirect more heat to that one room by adjusting vent dampers, heat registers or hot water valves. Anyhow, a better choice for a space heater of course would be to use a vented heater like a stove using a cheaper energy source than electricity. While a vented stove is not portable, who would not rather sit by the warm glow of wood stove instead of an electric heater?

Insulating Paint

Another over sold product is insulating paint. Often costing as much as $70 a gallon or more, insulating paints are sold on the idea that you can improve your home's insulation by simply painting the walls and ceilings. These products do work and some are great as vapor blockers for keeping moisture from entering the wall space. However in terms of insulation, while these produces do insulate, the possible insulation effect of something as thin as a film of paint is very small as shown by the complete absence of an "R" value insulation rating in the sales pitch. If the customer knew that in terms of pure conductance insulation, the insulating paint had an "R" value of less than 0.1 or more probably, less than 0.01, how many would buy the product? To make matters even worse, some insulating paints have made a claim of up to an R-19 insulating rating which is of course impossible and a number of companies have been pursued (as in sued) for making false claims. The high R-values are often based on the paint acting as a reflective heat barrier and not on the minor value of the paint insulating against thermal conductance. A heat reflective surface acts like a mirror by bouncing some of the infrared heat (light with a wavelength shorter than visible light) back into the room, while anything that touches the wall will conduct the heat right through the barrier as if it isn't there. Think of the reflective barrier as a large metal mirror that reflects the heat back at you and you feel warm, but if you touch the mirror, it feels cold and chills your hand. That is the drawback of reflective barriers, they only work for radiated heat and do little or nothing for conducted or convected heat. While reflective heat surfaces can work as part of an insulating system, they are inadequate by themselves. The average overall gain on an insulated standard wall is estimated to be about 2% for reflective barrier paint, so while these products can work, they are not worth the high prices charged for them and there are far cheaper heat reflectors available. White paint should do fairly well at reflecting infrared light since it reflects the entire visible spectrum.

Conversely, painting over an insulating paint with a dark colored paint will cover the reflective surface with an absorbing one and will block the reflection just as painting a mirror blocks the reflection. All heat reflective surfaces require an air gap next to the surface to work, since they only reflect the infrared light that is radiated across the gap. If there is no air gap, the heat is conduced rather than radiated and the radiant barrier is ineffectual. Since in most homes, many things touch the wall like window and door moldings, pictures, light switches, electrical receptacles and furniture; the effectiveness of infrared heat barriers is greatly reduced.

Some of the insulating paints sold are out right frauds, such as one containing hollow ceramic micro spheres with a vacuum inside each sphere that is suppose to provide a layer of vacuum insulation. The problem is that ceramics are fairly poor insulators and will conduct the heat right around the vacuum center in each sphere as if it was not even there, as will the surrounding paint film as well. This is called thermal bridging and it reduces the insulation value of the paint pretty much down to regular white paint.

Some companies also sell metal flake paint like aluminum paint to be used as reflective thermal barrier, and such paints do work as such, but only if they are not covered. Some companies sell these paints as a primer, but unless the top coat is transparent to infrared light waves, the top coat will absorb the heat waves and render the reflective base coat useless. It is once again, like painting the mirror, without an exposed surface for the infrared light to bounce off, there is little reflection of heat.

Reflective Foil Films

While reflective foil or radiant barrier products certainly are useful and work better than reflective paints, there is also a great deal of fraud and exaggeration in the sales pitches, (they even had a booth at the Wisconsin State Fair this year near the super mops and the kitchen wonders). Reflecting heat is a great way of staying cool, but a heat reflector has to have an air gap on the side receiving the heat and the surface needs to be clean and dust free to work. It has been found that reflective foil products installed in dusty attics lost 50% of their effectiveness in just one year due to dust accumulating on the reflective surface. Since dust does tend to collect in attic spaces due to using unfiltered outside air for ventilation, heat reflective products used in attics will eventually over time become covered with enough dust to render them ineffective. Blocking heat flow from the roof into the house can be addressed by increasing the attic insulation, having proper attic ventilation and the best choice is the use of roofs that reflect the sun. Sloped white or reflective roofs make far better heat reflective surfaces than foil films in the attic, because roofs are regularly washed clean of dust by the rain and the sky makes for an excellent air gap.

The use of reflective foils in walls has also been over sold, since the required air gap is often omitted and then there is no reflection of heat, or if the air gap is included, it can be a source of air infiltration. The increase in performance of an insulated wall when using an internal heat reflective barrier with an air gap has been found in tests to be minor.

"the air spaces and the strapping material (furring) used to create the air spaces will account for about 26% of the thermal resistance of the wall, whereas the low emissivity material itself will account for only about 5%." National Research Council Canada- http://wwwreno.nrc-cnrc.gc.ca/eng/ibp/irc/ci/volume-4-n2-7.html

What the above testing results of the NRCC are saying, is that the air gap was five times as effective as the reflective heat barrier. Clearly the space in the wall used for the air gap and foil film would be far more effectively used if filled with insulation instead. One major failing of foil heat barriers used inside walls is that the furring strips used to create the air gap, bridge the gap and thermally bridge the foil by pressing on the foil surface. This reduces the foil's effectiveness and is a limitation for all heat reflective surfaces installed inside walls, since the air gap in the wall is never complete and conductors of heat always touch the foil at many points. Once again, the heat reflective surface would work better if it were on the outside wall surface. A bright reflective white paint makes an excellent heat reflector and it has long been noted to reduce air conditioning costs, and is far cheaper than installing a foil heat barrier.

Foil reflective heat barriers are also sold for use underneath concrete slabs and for basement walls. Since there is often no provision for an air gap, the products of course fail to reflect any heat at all. Even when an air gap is included, chemicals in the cement, treated wood products or ground, often enter the air gap and corrode the reflective surface greatly reducing its effectiveness. The supports used to keep the air gap open underneath the weight of a concrete slab are by necessity strong enough to act as a significant thermal bridge and severely limit the effectiveness of a below grade reflective heat product even under ideal conditions. A far better choice for insulating underneath concrete is high-density foam board products, which are designed for use below grade.

Tankless Water Heaters

Tankless water heaters can be great money savers in certain applications such as for single point of use applications like for isolated faucets that are seldom used. However, for multiple uses that are frequently used, like the hot water supply in a family home, the savings can be much smaller. Tankless water heaters save money by eliminating the heat that is lost by a hot tank of water as it sits hour after hour. However, in a home where the water is used frequently there is little time for the water to cool sitting in the tank. I remember having to pull a tankless water heater from a home and replace it with a regular water heater because the homeowner had to turn on two or more faucets to create enough water flow to turn on the flow switch, which turns on the heater. If he only opened one tap, he only got cold water no matter how long he waited. This is still a problem with some tankless water heaters as is inconsistent water temperatures due to delays in firing up and delays in adjusting to changing flow rates. The potential savings is about $75 dollars/year for an average family and it will take about 22 years for the savings to pay for the higher cost of a tankless water heater compared to a water heater with a tank (according to Consumer reports). It is also highly unlikely that a tankless water heater will last that long which means a tankless water heater is probably a more expensive way to heat water for most people than the standard tank water heaters. Tankless water heaters are of course highly susceptible to scaling up due to hard water deposits and often require a water softener. A quality regular water heater with a tank is the better buy for the average family home, will give more consistent service and longer life, and will be cheaper to replace when it goes.

Chapter 3

Plenty of Options and What They Cost.

The first thing to look at when considering any heating method is how much it is going to cost to heat with. Fantastic wonder furnaces are worthless if you cannot afford the fuel they run on. The wise thing to do, is to compare the cost of each available fuel to see what they really cost. Now I cannot just tell you that fuel "X" is the best buy for you, because you are reading this book months or years after I wrote it and fuel prices have probably changed quiet a bit. Moreover, your local fuel cost is probably different from where I live anyway. Therefore, at the end of this chapter I will show you how to compare your current local fuel costs for yourself.

Solar Heating

While the "magic furnace" of insulation we considered in the previous chapter needs no fuel to reduce your heating bills, nearly all of the real heating systems require fuel that normally needs to be paid for. Except for one, solar heating, sunlight is free. While the costs of installation can be high, free "fuel" gives solar heating an enormous advantage in theory over all other heating systems. The problem with solar heat is it is normally coldest when the sun is not shinning. In winter time in the northern hemisphere, the sun is lower in the sky, the farther north you go, and the lower the sun is, the more atmosphere the light has to go through. This reduces the intensity of sunlight and further reduces the amount of solar heat available in the already short winter days. Many places like here in Wisconsin get many cloudy days in winter, with clouds often reducing the sunlight by 75% or more. Subtracting of all of these effects off the huge potential power in sunlight, leaves a meager amount left, which means that a solar heating system to heat a home would have to be huge. In my case, I was not sure if my roof was big enough to hold the size of system I would have needed just for doing a major part of my heating. Then I would have also needed a large heat storage for supplying heat at night and for bringing the house back up to temperature early in the morning. Therefore, the solar system would have needed to be large enough to heat the house in the day while also heating up a heat storage unit at the same time. Then there was the issue of if we got a few cloudy days, in wintertime we can go for a week and never see the sun, which would result in having to resort to using another source of heat as a back up. In short, solar heat works great in the summer but not so well in the winter, and the farther from the equator you are, the poorer it works.

I am not really down on solar, as a matter of a fact I did end up installing a solar system that works great. I put in a solar hot water system. You need hot water all year round, and for most of the time solar hot water heating works great. I am able to heat all my hot water for about 9 months of the year, then in the dark days of winter, my gas water heater fires up and fills in when my solar system falls short.

Since in this chapter we are comparing the costs of different fuels, we can put solar down as a free fuel, but the heating system only provides heat when the sun is out. Solar is by its very nature a supplemental heat and is not normally as a stand-alone heating system. So the solar fuel cost per MBTU (million BTU) is zero, but cold weather limited availability of sunshine is a problem. The costs of solar systems can be very high, a fair estimate for a having a hot water heating system installed would be about $3000 which will save about $200 a year, so it would take about 15 years to save enough money to regain the cost of the installation. If you heat your water with an electric water heater, which is about, twice the cost of using a natural gas water heater, your time to pay back would be shorter, about 7 years. The cost for a whole home solar heating system would be in the tens of thousands of dollars, and with the lack of long hot sunny days in the winter time, the time for the system to produce enough heat in value to pay for itself, is on the order of decades. In terms of getting a return on your heating dollar, solar heating your hot water makes sense, trying to heat your whole home, does not. Not everything worth doing makes sense in dollars however; some things are worth doing even if they do not make financial sense. The security of having fuel free solar heat for your house maybe something that is worth more than dollars to you. However, since for those of us living in the colder parts of the world, whole home solar heating is pretty much a dream in terms of feasibility and costs, a supplemental heating system that provides part of the home's heat maybe a more reasonable goal for a solar heating system. Wall mounted hot air solar panels with a fan powered by built in solar cells, cost about $2000. However, the time it would take for the panel to pay for itself is not even guessed at by the manufacturer and they produce less heat than an electric hair dryer. However, even just one of these panels might be enough to keep your pipes from freezing in a lengthy power outage if you have a well insulated home.

Coal

Of the fuels you have to pay for, coal is still often the cheapest common fuel to heat with, at a price as low as 100 dollars a ton, and with better coal burners having an efficiency of 75% or greater, a million BTU of usable heat can cost as little as $5.35 . Unfortunately for most coal users, getting coal at $100 a ton would be a real bargain as would having a burning efficiency of 75%. Old hand fed coal stoves have efficiencies of 50-65%, so if you were buying 50 lb bags of coal for $15 each and had a stove that was 50% efficient, a million BTU of useable heat would cost you $48, which at current electric rates would be more expensive than electric resistance heat. Which points out that any fuel can be a bargain or a waste of money; depending on how much you have to pay for it and how efficiently you burn it.

Comparing the true cost of various fuels is easy with some very basic math. It is simply a matter of seeing what the cost is for the amount of fuel it takes to produce a million BTU or MBTU. (BTU stands for British Thermal Unit; a BTU is the heat it takes to raise one pound of water one degree Fahrenheit.) For coal you take the price per ton, for smaller amounts such as bags, just multiply the price per bag by the number of bags it takes to make a ton, which is 2000 pounds. Then divide the ton price by 25, which gives you the price per MBTU. Then to get the price for usable MBTU, divide by the percent efficiency of your coal burner. Some people are confused by percents, but they are very simple, it is just so many out of a hundred. So a 50% efficient stove is heating the room with 50% or half of the total amount of heat that is produced from the coal while wasting the other 50% up the chimney. That is what percents are, now to divide or multiply by a percent; you have to make it a decimal percent, where 100% is 1 and 75% is .75. Dividing by the percent, efficiency will give you the approximate cost per usable MBTU, which is the amount of the heat that ends up in your house. Here are some typical efficiency percentages for coal appliances, for old hand fired coal stoves 50-60%, newer hand fired coal stoves 60-80%, automatic feeding stoves 70-85%, some top end units now claim an efficiency of 90%. Coal furnaces will have efficiency rates close to the coal stoves they are most similar to, and boilers in theory will too, but boiler efficiency is also affected by the water temperature.

Electric Heat

Electric heat is paid for by the KWh (Kilo Watt hour), which is one thousand watts for an hour, if you plugged in a 1000 watt heater for an hour, that is a KWh. On your electric bill will be a statement like "Total Electricity Used 389 KWh" and the amount charged per KWh, you can use the per KWh charge, or you can take the "Total Electricity Charges" and divide it by the number of KWh to give the true cost per KWh. In my case, my local electric company charges me 11.763 cents per KWh, but the true charge is 12.7 cents per KWh. Then take the price/KWh and multiply it by 293, which will give you the cost per MBTU, which in my case is $37.21. Electric baseboards and space heaters are 100% efficient since there is nowhere else for the heat to go. While electric furnaces and boilers do have some places to waste some heat, so they are normally assumed to have an efficiency of 95%. Divide the cost by 0.95 and you now have your cost per usable MBTU $39.17. Electric heat is one of the most expensive heating methods available; practically everything else is cheaper.

Air-Source Heat Pumps

It is not possible for a resistance electric heater to have an efficiency above 100% no matter what it costs or who is selling it. Heat pumps can have efficiencies well above 100% since they do not create the heat; they merely move it. Heat pumps can have efficiencies of over 200% and sometimes even over 400%, the efficiency is dependent on the quality of the unit and the outside temperature, with heat pumps being more efficient at warmer outside temperatures for heating. In southern climates, they can out perform gas furnaces in reducing heating costs. Such units are called air-source heat pumps since they are extracting the heat they supply, from the outside air. The problem is that the colder it is, the less heat there is to extract and the less efficient it is to use a heat pump. As you approach the freezing point, outside moisture tends to freeze on the outside coil blocking the air flow, preventing the unit from working just as can happen with the coils in refrigerators which is why air-source heat pumps have a defrost cycle just as refrigerators do. As the temperature drops below freezing, many air-source heat pumps are unable to extract enough heat to keep the house warm, which is why they have back up resistance electric heating elements. Here in Wisconsin, such heat pumps end up having to use far too much expensive resistance electric heat for them to be cost effective, I remember an electrician who had to have an air-source heat pump, but after one winter of electric bills, he was ready to switch to gas. In warmer climates, where the wintertime temperature is seldom below freezing, heat pumps can be a very efficient choice for home heating and a heat pump is also an air conditioner, which in warmer climate summers, is much appreciated. New heat pumps called All Season heat pumps, can work at colder temperatures, some as low as -15 F but with a drop to only 200% efficiency. At 10.7 cents for the KW, an average heat pump can create a million BTU for as little as $13.83 while an All Season heat pump could possibly create a million BTU for $11.17. The efficiency for air source heat pumps decreases with decreases in temperature, so that they are not as efficient in colder states, these problems are however overcome by Ground source heat pumps.

Geo-thermal or Ground Source Heat Pumps

In northern climates while the air maybe freezing, a few feet under ground the temperature is much warmer. Caves do not freeze, ground temperatures in the US ranges from 45°F in the far north to 75°F in Deep South. The ground temperature is warmer than the air in winter, and is cooler than the air in the summer, which gives a Geo-thermal heat pump an enormous advantage in both heating and air conditioning. A Geo-thermal unit will use 25%–50% less electricity than an air source heat pump and about 72% less than electric resistance heating with air-conditioning. At 10.7 cents a KWh, a Geo-thermal heat pump will produce a MBTU for about $9.46. Like an air source heat pump, the efficiency of a Ground source heat pump is dependent on the temperature it has to work against. The colder the ground, the harder it has to work, and it will take more electricity to produce a MBTU, while if the ground is warmer, it will cost less. So Geo-thermal units work better than air source heat pumps in all areas, even in fairly cold ground areas, they work well enough to often be cheaper to heat with than natural gas.

Corn

Corn for heating costs is competitive in price with coal, and with increasing coal prices corn is now in many places the cheaper heating choice. At $4 a bushel, 80% efficient corn stoves provide a MBTU for about $12.81, while corn prices will probably increase; corn will probably always remain one of the cheaper heating choices. In areas where corn is grown and available in bulk, it may be the fuel to consider. Buying corn in bulk requires either a farmer nearby who delivers or having a large truck that you can use to pick up corn in bulk from a local corn seller. Otherwise, the cost is much higher and corn is not such a bargain. Personally, I have a problem with burning food to heat my house. Buying corn to burn drives up the cost of corn for those who are eating it to survive. The only way I would burn corn by choice, is if I was growing it, since I would be planting it for that reason and not paying money to divert it from the food market, so I wouldn't feel like I was taking it out of the mouths of hungry people.

Wheat

Wheat at $5.32 a bushel, in an 80% efficient stove provides a million BTU for about $12.74. Once again, an inexpensive fuel source that is probably best suited for areas where wheat is grown and is available in bulk. Bread made from wheat has often been called "The Staff of Life" and today we burn it for fuel, seems like almost a sin in itself. However, it can be an affordable heating "fuel" for those who live in wheat areas.

Grass pellets

One of the possible future fuels being explored today is the use of bio-fuel pellets other than wood such as compressed pellets of different types of grass or agricultural by products such as wheat straw. So far, it appears that these future bio-pellets would have much larger ash content than wood pellets and would probably not work in pellet stoves without modifications. Some corn stoves have been used successfully to burn grass pellets (Harman's corn stove, Bixby Energy's Maxfire corn stove and CountryFlames' corn stove) and they may work in some multi-fuel pellet stoves. Grass pellets surprisingly have a heat content equivalent to wood pellets, but are not widely available and may never be. However, if they are some day, they may have a lower heating cost than any other fuel. Heating with grass pellets could be the next "big thing" and may even replace natural gas someday.

Miscellaneous Bio-fuels

A whole host of bio-fuels has been suggested for use in multi-fuel pellet stoves, including cherry pits, olive pits, wheat hulls, oat hulls, corn pellets, processed silage, various seeds, and all sorts of agriculture products and by-products. Most of these proposed fuels are not widely available and probably never will be, for many of them are not that plentiful to begin with. (Just how much of the USA could be heated with cherry pits?) Therefore, unless one of these bio-fuels is available locally for a low price, there is no reason to consider them realistically as possible fuel sources. A few of these bio-fuels are widely available, such as soybeans, nuts, seeds and grains. All of these except for some seeds most people would not want to eat are foods. Aside from the moral issue of burning what could have been someone else's dinner to heat your home, all of these biofuels being the fruit or seed of the plant, and not the plant itself, in theory will be more expensive than grass pellets.

Soybeans

At a cost of $9.57 per bushel burned in an 80% efficient multi-fuel pellet stove, a MBTU usable heat would cost $19.49.

Wood Pellets

Wood pellets at $190 a ton burned in an 80% efficient pellet stove has a cost of about $14.39 for a MBTU. A few years back when pellet stoves were new, 40lb bags of pellets sold for less than a dollar making pellets one of the very cheapest heating fuels. Now with 40lb bags costing over $5, the price per ton is over $250 and a MBTU of usable heat costs over $16.55

Wood

Wood is one of the few fuels that you can harvest and process yourself. Therefore, it can be a "free" fuel if one can forget about the cost of the chainsaw, log splitter, pickup truck, etc. Not to mention a whole lot of hours of back breaking labor that you can add to the price of your "free" wood. I cut and burn my own wood, I enjoy doing it, and since I am cutting dead trees in my yard, it is work that I would have to do anyway. You can save yourself the cost and labor of cutting your own wood by buying firewood. If you buy wood for $100 a cord and burn it in a 70% efficient wood stove, the cost per MBTU would be $5.71. While wood prices vary greatly locally, $100 per cord is less than the going price in many areas. For example, here in southern Wisconsin near Milwaukee I could easily pay as much as $200 for a face cord that generally does not come close to being a full face cord. Unless you live in a cheap wood area, or can cut your own wood, wood can be too expensive to heat your house for saving money. At my local wood cost, a MBTU would cost about $34.29 when heating with electric baseboards would only cost $31.25 at 10.7 cents a KW. Even if you cut your own wood, the costs of doing so can be more than the money you save by heating with wood making it a net loss. The trick to saving money by burning wood is to get your wood for next to nothing, by getting free wood such as wood scraps or being very frugal with the expenses in cutting your own wood. What burning wood is invaluable for is, as a back up heat source, since you can probably obtain it yourself locally and most wood stoves do not need electricity to run.

Even if you are buying firewood at low cost, burning it in a low efficient manner can make heat from cheap firewood, very expensive. For example, some Outdoor Wood Boilers have efficiencies as low as 28% and in general non EPA approved OWBs have an average efficiency of only 43%, and then they often lose 50% of the heat gained before it gets into the home, resulting in a usable heating efficiency for some OWBs as low as 14%. Burning $100 a cord firewood in an OWB with an overall system efficiency of 14% results in a cost of $32.47 per usable MBTU, which is more costly than using electric heat.

Natural Gas

Natural gas which at a $1.37 a therm, a MBTU of heat costs $17.56 with a 78% efficient gas furnace, which is a bit of a low efficiency since many newer gas furnaces are in the nineties. A 94% efficient furnace with gas at $1.37 a therm would only cost $14.57 for a MBTU, which would be cheaper than electric heat, oil, propane, kerosene, sometimes wood pellets and coal. It is important to consider the efficiency of furnaces when comparing heating costs since at the moment, a 78% NG furnace is more expensive to heat with than a pellet stove while a 94% NG furnace costs less.

Oil

Oil heat at $2.59 a gallon for fuel oil, with a 78% efficient furnace costs $24.57 for a MBTU. Now of course oil has been going up and down quite a bit lately. If heating oil were to drop to $1 a gallon, a MBTU of heat would cost only $9.48, which would be about as cheap as heating with a geothermal heat pump. If it dropped to 50 cents a gallon, oil heat would be cheaper than coal at bulk prices.

However, considering the direction oil will move in the long term, at $4.00 a gallon it would cost $37.95 for a MBTU, and at $10 it would be $94.87 for a MBTU. Changes in fuel prices can make a fuel the cheapest way to heat or the most expensive. The lack of predictability in future fuel costs highlights the wisdom of being able to heat your home with more than one fuel, that way if one becomes too expensive, you can switch to using the other hopefully cheaper fuel. Oil is currently more expensive to heat with than natural gas, that will probably continue to be the case, and it is to be expected that price difference will only get larger over time.

Propane/LP

Propane at $2.03 a gallon, burned in furnace with 78% efficiency, would cost $28.50 for a million BTU and with a 94% efficient furnace; a MBTU would cost $23.65. Propane is always more expensive than natural gas and oil since it is made from them. Due to the high cost of propane, and the huge winter time price increases for propane, propane is not an economical fuel choice. It only makes sense to use propane when cheaper fuels are not available, and with air source heat pumps having big improvements in efficiency and all season models that work well in colder weather and ground source heat pumps that work in all weather, if you have electricity you have heating options that are far cheaper than propane.

Kerosene

Kerosene at $3.80 a gallon burned in an 80% efficient furnace costs $35.19 or $28.15 for a MBTU in an unvented heater, so much for trying to use a kerosene space heater to save money in heating the house. The high cost of kerosene eliminates it from consideration as an economical heating fuel. It is too expensive to use for home heating if anything else is available, since at the present cost, it is the most expensive way of heating, even surpassing the high cost of electric resistance heat. Due to the high cost of kerosene, using it only makes sense for emergency heating use when other forms of heating are not available.

<u>Calculating fuel costs</u>

Fuel costs will have changed greatly by the time you read this, and the fuels that are now bargains in comparison to the other fuels, may not be the same ones when I wrote this book in 2008/9. You will need to use the formulas below to calculate the fuel cost per MBTU and then divide by your heating unit's efficiency (in decimal percentage form, like this 0.78) to arrive at the cost per usable MBTU.

<u>Electric Heat</u>

Price per kilowatt hour multiplied by 293 = cost per MBTU

<u>Air Source Heat Pump</u>

Take your unit's HSPF number and divide it by 3.4 and then divide the cost per MBTU for electricity by that number which will = cost per usable MBTU

<u>Ground Source Heat Pump</u>

Cost per MBTU of electricity divided by your COP number which will = cost per usable MBTU

<u>Natural Gas</u>

Price per therm x 10 = cost per MBTU
<u>LP</u>

Price per gallon x 11 = cost per MBTU

<u>Fuel Oil</u>

Price per gallon x 7.4 = cost per MBTU

<u>Kerosene</u>

Price per gallon x 7.4 = cost per MBTU

Coal

Price per ton divided by 25 = cost per MBTU

Wood

Price per cord divided by 25 = cost per MBTU

Wood pellets, Corn, Corn pellets, Grass pellets

Price per ton divided by 16.5 = cost per MBTU

Price per 40lb bag x 3 = cost per MBTU

Wheat

Price per bushel x 1.92 = cost per MBTU

Soybeans

Price per bushel x 1.63 = cost per MBTU

Chapter 4

Pros and Cons of Upgrading to a Higher Efficiency Heating System

One of the first things people think of when faced with higher heating costs, is replacing their existing heating system with a more efficient one to save money. The problem is that a new heating system is not free and installation costs for some can be quite high. However, in the long term, particularly when facing an uncertain future possibly containing some very large increases in the cost of energy, it can be a case of short-term cost verses long-term savings. The question is how long it will take the savings to pay for the replacement cost. If you need a new heating system anyway, then you certainly should buy an efficient system since the increased cost for a more efficient unit should easily be made up for in fuel savings over the life of the system. Now for those of you paying attention you noticed that I did not say "most efficient". The reason for that is often a manufacturer has a top of the line over priced Cadillac model that has an efficiency rating just a bit higher than the second from the top of the line model that is nearly as good and a much better buy. It makes sense for a manufacturer to offer an over the top model that is the "best" for those customers who's wallets are bigger than their brains. Efficiency is all about price verses operating costs, and if the price is too high, the unit will not have time to pay for itself before it kicks the bucket. Top of the line models tend to have extra features that are not on the cheaper models, sometimes that is because they are not really needed and tend to break down and really run up the repair bills. So often times the "best" is not really the best.

The next decision to make, is that once the replacement heating system is chosen, is deciding on what size to get. Most heating units have a BTU rating which is how many BTU (British Thermal Units, 1 BTU is the amount of heat needed to raise one pound of water one degree Fahrenheit.) the unit will produce per hour. An 80,000 BTU furnace will produce 80,000 BTU each hour. That is how much total heat the unit creates, but some of that heat goes up the chimney. The BTU rating is the input rating; the heat that you keep is called the output rating. If an 80,000 BTU furnace, is 90% efficient you will keep 72,000 BTU and 8,000 BTU will go up and out the chimney each hour that the furnace runs continuously. In replacing your existing heater, look for a BTU rating on it, and this will give you a starting point. Next you will need to know the efficiency rating, so you determine how much heat you are actually getting by multiplying the BTU rating by the efficiency (in decimal form where 78% is 0.78). The efficiency rating maybe found on the unit, or you may be able to estimate it by the type of exhaust system the heating unit has. The other factor to consider is how well the current heater heats the house, if it is big enough to do the job or if it is too big. If it is undersized, it will not be able to maintain your desired room temperature on the coldest days of the year. If it is too big, it will cycle on and off a lot even on the coldest days. An over sized heater costs you more money and all the cycling on and off can wear out the heater sooner. However, truth be told, there is little trouble with having an over sized furnace. The cycling problem is not the big deal that many make it out to be, since even a correctly sized furnace will cycle quite a bit since many high efficiency furnaces will cycle the burner on and off as needed to maintain a narrow temperature range on the heat exchanger. In theory, an oversized furnace may even run less since it will heat the home faster and spend less total time running. Wasting money on an oversized heater is still a very real cost since an oversized unit takes up more space, requires a larger flue and is more expensive to install. To get a large enough heater and yet not too large, consider the size of your current one and how well it does the job, also consider if you have improved the insulation value of your house. If your furnace heated the house fine and you have since insulated heavily and cut your monthly fuel bill in half, you could consider getting a furnace with half the rating of the old one.

If you have no way of knowing the BTU output of your current heat source, you could look for a house similar to yours in size and insulation and see what size of furnace that they have and how well it works. The standard method is to use what is called the manual J load calculation, which involves knowing the size of the house in square feet and the amount of insulation in the walls and ceilings. Since the math involved can be lengthy, it is often now available as a software program, the various numbers such as square feet are entered, and the program figures out the amount of BTU needed to heat the house on the coldest days of the year. There are some free on-line J load calculators, here are the web addresses for two of them.

http://www.heatload.com/forcedair/

http://www.h-mac.com/heat-load-calculator/heat-load-calculator.php

The manual J load calculators will give you the minimum amount of BTU needed for heating and since furnaces and other heaters only come in certain sizes, you will need to buy the size just above the result of the calculation. If the result seems way off, it could be wrong, particularly if any of the numbers you entered were wrong, or the results can be correct. It is common for some furnaces to be twice the size they need to be. If a contractor installs a furnace that is too small to heat the house, he has a problem, but if it is over sized, it will still work and he sells a bigger unit and may make more money. Therefore, the tendency is to error on the large size and install an oversized unit, and what is even worse is that most contractors do not bother to do any calculations, so some furnaces can be massively over sized. The average contractor can probably tell you over the phone by asking a few questions, what size heater he would recommend, bear in mind that his guess will be on the high size of course. However, if you actually do the calculations you may find that a smaller unit will do the job.

Electric Heat

With electric resistance heat like baseboards, there is no exhaust to waste heat, so all electric heaters are 100% efficient, so it is not possible to improve efficiency by getting newer ones. Electric furnaces and boilers are often considered to be 95% efficient since they can lose some heat in transferring it to the living spaces of your home. If you have an unfinished basement, the heat lost there is considered wasted, but since you may use the basement it may not be wasted heat to you. Since the heat is "lost" in moving it, not in creating it, there is no point in trying to get a more efficient electric boiler or furnace. System efficiency in electric boilers is improved by reducing heat losses in the piping by increasing the pipe insulation. With electric furnaces, the ducts need to be sealed and insulated. The biggest gains in reducing the operating costs of electric heat is to weather strip and insulate the home as much as possible, which will have the greatest pay back since electric heat is normally the most expensive way of heating a home.

Since electric heat is so expensive, great savings can be had by switching to something else. Often electric heat is used because other heating options are not available or too expensive in your area. However, if you have electric heat, you could convert to a heat pump, which could cut your costs by about 60%, or a geo-thermal heater, which would cut your costs by about 72%.

Heat Pumps

Newer air source heat pumps can have twice the efficiency of older heat pumps, so you may be able to cut your electric heating bill in half by upgrading to a new high efficiency heat pump. Heat pumps efficiency ratings are given by a HSPF (heating season performance factor) number, which is the ratio of watts used to BTU produced. An old heat pump with a HSPF of five, will produce five BTU per watt used of electrical power, while a newer heat pump with a HSPF of 10 will produce 10 BTU per watt used. Most heat pumps made before 1992 had a HSPF rating below five, while today heat pumps can have a HSPF rating of 9.5 or higher. Locate on your heat pump its labeled HSPF number, and its SEER (seasonal energy efficiency rating) number, which is its air conditioning efficiency ranting. The SEER number will normally be much higher than the HSPF number, because it is much easier to extract heat from an air-conditioned house at 74 F than it is trying to extract heat from 40 F outside air. To figure out what it costs for your heat pump to produce a MBTU, take your electrical rate per KW and multiply it by 293, which will give you the cost for a MBTU with electrical heat. Now take your HSPF number and divide it by 3.4, which will give you the efficiency of your heat pump. Now take the number for the cost of MBTU for electrical heat and divide it by the efficiency (in decimal form) of your heat pump, the result is your cost per MBTU.

If you are spending a $1000, a year, with a heat pump with a HSFP below five, replacing it with heat pump with a HSFP of 9.5 will save you about $500 a year and pay for a $3500 installation in 7 years. If you have a heat pump with a higher HSFP number, the pay back will be smaller of course, and it will take longer to pay for the costs of a new more efficient heat pump.

There are a number of steps that you can take to improve the efficiency of your existing heat pump. The biggest one, is if natural gas is available, is to add a high efficiency gas furnace to create a hybrid heating system. The two heating units are both wired to an outdoor temperature sensor, so that when the temperature is above about 40 degrees, the heat pump runs since it is more efficient than the gas furnace in warmer temperatures, and below 40 degrees the gas furnace runs since at colder temperatures it is more efficient than the heat pump. By combining the two, the hybrid system has an overall efficiency above either heat source by itself.

Dirty air filters are a common problem that is easy to fix. If you do not know where your filter is, the two most popular places are inside the air return vent, which should be the big vent in the hallway or in a slot right next to the indoor heat pump unit in the cold air return duct. The filter has to be located somewhere between the return air grill, and the indoor coil.

Another efficiency tip with heat pumps is that if you do not have a heat pump thermostat and you set a lower temperature at night, when the heat pump gets the sudden request in the morning for more heat than it can do at once, the electric back up resistance heat may come on. Since resistance heat is far more expensive than the heat pump, it will waste whatever you saved by lowering the temperature at night and then some. A thermostat intended for use with a heat pump will be programmed not to call for the electric heat when coming off a lower temperature setback.

One other basic trick is not to run the fan on the "on" setting, since it will run all the time and waste electricity, the "auto" setting will only run the fan when needed and will use less electricity.

In inspecting heat pump heating systems, it was found that more than half had major problems with low airflow, leaky ducts and incorrect refrigerant charge. Your heat pump may have a fan that is belt driven, and belts wear out and need to be replaced now and then. If the belt is slipping, your fan will not be moving the air as much as it should and your heat pump will act as if the coil was dirty. The way to tell if the belt needs to be replaced is to see if it has cracks on the inside surface of the belt or if any of the cords are showing on the edges or back. Other signs of wear are fraying, or chewing, where an area on the belt is visibly worn as if it had been sanded by rough sand paper. This type of wear happens when the belt has stretched enough from use that it is slipping and the drive pulley is wearing it by spinning on it like a grinder. Replacing a belt is easy, with the power turned off, walk the belt off the larger pulley by moving the belt to once side while rotating the pulley by hand. The belt should be loose enough to ride up over the edge and pop off the pulley. On the back side of the belt is the size, but the easy way to get the right size, is to take the belt to a place that sells them, hardware store, auto parts store, garden tractor store, etc, and put the belt on the counter and say "I need a belt like this.". Once you have the new belt, compare it in size to the old belt. It should be a bit shorter, maybe about half an inch or more depending on the length and how long it was in use. If the new belt is longer or much shorter than the old belt, it is the wrong one. The new belt should be the same width, or slightly wider, maybe about a quarter inch wider as the old belt may have narrowed a bit as it wore down into the V pulleys. To install the new belt, place it over the smaller pulley and try to put it over the large pulley and turn the large pulley as you push the belt onto it. As you turn the pulley the belt should pop into the groove, just be careful not to pinch your finger. If the belt is too short to go over the pulley, loosen the motor mount and move the drive pulley closer to the big pulley. Once you have enough slack to get the belt on, move the motor mount adjustment back out until if you press with one finger with about 5 pounds force, the belt only deflects inward about half an inch. While you are playing with the belt, check the motor to see if the bearings need to be lubricated. Some motors have sealed bearings, but many older fan motors need oiling every year. Three to seven drops in each bearing oil well, normally a plastic plug cap that you remove to drip in the oil. You may have to remove the motor and turn it over so the caps are on the upper side, so you can drip the oil in. Yes, life would be so much easier if the oil wells were always on the top side as they should be. Some motors may have little metal nipples; these are grease fittings for connecting a grease gun for pumping grease into the bearing. The rule of thumb for pumping grease is one pump per bearing for small motors (under 3HP), two for mid size (3-5 HP) and three or more for the big ones. You do not want to over grease a motor since any excess grease maybe pumped into the motor shorting it out. Over greasing, is one of the leading causes of industrial motor failure.

Another cause of poor airflow is dirty coils; the operating efficiency of many heat pumps that have been in use for a few years can often be nearly doubled by cleaning the coils and changing the air filter. The outside coil will need to be cleaned even more than the indoor coil; the amount of dirt that can hide in an outdoor coil has to be seen to be believed. Dirt can plug the air passageways between the coil fins, greatly reducing the rate that heat can be transferred by the coil, reducing efficiency sharply. It is a simple matter to clean the coils. For the outside coil, buy "condensing coil cleaner", the non-acid type is safer to work with and does not take paint off, and foaming cleaners help lift the dirt off the coil. The cleaner is mixed with water, and sprayed on the coil using a plastic garden sprayer of the type normally used to spray pesticides or liquid fertilizers. Even the non-acid cleaners are chemically active, so be sure to wear protective clothing, gloves and eye wear. One trick I have for safely spraying on the coil cleaner is to unscrew the spray nozzle so the spray comes out in a solid stream. I hold the nozzle just an inch or two away from the coil so the chemical goes directly into the coil and little if any is misted in the air to blow in your eyes or get on other things nearby. The foaming cleaners should foam up the coil, pushing the dirt out with the foam. Once the foaming slows down, take a garden hose with a spray nozzle and set it not to solid stream, but back it off a bit, so you have a spray pattern about 3 to 6 inches wide at a foot. You want a hard spray to wash out the dirt, but not so hard that you bend over the fins on the coil. Start at the top of the coil and spray left to right and back, while slowly working towards the bottom of the coil. When you first start spraying, the water running off the bottom of the coil will be dirty, but by the time you reach the bottom of the coil, the water should be clear. On really dirty coils it may take more than one cleaning to get all the dirt off. If you have thick mats of dried grass on the coil, you will have to brush them off with a hand brush before cleaning. Bent fins can be straightened with a fin comb, which you can buy for a few dollars.

To clean the indoor coil, buy "Evaporating Coil" cleaner and use the sprayer after it is rinsed out. The cleaner is mixed with water, be careful about getting it too strong, or the soap in the cleaner will act as bubble soap and the system may blow bubbles out the vents. The cleaner can be rinsed off with water or can be left to self-rinse if you run the air conditioner, the water that condenses on the cold coil will wash it off. There will hopefully be an access door you can open to reach the indoor coil, if there isn't one, you maybe able to reach it by removing the air filter and spraying in through the opening using a flash light to see what you are doing. Other options are making small holes that the spray nozzle will fit through, and taping the holes with duct tape when done, or cutting and installing an access door. You maybe able to skip cleaning the indoor coil, since it is normally exposed to much less dirt than the outdoor coil. Regular use of an air filter also helps keep the indoor coil clean as does if the air in the house has is not been filled with cigarette smoke or grease from a lot of frying.

Heat pumps in general, waste 10 to 30 percent of the heat or cooling that they create by blowing it out through leaks in the ductwork. With heat pumps, ductwork is often located in unheated and non-air conditioned spaces such as attics and crawl spaces. Just imagine an open seam on a section of ductwork, with the fan air pressure blowing the hot air out into a cold winter attic or blowing air-conditioned air out into a hot attic. In such spaces the lost hot or cold air will be a rock dropped into the ocean; it is gone with out a trace. The only way to detect such loses is to go over the ductwork and inspect every seam for air leaks while the fan is running. Repairing such leaks is child's play; just tape them up with duct tape. Larger gaps between sections may need to be reconnected and fastened with sheet metal screws or missing sections replaced and large holes capped with sheet metal secured with sheet metal screws and taped. The ductwork should also be heavily insulated, and the insulation should be checked and repaired or replaced as needed or installed if there is not any. Foil backed fiberglass insulation works great and the seams can be sealed with foil tape, which if done neatly, it makes the ductwork look brand new and very efficient looking.

If your heat pump has too little refrigerant charge or too much, it will not run right and will be wasting energy if it even works at all. Too much charge can only occur if the system was over charged when it was installed or last serviced, while too little refrigerant is usually the result of a small leakage over time. Since there are normally no gauges to tell you how much refrigerant is in the system, your best indication of if you have a proper charge is system performance. If the heat pump works great, your charge is probably about right. However, if you have performance problems that are not cleared up by the steps outlined above like cleaning the coils and checking the belt, etc, you should have the refrigerant charge checked. The only way to check the refrigerant charge is to hire a certified air conditioning technician to check it. With the current EPA laws on the servicing of refrigeration systems, you must be an EPA certified refrigeration technician to check the charge on a refrigeration system. A person can be fined $25,000 by the EPA for venting refrigerants and just having a refrigerant manifold gauge set to check your charge in your possession could make you the possible target of such a fine. There is also a $10,000 reward offered by the EPA for reporting anyone who violates the EPA laws on the proper handling of refrigerants. You also need to be an EPA certified refrigeration technician to legally buy the necessary refrigerants to recharge the system. So the would be do-it-yourself person is legally locked out from handling or even checking the pressure of common refrigerants used in home air conditioning systems. Without an EPA certification, you are limited to fixing things outside of the refrigerant tubing system.

Geo-thermal or Ground Source Heat Pumps

Despite the newness of GHP (Geo-thermal heat pump), it can be worthwhile to upgrade to a newer one since some new GHP have twice the efficiency of older GHP. The heating efficiency of GHPs are rated by their Coefficient of Performance or COP (efficiency rating) which is the ratio of BTU output divided by BTU in, which is roughly equal to a HSFP rating divided by 3.4, so that a COP rating of three is about equal to a HSFP of 10.2. The COP ratings of GHP range from under three to over six, and the EER rating for cooling which is similar to the SEER ratings for air conditioners, can range as high as over 30. Ideally, in replacing an old GHP with a new more efficient one, you may be able to reuse your existing ground loop, so the cost of upgrading would only be the cost of replacing the heat pump itself, and would not include the cost of installing a new ground loop.

For improving the efficiency of your current GHP, most of the information on improving the efficiency of Heat pumps applies since the two have many components in common. The key difference is that GHP does not have an outdoor coil to clean, and some GHP heat the home by means of a radiant floor loop, so some GHP do not have fans, belts or air filters. GHP are considered one of the lower maintenance heating systems. On most GHPs, you do have air filters, ductwork and fan belts to check, and an indoor coil that can be cleaned. The ground loop water pump filter should also be cleaned every three months, and if you have a radiant floor loop, that pump's filter should be cleaned as well. Also like with heat pumps, if even after checking these things you still have performance problems, have the charge checked by an EPA certified refrigeration technician.

Natural Gas

On natural gas furnaces, it normally does not pay to upgrade to a higher efficiency furnace if you already have one that has plastic

PVC pipe for the chimney or exhaust vent. PVC vented furnaces are high efficiency furnaces, also called condensing furnaces, with an efficiency range of 89% for the worst to 97% for the best, so the maximum possible savings for upgrading is only 8%. Most of the condensing furnaces are in the 90-94% range, meaning that your probable savings if you up graded to the "Best" model would only be 3-7%. With an annual gas bill of $1000 a 5% savings for the "Best" would be about $50 and with an installed cost of $3500 would take 70 years to pay for it, which would be hard with gas furnaces having an average lifetime of only 20 years.

Shockingly, not all new gas furnaces sold are high efficiency, it is still legal to sell gas furnaces with efficiency rates as low as 78%. These "mid-efficiency" furnaces are from 78% up to maybe 88%, but anything above 81% tends to have condensing problems which since gas condensate is corrosive, can lead to heat exchanger failure and corrosion damage to the stove pipe and chimney, so nearly all of these furnaces are about 80% efficient or less to avoid this problem. These mid-efficiency furnaces have exhaust temperatures that are too hot for venting with PVC, and are vented using metal stovepipe and chimneys. It makes no sense to buy a mid efficiency furnace any more, gas is just too expensive, and since a furnace is expected to last 20 years, the out look for future gas prices makes it a certainty that within the next 20 years you will be kicking yourself for not buying a better furnace. Replacing an 80% efficient furnace with a 95% one with an annual gas bill of $1000, you would save $158 a year and with an installed cost of $3500 would take 22 years to pay for itself.

Now if you have an old gas furnace, with a pilot light, dating from the early 1970s or earlier, the efficiency is around 65%. If you replaced it with a 95% furnace with an annual gas bill of $1000 you would save $316 per year and the new furnace at $3500 would pay for itself in 11 years.

LP/Propane

Heating with propane is very much like heating with gas, in fact most propane furnaces are modified natural gas furnaces. Like NG (natural gas) furnaces, LP (Liquefied Propane) furnaces have had the same increases in efficiencies and the same percentage gains in efficiencies can be had by installing a newer higher efficiency furnace. The difference between LP and NG is that LP is more expensive than NG, which makes any gain in efficiency much more of a financial gain. The gain in efficiency of replacing a old 65% efficient furnace with a new 95% efficient furnace results in the same 32% reduction in fuel use as with NG, but with LP costing about 30-40% more than NG, that also reduces the time it takes to pay for a new furnace by 30-40%. The high cost of LP makes insulating to reduce heating costs, even more important.

LP gas does have some very fundamental financial differences from NG. NG users are used to small increases that they can do nothing about, while LP users can often pick and choose from among a number of different supplies, and such competition can help hold down prices. LP is however very prone to supply shortages that occur in wintertime with near 100% certainty and result in some rather sudden and severe surges in price. This wintertime price surge is so predictable that many LP suppliers offer their customers the option of locking in the price by prepaying for their winter fuel. However, unless the supplier has an enormous storage tank farm, he will still have to buy LP at wintertime high prices to supply his customers, so that the reduced rate offered may not be as low as what LP costs in the summer. While such prepay plans are a great bargain, an even greater savings may be had by buying enough tanks or a large enough tank, to last for the entire heating season. Then you can buy LP in the summer at the cheapest rates and have enough to last until the price is low once again. Of course you have to pay for the larger tank, while a nearly as large savings maybe available with a dealer's prepay plan.

As you hopefully noticed in the preceding chapter on comparing the cost of heating with various heating methods, LP was second in cost only to heating with electrical resistance heating. Therefore, you could reduce heating costs by switching to any of the other alternatives. NG is of course the most logical option to switch to, but if it was not the fuel of choice when your furnace was put in, it was probably because it was not available. Since that time, your local gas company has undoubtedly been busier than a butcher shop dog burying bones, so NG may now be available or may be available soon. It would be wise to call your local NG Company and find out if NG is available or will be, to avoid going to the expensive of perhaps switching to oil only to have NG available next year.

Even when NG is available, many LG users still do not switch due to the cost of switching over, which can be $100 to $200 dollars per appliance, if you make a list of everything that uses propane in your house it can really add up. The simple solution is to have only the furnace converted to NG and keep the other small appliances on LP, and then as they need to be replaced, they can be replaced with NG appliances. Without the furnace on LP, the tank will probably easily last the whole heating season so it can now be just filled when LP is cheaper in the summer. To do this sort of gradual change over, when the furnace is hooked up, have NG lines run to each appliance, but not connected and leave the LP lines in place. It would also be a very good idea, to clearly label the lines so no mistakes are made in the future.

Many LP users switched to LP from electric heat, to save money. While LP remains cheaper than electric resistance heat, electric heat pumps are much more economical than LP. In areas where it is seldom below freezing, air source heat pumps can heat for half the cost of LP, and geothermal or ground source heat pumps can heat for a third of the cost of LP. The reason we have not seen a whole scale switch from LP to air source heat pumps, is they are less efficient at cold temperatures. Geothermal heat pumps over come this problem by using the ground rather than the air, but the installation costs can run about $20,000 to $30,000. If you were using a $1000 a year heating with LP, switching to Geothermal would save you $667 a year, and it would take 30 years to pay for a $20,000 installation.

Another option for LP users is to install a pellet stove, since while heating with wood pellets is about as expensive as NG, it is 30 to 40% cheaper than LP.

Fuel Oil

Oil furnaces are in theory only used today where natural gas is not available, since oil is now more expensive to heat with. Depending upon the relative prices of natural gas and fuel oil, gas can be 25 to

40% cheaper. In addition, of course oil furnaces require far more maintenance and parts than gas furnaces, for units with comparable efficiency.   It is estimated that 35% of the oil-heating units in residential use, are over 20 years old and have efficiencies of about 56%–70% while new furnaces are required by law to be at least 78% efficient and some are up to 96.7% efficient. Replacing a 65% efficient oil furnace with a 95% efficient one, with an annual oil bill of $1,000 would save $461 a year and pay for an installation cost of $3,500 in less than 8 years.

The problem with oil burners is that they last too long, and over time, they turn into old inefficient dinosaurs. Old furnaces had a low efficiency to start with, and they become less efficient as they age until they turn into a real Smokey fire-breathing monster that is best sold for scrap and replaced with something that has a much lighter appetite. The best choice is to switch to a more affordable fuel; the second is to get a high efficiency oil furnace or boiler. A third choice that is cheapest in the short term, is to upgrade your existing oil burner to improve its efficiency.

If you have a tall chimney, such as is found in a two or three story tall home with a steep roof, your draft could be excessive and a Barometric flue damper could reduce the excessive draft and increase your efficiency by 5%, of course you probably already have one, since this is a very old trick. The next trick is to install a smaller nozzle in your burner, reducing the furnace's heat output which in effect makes the heat exchanger bigger, reducing the amount of heat that goes up the chimney and also reduces the on and off cycling. This can increase efficiency by 10%, but if your furnace has a hard time keeping up in the winter, this may not be your best choice. You could however increase your home's insulation so that far less heat is needed and then also reduce your furnace's output, which would be in effect doubling the savings. The biggest trick for improving the efficiency of old oil burners is to replace the old burner with a flame retention burner for about a 20% increase in efficiency. Flame retention burners have been around for decades so even most old oil heating units already have one. The other problem with flame retention burners is that they burn hotter than the old burners and there is a chance that you will burn out your heat exchanger in as little as one to two years. If you do decided to install a flame retention burner, you may be able to extend the life of your heat exchanger by down sizing the burner, and you could increase the amount you could downsize and increase the lifespan of your heat exchanger further by reducing the heat needed by insulating your home.

I would be amiss, if I failed to remind you that the simplest way to improve the efficiency of an oil furnace or boiler is to clean it. As you know, oil is not a clean fuel, and the heat exchanger will get a build up of unburned oil and oil ash, that will insulate the surface of the heat exchanger and reduce the efficiency of transferring the heat. Every year, an oil burner needs to be opened up and cleaned out with a metal brush used for cleaning furnaces. The burner nozzle may need replacing, and the arc rods may need cleaning and adjustment. The key adjustment on an oil burner is adjusting the inlet air; too much air wastes heat up the chimney while too little air soots up the furnace with unburned carbon. The old time trick is to reduce the air until the furnace starts to smoke and then back off and increase until the smoking stops and give it just a bit more for some leeway. Such fly by the seat of your paints will not give you the most efficient air/fuel ratio possible, unless you are lucky or are much better than most at doing this. A CO_2 meter or flue-gas analyzer some times called a combustion analyzer is necessary for correctly setting the air/fuel ratio, to measure the percentage of CO_2 in the exhaust and adjust it to the desired level of 10%, which means the burner is getting just the right amount of air. If you learn how to maintain your heating system and repair it, you will not have to pay someone else to do it for you. You can get all the parts and tools you need from supply houses like Johnstone supply, which also has a number of stores across the country where you can go and pick up parts when you need them right away. If you are not the do-it-yourself type, it pays to have an oil burner cleaned and adjusted once a year by a service person to keep it operating efficiently and safely.

Coal

If you are still burning coal, you are either behind the times or ahead of everyone else since we seem to be coming full circle with coal once again becoming the fuel of choice for many. The efficiency of most older coal stoves is about 50 to 65% while new coal stoves are about 60% to 80%, automatic feeding stoves are 70% to 85%. Due to a lack of regulation and testing, it is often impossible to know or even compare the real efficiency of one coal burner with another. Some older coal stoves have efficiencies that are sometimes higher than some of the new stoves, thus buying a newer unit is no guarantee in itself of reducing fuel costs. You maybe better off weather stripping the house. There are coal stoves with efficiency claims of 88% to 90% (Keystoker coal stoves http://www.keystoker.com/index.html) and replacing a 50% efficient coal stove with a 90% efficient one, with a $1000 annual coal bill would save $444 and pay for an installation cost of $3500 in 8 years. Due to the historically low cost of coal, your annual coal cost maybe much lower, which greatly increases the number of years it takes for a more efficient stove to pay for itself. Coal prices are affected by oil prices and we have and probably will see large price increases in the near future. Even now, Pocahontas coal in 50 lb bags can cost over $15 a bag, which is $600 a ton. If coal prices continue to rise, it changes things and makes upgrading to a more efficient coal burner an economic necessity, if you are going to continue heating with coal. A recent and probably temporary drop in the price of natural gas, put heating with gas below the cost of heating with coal in some areas in the United States, which is just part of the trend of escalating coal prices.

Wood Pellets, Corn and Grain.

Wood pellets, corn and most grain stoves, furnaces and boilers are all so new that there is not enough of an improvement in efficiency in most cases to make it economical to replace an older unit with a new one since they both will have about the same efficiency (all about 80%). There are a few high tech pellet stoves and multi fuel stoves that have an efficiency in the high nineties, like Bixby Maxfire with a claimed efficiency of about 97% which retails for about $4,500. If you burned three tons of pellets each winter at a cost of $750 at per bag cost of $5, and switching to the Maxfire reduced your pellet burning by nearly 20%, you would save $150 a year and it would take 30 years to cover the cost of the stove. Then there are also installation costs and expected costs for repairs, which makes it unlikely that you could save money by switching from a regular pellet stove to a high efficiency pellet stove while still burning wood pellets. However, a larger savings at a lower cost is possible by switching from wood pellets to corn or grain, and in the future, grass pellets may be an even better bargain. The price for wood pellets has risen to the point where in some places it is now cheaper to heat with natural gas, and it was logical to expect pellet prices to rise to that point. For if, heating with wood pellets is much cheaper than heating with gas, people will switch to pellets, and with more people buying pellets the price rises until it is no longer a bargain and people have no economic reason to switch to a pellet stove. Unfortunately, the same principle may apply to corn and grain, since they are much cheaper to heat with, many will do so, until the price rises to the point where it is not a significant savings to switch to them. This means that the price for corn and grain will rise and just as other fuels like natural gas and coal rise in price when oil does, so in the future the price for corn and grains may very well rise proportionately in step with oil prices if their use as fuel becomes wide spread.

If you replaced your wood pellet stove with a stove that can burn corn (both with an efficiency of 80%), currently with wood pellets at $5 per 40lb bag, a MBTU costs about $18.75 while for corn at $4 per bushel (56lb) a MBTU costs $10.81 .

All three of these fuels are best bought in bulk when they are cheapest. For wood pellets, they are cheapest, or should be, in summer before the retailers place their orders for the fall, about late spring until mid summer. Unfortunately, wood pellets are now in such demand, that there is little reduction in price even in the summer in most places. Locate the nearest manufacturer of wood pellets and order at least a year's worth or more to get the lowest price. For corn, the lowest price is often at harvest time in the fall in your local area, and remember we are taking about field corn not sweet corn. Sweet corn is harvested in the late summer, while field corn is left in the field until the kernels have dried in the hopefully dry fall air. Buying corn in bulk means that unlike wood pellets, the corn will be unbagged. You will need to be able to store the corn in a dry location that is inaccessible to rats or other animals. Your best deal will be to buy enough for the heating season from a local farmer, who will probably be thrilled to sell to you, since you need to heat your house every year, making you a repeat customer. Make sure that the corn is dry, in a dry fall, the corn will be dry enough from air-drying in the field, but if the fall is wet, the corn may need to be dried by the farmer. The corn needs to be dried before being stored or it would get moldy, so drying is a normal procedure. Check bulk corn prices and offer the farmer a price a bit above that, and he should jump at the offer since he does not have to take the corn to a distance mill, and may be willing to throw in free delivery.

Grains are similar to corn, except for that they are harvested earlier and their fineness will require different handling. If you do not wish to buy in bulk, you can buy corn and grain in bags from your local feed store, but you will pay a much higher price of course. Pellets are also available at many building supply stores, at prices slightly higher than buying in bulk.

Wood Heat

Great gains in efficiency are possible in burning wood for heat; some of the possible gains are almost beyond imagining. Open fireplaces have an efficiency of only 15%, while a fireplace insert has an efficiency of 70-80%, which means that the same heat output can be produced in the insert while using only a fifth of the wood that was used in the fireplace before. That is an 80% reduction in wood use. In wood stoves, the new EPA rated stoves are far less smokey and produce the same amount of heat while burning about half the wood. Therefore, if you burn 10 cords a year, and each cord cost $150, a new wood stove with twice the average efficiency of the old stove, would save you $750 a year, and cover an installation cost of $3500 in less than 5 years, that however, is a very rough estimate based on some broad generalizations.

Old non EPA wood stoves when running with a reduced air inlet setting, are only about 35-40% efficient, which is nothing short of terrible, but when running hot with plenty of air, their efficiency shoots up to 70-75% efficiency. While the new EPA approved wood stoves with a reduced air inlet setting are about 70-75% efficient and are up to 80% efficient when running hot. The reason for this is that with the old stoves, at low setting the temperature in the fire box dropped and a lot of creosote was not burned and even some of the wood was not completely burned either at times leaving behind black ash. However, if the stove inlet damper was opened up, enough air entered the firebox for the fire to get hot enough to burn the creosote and completely burn the wood leaving only white ash behind. The EPA approved stoves use various tricks like directing the smoke back down into the hottest part of the fire to burn the creosote even when the fire is smaller, which allows more complete combustion even while on a reduced setting.

Therefore, to improve efficiency if you have an old wood stove, you can replace it with a new EPA approved one, which will double your efficiency when running with reduced air inlet. On the other hand, you can keep your old stove and only burn hot fires for which your old wood stove will be or will very nearly be as efficient and clean burning as an EPA approved stove. Now the very reason everyone cuts back on the air inlet on the wood stove is to keep from overheating the house. They are trying to match the heat output from the stove to the heat load of the house. The trick for doing this with hot fires is, instead of reducing the air available to the fire, you reduce the wood. The normal operation of a wood stove is to keep a fire running all the time and adjust the size of the fire to match the heat loss of the house to keep a constant temperature. The new EPA approved stoves can do this without smoking and wasting wood, while the old stoves could easily drop their efficiency down to 35% and smoke out the neighbors with a really unhealthy nasty sooty smoke. If you want to load up the stove and let it run, you really need to buy a new one. To run an old stove efficiently and cleanly you need to change your whole outlook, and how you operate your stove. To do it right, the first step, is to forget about maintaining a constant temperature in the house, which is only possible with a constant fire. With brief hot clean fires, you need to think in terms of a temperature range of perhaps 68 to 72 degrees. You let the house cool down to 68 degrees and then you load the stove up with enough wood to raise the house back up to 72 degrees as a target that you are shooting for. With practice, you will learn how much wood it takes to heat the house under various conditions. By doing a rough estimate, of how many degrees you wish to raise the temperature in the house against how cold it is outside, will give you an idea of how much wood to put in the stove. Then you light the fire and run the stove with the control damper as wide open as you reasonable and safely can, without over heating the stove. Once you set the inlet damper, you let the fire burn and you do not have to attend to the stove until it is time for the next fire. If you guessed right on the wood, the stove will raise the house to your target temperature and then the fire will be burning out by then. The surge in heat in the wood stove, in the chimney, in the hot air in the house and the house itself, will maintain the temperature for a while and then slowly drop. The daily pattern of firing your wood stove is to allow the temperature to drop over night as you normally would, and then in the early morning to light a large fire that will bring the house up to your target temperature. Then you let the house cool back down to the low end of your temperature range and then light another fire sized to bring the house temperature back up to your target temperature once again. You can extend the time between fires by increasing the insulation in your home, which reduces the rate at which your house loses heat. Stored heat in the house in the form of hot masonry will also extend the time between fires. If you have an exposed fireplace in the center of the house that also houses the flue for the wood stove, you have a heat sink that stores heat for you. If you have a concealed masonry chimney that is not on an outside wall, you can tap into it as heat storage by installing a vent near the floor and another near the ceiling in the drywall, which will allow the air warmed by the chimney to flow into the room. If you do this trick, make sure that the chimney is fire stopped at the floor and ceiling in the space between the chimney and the surrounding wall, so that air cannot flow up from a basement or up into an attic. If there are no fire stops, fiberglass insulation with foil backing or no backing, can be stuffed into the gap like a weather seal, to seal the gap. The danger in having an open space without any fire blocks around the chimney is that if a fire were to start, the free flow of air would allow the fire to rapidly spread upward into the attic. Even just the vents for recovering the "free" heat, could feed air to such a fire, and may pose a small increased risk. On the other hand, the vents may also allow you to quickly detect any smoke leaks from the chimney before they become the source of a possible fire. Other tricks to extend the time between fires by increasing thermal mass, is to add firebricks to your wood stove. Many old stoves have as few as the manufacturer could get away with, and some have space where a second layer can be added over the ones already there. If you have a non-EPA approved stove, look inside your firebox and see if you could add some more. Adding firebricks raises the temperature at the base of the fire and increases the cleanness of the burn while increasing efficiency if done right. The idea here is to insulate the fire, not just stuff bricks in the way. The firebricks work best on the bottom and lower sides of the firebox, think if it as lining a warm nest for the fire. Once the fire is out, the bricks will still be very hot, and will gradually give off heat as they cool. Remember that one brick in the firebox will store the heat of ten bricks in the chimney.

If you have a well-insulated house and some thermal mass, you may only need to make one fire in the morning, for most of the winter. On the colder days, a second fire in the evenings may be necessary, and on the really cold days, a mid day fire may also be needed. By doing these hot fires now and then, rather than constant firing, your old wood stove will burn clean and use half the wood you would otherwise. If your house is poorly insulated, on cold days you will need to make more frequent fires, and as it get colder, transition into one long hot fire. This type of brief hot firing is definitely trickier than constant firing, which is why buying one of those expensive new EPA rated wood stoves may be the smart thing to do.

The biggest gain in wood burning efficiency is to properly dry your firewood and keep it dry. Cut your wood early enough that it has time to dry before you need to use it. Never burn wet wood or green wood unless you have a heating emergency and it is all you have. For burning wet wood wastes wood, for it can take half of the energy in the wood to drive off the water, and doing so reduces the temperature of the fire, which leaves the soot and creosote unburned. Some manufacturers will state that their stove or boiler, can burn wet and green wood, which is true in the same sense that you can use your golf clubs to pound nails. Sure, you probably could do it, but that still does not mean that you should. On the other hand, it is also a commonly held myth that wood has to season for a year before it can be burned. Wood does not have to be seasoned; it only needs to be dry, which it can do in less than a year. It is possible: under ideal conditions, to dry wood in as little as two weeks. I do not know about you, but I know that I do not have idea conditions for my woodpile. However, I routinely dry my wood in three to six months. The trick is to stack your wood in rows with enough space between them so that the air can flow through the pile and also flow in one end and out the other. You also need a tarp to keep the rain off the pile. What works is to cover the pile with a tarp over the top, but leave the ends of the rows exposed so that the air can blow through underneath. Also if possible, remove the bark and split the wood, which will dry the wood much quicker. That is the idea, but I only manage to knock the bark off the dead wood and elm does not split nearly so ideally. If I was able to get all my firewood into such idea pieces, I could probably dry my wood perfectly in the Wisconsin month of August before the month ended, in time for the start of the heating season next month. (Depressing isn't it?)

Wood Burning with an Outdoor Wood Boiler

It has been noted *"OWBs may be among the dirtiest and least economical modes of heating"* (NY Attorney General's Report). The state of Washington has already banned all OWBs and as of March 31, 2008 it is illegal to sell or import non-EPA approved OWBs in the states of Maine and Vermont, and many local townships and counties have also banned OWBs as well. OWBs have attracted enormous opposition. The reason for such down right hatred is caused by OWBs low efficiency since what you don't use as heat goes up the stack in the form of smoke, often in the case of OWBs, huge dark clouds of choking thick smoke that people don't like breathing. In terms of efficiency, Outdoor Wood Boilers are a disaster with an overall efficiency rating that is sometimes as low as fireplaces. Common OWBs in efficiency tests scored as low as 28% with an average efficiency of only 43%. As bad as these efficiency ratings are, they only tell half the story. Since the boiler is outside and still has to get the heat into the house, and it is common for OWBs to lose 50% or more of their heat in the ground lines, resulting in a total system efficiency as low as 14% with an average of only 22%. In some cases, even as dismal as these figures are, some OWB users burn wet wood and greenwood which can cut the efficiency of use in half again, wasting heat to drive off the water as steam, resulting in as little as 7% of the potential heat value in the wood ending up as heat in the house. While few OWB owners are working uphill against such long odds, OWBs are well known for their monstrous appetites for huge quantities of firewood and being prodigious producers of thick sooty smoke. It is a given that a OWB will consume more wood to heat a home than an indoor boiler due to the very nature of it's design. But the picture for OWBs, is not all dark, there is now a bright spot on the horizon, new EPA approved Phase 2 OWBs with efficiencies of 66-88% which for the same heat output, burn half the wood and produce only a tenth of the smoke of the old OWBs. If a Phase 2 OWB is installed with properly insulated ground lines, and only properly dried firewood is burned, huge gains in efficiency and smoke reduction are possible. With efficiencies as high as 88%, with well-insulated ground lines total system efficiencies of 70 to 80% are possible. Which is close to the performance of efficient indoor water boilers, if you can over look the loses that occur while the OWB idles when in contrast an IWB is storing heat in a water tank or is not fired to prevent over heating. A new EPA approved phase 2 OWB costs about $10,000 and will cut firewood use about in half, so if you are burning 10 cords a year at $100 a cord, you would save $500 a year and it would take 20 years to pay for the cost of a new OWB, then there are the installation costs. Of course, if you are paying for and burning much larger amounts of wood, the time it would take to pay for the new OWB is reduced accordingly.

If you have, a new EPA approved phase 2 OWB or any of the EPA approved OWBs, there is not much that you can do to improve efficiency. Aside from installing well-insulated ground lines, increasing your chimney height to improve natural draft and for getting the smoke up out of the way and burning properly dried wood. If you have a non-EPA approved OWB, there are quite a number of things you can do to improve efficiency, which will also reduce the amount of wood you need to burn and the amount of smoke you put in the air. The efficiency of any wood fire is very dependent on the temperature of the fire, colder fires often fail to burn much of the creosote and even soot resulting in a very smoky fire. Many OWB fireboxes do not have any firebrick, but instead are bare metal with water right on the other side, resulting in a very cold surface being exposed to the fire. Since water temperatures in OWB will nearly always be below 200 degrees and creosote burns at 1000 F, these primitive designs result in the near equivalent of trying to burn a hot fire inside of a block of ice. A firebox needs to be lined with firebrick to allow the fire to reach the high temperatures necessary for efficient combustion. Firebrick acts as high temperature insulation, allowing the fire to reach higher temperatures while shielding the metal of the firebox metal from temperatures that would damage it. You can lay a tile like floor of firebricks being careful not to cover any air inlets, and then stack a wall of bricks up the sides of the firebox, creating a hot spot for the fire to burn in. On many OWBs, the stack is too short to create an adequate natural draft, one solution is to add an insulated chimney extension, and the other is to install a draft inducer (about $1000). Draft inducers are a type of exhaust fan installed in the chimney or on the chimney cap, and are turned on and off normally by a heat sensor installed in or on the chimney base where it can detect the heat of a fire burning. On OWB with only natural draft, a draft inducer can over come the problems of poor air flow and assure enough oxygen reaches the fire for complete combustion. An insulated chimney extension can do the same, by increasing the natural draft and a taller chimney will help get the smoke up and away from people and things on the ground.

The biggest improvement in operating a standard OWB is to only load enough wood into the firebox to bring the water temperature up as needed. In other words, do not over load the OWB with too much wood, for once the heat demand is satisfied, and the house is at temperature, the OWB will shut down or idle. This is when OWBs smoke, when they are idling or coming off idling. You can't really turn off a wood fire, the wood is hot and wants to burn, and it is impossible with today's products to totally shut off the air, and even if you could it would be very unwise since then the fire really would go out but the flammable gases would still be emitted and would build up. Such gases need to be burned off to avoid the risk of a flash over or even an explosion, one solution as is used in more efficient wood burning stoves, is to reduce primary air to the fire while still providing secondary air to burn off the gases. Unfortunately, this concept has not been used or at least successfully used by standard OWBs or they would not be the smoky monsters that they are. On a natural draft OWB it may be possible to add secondary air, by drilling a hole in the front wall of the OWB in an area where it is "single walled" and there is no water jacket. Then run a one and one half inch threaded pipe in through the firebox along one side and back up to a point above the fire where the flames can reach it. If done correctly, the pipe will add enough secondary air and burn off the soot and some of the unburned gases. The secondary air pipe or pipes, need to be sized to provide 20% of the air that is coming in through the regular damper, the primary air that goes to feed the fire. Making such modifications to an OWB is largely a matter of trail and error, and you will need to observe what works and what does not and make changes as needed. Considering how primitive some OWB designs are, it should not be too hard to vastly improve both efficiency and reduce smoking.

Another modification to reduce idling and smoking, is to add more water volume to the system by adding a large tank in the house or one in each heated building. In this modification, the OWB now instead of heating the home or multiple buildings, heats one or more large tanks of water. The tanks act as heat storage, and can be sized to hold all the heat that an OWB can produce from the maximum wood load that it can burn without being over loaded. Each tank can also be sized according to the heat needs of the building it is supplying, so that when one tank needs heat the others do too. Then a fire can be made and all of the tanks brought back up to temperature. Each tank can be heated by a heat exchanger to reduce the amount of anti-freeze needed or can be piped directly. Then the building heating system pumps water from the tank as heat is needed. The tanks also have the advantage of being indoors and any heat leakage helps heat the building, instead of trying to heat the outdoors as the case with standing heat loses from the OWB. This idea works better with OWBs that have smaller water capacity, since the heat stored in the OWB is lost if the unit has time to cool down between firings and has to be brought back up to temperature. This loss can be reduced on many units that are poorly insulated by removing the covering panels of the OWB and adding insulation, which will also reduce heat losses while burning as well. All OWB manufacturers will state that their product is already fully insulated and no additional insulation needs to be added. However, I would suggest that you check for yourself and see if that is true or not, since OWB manufacturers have quite a history of making statements about their products that seem to be more the result of wishful thinking than reality.

Chapter 5

Insurance

When it comes to insurance companies and their agents, I tend to think of Snidley Whiplash in his black hat and cape, with his over sized handle bar mustache that he would run his fingers over as he chuckled evilly as he planned his next evil deed. While there are, in my opinion some companies and agents that do seem to live down to that standard, some are fair and reasonable. The concept of insurance is that a loss that would financially wipe out one, if shared can be absorbed by a group. Which makes good sense, few people could afford to replace their home if it burned down, but a whole community can afford the cost of replacing a home. Therefore, we all pay our insurance premiums so that our risks are covered or shared by all who have insurance with that particular company. Insurance is a noble enterprise with worthy goals, the problem is that insurance companies like to make money and do not always like to pay claims as they should and many people with insurance like to understate their risks so they can under pay the insurance company or even make false claims to rip off the company. This cheating on both sides, leads to a lack of trust, while in the past things may have been agreed to with a handshake, today we have very long forms that list exactly what is or is not covered and for how much. While insurance companies like to encourage their customers to feel all warm and fuzzy, that they can completely trust the insurance company to take care of them that of course is nonsense. Insurance companies are run by accountants and you are just one of the numbers. An insurance company looks at you and everything you do, not in terms of what a nice person you are, but in terms of a premium/risk ratio. Like if you decide to start a fireworks factory in your garage, the insurance company will decide that this increases the odds that you will soon be making an insurance claim, so they will either greatly increase your premiums or cancel your insurance. To stay in business insurance companies need to control their risks, it does not matter if you go golfing with your agent or not, it all comes down to the numbers game of averaging more in premiums than you pay out in claims.

It is not that insurance companies are cold hearted, well OK maybe they are, but you just have to remember that they look at things differently than you do, for everything is looked at in view of being a possible risk for filing an insurance claim. Adding insulation or weather stripping your home is not an insurance issue, for there is no increased risk associated with it. You should have no problems with your insurance company with any of those activities as long you do not do any damage to your home that results in your later making an insurance claim.

Adding a solar system is risk wise, not much of an insurance event, but you should inform your insurance company about it, if you wish for them to cover it. Much like if you bought some expensive furniture and wanted to make sure your insurance company will pay for it if the house burns down. Insurance companies do not like to pay for things that they did not know that you owned. A solar system should be included on any list made of things insured in the home.

Before you consider installing any new heating system, you need to consider the impact it will have on your homeowner's insurance policy. Heating systems tend to be expensive and since they also generally involve burning something, they can be a cause of home fires. If installing a new heating system results in a large increase in your insurance premium, adding the system may not be cost effective. Not telling your insurance company is not wise either, since an undisclosed risk, could give your insurance company a legal justification for refusing to pay any future insurance claims. While there still maybe some insurance companies who will drastically raise your rates or drop you for installing a wood stove, they would be the exception rather than the rule. Most insurance companies today are very open minded about alternative heating, if you follow their guide lines, which do turn out to be very reasonable.

I asked American Family Insurance what their policy was on someone installing a wood stove, and I received the following response from one of their agents.

"If the wood stove is installed according to code it does not matter who installed it. The stove must have a UL label. The agent does go to the home and takes a picture of the stove. We have a wood burning booklet that we offer to people. It shows recommended clearances from walls and floor. If we approve the stove there is no extra charge on the homeowners."

American Family Insurance's policy is very fair and reasonable on wood stoves, if your insurance company gives you any grief, you can always switch to American. Notice what the insurance agent stated about *"recommended clearances"*, that to get or keep insurance, the system has to be installed according to code standards. The term *"code"* refers to safety codes, building codes, electrical codes etc. While there maybe safe non-code ways of installing a heating system, your insurance company will only insure your home if your installation follows the various codes involved. It is not just the do-it-yourselfer that sometimes fails to follow the codes, there also are contractors who fail to do work that is up to code, and these are the guys with 10 thumbs that you should avoid like the plague that leave a disaster wherever they go. Obviously, no one in their right mind would insure anything that they had touched, and that is why we have code standards. Codes are designed to prevent accidents waiting to happen, from being built in the first place. Many code standards are literally the result of combing through the ashes to find out what went wrong and figuring out how to prevent it from happening again. Nobody wants their home to burn down, code standards are designed to prevent that from happening, so it is in your best interests to always follow code standards and make sure any contractor that you use does so as well.

Insurance and Outdoor Boilers

One of the biggest reasons that people decide to install an outdoor boiler rather than having something in the house, is because they worry about their insurance. As the response above from American Family Insurance shows, some insurance companies do not have a problem with properly installed wood stoves. If you would rather have an indoor unit rather than an outdoor unit, check with your insurance company, they may not have a problem with it. If you do not check, you may find yourself having to go out in the cold for years to make a fire just because you were unwilling to make a phone call. Other than the insurance issue, outdoor boilers have few advantages while having many disadvantages. Even if your insurance company was more favorable towards outdoor boilers, you would probably be better off if you got an indoor unit and switched insurance companies. Any money saved on premiums with an insurance company for having an outdoor boiler is more than offset by the greater expenses in installation and operation.

Insurance and Doing-It-Yourself

If you like to do things yourself, just be sure that you check the code requirements before you even start on your project and do not get in over your head. Perhaps you can do part of the project yourself while having a craftsman like an electrician do the electrical wiring for you. Be sure to do a neat looking job so that if your insurance agent comes in and has to send a picture of it to his home office, that it looks like who ever installed it, knew what he was doing. Sloppy work is going to make your insurance agent nervous, for he is not a craftsman or contractor and does not really know the trades, so he is not really going to know everything about what you did. However, you can bet that he will certainly see sloppy mistakes and will assume that work that he cannot see or may not fully understand is of the same poor quality workmanship. Therefore, if you put in a gas furnace and the ductwork looks like a series of tin cans taped together, he is going to worry about how the gas line was run and who did the electrical. Now if the ductwork looks great, maybe even the same "tin cans" but with a neat foil insulation with neatly foil taped joins, he will probably not have a worry in the world. Any smart contractor knows that the appearance of the finished job is very important, for it affects nearly completely, what people think about the job. This is why electrical conduit is always run vertically or horizontally with 90-degree bends, rather than at crazy angles looking like spaghetti. There is nothing in the electrical code stating that conduit has to be vertical or horizontal, but just try to get approval if it isn't. A job has to look professional, sloppy work is a red flag of possible trouble and inspectors will tend to look until they find it, things that otherwise might have been OK will suddenly be noticed and have to be redone if they are not perfectly up to code. Once you have been "red flagged" by an inspector, they will be extra cautious in the future, expecting you to make more mistakes. Therefore, you need to correct the problem perfectly and anything else that can be pointed to, and tidy up the job so it looks better. If you can't really change that much, because everything is already up to code, at least sweep, dust and clean up the job site. You would be surprised at the difference it can make since so much of how we look at things is subconscious and even things that shouldn't make a difference can strongly influence how we see things. So before you have your insurance agent over to check out your new installation, clean the house. Seriously, clean the house and reduce the clutter as much as you can, a neat looking house will affect how the agent views you and your installation and whether or not he sees you as an excessive risk. If your insurance agent comes into your living room to see your new wood stove and sees huge plies of newspapers stacked on every piece of furniture in the room, he may figure that it is only a matter of time before someone puts a stack of paper on the stove and starts a fire.

Now while your insurance agent is over, I would be surprised if he failed to try to sell you more insurance. My word of advice is if you remember that the concept of insurance is to cover losses that you cannot afford, since coverage costs money, it makes no sense to insure losses that you can afford. Since insurance companies make money, you can save money by being in effect your own insurance for minor losses. Keep some money on hand for a rainy day to cover unexpected events, and have as large a deductible on your policies as you are comfortable with, that way your insurance premiums will be smaller. Insurance is more expensive in coverage for nickels and dimes than for dollars, because smaller claims are more frequent. With a high deductible, you eliminate the possibility of making nickel and dime claims, and with less risk of making a claim, you become a lower risk and should receive a lower rate. While you need insurance, it does cost money, so it makes sense not to buy insurance that you don't need.

Chapter 6

Adding a New Heat Distribution System to an Existing Home

A single heat source like a space heater or a stove, often fails to heat the entire house since the heat is not delivered to all the places it is needed. A hot stove can overheat the living room while the pipes freeze in the back bathroom. To really heat a house, the heat has to be put where it is needed, and heat is needed where you are losing it. An interior room with no outside walls needs little if any heat, while corner rooms need a lot since they have two cold outside walls. Rooms with many windows need more heat than the same kind of room with few windows. The main heat loss in an average home is through the ceiling into the cold attic, but that heat loss is even for the entire house, and any heat present will rise to the ceiling. The second big loss is the outside walls and especially through the windows, since a pane or two of glass has far less insulation value than a properly insulated wall. This is why heat needs to be added at the base of the outside wall, so the heat can rise like a curtain of warm air shielding the occupants from the cold walls. Heat particularly is needed at the floor below each window, and if heat is to be added at only one point along a wall, it should be below the window, which is the coldest part of the wall.

The targets for any heating distribution system are those cold spots below every window; forced air systems put a heat vent under the largest window in every room and sometimes under every window. Other heating systems are less focused like electric baseboard heaters and hydronic radiators, which to provide the heat needed for the room, would be too long to fit under the window and may be run along the outside walls in the coldest spots or even along the entire outside wall. Then there are heating distribution systems that don't try to focus on any one target, but simply heat the whole house from the bottom up, by heating the entire floor as is done with hydronic radiant floor heat. One problem with heating the whole floor is if the floor is heated to the same temperature in an interior room as an outside room, the interior rooms will be overheated since they do not lose as much heat as the outside rooms, hence the need for controlling the heat delivered to each part of the house.. Each heating system has its advantages and disadvantages, and difficulty of installation in an existing home.

Heating Without a Distribution System

Using a single stove for home heating often results in only partial heat in the area where the stove is. People have come up with a number of ways of moving the heat so that more of the home is heated. One of the simplest, is if the home has a forced air system, is to turn the fan on and let it move the hot air around the house. This works better if the heat can be directed into the cold air return. If the system has air conditioning, there may be a warm air return vent on the wall above the cold air return that can be opened. If the warm air return is in the area heated by the stove, the forced air system will move the warm air throughout the entire home. Some use small electric fans to move the air to the warm or cold air intake, or just to move the air through a doorway into the next room. Small electric fans designed to fit in an upper corner of an open doorway are sold just for this purpose. Another basic trick is to leave all the interior doors open so it is easier for the warm air to move through the house. However, often none of these tricks works well enough, and then the old time solution is sometimes used, just put a stove wherever it is needed. While a single stove can often only heat part of a home, several can do it easily. Old homes often had a fireplace or stove in practically every large room, and you thought that your fuel bill was bad. A modern trick to avoid having to have all those stoves is to simply put the stove in the basement and try to heat the home by heating the floor. This one sounds great and many people tried it in the 1970's, and at least here, in Wisconsin with our cold winters, it didn't work very well. The problem was they had a hard time trying to get enough heat to flow up through the floor to make up for what was being lost through the ceiling and outside walls (this trick does work for homes with well insulated walls and ceilings, since not as much heat is needed). To increase the heat flow, it was necessary of course to raise the temperature in the basement to make the floor warmer, and the flaw was that the basement walls were not insulated. Heating the basement to 80 or 100 F or even higher, to try to get enough heat upstairs, resulted in enormous amounts of heat going out through basement walls. The homeowner may not have realized where his heat was going, but what he did notice was that he was burning a lot of wood and the house was still not very warm. The next thing that was tried was to leave the door open at the top of the basement stairs to let the hot air flow up into the first floor. For some this worked and they would regulate the temperature by partially open or closing the door, and after awhile they knew how far to open the door for a desired temperature and would yell at you if you went through the doorway and failed to return the door to the correct "setting". However, even with the "correct basement door setting" there were still cold spots in the house where the heat failed to reach. To really heat a house, the house has to have a distribution system that supplies heat to where it is needed.

Forced Air Systems

Forced air systems are the most common heating distribution system for homes, since it can also be used for distributing central air conditioning and is considered cheaper to install and maintain than other distribution systems. The simplest of all distribution systems, a forced air system consists of a connected series of sheet metal boxes with a fan to move the air through them. The fan is normally in the furnace and blows the air through the airside of the heat exchanger and into a large metal box that connects to the main duct that takes the heat to both ends of the house. The normal set up is to put the furnace in the center of the house, with a main duct line running down the middle. Then off the main duct, smaller ducts branch off and extend to a heat register underneath each window. Depending on the size and layout of the house, the main duct branch may be more than just one branch and may have bends to reach where the heat needs to go, and may even have risers taking heat to the ductwork for heating upper floors. Some homes can have more than one forced air furnace each with its own duct system.

In homes with a basement, the furnace sits on the basement floor and a fan in the bottom of the furnace blows the hot air out the top of the furnace, this is called an updraft furnace and is the most common type. A sheet metal box called a plenum rises from the top of the furnace and connects to the main duct. The old gravity systems didn't have a fan; the plenum was the chimney that created the draft that moved the air. A large wide and tall plenum is stronger for moving air in gravity system, and our plenums today tend to retain some of this old design influence and are a convent place to put an air conditioning coil or the heat exchanger from an outdoor boiler. Since the main duct runs the length of the house, it normally runs across the bottom of the floor joists in wood framed homes, and the branches going to the heat registers come off the top of the main duct and run between the floor joists out to the outside wall where the heat register is located. Once the heated air is blown into the rooms, it cools and needs to be returned to the furnace to be reheated. This is done by locating in the center of the house usually in a hallway, one or more large cold air return grills which connect to a return air duct that runs back along next to the main duct and is connected to the furnace. The return air duct needs to be just as large as the main heating duct since it is the return path for the air that is being blown out into the house. The return duct normally has to drop down next the furnace and connect to furnace fan compartment so the fan can draw air in from the return duct and blow it up through the heat exchanger and out into the heating ducts. The point where the return air duct connects onto the side of the furnace is where the air filter is normally installed.

In a crawl space, a side draft furnace is some times used, which looks like an updraft furnace lying on its side. The cold air return is connected to what would have been the bottom of the furnace, and the other end is connected to the main duct. The furnace is supported by hanging it from the floor above by means of metal straps or hangers. Sometimes with crawl spaces, the furnace is installed on the first floor and blows the hot air out the bottom into the main duct down below. This type of furnace is called a down draft furnace is like an upside down updraft furnace.

Some homes have neither basements nor crawl spaces to run ductwork in, such as homes built on a concrete slab, then the ductwork and a side draft furnace is installed in the attic. The furnace lays on its side across the tops of the ceiling joists, and the main duct feeds branches that feed heat registers either in the ceiling that try and "push" the heat down, or have ducts in the spaces between the two by fours in the interior walls with a vent near the floor. Ductwork in the attic is considered the least desirable way of routing heating or cooling ducts, since in the heating season the attic is cold and in the cooling system the attic is hot, which results in large energy losses.

Installing a Forced Air System

If possible, a forced air furnace should be installed in a basement, even if only a crawl space. A location underneath the home to be heated is the best location. Heat naturally rises and is best supplied from below. Crawl spaces can be converted into a heated space by sealing the ground in the crawl space with plastic or some other type of sealer, perhaps pouring a concrete floor. Once the ground has been sealed the crawl space vents can be removed and the holes sealed. The sill area can be insulated and the exposed foundation walls insulated as well. Foam can be applied to the outside of foundation walls or foam insulation can be installed on the inside of foundation walls and covered with half-inch thick cement board. With the space underneath the house insulated, any heat given off by the heating system stays inside the house rather than being wasted. Ductwork or piping in unheated crawl spaces loses a lot of heat. The surface area of ductwork is quite large and to cover all the exposed surfaces with insulation equal in to what should be in the exterior walls would be difficult, so difficult that it is often easier to insulate the foundation walls instead. By insulating the walls of a crawl space, the cold and heat is kept out from under the house and heating and cooling loses through the floor are greatly reduced.

If it is not possible to stand an updraft furnace underneath the house, a side draft furnace could be used. Another possibility is to install a downdraft furnace in a closet on the first floor and have the furnace blow the hot air down in the duct system. Downdraft furnaces are easier to service being located on the first floor rather than in a tight crawl space under the house. Digging out part of the crawl space dirt floor for building a partial basement with a furnace room should be considered. It may be possible to build a furnace room that could hold two furnaces ducted in series, so that either fuel could be used. Some choices could be a LP (newer local codes may forbid new LP in basements) or gas furnace with wood or coal as a second furnace. A coal chute or basement outside entryway for bring in wood could be built as well.

The hardest part in installing a forced air heating system is making the ductwork. Ductwork is made by skilled sheet metal workers using the tools found in a sheet metal shop, some of which are too large to fit in the bed of a pick up truck. Making your own ductwork is nearly impossible, but most of what you need is available at building supply centers and better hardware stores. These stores will have the all of the small ducts, but will often not have the larger sizes. The larger size pieces can be ordered from your local sheet metal shop, which is the back workroom of the larger heating contractors who make their own ductwork, and yes, this is the convenient but probably expensive way of doing it. You can also order the larger pieces from some one who stocks them and thus eliminate the cost for custom work; there are a number of such sellers on the internet. The other way of getting large ducts is to make them yourself. Now unless you are a skilled sheet metal worker with the necessary tools, you will have to cut a few corners. You can do this by using 1/2 or 3/4 inch galvanized angel iron for the corners and cutting sheet metal panels for the duct sides and pop riveting them to the angel iron to make a duct. Crude, but you can make a workable duct this way without large tools. You can make a plenum the same way, to connect to the top of the furnace to the main duct. Then each branch, which is normally a round duct, is connected to the top of the main duct with a 90-degree elbow, and run between the joists to the outside wall. At the end of the round duct, an adapter that connects to the bottom of the register is used. A hole is cut in the floor for the adapter to fit under the heat register that is installed on the floor against the outside wall.

For working with sheet metal, you will need a few basic tools, such as a side jaw cutter. This type of cutter has offset jaws so your hand stays above the metal, this makes it a lot easier to use and really cuts down on the cuts, on your hands that is. A drill and bits, and a pop rivet gun, sheet metal vise-grip with 3 or 4-inch jaws is great for bending. Do not for get a good pair of gloves, sheet metal is sharp when cut. A couple of two by fours and a hammer are handy for making simple bends.

To do the job, use as much of the ductwork pre-made as you can, to improve the quality of the ductwork. The pre-made pieces are put together with metal splines that are pushed in the side to connect the ends together in a nearly air tight joint, and at the corner the ends of the splines are bent over together to seal the corner of the joint. The main line and all the ductwork are mounted on metal hangers two inches or more below the wooden joists to keep the wood from being lit on fire if the ductwork is ever filled with flames from a failed heat exchanger. Always keep some space between the heat supply ductwork and any wood for this reason, while the cold air return duct can touch wood or even have exposed wood in it, since the way the cold air return connects to the furnace precludes flames from the heat exchanger entering it. The plenum connects to the top of the furnace with splines or by over lapping the metal of the plenum and the furnace and pot riveting them together. The small branch ducts are cut into the top of the main duct by cutting a round hole to fit a duct-to-round adapter. The adapter has metal tabs that are bend and pressed up against the inside of the duct. Then the elbow is slipped over the adapter. The standard procedure with sheet metal pieces that slip inside each other is that the down stream part always goes over the upstream part, so any air that leaks out of the joint has to turn back against the airflow rather than being blown straight out. The rounds come open or unseamed, so they can be nested inside each other to save space. Measure and cut to length before closing the side seam, to close the seam, press the two corners in at one end of the duct and slip the folded side into the groove on the other. Then keep slipping the fold into the groove working up the round duct and let the seam pop up, which locks the fold into place. You can also still cut the round duct after it is seamed; it is just harder to start the cut. To start a cut in the middle of a piece of sheet metal on thin metal, push the tip of the cutter into the metal to make a small hole to cut from, or on thicker metal drill a hole large enough to get the cutter started.

With an elbow attached to the adapter mounted in the top of the main duct, attach one round after another to reach out to the outside wall, supporting the round duct with supports, which are metal folded straps or metal hangers used for securing electrical boxes between joists. Allow room at the end for the adapter that connects the round to the hole in the floor beneath the register. The adapter has metal flaps that extend up through the rectangular hole you cut in the floor to fit it, and the flap ends are bent over and nailed to the floor to secure it. Each joint in the duct is riveted with three pop rivets or three short sheet metal screws. Tape all the joints with foil tape or duct tape to make the duct airtight. To regulate the airflow in each duct, a heat register with adjustable damper can be used, and/or a damper is installed in the round duct. The dampers are nice for basement jobs, since to balance how much heat goes to each part of the house, you just reach up and adjust little handles on each damper as needed and your adjustments stay. If you just have register dampers, everyone and their brother are always changing the settings. However, if your ductwork is in a tight crawl space, you will probably prefer to adjust registers rather than always having to crawl under the house to make adjustments.

To plan the lay out of the duct system and to get an idea of the sizes of ducts needed, look at other homes with ductwork and see how they are laid out. Ideally, try to find a home as much like yours as you can and see how the ductwork is run, and copy it like a pattern, providing of course, that the ductwork is worth copying, that it is a properly installed job with good workmanship. If you wish to have a system that heats by gravity flow, or can do so at least in power outages, oversize the duct by 50% and slope them for upward heat flow when possible. The ductwork over wood and coal furnaces is often recommended to be installed with six inches of clearance space between duct and any wood, within six feet of the wood or coal furnace, and two inches farther way.

Hydronic Heating System

Hydronic or hot water systems are of course heated by a boiler. For the life of me, I just do not see why we call a "hydronic heating unit" a "boiler" when it does not boil anything, only steam boilers really do any boiling. However, who said there was much logic in the way some things are named. Well then, the water is heated in a "boiler", and then pumped through pipes to radiators or through tubing in the floor for radiant floor heating. Hydronic heating systems are very flexible since the pipes are far smaller than ducts and can easily be routed in smaller spaces for far longer distances than ductwork. Plus in the old really not so long ago days, the piping was all threaded pipe that you really had to be a skilled plumber to be able to cut, thread and screw together a complicated pipe system. Now you can run the whole thing with plastic PEX tubing in far less than a tenth the time it took to run the old stuff while needing only some basic skills. Hydronic heat is often called "Rich man's heat" due to its better performance over forced air in not causing drafts, reduced noise in operation, for not creating dusty rooms and for the historically higher cost in installation and repairs. Nearly all of the historical problems with hydronic heat have been over come by newer ways of doing things. The traditional higher installation cost has largely been eliminated by newer piping methods like PEX tubing, which is cheaper and quicker to install than ductwork. The higher operating costs have largely been eliminated by better controls, such as turning off the circulating pumps when they are not needed, rather than running them continuously. Repair costs have also been reduced by the simpler piping methods, which make repairs easier and quicker to do.

Hydronic heat is delivered by means of baseboard heaters run along outside walls or strategically placed underneath windows. The cheap ones have a thin metal cover over a finned copper pipe and the expensive ones are a one-piece cast iron part with build in concealed ribs for warming the air. If you have the money, definitely get the better radiators, the covers on the cheap ones get dented and bent over time while the iron ones seem to last forever. Often times there will be a control valve with a setting from zero to nine for setting the temperature level located on each radiator, or they can be controlled by a room thermostat that operates an electric solenoid valve located in the hot water supply line under the floor leading to the radiators.

Radiant floor heat is piped inside the floor so there are no radiators, since the entire floor is the radiator. Often claims are made that radiant floor heat is the most efficient heat, which of course is pure nonsense, for heating the floor isn't any more efficient that using a baseboard radiator or forced hot air. The better efficiency claim is based on the concept of radiant heating, that with the entire floor radiating heat up at you, you will feel warmer at a lower air temperature. Therefore, the only way radiant floor heating is more efficient is if you turn down the thermostat, which is the only potential savings with the system. The problem with the concept is it fails to consider that if the walls and ceiling are cold, which is a lack of radiant heat, radiant heat from the floor may fail to be enough to make up for low radiance of the other surfaces. To compensate you may turn up the floor heat to balance the loss so that you feel warm, wiping out any savings. While in a well-insulated house, with warmer walls and ceiling, the radiant effect will work better and you will feel warmer at a lower air temperature.

Installing a Hydronic Heating System

In hydronic systems, the building water supply connected to the heating system must have a shut off valve, then a backflow preventer and then a pressure regulator to reduce the water pressure to the pressure in the system. The boiler has to have a pressure gauge and a temperature gauge, a low water cut off, and a safety pressure relief valve. All flooded pressurized hydronic systems also require an expansion tank, which has an air space to allow for the expansion of the water as it is heated.

It is ideal if the boiler is centrally located so the piping is short and all the runs are about the same length, but the boiler can be placed just about anywhere, even out in the backyard as is done with outdoor wood boilers. Boilers are normally placed in basements with the piping run across the bottom of the basement ceiling to the points along the outside walls where the radiators are installed. In the case of homes with crawl spaces, the boiler is often installed in a utility room and the piping is piped in the crawl space to the outside walls. In homes without crawl spaces, the piping is piped from the utility room through the attic, interior walls and some times even in exterior walls.

The heating pipes must be protected from freezing; I know that sounds strange, but heating pipes tend to be the first thing that freezes. As hard as it is to believe, hot water pipes do freeze before cold water pipes. The reason is that when water is heated, the minerals and dissolved gases in the water are altered in a way that results in changes that allow the water to freeze quicker than water that has not been heated. Since the water in hydronic heating lines, has of course passed through the boiler, the water will freeze quickly in cold conditions if the water stops moving. How freezing occurs is an ice plug forms and blocks the pipe and begins extending down the pipe in both directions as the water crystallizes on the surface of the ice plug. You can freeze a pipe solid without breaking it, since contrary to popular belief; ice does not expand and cannot break any pipes by itself. What does expand is the water as it crystallizes, so the pressure is not in the ice, it is in the water if it is trapped by ice. As the water expands, it creates a hydraulic pressure that has the strength to burst any pipe. Pipes are only burst by ice in one of two ways, a ice plug blocks a dead end such as water trapped against a closed valve, and as the water expands as it crystallizes, there is nowhere for the pressure to escape too. The second way is if water is trapped between two ice plugs, as they grow towards each other, the water is squeezed between them. Having seen far too many pipes burst by freezing, I have never seen one broken by the ice itself, every single one was split, cracked or burst apart by extreme high water pressure. In copper pipe, which stretches quite a bit, the pipe often blows up like a balloon and forms a "frost blister" that pops with a split in the thinned copper wall of the pipe. In threaded pipe, a fitting splits apart or threads are stripped by the high water pressure as pipe connections are blown apart. If ice really expanded, there would be a fine crack running the entire length of the frozen section, but that is never the case. Expanding ice is a myth. Once you know that, you will be able to understand how some lines can freeze without damage, if the water was not trapped by the ice and how others were burst. PEX tubes or hoses can be largely frost proof, because PEX stretches. If water is trapped by an ice plug, as the pressure increases, the PEX blows up a like a balloon and the water may be able to leak pass the plug.

Insulating pipes does not stop them from freezing it just slows it down. What keeps the pipes unfrozen is the heat in them, and if the flow stops, the heat is turned off and the pipe begins to cool. Insulation slows the rate of heat loss, but since no insulation is perfect, given enough time even the best-insulated pipes will freeze. This is why hydronic heating lines should never be run in unheated spaces or in outside walls where they are exposed to cold temperatures. This is why hydronic baseboard radiators on outside walls are piped through the floor rather than the outside wall. Running a line in an outside wall is the last choice, and if it can't be avoided, be sure to put the line on the inside of the insulation in the wall as near to the interior side of the wall as possible.

The standard piping layout is water is pumped through the boiler and out to the radiators and back to the boiler in a loop. In systems where control valves or zone valves can shut off lines, it is common to put a small loop at the end of the main line to allow for circulation even when all the branches are closed. Otherwise, it can take much longer for the hot water from the boiler to reach a single radiator needing heat if all the water in the system has to flow through it before the hot water can reach it. To allow for expansion of the water as it is heated, an accumulator or expansion tank is connected to the main line; an accumulator has a balloon like air bladder in it that is compressed by the expanding water. To branch off the main line into the many small lines, a manifold is some times used which is a pipe with a number of valved connections for piping the branches lines.

Plan the piping lay out carefully; try to see other hydronic systems in houses similar to yours so you can have an idea of what you are trying to do. Remember to do a neat installation, no angled pipes or weird knots of pipes. Know where a line is going and how it is getting there before you start running it. Be sure to secure piping with the correct pipe hangers within the required spacing. (Often this is every 4 feet for steel and copper and every 2 feet for PEX) If you are running PEX, you will have to work extra hard to create a neat looking installation since PEX tends to look like spaghetti. Many use copper or galvanized pipe for key places like to run up from the boiler to the pump and manifold and then run PEX, and also to use metal pipe for piping in and out of things like pumps that need to be secured by clamping the piping in hangers to hold them.

Sizing of radiators is critical, if they are too small, they will not be able to heat the room and if they are too big, you are wasting money on them. Since an oversize radiator can be throttled back a bit and will work just fine while an undersize radiator has to be replaced by a larger one. Radiators are nearly always deliberately oversized by a safe margin to allow for some heat losses being bigger than expected. The actual calculations to determine the correct size of each radiator in each room is a lengthy consideration of the climate, house insulation, air infiltrations rates, type size and number of windows, etc, etc. Few installers do the calculations, they simply know what sizes to use in most situations. To find what those sizes are, simply go and look and see what is used in similar homes in your area. One good rule of thumb is to size the radiator for the width of the window above it. In a well insulated home each radiator can be the width of the window above it while in a poorly insulated home the radiator may need to be in length a multiple of window above it like 1.5 times or twice as long. Just go and see what the ratio is used in homes in your area that are built like yours with about the same amount of insulation which will probably be homes built when yours was built. Also consider the temperature of the water used in the heating system, hotter systems can get by with smaller radiators while cooler ones like ones used with Heat Pumps need to be larger. My advice is also not to have a radiator narrower than the window above it, for appearance and practicality of space when putting furniture against the wall, it looks best if the radiator is the same width as the window above it and if the radiator is oversized it can be throttled down to work. While you will waste money on some oversized radiators, a radiator narrower than the window above looks undersized to the eye and has a dinky toy feel to it.

Installing Hydronic Radiant Floor Heating

Floor heating can be installed in an existing home. There is an endless ways of installing radiant floor heat. There are wet systems, which are cast in concrete, and then there are dry systems that are installed in a built up floor. Some dry systems are installed with cement boards over or under them; maybe with tile on top, others are put underneath plywood with finish flooring on top. Then there are the under the floor systems that are installed between the floor joists with a heat reflective film across the bottom of the joists. Under the floor systems while they have to heat through the thickness of the floor above by heating the air underneath it, which make them slow to respond, have the advantage of having little chance of being punctured by a nail and are easily accessible for repairs. The hardest to repair are the wet systems since the tubing is cast in concrete and just locating the leak is not a very promising proposition. The dry built up systems can be disassembled to look for the leak, of course that is after the tile or other finish flooring above is removed. The under the floor system is the logical choice for homes with basements or heated crawl spaces.

The heating tubes in the floor or under the floor, are laid with each room having its own valve for adjusting the amount of heat delivered compared to the rest of the home for balancing the system. By adjusting the water flow through each room's tubing, the heat delivered can be increased or decreased to match it to the heat losses for that room. A house thermostat will control the boiler pump or even the boiler water temperature, which will control the overall temperature of the house, but if one room is colder or hotter than the rest of the house, adjusting the flow to the room will adjust the temperature in respect to the rest of the house. That is what balancing a heating system is all about. The individual rooms can also have their own thermostat that controls the valve in the line for that room, allowing each room to respond to changes in demand for heat. The furnace pump is turned on whenever any of the thermostats calls for heat.

The return lines from each room also need to have a valve, so if a floor tube starts leaking, that room line can be shut off, isolating the leak. Otherwise if the leak cannot be valved off, you will be faced with trying to keep operating a leaking system that could be damaging structure of your home or having to turn the heating system off in the middle of winter. Valves are expensive, but not as expensive as not having one when you need it.

Steam Heating Systems

Steam heat in the home is a fossil from the past, since it has been replaced by hot water hydronic heating systems, which are more efficient and safer. Most people today do not even realize just how dangerous steam can be, in its day; steam boiler explosions that destroyed whole buildings were common. Steam is very dangerous, because it is a vapor, which is a gas, and in most systems it is under a fair amount of pressure. The difference between liquids and gases in pressure vessels is that gases, when released expand, and liquids do not. A broken plug on a compressed air tank is shot across the room like a bullet by the out rushing expanding air behind it, while a broken plug on a water tank pops off and falls to the floor with only the pressure piped into the tank pushing out. Since water does not compress or expand like gas, a water vessel losses all its pressure with any leak. Steam boilers are safety checked by hydrostatic testing; they are completely filled with water, and then pressurized. The pressure is raised to the test pressure for that boiler and it is perfectly safe since if anything breaks, the water pressure is released at once by the loss of any water and the broken boiler merely drains like a pool with a hole in it. While steam escaping from a large break will cause the boiler to explode as all the water in the boiler is under high temperature and pressure, and will flash into steam as the pressure is released. The escaping steam from any break is of course steam, which is hot enough to cause steam burns. These dangers of steam were known and later steam heating systems reduced the risks by operating at lower pressures. Like only half a pound pressure per square inch (PSI), or even partial vacuum steam systems that also reduced the temperature of the steam and reduced the burn hazard and eliminated the danger of steam leaks since the system was at less than atmospheric air pressure. However, once electric pumps were used to circulate the water in hydronic systems rather than having to depend on gravity, the principle advantage of steam flowing to where it where it was being condensed was gone and hydronic heat took over the market.

For residential heating, steam heat is inherently less efficient due to higher temperatures needed and the energy need to create steam. The higher temperatures results in excessive temperatures in the lines and radiators resulting in larger line losses and greater burn hazards for any one touching the radiators. Steam boilers also require more maintenance and have a greater danger of exploding. For these reasons steam heat is no longer made for or installed in homes any more and existing steam heat systems are often ether replaced or converted to hydronic heat. Steam heat for residential heating is a dead dinosaur and few if any heating service people will know much of anything about servicing or repairing them. If you have an old steam heating system, you will probably have to learn how to service and repair the system yourself. The book for learning how to do that is *"The Lost Art of Steam Heating"* by Dan Holohan. (http://www.heatinghelp.com) To save on heating with a steam heat system, your best option is to convert it to hydronic heat or replace it.

Chapter 7

Solar

There are two basic types of solar systems, passive and active. Passive solar has no pumps or other active or moving parts, while active solar systems do. Passive solar is pretty much what I would call strategic use of windows. Windows are placed on the south side of the house in such a way that they catch the maximum amount of sunlight in the winter and far less in the summer when the heat gain is not needed for heating. This is generally done by having an over hang that shades the windows in the summer and then when the sun is lower in the winter, it shines underneath the overhang and into the window. Inside the home the heat in the sunlight is absorbed by things like a dark title floor over concrete or a dark colored masonry wall. Then at night a insulating cover may be closed over the inside of the windows to keep the heat in, and the absorbed heat in the wall or floor keeps the house warm for the night, at least that is the way it is supposed to work. While passive solar clearly does work, the amount of heat you can gain from southern windows in a cold climate pails compared to what you can lose, depending on the effectiveness of night time window insulation it can be a narrow advantage or even a big loss. The colder the climate, the more heavily insulated a passive solar home needs to be, for as the winters get colder and the days are shorter, the sunlight gets weaker. Currently, with the materials we have today, passive solar homes are a very tough proposition to get to work in truly cold areas. However, that may change in the very near future with vacuum insulated windows which have an insulation value of R-10 equal to two inches of foam hopefully becoming available soon. With windows of this sort, passive solar homes may suddenly become much more feasible in cold climates, and passive solar home designs may suddenly become the norm.

Obviously, passive solar homes for best results ideally should be built as such, since retro fitting an existing home that extensively is difficult. You can do some simple passive solar heating tricks in your house with little expense. Like opening your drapes to let the sunlight shine in to warm the house and closing them when the sunlight is gone to keep the heat in. Awnings can be installed over windows that get the sun, and positioned so that the windows are shaded in summer and not shaded in winter. Heat reflective window films could be selectively used in the non-solar used windows to help keep heat in and reflect unwanted heat from windows that get too much sun in the summer. My southern windows catch the sun in the winter, and I try to open those shades in the daytime. I do notice a slight heat gain on sunny winter days if it isn't too cold, like when it is about 40 or above, the heat gain can be enough that I don't have to light a fire when on a cloudy days I do.

Active solar systems are flexible enough to be added to just about any home and they often were in the 1970s. While most of those old systems have disappeared as the homes were reroofed over the years and it was determined to be too expensive to reinstall an old solar system that probably no longer worked any more. For quite a number of years you could see all sorts of various contraptions that looked like props from some science fiction movie mounted in an endless assorted ways to every kind of house you could imagine. When it came to installing a solar system and getting a sale, the solar contractor's imaginations knew no limits.   The 1970's did demonstrate that it is possible to add active solar to just about any kind of house, while not always in a tasteful manner.

Active solar systems come in two basic types, hot water or hot air. In a hot water system, water is pumped or flows due to hot water rising naturally, through the collectors and back down to a tank or heat exchanger. While in hot air solar systems, air is blown by a fan through the collector and through flexible insulated ducts directly into the house or through a radiator like heat exchanger through which water is pumped from the hot water heater.

The solar industry has always been big on the promise of free energy from the sun, but has often fallen short on delivering that energy economically and has sometimes even failed to provide anything near the amount of energy a given solar system is suppose to produce. The difference between fantasy and reality is in the math, for things that are real, the numbers add up, while for fantasies they do not. Salesmen can and do say anything to make a sale, and with the newness of solar to most people, some feel they can get away with the most outrageous lies. In the 1970's the solar business was rife with grossly exaggerated claims of performance, reliability and service. Potential customers were assured that a small window connected hot air panel would heat their whole house for free. The actual performance of course was more like less than 5% of the total needed heat for the home, and then only when the sun was out. Hot water systems were stated to provide 100% of the heat for hot water use, when even today 70% is the average for most systems. The solar systems were often sold as being maintenance free, or having much lower service costs than what they really had. Many solar systems in the 1970's had service costs above what they were saving in energy costs, making having the system a net loss even if getting the system had been free. To keep the sales rolling in, some solar companies offered free repairs on their solar systems for 25 years, of course once the solar tax credits disappeared, so did most of the solar companies. The customers were left holding the bag with solar systems, like one that had four panels that tracked the sun and focused the light on black pipes (SOL R BEAM tracking system). In some of these models, the electronics for tracking the sun included an E-PROM chip on a board mounted in a metal box on the collector's metal rack mounted up on the roof. The problem was that an E-PROM being an electronically programmed chip, are sensitive to static electricity. Some homeowners stated to me that if a thunderstorm flashed so much as a single lighting bolt with insight of their home, the solar system stopped tracking. Repairing this was easy, just had to replace the $200 circuit board each time it happened. The homeowner was hit with a bill for the $200 board plus labor, and this could happen several times each year. This is why you do not see this type of system any more and if you do, it no longer tracks the sun. While the passive systems have no moving parts and hence have little or no maintenance costs aside from what you would expect for windows and floors, active solar systems can be a can of worms when it comes to things not working. If you are considering an active solar system, be sure that it has been rated by the Solar Rating and Certification Corporation (http://www.solar-rating.org/RATINGS/RATINGS.HTM), and check to see what the rated output of the solar system really is, rather than just believing whatever a sales person tells you. You would also be wise to check out any solar installer you are considering by checking around and call the Better Business Bureau. Ask to talk to previous customers and go see what the installed system looks like after it has been in use for a few years.

Solar hot air systems are breakdown wise, basically bulletproof. While many hot air systems were installed in the 1970's, I hardly ever worked on any of them due to the simple fact that there was not much to break. The moving parts consist of a fan, a controller, maybe some motorized dampers and if also heating hot water, a heat exchanger and a pump. One system I liked was the 'black wall' as I like to call it, a wall mounted black box with a glass cover. Since it is not on the roof, many of these systems are still in place and presumably still working. While the hot air systems have great reliably, their efficiency is less than hot water systems. Water carries much more 'heat' than air, that to warm something you would really have to blow a lot of hot air at it, compared to pouring hot water over it. Air simply does not hold a lot of heat, meaning a lot of air has to be moved through the collector to carry the heat into the home, and this air is moved through flexible ducts with comparably little insulation and frequently with numerous air leaks. While water leaks are very apparent, air leaks are harder to spot and seldom case any notable problems. On an older hot air system, it is not unusual for the tape used for sealing the duct connections, to have dried and cracked or even peeled off leaving open joints. The lower efficiency and the generally poor insulation on hot air systems, makes them a better choice in areas that do not have really cold winters, but they do work even here in Wisconsin, just not as well as a hot water system can. Hot air systems do have an advantage in that air does not freeze and cannot break pipes as water does. Here in Wisconsin some hot air systems for heating do well in the fall and spring, but might as well head south for the winter. For heating hot water, they do great in the summer, and start having problems keeping up, as the weather gets colder. With hot air systems I would expect a longer period of time in the winter when a back up water heater will be needed compared to a hot water solar system.

Hot water solar systems come in quite a number of different types and forms, from plastic mats with pool water pumped through them for pool heating to glass enclosed flat collectors and evacuated tube collectors. There are so many different types that I am just going to focus on the flat plate collectors and the evacuated tube collectors since they are the most common and the most likely choices for heating hot water or your home.

Flat plate collectors are simply a flat glass covered insulated box with a black copper sheet with copper tubing attached to it. The sun heats the black surface, the glass keeps the heat in and the insulation keeps the heat from going out the bottom of the box. This is solar heating in a nutshell, and for heating hot water probably the way to go. Flat plate collectors have become so very common because they work well and are not that expensive. Some of the endless variations on the basic design are in warm climates, to add a water tank as part of the panel, eliminating the pump and controls. Or as in some designs such as the Copper Cricket (no longer manufactured), the pump and controller is eliminated by a thermosiphon design, in that there is a air gap and the panel has to 'boil' over the water into the return pipe. Some systems include solar cells to power the pump and sometimes the cells act as the controller, running the pump whenever there is enough sun to do so, with a bi-metal high limit switch to stop it once the water tank is hot enough.

Evacuated tube collectors have an insulated header or pipe across the top of the collector into which are connected a number of glass tubes that slope down away from the header. Each glass tube is vacuum insulated with a black copper element in the center; inside the element is a hollow copper pipe with a refrigerant that is a liquid in the lower end of the tube. As the refrigerant is heated, it turns into a hot vapor and rises to the high end of the tube, which has a copper bulb that projects inside the header pipe. This design results in a double heat trap, having both a vacuum break and a refrigerant cycle separating the heated water in the header from the outside air. I installed this type of system on my home because of how well this type of collector works in cold temperatures, and the performance on sunny but extremely cold days has been phenomenal. With this system, outside air temperature hardly matters at all. High temperature water output in cold outdoor temperatures is what evacuated tube collectors do best and is the only area in which they out perform flat plate collectors. Flat plate collectors can be one-third the cost of evacuated tube collectors and out perform them in nearly all temperature conditions except for the very coldest. If you are looking at trying to heat a house in cold sunny winter conditions, evacuated tube collectors are the best choice since they will give you the highest water temperature in really cold conditions. I would recommend flat plate collectors for nearly everyone else for hot water heating, since in really cold conditions where evacuated tube collectors would be better, there is often by then too little sun light to make the difference worth wild. The reason I went with evacuated tube collectors myself, was I was able to order them direct from China for a fraction of the normal cost (Sunline Solar Inc. http://www.sunline.com.cn/) for about what flat plate collectors cost. ($300 for a direct roof mount 30-tube collector, $600 for larger 30-tube collector on a stainless steel rack) Many Evacuated tube collectors require heat dumping in sunny weather, in that if the tubes are not cooled by water the refrigerant in the tube will over heat and possibly destroy the tube, Sunline Solar tubes do not need heat dumping and will not burst if left out in the sun. This is a very important consideration, for if there was a power failure on a sunny day; your evacuated tube collectors could be ruined. Obviously, systems that have to run in sunny weather to avoid damage should have all of their electrical power supplied by the sun to avoid catastrophic failure due to a power failure. Of course, you could still have a pump fail or a pipe leak, so an easy way of covering the tubes quickly and easily in an emergency would be a very good idea. Personally I have always thought that the makers of evacuated tube collectors should have a heat triggered bi-metal spring device on the header that when overheated would rotate a polished metal reflector from the lower side of each tube to the upper side, for preventing over heating and could be used as a hail shield. With evacuated tube collectors, you still have to worry about vacuum leakage with an estimated lifetime of only 15 years for the tubes keeping their vacuum. While flat plate collectors use tempered glass, evacuated tube collectors use a softer untempered glass that can be fused for making the vacuum seal, making them much more susceptible to hail damage. Since the heating loop I installed with my system has not done that much, when I replace the collectors someday, I will probably install flat plate collectors.

To avoid having your solar installation make your house look like a reject from a 1970's science fiction movie, it looks much better if the collectors are mounted directly on a south facing roof, rather than being mounted in a rack above the roof. My system is rack mounted and looks pretty bad. The reason many solar collectors were rack mounted was that the roof did not have a south slope or the angle was too low. Ideally, a solar collector should be mounted so it faces the sun at noon at the time of the year when it is used the most. This angle is generally your latitude, if you were at the equator, at 0 degrees with the sun straight over head at noon, your panel would be flat mounted, at the north pole 90 degrees north, your panel would be vertically mounted to point at the noon sun on horizon. Your latitude is the angle that the sun is overhead on the equinoxes when the sun is directly over the equator. Since the earth spins at a 23 and half-degree angle in respect to the plane of its orbit about the sun, the sun at noon is 23 and half degrees higher in sky at the summer solstice than it was at the equinoxes and 23 and half degrees lower at the winter solstice. With this 47-degree range between the high sun of summer and the low sun of winter, your collector will seldom be directly facing the sun. Collectors that track the sun roughly double the energy collected. For thermal solar collectors it is not cost effective to use a tracking mount, it is cheaper to install extra collectors and avoid the cost, complexity and repair costs associated with operating a tracking unit. Tracking units really only make sense for photovoltaic, solar cells, since due to the high cost of the cells, using an expensive tracking unit makes sense since otherwise you would have to buy twice as many.

The correct angle for mounting solar collectors is basically your latitude, for systems used year round. Pool heaters used mainly in the summer time when the sun is higher overhead, could be more efficient if mounted at a lower angle. However, if the heater is not used in the hot summer, and is rather used to extend the swimming season, then the collector would probably be better mounted closer to the angle of the latitude. While home heating units may work best mounted at a steeper angle so that they face the sun when they are used most. Since it can be hard to predict when the "most use" time of the year will be, the middle of the road angle of your latitude is probably a pretty good angle to choose. Of course, it is unlikely that your house just happens to have a south facing roof with the perfect angle. The solution is simple, just add collectors to make up for a less than ideal setting. For heating hot water for an average home, two flat panels mounted on a south facing roof with a clear view of the sun for most of the day will probably do the job. Therefore, if the roof angle is poor or the roof does not face directly south or is shaded for part of the day, adding a third collector may be able to make up the difference. Solar systems can even be mounted on east and west facing roofs, which does mean increasing the number of collectors to get enough sun to heat the hot water. For such a system it would probably be best to split the collectors on two different loops each with their own controller, so that each collector will run when it is hot since each will get the full sun at different times of the day. With a little bit of creative thought and ingenuity, it is possible to direct mount solar collectors to your roof without using ugly racks.

Now for a word in favor of ugly racks for solar collectors, "snow". If you get a snow-covered roof for most of the winter, you can expect any roof mounted solar collectors to be snow covered for most of the winter as well. If you have a low slope roof, using a rack to raise your solar collectors to your angle of latitude or above, may give your collectors enough slope for most of the snow to slide off. This is why I chose to use a rack, and it has worked out well for my system, which is an evacuated tube system without any reflectors, which can catch snow. All I get is a light coating that is normally gone in a day or two. If I had roof mounted, my collectors would be buried under several inches of snow for a good part of the winter. Another point to consider is that while evacuated tube collectors lose too little heat to melt the snow off, most flat plate collectors will often melt the snow off if part of the panel is exposed to the sun.

At this point in this chapter, you are probably thinking that you could indeed fit a solar system on your roof, but you also have to consider if it will fit your wallet. A typical solar hot water system will cost about $2,000 to $4,000 dollars or maybe much more. Some systems cost much more than others and some installers charge much more than others, the sky is the limit for the cost of installing solar. You can of course save quite a bit of money by installing it yourself, but remember that if you get a contractor who gives you a fair price, the savings may only be a few hundred dollars and the work is skilled and has to be done right. A bare bones price for the cost of the materials to install a cold climate hot water solar system is about $1,500.

Installing a Solar System

To help you decide if you want to install your own solar system, I will talk you through a basic installation. Once you have picked out where on the roof or yard you wish to install your system, next you will need to figure out how to do the plumbing. For most hot water systems 3/4 inch copper pipes will need to be run from the collector to the storage tank or water heater. In areas that do not freeze, it is possible to simply pump the water from the existing water heater through the collector whenever the collector is hotter than the water in the tank. In freezing areas, an anti-freeze/water mix is used and is pumped through a heat exchanger that is either inside a storage tank located "upstream" of the existing water heater or is piped to the tank with a second pump to move the tank water through the exchanger when the solar pump is running. As you can see, hot water systems in hot areas are simple and cheaper than systems for cold climates. Solar systems in cold climates also tend to lose half of the heat that they collect in the piping between the collectors and the storage tank. This means that you should design your installation with the shortest most direct runs possible to reduce this huge loss of heat. You basically want the collectors on the south roof above where your existing water heater is located, and run the lines down inside an interior wall, and have a direct and simple pipe runs to the pump and tank and also heavily insulate the lines. I found that pipe insulation is expensive and often too thin to really insulate the lines, and doubling the insulation by putting one layer over the outside of another, made it too expensive. A cheaper and possibly better choice is to go to Wal-Mart and buy pool noodles. The company that makes the pool noodles is a pipe foam insulation manufacturer. Wal-Mart sells an assortment of these colorful noodles in different shapes. I just picked out the thick large ones that would fit over a 3/4 inch copper pipe with a 7/8 inch diameter hole in the center and with an outside diameter of three and half inches compared to normal pipe insulation that has a diameter of only 3 inches. These large noodles are also just the right size to fit inside a standard 2 by 4 wall. For extra insulation in the unheated attic, I wrapped the pipe insulation with bubble foil reflective insulation using foil tape to secure it and then on the roof I covered the foil with white vinyl tape. Another trick to save heat is to design the system so that the water drains back down into a tank above the pump when the pump shuts off. That way when the system starts in the morning, it does not have to heat up water that has cooled all night sitting in the unheated attic and on the roof, which could be at sub-freezing temperatures. A drain back system like this also avoids the problem of the collectors steaming off in the summer time, since water is drained from the collector when not in use.

The collectors are mounted to the roof by long bolts that pass between the rafters and through a 2 by 4 laid across two rafters, giving the collector a grip on two rafters at each line of anchors rather than just one. Drilling and lag bolting into the top of a rafter weakens the rafter and if any water leaks down the lag bolt, it will enter the center of the rafter rotting it and destroying the holding power of the lag bolt. It is better to drill through the roof between rafters and silicon caulk the hole heavily, caulk the bolt, and insert it in a twisting motion to insure that the singles or other roofing material is well sealed to the bolt so there is no path for water to follow. Inside the roof, a short piece of lumber equal in thickness to the rafters is nailed between the rafters on both sides of the bolt to carry the weight of the collectors to the rafters. A cross board is placed over the bolt that crosses both rafters, so when the nut is tightened down against a large washer, the board presses up against the bottom side of the rafters, securing the collector to the roof. In the event that you end up with a leak at a mounting bolt, here is my secret fix that always worked wonders. People do not know that water flows underneath the top layers of shingles, and across the top of the bottom layer, so they only seal the top layer. To divert the water away, simply seal the spaces between the tabs in the two rows above the leak, for a foot or so to each side above the leak. This prevents the water from flowing under the tabs and to the leak, which is normally never the top shingle, but rather the bottom one. Use 100% silicon caulk and you should only have to do this once.

The lines from the collector are normally 3/4 inch copper pipe, which is soldered together with copper fittings which are cleaned, fluxed and heated with a torch until hot enough that the solder flows when touched to the joint, and the tight fitting draws the liquid solder into joint by capillary action. Soldering is an art, not a science. The soldering of copper pipe is tricky and takes practice to develop a skill for it. It is easiest to solder joints when the pipe is horizontal and you have easy access to the pipe, and hardest when the pipe is vertical and you have to get the solder to flow up into a joint when you can hardly reach the pipe, let alone see what you are doing. Which is why it is best to pre-solder tricky sections together before putting them in place. It is also sometimes wise to use compression fittings on some connections where solder would be difficult or inconvenience for future disassemble; one such place is at the collectors. If you ever need to remove the collectors for reroofing, it would be much easier if you could simply open the fitting with a wrench, rather than having to cut the lines and resolder later. Speaking of reroofing, that is what kills most roof-mounted solar systems, the cost of having to remove and replace the collectors is too much for many people and they end up simply removing them instead. This could be avoided if the collectors were flashed to the roof with the piping exiting the panels on the back, this way the collectors are part of the roof rather than on top of the roof, so they are not removed for reroofing any more than you would remove your chimney. The downside of flashing a collector to the roof is any leak in the collector is a leak into your house.

The lines from the collector will normally come out of sides of a flat plate collector and will then have an elbow and enter the roof at a 90-degree angle and enter the attic space. It is difficult to get roof flashing with a small enough opening for a tight seal for 3/4 inch copper pipe, so generally, a 7/8 inch hole is drilled and the pipe is caulked in the roof. Of course, the elbow and a short piece to reach the fitting that will connect to the collector, is soldered together before the pipe is inserted in the roof and caulked. The heat of soldering tends to burn the caulk resulting in a roof leak, which is why this joint is best done before hand. If a compression fitting is used here to connect the pipe to the collector, no heat is needed for the connection to the panel. A compression elbow works well here, since when the collector when lifted, it will lift off the pipe coming out through the roof. Inside the attic, slope your lines so the water will drain down to the drain back tank, or just so the lines will drain for servicing if you have to resolder a line. From the attic space, the lines are normally routed inside an interior wall cavity between the studs. Locate a wall space without any vents, pipes, electrical wire or other obstructions in it, and drill a hole in the top of the wall in the attic. In the attic, you can locate the tops of the walls by looking underneath the insulation since the walls were installed before the ceiling drywall was. There will normally be two 2 by 4's in the top of the wall, drill a half inch or larger hole and peak in with a flash light and a coat hanger wire. Use the wire to "feel" where the studs are and mark their locations on the wall top, and use the flashlight to look for pipes and wires. To see them you will probably need a larger hole, the 1/2 inch hole is hard to see through, but some people with better eyes then mine seem to be able to do it. If the wall cavity is clear, locate the bottom of it in your basement. There are some tricks to doing this, measuring from various things etc. What works best is to simply take a small drill bit, 1/8 inch or smaller and drill a small hole in the floor right in front of the wall cavity. If you do not know where the cavity is exactly, you may need to drill a small hole in the drywall from the attic and stick a wire down through the hole like a marking flag. Then do the same with the floor and look for your flag wire in the basement. Then if the cavity will work for routing the pipes, cut out the wood at the top and bottom of the space, which is done by drilling into the wood and using a keyhole saw or Sawzall to remove the wood.

At this point now, you have a clear shot from the pipes in the attic to the tank in the basement. Make up the lines for the run inside the wall to the attic, cut them to length and slip the pipe insulation over them and shove them up inside the wall cavity and tie them in place temporally, while you finish the soldering in the attic. Last, you do the runs from the lines to the tank.

Drain Back Systems

For drain back systems, the normal piping set up is the return line from the collectors enters the top of 3 to 5 gallon drain back tank and out of the bottom of the tank to the pump, a small circulating pump with bronze housing and stainless steel impeller. Then the line runs down to the low point on the system with a drain valve for draining the piping for repairs and then into the heat exchanger. The other side of the heat exchanger is piped to the line going back up to the collectors. There should also be a valve underneath the drain back tank and a valve below the pump so the pump can be removed without draining the system. There is also a pressure relief valve, 15 to 25 PSI mounted on the drain back tank, to release excessive pressure if the system were to over heat and steam. The relief valve should have a drain line extending to within 2 inches of the floor, so that nothing is sprayed with steaming hot water if it ever opens. To fill the system, open the drain back tank by opening a plug in the top of the tank or by removing the pressure relief valve. If you have an opening on the top of the drain back tank, you can use a funnel and pail to pour the water/anti-freeze mix into the tank until it is full. If you are filling through a valve above the tank, put a hose on the valve, put a funnel in the hose end, hold it above the valve, and pour water into the funnel until it comes back out. Once you have filled the system, turn on the pump and listen with your ear next to the drain back tank for the sound of water falling back into the tank. If you do not hear it, check your valves, one may still be closed blocking the flow. If that is not the problem, it could be that your drain back tank is too small to hold the amount of water that the system needs to circulate. What you can do is add water, while the pump is running since the tank is drained by the pump, until it starts to return to the tank. Then close the filling valve or put the plug or relief valve back in before turning off the pump or the fluid will flow out the opening since there is now more fluid than what the drain back tank can hold. Your level is now above the top of the tank, and when the system is off, the level will be between the tank and the top of the collectors. As long as the fluid level in the system when the pump is off is below the level at which your piping enters unheated areas like an attic, the fluid will not be overly chilled by the winter cold and you will not have the big heat loss that flooded or filled systems have.

A drain back system can be operated in a cold climate without anti-freeze since when there is no heat in the collectors, the system shuts off and the water in the collector loop drains back down into a tank located in a heated part of the house. Drain back systems were designed for this very reason and many were installed this way. Once of my first jobs when I worked as a solar repairman, was to go around and drain the water out of a quite a number of drain back systems and replace it with a water/anti-freeze mix. What they found of course was that all it took was for the controller to malfunction and you could frost damage all the collectors and the entire collector-piping loop. It was soon realized that using anti-freeze was cheap insurance to spare yourself the cost having to replace your collectors, frost split piping located inside walls and repair water damaged ceilings and walls.

Filled Systems

On flooded systems, there is no drain back tank, and the system-piping loop is completely filled with the water/antifreeze mix. Since there is no drain back tank with air in it to absorb the expansion of the water as it gets hot; remember it is a closed loop, an expansion tank is used. A pressure gauge, and a pressure relief valve is installed on the line. A steam/air automatic vent is sometimes placed at the high point on the system, normally on the pipe on the top of the collector on the roof. In addition to the two valves isolating the pump, there are two hose bib type drain valves on each side of the valve above the pump. To fill the system, the valve between the bib valves is closed, and a pump is used to pump the water/antifreeze mix into the bottom bib valve. It flows through the system up to the collectors and back down to the top bib valve, which is open with a hose draining into the pail that the portable pump is pumping from. To fill the system, you fill the pail with your mix and turn the portable pump on and as the level drops you keep adding more until the mix is returning to the pail as fast as it is going out and the level remains constant. If the level in the pail drops too low and you are out of mix, turn off the pump and close the valves to keep the fluid from draining back and over filling the pail. Then once you have more fluid mixed up, turn on the pump, open the valves, and pour in the mix. Once the system is filled, you will still need to run the portable pump for a while to flush out any air bubbles in the system.

Then once that is done, close off the return valve and let the portable pump put some pressure on the system before closing the inlet valve and shutting off the portable pump. Now open the valve between the inlet and outlet bib valves, turn on the system pump, and check for flow. Some systems have flow valves for doing this, but they are not really needed, for all you have to do is feel the pipe coming back down from the collectors to see if it becomes hot. The return line can get hot enough to burn your hand if you are not careful, while the somewhat cooler supply line going back to the collectors will be about 20 degrees warmer than the storage tank which when the tank gets hot, can burn your hand too. By feeling the difference between the two lines, you can feel what your system is actually doing. Some systems have a temperature gauge installed in each line for monitoring the solar system, if the system also has a flow meter, you can calculate the amount of heat being collected.

Storage Tanks and Heat Exchangers

The solar heating loop can transfer heat to the water in the hot water heater in a number of ways. One way is to mount a heat exchanger next to the water heater with a pump that pumps the hot water tank water through one side while the solar heated mix is pumped through the other side. Some try to eliminate the pump for the water heater water, and depend on thermosiphoning to move the hot water into the tank. This does work, but the problem is that the hot water goes to the top of the tank and stays there and can get so hot that it opens the temperature/pressure relief valve on the water heater while the bottom of the tank is still cold. Normally your sensor for your controller is mounted on the side of the tank, so it may not see this over heating and since the heat is all concentrated in a small volume at the top of the tank. There is very little storage of hot water with this set up. If a pump is used, the hot water will still rise to the top of the tank, but the movement caused by the pump will cause more mixing in the tank so the water in the bottom of the tank is also hot and this makes for a much larger volume of hot water.

The most common system set up uses a preheat tank that the cold water enters before it goes into the water heater, and this tank has a special built in coil in the bottom that the hot fluid from the collectors is pumped through. If the tank is designed right, the rising hot water inside the tank will turn the water in the tank over as it rises, mixing the water, so the whole tank is heated instead of just over heating the water at the top of the tank, tripping the relief valve. The hot water from this tank enters the water heater so your water heater is being filled with preheated water. The disadvantage is that if you are not using much hot water, it can cool off while sitting in the heater and your water heater will have to run to keep it warm.

Solar preheat tanks with built in heat exchangers can be expensive, over a $1,000 dollars, so sometimes cheaper tanks like large electric water heaters are used instead. How this works is the tank is never wired for electrical heating, instead a heat exchanger and pump are used to heat the tank by pumping the tank water through the heat exchanger. You have to pay for the pump and heat exchanger, but you have the advantage that when the tank goes, you can replace it with another cheap tank. A quick scan of things for sale will often reveal a number of old electric water heaters for sale, since their owners have recently discovered it is far cheaper to heat hot water with natural gas.

Mixing Valves

An absolutely critical piece of a solar hot water heating system is the mixing valve. Normally with solar systems to maximize the amount of heat that can be stored in a tank, the water is heated to about 160 to 180 degrees F. So that even if the water cools over night, it is still hot enough in the morning that the regular water heater will not be needed. Whereas if you only heated water to the normal use setting on water heaters, practically every passing cloud could result in a drop below the water heater setting causing the regular water heater to fire up. However, by solar heating the water to a much higher temperature, there is a wide reserve of stored heat that you can draw on without causing the regular water heater to start up. Now if your solar system is running well, you could have 180 degree F water coming out of the water heater, which is a really dangerous temperature for residential use and someone could be badly burned. The solution to the problem is to install a thermal mixing valve. How these valves work is they have a cold water connection and meter cold water into the hot water line to reduce the hot water down to a temperature you set with a dial on the valve or that they come preset for. Inside the valve is a metering valve controlled by a bi-metal spring. Back when I was working on solar systems in 1988, I saw a lot of these valves and practically none of them still worked. Apparently, as the valve adds cold water, the minerals drop out just like they do in your water heater and they can coat the valve and plug the metering seat. The mixing valves made today can be opened for cleaning, just soak in vinegar to dissolve the minerals or use something like lime remover if you have to, just be sure to rinse well before putting it back together. Keep an eye on your water temperature, and if you suddenly can get very hot water at the tap, you may need to clean your mixing valve. When you install the valve, put a valve near it in all three lines so it can be easily removed and cleaned without having to drain any water lines. Be sure to install a line thermometer after the mixing valve, so you can check the temperature.

Solar System Controllers

The solar system pump is controlled by a differential controller, which has two remote sensors, one on the top of the collector and one on the hot water tank that is heated by the solar system. Each one senses the temperature and whenever the collector is several degrees warmer than the tank, the pump is turned on. Then when the collector temperature drops enough that, there is little heat to be gained above what is already in the tank, the controller shuts the pump off. Once the solar heated tank reaches the set temperature, the pump is shut down so the tank is not overheated. Differential controllers are very reliable and normally cost less than $200 and sometimes you can get one for about $100. One word of experience, when you wire the sensors to the controller, use a shielded cable for the sensor on the collector, and ground the shield. That way if there is a lighting bolt nearby, it will not set up an induced voltage in the wires running down to the controller that could overload it. Your collectors should also have a ground wire for lighting induced voltages, if piped with copper pipe that may be good enough. But if your system is in danger of actually being struck because of its location, like on a rack above the roof on a exposed hill. Install a lighting grounding cable so if the collectors are hit, the bolt should be directed by the cable to the ground outside the house rather than coming down the piping inside the house.

Hot Air Solar Systems

While installing a hot water solar system can be very complicated, hot air systems are much less involved. The company Your Solar Home Inc. (http://www.yoursolarhome.com/index.html) sells hot air solar collectors that can be mounted on a south wall that merely requires cutting two holes for the vent ducts similar to dryer vents and wiring a thermostat. A built in solar panel provides the electricity to power the fan and control, so no electrical wiring or piping or any connection with anything else is required, making this one of the easiest systems to install. These units are a bit costly at about $2000 for the 1500g Solarsheat measures about 7 feet tall by 3 and half feet wide. The units can also be roof mounted as well, but then require an extra fan. Your Solar Home Inc also sells a "Solar Furnace system" which they state is a "*turn key solar heating, ventilation and domestic hot water solution and uses both hot air and hot water collectors. It can provide whole house heating, ventilation and hot water supply for a home from 0-3000 sq ft.*" Sounds fantastic, but it costs $5449 and the price does not include installation. Your Solar Home Inc also states that the Solar Furnace system will "*reduce your heating and electricity bills - savings from 20% up to 60%*". Which means if you have a house with the standard 3 and half inch insulated walls, this system will probably supply only a fifth of your yearly hot water and heating needs. While if you have a well insulated the system may provide nearly two thirds of your yearly hot water and heating needs. The Solar Furnace system is also available as a retro fit for existing homes.

Hot air solar can also be cheap to install, there are a number of plans for sale that basically describe how you can built a glass covered black box that the sun warms and includes a controller that turns on a fan to blow the solar heated hot air into the house. These home built collectors need an insulated back, unless the house wall is the back, and a frame that holds it together now and tomorrow. You need good quality aluminum or galvanized steel frames that will not rust or rot away and tempered glass for the front and a good seal between the glass and the frame. Then inside the box there is normally a black wire mesh or plates that are heated by the sunlight, and air is blown behind the plates to keep the heated air somewhat away from the cold glass. The air is moved into and out of the collector through two vents cut through the wall into the house. These vents need to be designed so at night, warm air from the house is not flowing out into the collector. Some use powered dampers, flow opened dampers, or running both vents upward into the house since heat tends to rise rather than sink. The problem with home built collectors is leaks, both air leaks and water leaks from rain entering the collector. The wind can also find its way in through any air leaks in the collector and cause a draft in the home, which can cause a large loss of heat. Hot air collectors need a good design and need to be well built if they are going to be a net energy gain rather than a net loss. It will also be difficult for a homeowner while buying quality materials at retail prices, to build a quality hot air collector for less than the cost of simply buying one at a fair price.

Another point to consider on hot air collectors is that people who have them, state that they produce about as much heat as a south facing window on a sunny day. The advantage is that while the window loses heat at night, the collector does not, which is only true if it doesn't thermosiphon heat out at night which some of the collectors have been reported to do, even though the manufacturers claim that they do not.

Obviously, to solar heat a home, the home needs to be as well as insulated as possible and a back up heat source will still be required. Pumps and controls along with other parts can be expected to fail and will need to be replaced, with the added costs of service calls if a contractor is to do the repair work many solar systems may still end up being an economic loss. Before installing a solar system, consider the complexity of it and whether or not you will be able to do the repair work yourself. When I worked as a solar repairman, what often made the difference between a system being a gain or loss financially, was my labor charge. If the homeowner had bought the parts and done the work himself, then the solar system savings would have covered the costs. Hot air systems like Your Solar Home Inc's Solarsheat collectors are so simple that they will probably be super reliable with only a low voltage fan to wear out and shouldn't be a hole in your wallet like many of the 1970s solar systems turned out to be.

Operating a Solar System

On passive solar systems, there are no moving parts and no controls, except for you. You are the control and the moving part of the system. You have to open the curtains in the morning to let the sun in and close them at night to keep the heat in. Therefore, in some ways passive solar takes the most work. There are automatic designs where insulated curtains or blinds are raised and closed automatically, but then the system is not a very passive passive solar system any more, might as well throw in a pump or two.

On hot water solar systems, you will need to set the temperature that the differential controller will heat the tank to, normally a temperature between 160 and 180 degrees to maximize heat storage, or a lower temperature to help the tank last longer. Higher temperatures particularly above 180 F shorten tank life, for at higher temperatures chemical reactions take place quicker, which increases the rate of corrosion in the tank. One operation trick I have is to set the preheat solar tank at the 160-180 range, but set the gas water heater at only about 105 degrees, that way when the water in the bath is above 105 I know that I am using solar heated water and I can take a long shower. However, if the water is cooler I take a short shower because the gas heater is running and I have to pay for the gas. The mixing valve of course limits the maximum temperature at about 115-120.

You may need to clear snow off the collectors, or you may feel that the risk of damaging the collector or falling off the roof is not worth the small gain in solar heat. As you get older, you get better at doing this sort of rationalization.

On hot air systems for home heating, there is little to do other than setting the temperature you want the system to try and heat the house to. The glass front may benefit from some glass cleaning once and a while, if mounted under an overhang where the rain may not reach it, a dirty window lets in less light after all.

Chapter 8

Electric Heating Methods

If the dream of electricity too cheap to meter from nuclear power had come true, every house would have electric resistance heat. Electric resistance heat is wonderful from many points of view, it is easy and inexpensive to install and requires almost no maintenance at all and has no moving parts. In the home, there is no exhaust gases to worry about, no chimney, no storage tank and no fuel leaks. Electric resistance heat wins on just about every point except for one, economy, for it is just about the most expensive way of heating a house that there is, short of making a fire out of dollar bills in the fireplace. Costing over twice as much as natural gas to heat a home, electric heat is today the last choice for heat. Electric resistance heat once made good sense when nothing else was available, for it was a case of electric heat or no heat. However, in areas today where the only heating power available is electric power, heat pumps can be installed which will out perform electrical resistance heating by a factor of three or more. In other words, heat pumps can supply the same amount of heat for as little as a third or even a tenth the cost of electric resistance heat. Electric powered geothermal heat pumps are one of the most efficient to operate heating systems available today and have one of the lowest monthly heating costs.

Electric heat can still make good sense for super insulated homes that in theory do not need any heat. That way if it becomes obvious the design is not adequate for all situations after all, backup heat will be available. Since little heat would be required, an inexpensive electric heating system that requires no chimney, air intake or fuel tank, can keep the costs down on a backup heating system that will hopefully see little use and have little run time to pay for the costs of a more expensive but more economical to operate system.

Electric resistance heating comes in a number of different forms. The most common are baseboard heaters, which are placed where heat vents would be, underneath the windows on outside walls and each one has an adjustable heat setting or can be controlled by a room thermostat. Another type is a central electric furnace that is like a giant toaster with a fan connected to the ductwork, or an electric boiler, which is just a big electric water. An electrically heated hot air furnace is just like a gas furnace, only it just costs twice as much to operate and the same is true of an electric boiler, just an expensive way to operate a hydronic heating system. While the other furnace and boiler parts will be the same as other systems and experience the same breakdown rate, the electric elements can out last and out perform the gas equivalents and since there are no heat losses due to having to vent exhaust gases, electric resistance heat is often 95-100% efficient. If only electricity was not so expensive.

Electric Radiant Heat

Electric radiant heat is the most comfortable and low maintenance heat period. However, it is expensive since it is electrical heat. A number of suppliers of radiant electric heat systems make claims that electric radiant heat is the most affordable and most efficient form of heating, which of course is a bald-faced lie. What they mean by efficient is that with electric heat, none of the heat is wasted up a chimney and this of course makes nearly all electric heat 100% efficient. The supposed advantage of radiant electric heat over other forms of electric heat is that with radiant heat you feel some of the heat directly and may feel comfortable at a somewhat lower room temperature and can thus save energy by maintaining a lower temperature in your house. If you continue to heat to your normal house temperature, the "savings" of radiant electric heat disappears. Like other forms of electric resistance heat, it is currently about two and half times the cost of heating with natural gas and four times the cost of heating with a geothermal heat pump.

Electric radiant heat is also installed in places that hydronic radiant heat is not normally ever installed in, like walls and ceilings in a thick coat of plaster, making the entire plaster surface warm to the touch. Being surrounded by heated surfaces other than windows and doors, is like being inside an electric toaster, and you will probably want to turn down the thermostat a few degrees to feel comfortable. One problem with this type of heating is if it is used only in part of the house and the temperature is the same throughout, the part of house with it will feel too hot or the other areas will feel too cold without it. I know of one case where they do not turn on the radiant heat because it feels too hot in the one room that they have it in. Electric radiant heat has the advantage of that it will never spring a leak, you will never have to rip up a floor or open a wall or ceiling to fix a leaking hot water pipe that has caused thousands of dollars in water damage. Even if a wire breaks, the rest of the system will still work and it is not the total disaster that radiant hydronic leaks can be.

Installing Electric Heat

Older homes often had 60 amp services, which was plenty for the 50's then in the 70's came 100 amp services, in the 90's 150 amp services and now 200 amp services are common. For electric heat, the rule of thumb is 10 watts per square foot, for a 2,000 sq ft house that would be 20,000 watts, which with 220 volts would require nearly 100 amps. Not too many electrical services are installed with enough amps to spare for an extra 100 amp load.

Since the amount of electricity needed to heat a home is larger than the size of the standard electrical service that older non electric heated homes normally have and is more than what most newer homes can spare, it will be necessary to have a new larger electrical service installed. The electric power company (in most areas) will not connect to the new service without the necessary permits, which requires having the work done by a licensed master electrician. So the do-it-yourself person cannot do it unless he happens to be a master electrician. There is one loop hole for the do-it-yourselfer, hire an electrician to install a larger service for a "future" electric heat installation, that way the electrician can pull the necessary permits and the power company will connect to the new larger service. Of course you certainly should not do electrical work if you do not know what you are doing; electricians have licenses for a reason. Few things are as dangerous as electrical work done by a non-electrician. It is all to easy for someone who thinks he knows what he is doing, to create an electrical time bomb that seems to work just fine but later kills someone or burns the house down.

Installing Electrical Baseboard Heat

The first step is calculating the heat load, determining that amount of heat that is needed on the coldest day of the year to keep your house at an acceptable temperature and the amount of electric baseboards it will take to supply that heat. Normally that would be about 10 watts per square foot, or 1500 watts for a 10 by 15 foot room, which at 220 volts would take 6.8 amperes. For rooms with many large windows or poor insulation, you may have to double the heat needed to 20 watts per square foot. Standard electric baseboard heaters normally supply 250 watts per foot of length of the heater, so for 1500 watts about 6 feet of baseboard heater would be needed. The 6 feet of heater can be installed as one unit 6 feet long or as several smaller units with a total length of 6 feet. The baseboard heaters will need to be located along the outside walls, normally underneath each window to counteract the cold air spilling down off the windows. Placing the baseboard heaters can get tricky since they can not be located underneath an electrical receptacle to prevent a cord from resting on the top of the hot baseboard heater; this problem is avoided with some baseboard heaters that have the electrical receptacle built into the baseboard eliminating the need for receptacles above the heaters.

Most baseboard heaters have a temperature control, normally a dial number 0 to 9 for setting the heat, while some are wired to be controlled by a room thermostat mounted on the wall. Due to the high cost of electric heat, it makes sense to have a good control system so that more heat is not used than is needed. A wall thermostat will give much better control over temperature than dial thermostats on the baseboard heaters will and will save energy. The thermostat cannot be located above a baseboard heater or the heat from the heater will heat the thermostat causing it to turn off the heat before the rest of the room is warmed up. The thermostat should not be located on an outside wall since the cold wall surface would throw off the temperature reading for the room by causing the thermostat to over heat the room in an effort to warm the cold outside wall to the set room temperature. The thermostat should be located on an interior wall where it will read the average temperature of room; such a location is near the center of the room and away from cold drafts or bright sunlight shining in through windows directly on the thermostat. A thermostat for baseboard heaters is a line thermostat meaning that it opens and closes the electric lines that supplies the electrical power to the baseboards, in contrast to regular thermostats that operate on 12 or 24 volts and use the low voltage to operate a relay that controls the furnace. The big difference here is that while regular thermostats only have low voltage wires and are pretty harmless, line thermostats for electric heaters have 220 volt power circuits routed through them and are quite dangerous for the uninformed to be sticking their fingers into. These thermostats consist of a plastic cover with a temperature dial which when turned; turn a screw that adjusts the spring like bi-metal temperature switch. A bi-metal snap switch is made of two different metals fused together in such a way that when cooled, one metal will contract more than the other causing the switch to snap close, turning on the power to the heaters. The snap switches are mounted on top of two electrical switches that they operate by pressing down on a plastic button. Inside the plastic housing of the switches are the actual contacts that control the power. This thermostat assembly is mounted in a electrical box like a wall switch, so that the temperature sensing plastic covered snap switch is exposed to the air while all the high voltage parts are enclosed inside the electrical box mounted in the wall. The thermostat should be mounted in the wall at a height of 60 inches like a light switch, where it will better sense the average temperature of the air in the room and the height above the floor will help to keep little fingers away. The electrical cable from the electrical panel has to be run to the thermostat electrical box and connected to the "line" contacts and then run from the "load" contacts to the baseboard heaters.

All electric switches need to open and close quickly, since if the switch contacts moved slowly, the current would continue to arc across the gap until the gap was wide enough to break the circuit. The switch by opening very quickly breaks the current flow before much arcing can occur, but each time even the quickest switch opens, there is always some brief arcing. Eventually the arcing will burn away the contacts until they no longer work. Since line thermostats have 220 volts running through them, the contacts will someday wear out and they will have to be replaced, but in normal use they should last for many years.

The baseboard heaters all need to be wired to the electrical service panel. This is one area where electric heat really shines, for routing electric wires is much easier and takes far less space than running hot air ducts or hot water pipes. Electric wires can be run in outside walls where hot water lines could freeze, and thru unheated spaces without thermal insulation. Electric heat is the most flexible of all heating systems. The electrical cables or conduit and be routed underneath the floor in the basement or crawl space, or through attic spaces. Once at the electrical panel, each branch circuit will need to have it's own disconnect that can be locked or a breaker in a lockable panel. The wires in the circuits will need to sized at 125% of the full load, which works out to 12 amps on 15 amp circuit and 16 amps on a 20 amp circuit so that they are not overloaded. Nearly all heating circuits are 220 volts since it makes little sense to run a hot wire at 110 volts with a neutral return wire, when by using two hot wires each at 110 volts to ground but 180 degrees out of phase with each other, (split phase) the voltage is doubled creating 220 volts while not requiring an additional wire. A 220 circuit uses half the copper wiring that an equivalent 110 circuit uses. How this works is that by adding the two currents together, you get nothing, since the current of one line neutralizes the current of the other line when they are 180 degrees out of phase to each other. Producing a flat line or floating ground point in the middle of the load, without any need for a return path to the panel. This works because AC current is an alternating wave of positive and negative waves, two waves perfectly out of step with each other will cancel each other out perfectly. The hills in one wave fill the valleys in the other, leaving a level flat line at zero volts and zero amps.

Each baseboard heater will have its own electrical box built in for wiring, otherwise an electrical box will have to be installed in the wall behind the heater, but the heater will have to be removed for access to the electrical box. Access is necessary since all splices or connections in electrical wires must be done in an electrical box and all electrical boxes must have removable covers that are accessible so that the splices can be checked which trust me is very important when you are trying to locate a broken wire. It is illegal to wall over an electrical box, if you do so, you must install an access door. The wiring from the electrical panel will need to be routed to the thermostat without any splices or any splices must be in an accessible electrical box. Then from the thermostat the wires are routed to the first baseboard heater and then to the next. Since in remodeling work, the electrical wiring will have to be routed through existing walls, flexible cables like Romex or flexible armored cable will require far less openings cut into the walls for installation than conduit .

I would like to reemphasize here that all electrical work should be done by someone who knows what they are doing. I have not spelled out all the details such as proper grounding and other electrical requirements, for such details you would need a good book on home electrical wiring and basically study to be an electrician. Therefore, unless you are an electrician, you should hire one for most electrical work. However, even if you hire someone, it is good to know what the job entails and what to expect.

Installing Electric Radiant Heat

While installing baseboard heaters is pretty easy, radiant heat is much more involved since the heating cables will need to be installed inside the floor, wall or ceiling. The most common is in the floor since heat rises, while heat in outside walls are nice for stopping the cold from coming in. Floor heat is done by heating tapes, cables, mats or panels built into the floor. Some systems are encased in concrete and some are installed in modified wood floors. How the floor is modified is, it is stripped down to the sub floor and a half inch thick tile backer board or cement board is screwed to the floor. Then electric heating mats are laid down on the cement board and are covered with thin set cement and the new finish floor is installed over the cement. Nearly any kind of floor can be installed over the thin set cement, but not thick carpeting, which would block the heat, as would a solid hardwood floor.

Installing radiant floor heat in an entire house is an expensive and time-consuming project, which will result in an expensive to heat home. The steps needed to be taken to install are considerable, an enlarged electrical service, removal of all finish floors, cementing in the electric heating mats, wiring the mats to the thermostats and back to the panel and then installing new finish floors in the entire house. For what the project would cost you could probably afford to install a geothermal heat pump and have air conditioning to boot.

There are a number of outlets selling radiant flooring heating mats to the do-it-yourself market; here are the web addresses to two of them. Please remember that they are trying to sell you something and will lie about the "efficiency" of radiant heat by implying that the 100% efficiency of all electric heating some how makes radiant cheaper to use than other heating systems, which is not true. They will also exaggerate about how easy the products are to install and may even leave out important details to make the installation seem much easier than they really are.

http://www.radiant-floor-heating.com/index.htm
http://www.heavenly-heat.com/easymat.php

Installing Air Source Heat Pumps

An air source heat pump is basically a backwards air conditioning system; instead of pumping heat out of the house, it pumps it in. The key difference is that a heat pump has a reversing valve that reverses the flow of the refrigerant that reverses the system and turns an air conditioner into a heat pump. Air source heat pumps work best at temperatures above 40 F even though some new heat pumps claim to work well at temperatures below zero, for as the air gets colder there is less heat available to be extracted. At temperatures below 40 F, other heating systems such as gas furnaces are more economical to heat with. A hybrid system using a heat pump at outside temperatures above 40 F and gas or some other fuel for temperature below 40 F will save money over either system by itself. Installing an air source heat pump is installing an air conditioner and will require the skills and licenses that an air conditioner contractor has.

An air source heat pump designed to heat an entire house, will consist of an outdoor pad mounted unit, which is piped to a indoor furnace like unit with a fan connected to the ductwork. The heat pump compressor will draw a considerable amount of power and will be wired for 220 volts. Many heat pumps like many air conditioners come precharged, the coils and lines have seals on the ends and are prefilled with refrigerant. When the lines are connected into the fittings, the seals are cut and the lines are opened with the refrigerant ready to go. There are kits available for complete heat pump systems consisting of both the indoor coil and the outdoor units and the precharged lines to connect them. These kits are generally sold to contractors who wish to install air conditioner or heat pumps, but do not have a refrigeration license; since the units come recharged, they do not need one. The problem is if one of the fittings is incorrectly assembled so that the seal is cut but the fitting is not completely seated, it can leak and if the charge is lost, a licensed refrigeration technician will be needed to recharge the system.

A heat pump kit is normally a forced air system, though there are water systems for hydronic heating systems. A radiant heating system that is heated by a boiler can be converted to being heated by a heat pump, but the temperature of the hot water put out by the heat pump will probably be much lower than what the boiler put out. This reduction in temperature will reduce the amount of heat each radian floor section puts out, and with the lower water temperature, there may not be enough heat to heat the house on cold days. Replacing a hot air furnace with a heat pump may encounter the same problem; the cooler air may not provide enough heat to heat the house. As long as the new heat pump has a rated output equal or greater than the old furnace, the problem may be solvable by increasing the fan speed to move more air to make up for the lower heat content. This solution has its limitations for if the air speed in the ductwork is increased too much, it will make wind like noises and will create drafts that will make you feel colder like a breeze on a warm day does. Hot water systems have the problem that increasing pump speed will keep the water a bit warmer in the lines, but it does little beyond that to increase flow of heat in to the rooms, the solution often used is to double the radiators. A good heating contractor maybe able to help address these problems and make any necessary changes like increasing the size of the ductwork to correct them before the system is installed instead of trying to fix them later.

The heat pump looks much like a gas furnace, a large metal box, and connects to the ductwork in the same manner and consists of little more than an air conditioning coil, a fan and the controls. The coil of course needs to be connected to the coil and compressor in the outdoor unit. In a remodeling situation, where you are replacing an existing furnace or installing the heat pump as a secondary furnace, the location for the heat pump indoor unit is already set. The outdoor unit is normally located outside as nearby as possible to keep the refrigerant lines short. Normally outside air conditioners compressors, are never placed in front of the house or where they are visible from the road. This is not just due to the price of copper and the risk of the coil disappearing, it is because compressors are noisy and considered unsightly. The other place compressors should not go is near bedrooms so a noisy compressor does not keep you up at nights. Therefore, you may end up running the refrigerant lines the long way out the back. The outdoor compressor unit will need to be set on a precast concrete pad or you can mix up some cement and pour your own pad. However, the precast pads are pretty inexpensive and though heavy are not too hard to move with some help or a good hand dolly. The electrical code requires a disconnect switch by the compressor unit, normally mounted on the house wall.

While the heat pump whole house models are hard to install, smaller through the wall heat pump systems are easier. These systems come as a kit and are designed to heat and cool a room or two. There is a wall-mounted unit that can be wired into an existing 110-volt circuit and an outdoor unit that is set on a concrete pad. A small hole needs to be drilled through the wall for the refrigeration lines and wires, and the lines are precharged. These units are sold as plug and go units, meaning that they take little work to install compared to the central units. While these units are not designed to heat entire house, they can heat a very small house or more than one unit could be installed, but one large central unit would be cheaper than several small the wall units.

The last option for heat pumps is window units. Some window air conditioners are available with a heat pump option. While a window mounted heat pump would be a joke in a northern state, in a warmer climate where little heat is needed, an air conditioner that doubles as a heat pump could work very well. Such units can be 2 to 3 times as economical as using electric resistance heat and should be capable of supplying the minor heat a home in the Deep South needs.

Installing Geothermal Heat Pumps

Like the air source heat pumps, a geothermal heat pump can be used to heat air or water. What is different is that there is no outdoor unit; the compressor and its coil are located inside the indoor unit. The only thing outside is plastic tubing that is buried underground and enters through the basement wall if you have one. The key differences in geothermal systems are the type of ground loops that are used. There are open and closed loops, in closed loops the loop goes out and comes back in with the same water in it, in open loops the water is dumped down a well or into a body of water like a lake and other water is pumped back in. In geothermal heating and cooling, having a body of water from which to pump water from is solid gold; it is the best situation to have. Water holds an enormous amount of heat and having a lake full of water just waiting to be pumped eliminates the largest cost of a geothermal system, the cost of drilling wells or burying hundreds of feet of coil 3 to 6 feet underground. Geothermal systems using lake water can be open or closed, the closed systems have a slinky of coiled plastic tubing that is spread out and anchored on the lake bottom while the open systems are just an intake pipe and an outlet pipe. The closed system costs a bit more for the plastic tubing, but it eliminates algae and little fish from clogging up your heat exchanger coil.

The deep geothermal systems, which are used where there is limited yard space to work with use one or more wells drilled deep into the earth, normally about 200 feet but sometimes as much as 600 feet or more. The wells when used in an open system have the water pumped into the well and then pumped out from the same well at a different level or pumped out from a nearby well so the water has to flow through the ground. Open systems are prone to mineral problems while closed systems are not. In closed systems the plastic tubing is routed down to the bottom of each well hole and back out and down the next, the tubing is in contact with the ground water, which fills the well bores to the level of the water table. In areas with high water tables, the wells may not need to be very deep to have good ground water contact while in areas with a deep water table the wells will need to be much deeper.

Shallow geothermal systems consist of a continuous buried plastic loop, the loop can be a slinky like coil buried in a wide trench, or a long single tube buried in a narrow but very long trench. The tubing can also have branches and have smaller tubes in all sorts of patterns. For most settings, the simplest and best coil layout will be the slinky since it requires the least digging. Some other possibilities for keeping down costs are machines that slice the ground and insert a plastic tube without making a trench; the gas company loves those things. The problem is that in many areas, the ground loop has to be buried deeper then these machines can reach or the ground is too rocky for them to work.

Geothermal systems can cost about $20,000 and a good part of that is for the ground loop, so you can see how a handy lake can greatly reduce the cost. The rest of the installation consists of the pumps and the heat pump unit itself that looks like a conventional furnace or boiler. The ground lines on closed loops will need to be purged of air and filled with water or a water anti-freeze solution, one do-it-yourself geothermal system ships its ground lines prefilled. Then the lines will need to be connected to the pumps and also to the heat pump heat exchanger. The heat pump will need to be installed and connected to the hydronic heating system or the ductwork and supplied with electrical power.

Installing a geothermal heat pump is not generally considered a project for the do-it-yourselfer, yet there are companies who sell geothermal kits to the DIY market. While just the necessary excavation or well drilling for the ground loop should eliminate all but the most hardy and over equipped DIYs. Last time I checked I did not have a backhoe or well driller in my tool set, yet there are those who do install their own geothermal heat pumps. What they do is hire contractors for the parts of the job that they cannot do, or they are superman with a shovel. One website states *"Our goal is to provide tools, resources, support and our expertise to help people get DIY, Do it Yourself geothermal heat pumps installed and operational.*" http://www.geojerry.com/ , though not necessarily at a bargain price since they charge $990 dollars for sizing your system and providing the information on how to install it. Here is another site that offers a DIY geothermal heat pump http://advbuildingtech.com/TerraLink.htm . Another option is to buy the heat pump and the other parts from the suppliers directly, some suppliers even offer kits for contractors, but you would be on your own in some pretty deep water.

Operating a Heat Pump

Operating a heat pump involves not much more than setting the thermostat. Once set, they will provide year round heating and cooling at a low cost. Some geothermal installations are sized to barely heat or cool the home and will struggle to bring the temperature back up after coming off a nighttime setback setting. For reasonable comfort, it maybe best not to use a setback thermostat on such systems and instead attempt to maintain a constant temperature at all times. When air conditioning, some geothermal systems are known for being cold and clammy, but this has little to do with the type of system and more to do with how it is operated. Clamminess is caused by a failure to reduce the humidity due to the evaporator coil being above the dew point. The coil must be below the dew point to condense out the excess humidity. The coil temperature can often be lowered by increasing the demand for cooling by lowering the desired temperature setting on the thermostat, and then once the clamminess is reduced, the temperature setting can be reset. The reason some air conditioners cause a clammy humid coolness is due to being oversized and being able to cool the building without removing enough humidity. This problem can be avoid by having more than one stage of cooling, so the unit is better matched to the load, and the evaporating coil runs enough to adequately reduce the humidity.

Chapter 9

Natural Gas

Natural gas occurs in gas pockets and in association with oil deposits deep inside the surface of earth. It was a product without much of a market until in 1803 when Frederich Winsor patented a gas lighting system, and gaslights started to appear on city streets and in homes. Lighting remained the main use for natural gas until the year 1885 when Robert W. Bunsen's lab assistant Peter Desaga invented the Bunsen burner, which his boss promptly named after himself. The Bunsen burner was the first way of safely burning natural gas as a heat source and was adapted the very next year by the company Pettit and Smith for use in the first gas heater, the age of gas heat had arrived. Our modern forced air gas furnace had to wait until the forced air coal furnace was developed in 1935 and was soon adapted for use with natural gas. The last piece of the puzzle fell into place with the building of the gas pipeline system in the 40's and 50's that allowed for natural gas to be distributed widely from coast to coast in the continental United States. Today over half the homes in the United States are heated with natural gas with 70% of new homes built to use natural gas. The number of homes heated with natural gas has continued to rise while the amount of gas used has not increased as much due to the higher efficiency of newer gas furnaces. Natural Gas remains one of the cheapest, most efficient and easy ways to heat a home.

Natural gas is mostly the gas methane (80-95%) with possibly a small amount of ethane and often some hydrogen with some minor traces of other gases. Natural gas if found by itself in a gas pocket is very nearly pure methane and is called 'dry'. Natural gas found with oil is 'wet' having heavier hydrocarbon gases such as ethane, propane and butane along with other gases such as carbon dioxide, nitrogen, helium, argon, carbon monoxide and hydrogen sulfide. Wet natural gas is 'dried' by removing the heavier hydrocarbon gases such as propane, which have their own markets, and removing the other gases including helium, which comes primarily from natural gas refining. To the now 'dry' natural gas, the chemical butanethiol commonly know as 'skunk oil' is added. The reason skunk oil is added is because it stinks, and natural gas without it is odor less, it is the smell of the skunk oil that we think of as the smell of natural gas. This distinctive scent is added for safety so that gas leaks can be readily noticed long before there is time for the gas to accumulate to high enough levels to form an explosive gas/air mixture. In coal mines, methane gas represents a grave danger since unlike natural gas with its distinctive scent; methane is odor less and can accumulate to explosive concentrations unnoticed by mine workers. Natural gas is piped into homes after the meter at a pressure of about 0.25 PSI or 7"WC (pressure at the bottom of a column of water 7 inches tall) so that any leaks are slow and fairly small and will be noticed by smell well before the gas can build to dangerous levels. Normally the smell of natural gas has to be practically overpowering before there is enough in the air for an explosion.

Natural gas is sold in units of 1,000 cubic feet (MCF) which contains 1 million BTU (or by therms, 100 cubic feet) which is about the amount of heat needed to heat the average home for one day on a average cold winter day. A quick way of seeing how your house compares to the "average home" is to look on your gas bill for the number of MCF or therms used per day in the winter, the "average home" uses 10 therms per day or one MCF per day. I hope that your usage will be well below the average amount or you need to do some serious insulating.

Natural Gas is distributed by pipeline and is produced all year round; the majority of use occurs in the winter time causing summer time NG prices to fall. The major gas companies buy up large amounts of NG at low summer time rates and inject it in old depleted gas wells, underground porous rock formations and salt caverns. Then in the winter time, they draw on these vast underground stores, which can contain enough NG to carry the U.S. through the winter. Without this giant storage capacity, NG prices would be more unstable than LP prices.

Another solution for winter time NG shortages is SNG; Synthetic Natural Gas. SNG is a substitute for NG and has been used in place of it without any modifications to supply systems or NG appliances. SNG can be made by mixing LP with air, at about a 60/40 ratio, depending on the propane/butane ratio in the LP. Propane and butane both burn hotter than NG, which is mostly methane, but by diluting them with air or another gas like nitrogen, the SNG burns like NG. Synthetic Natural Gas is also produced from petroleum waste products, lignite coal and biofuels. (SNG from biofuels are termed Bio-SNG) Sizable amounts of SNG from lignite coal are injected into the national NG pipe line system, so some of the NG that you use may actually be SNG made from coal. Bio-SNG may someday soon also be injected into the NG pipeline system and is hoped to be the start of a switch from using NG from fossil sources to renewable plant sources.

In the United States and other parts of the world, we have been looking at a declining supply of natural gas as the old gas fields production levels dropped with each passing year and gas terminals were built for importing liquefied natural gas. But then things changed, unconventional natural gas such as "tight gas" have entered the gas market and increased the supply of NG and has resulted in a drop in price. Tight gas is found in non-porous rocks that are gas tight which traps the gas in the rock, this gas was largely unextractible in the past. Now the non-porous rock is fractured by high pressure water so the gas can flow out. In 2007 unconventional natural gas made up 47 percent of the NG used in the United States and it is expected to soon make up over half of the U.S. NG supply. This large increase in NG supplies has lowered prices and will probably help keep gas prices low. However, Gas wells in nonporous rock formations may not produce gas as long as conventional Gas wells do and it is feared that UNG production levels could drop very suddenly someday. Such a sudden decrease in the NG supply would be catastrophic since there would suddenly not be enough keep the residential market supplied and many homes would be without heat as prices would spike to unbelievable highs.

Ways of Heating with Natural Gas

The most common natural gas heating appliance has to be the gas water heater. Even homes heated by other means will sometimes still have a gas water heater. Often able to heat hot water for a third or less than the cost of an electric hot water heater, gas hot water heaters are often the most economical choice for year round water heating. Another very popular natural gas appliance is the gas range. Most cooks greatly prefer using gas burners over electric. Gas clothes dryers also far out perform electric clothes dryers doing the same job at a third or less of the cost of electricity. The big star of course is the natural gas furnace. With efficiencies in the high nineties and nearly maintenance free, natural gas furnaces are the number one choice for home heating. There are also natural gas boilers, space heaters, air conditioners, even refrigerators.

Installing Natural Gas

For natural gas to be available there has to be a gas pipe buried in the street in front of your house. The simple way of checking on the availability of natural gas in your area is to go around and check and see who has gas meters. You can also call your local gas company and ask if service is available for your address. The cost of converting from oil to natural gas runs about $3,000 to $7,000. The costs include running a gas line from the street to a meter on the side of the house, and running gas piping inside the house and installation of a gas furnace or conversion of an existing oil or LP furnace to natural gas. Oil furnaces should no longer be converted to burn natural gas as they are too inefficient and the new gas furnaces are far cheaper to run and will pay for their added cost in just a few years. Since natural gas lines are buried underground, installing NG will involve trenching a ditch from the gas line under the road to where the meter will be installed. Contractors with newer equipment will have a trenching machine that will cut a trench just wide enough to lay the plastic gas line or they may even have a slicing type pipe layer that cuts the ground and lays the line without even making a trench. Therefore, the disruption to the landscaping around the home can be minimal. Replacing an existing furnace with a gas furnace and running the lines to it, is also a simple job for most contractors since due to the large number of people switching to natural gas, they have plenty of practice. If installing natural gas, be sure to have lines run for future appliances so that when your existing electric drier or water heater goes, that you will have a gas line ready for hooking up a gas replacement.

Now for the do it yourselfers, running natural gas pipe is nearly as easy as running water pipe. However, while with water pipe if you mess up you get wet, with NG a leak can be a lot more serious, so obviously you shouldn't be playing with gas pipe unless you know what you are doing. If you have run much threaded pipe, gas piping is easy and simple to do. On a home, the average main line is one inch or three quarter inch black pipe with three quarter pipe for branches and half inch pipe for single appliance lines. It is best to run the larger size three quarter inch as close to the half inch flexible hook up that many appliances have, to reduce restrictions in the line. Some larger appliances may require a 3/4 hook up instead of the more common 1/2 inch size. The common gas piping layout is a one inch pipe from the meter running across the bottom of the floor joists to near the furnace and 3/4 inch branch lines going to the water heater, kitchen stove and clothes dryer. The gas pipe will need to be well fastened to the bottom of the floor joists with pipe hangers every four feet or less. The threads on gas line need to be sealed with pipe dope, most will work well with gas, check the label to be sure. TFE or Teflon pipe dope works very well for gas, having a nice thickness to the dope that keeps the gas from leaking even from pipe that has been only hand tightened or has less than perfect threads. They also now make Teflon tape for gas pipe; the tape is yellow instead of white and presumably is less prone to strands and stretching. You are not suppose to use regular Teflon tape on gas lines due to the possibility of a Teflon strand blowing down the pipe and blocking a gas line or jamming a gas valve open. The big problem with Teflon is when you wrap the threads on a pipe; the tape can stretch across the end of the pipe like stretch wrap blocking the pipe. In a water pipe, the water pressure will burst any such Teflon blockages, but with NG having a pressure of only 0.25 PSI the pipe would be blocked, the new gas tape avoids this problem.

Have you ever wondered why black pipe is used for gas pipe instead of galvanized pipe? The old plumbers will sometimes say that galvanized pipe is not used because the zinc can flake off inside the pipe and block gas valves. Zinc does not flake off and metal flakes would be too heavy to be moved by NG at only 0.25 PSI. A better reason is so you can tell it from the water lines, black pipe helps to identify gas pipe as being gas pipe. The real reason is that historically galvanized pipe was more expensive than black pipe and NG is not as corrosive as water so black pipe was used to save money. We really should use galvanized pipe for gas lines, nothing gives me the willies like seeing old really rusty gas pipes. However, due to the strength of the well established myth about not using galvanized pipe for gas pipe, a number of local building codes and building inspectors forbid using galvanized pipe for gas pipe.

When running threaded pipe always put a union in here and there so if you have to go back and fix a leak, you do not have to disassemble the whole piping system. Every branch line should start with a union near the main line, so the branch can be disconnected so the main line can be turned to tighten any leaky joints. You should be buying at least one union for every tee. Every branch will need a valve at the end and a cap or plug for when no gas appliance is to be installed right away, so no one can open the valve and let the area fill with gas. The theory being that if you know how to remove a plumbing cap you will know better. On very Long Branch runs, it is often smart to install a valve on the start of the branch line as well as the end, so the line can be shut off if it ever leaks without having to shut the whole system down. For example if you have a gas line that runs from the house to a heater in an unattached garage. If the line in the garage or going to the garage was damaged, you would have to shut the gas off at the main valve on the gas meter and the house would have no heat or hot water, unless you had put in an isolating valve. Though valves cost money, it does not pay to go short on them. Also try to buy gas rated valves that are non-reducing, that when you look through the valve when open, the inside opening is the full size of the inside of the pipe. Many cheap gas valves have a small opening when open and will restrict the flow of gas. What works nice on gas lines is brass ball valves with a stainless steel ball with Teflon seals that are rated for gas.

A Plumber running threaded pipe will normally have a threading machine for cutting and threading pipe. Since such is far too expensive for having around the house, a hand plumbing pipe threader with threading dies for the sizes of pipe you will be working with, maybe the way to go. A pipe cutter is also necessary. If you do not want to buy a threader or thread pipe, you can make due with an assortment of nipples in different lengths. Running pipe without cutting any pipe is done by running the longest lengths that will fit, and then making up the remaining distance with the largest nipples that will fit. How this works is you run full pipe lengths of ten feet, until you are within ten feet of where you want to go. Then you use the next largest size precut pipe section that will fit, like a four foot or two foot precut pipe shorts sold at most building supply stores. Then throw in nipples to make up the last few inches. Like if you need 11 inches, you could use a six and a four. You will need a lot of couplers if you run pipe this way and remember to allow at least the pipe diameter for space for every coupling.

To do plumbing work you need two wrenches, one to hold the first part and the second to turn the other part to thread the two together. You cannot do plumbing without pipe wrenches, just one wrench will not do either. The whole concept is to turn the thread between the two wrenches tightening the threaded joint without over twisting the pipe that has already been installed.

When sealing the joints with paste, brush the paste on only the male threads filling the threads half way. For gas pipe rated Teflon tape, wrap the male threads starting from the threaded end of the pipe and wrap all the threads with about three layers of tape. Some say to start the tape back a thread from the end to keep the tape from projecting inside the pipe, which is good advice but can be tricky to do since the threads are small.

When routing threaded pipe you have to "help yourself" as an old pipe fitter liked to say. Many novice plumbers make the mistake of making life hard on themselves by routing pipe with the least possible fittings, while this may sound smart it isn't. Picture two pipes running next to each other and the job is make a cross connection between them. The novice plumber installs a tee in each line and tries to make a connection between them with two nipples and a union, which is nearly impossible to do. In order to close the union the plumber will have to tighten the union tight enough to pull one of the pipes toward the other to close the gap and the tees will have to be perfectly aligned. The experienced plumber installs his tees with the openings pointing at a 90 degree angle to the other pipe and puts in nipples but then installs four elbows forming a three sided box with a union on the side between the pipes. This way the elbows can be twisted in and out a bit to allow the union to be tightened without counting on being able to move one of the pipes and the tees don't have to be aligned perfectly. The common application of this wisdom is not to make a right angle turn in a main gas line with only one elbow; the elbow may not even be a perfect 90 degrees anyway. You are better off using two elbows so the angle can be adjusted to what you need and which will also allow you to put the pipe running next to the floor joist, up next to it and then piping back down to run across the bottom of the joists with two elbows at the next turn. The same method can be used for hooking up to gas valves on water heaters and other cases where you may have a direct pipe connection. The other option is to do the connection with a flexible gas line as is done for gas ranges and gas driers. It is still customary to install drip legs just before connecting to the gas valve on furnaces and water heaters. The last fitting used is a tee connecting to the furnace gas valve, with the gas line feeding down from above with a three inch nipple coming out the bottom of the tee with a cap on the end. The idea being that any oil in the gas line will drip in the drip leg and not be carried into the gas valve to foul it up. The oil the drip leg was supposed to catch was the oil from the pipe cutting machine that could still be on the threads that the pipe doping might not have removed. Therefore, it is from highly unlikely to impossible for there to be any oil in the line for a drip leg to catch, but it is still custom and something some inspectors look for, so it is wise to throw one in.

Obviously running threaded gas pipe is a of lot work which is why there is now CSST Corrugated Stainless Steel Tubing for running gas lines. Approved by the National Fuel Gas Code in 1988, CSST is a lot like a armored cable but made with stainless steel covered inside and out with a flexible plastic jacket. The stuff looks like yellow liquid tight conduit, which is a flexible water proof conduit often used for making the connection between a motor and rigid conduit. Though many of the makers of CSST require contractors to take a training course on how to install it, CSST is sold in many building supply stores that cater to the Do-It-Yourselfers. Often times there will be a stack of instructional pamphlets on how to install it, but it is more than a little bit scary to think of an army of handymen out there installing gas lines based on what they read in a pamphlet.

A CSST gas pipe system is laid out in one of two ways; the series system, which is the standard method of starting with a large size and reducing it, as lines are branched off. Then there is the parallel system where the line for each appliance is routed back to a manifold. The advantage of the parallel system is everything is run in 3/4 or 1/2 inch size and no larger sizes are needed, the down size is it is a messier looking installation with a bunch of lines running back to the manifold. Adding a new branch to a parallel system requires adding another outlet to the manifold and routing the new line from there. The series layout requires larger sizes of CSST but looks much neater and is easier to add branches to later if the pipe is large enough to handle the addition.

The big bogyman in CSST right now is lightning hits. I know it sounds ridiculous to think of gas line getting hit by lighting since it is supplied from underground and used inside the house, so how could it be hit by lighting? What they have found is that a nearby lightning strike can induce a very large voltage on any thing metal which acts as a receiving antenna and this voltage charges the metal jacket of the CSST to a high enough voltage that the electricity can jump from the CSST gas line to a ground. This electric arc can burn a small hole in CSST, which would not be much of a problem if it wasn't a gas line. The trouble is the hole lets out the gas which is ignited by the hot arc and of course the heat of the burning gas burns the plastic covering of the CSST. Having a CSST line turn into a flaming torch can start a house fire. This is why they have tried to come up with some code changes to address this problem. The code requirement now is to have a six gauge or larger copper grounding wire connected to the CSST at the point it enters the building and also connected to the ground for the electric system. This way if lighting induces a voltage in the CSST the ground wire will prevent it from reaching a high enough level for arcing to occur.

The older alternative to CSST is soft copper tubing connected with flare fittings, which is legal in many areas. CSST is cheaper and easier to install than soft copper, but some may feel safer with copper tubing over CSST, which is mostly plastic, and the plastic may not age well in decades to come. The possibility is that CSST will only last so long before the plastic in it dries out and becomes brittle and prone to cracking and leaking. Soft copper is available in sizes up to 2 inches and can be used for the entire gas piping system if desired and if allowed by local code. One problem with copper gas lines was that in some areas NG had hydrogen sulfide in the NG, which is called sour gas and is corrosive and may eat a hole in the thin copper tubing. Today however, all of the NG sold has been purified and the hydrogen sulfide has been removed along with the other impurities. Hydrogen sulfide is easily detectable in NG since the exhaust gases will smell like rotten eggs and be rather poisonous. The one problem that still exists for soft copper tubing is that it is even more easily damaged than CSST and should be protected by nail guards when routed inside walls where it maybe pierced by a nail. The tubing should also not be routed where it may be damaged by being kicked or stepped on.

Needing not much more than a flaring tool, tubing cutter and some wrenches, soft copper is easy to run. Like all piping, it will need to be neatly installed and well supported, probably every 4 feet. Like CSST, the long lengths of tubing will reduce the possible places for NG leaks by reducing number of joints. While a threaded NG piping system in a house may have over a hundred joints, soft copper tubing or CSST may have less than a dozen.

Leak Testing

Once the gas piping is installed, it has to be tested for leaks. The standard method is to use a leak detection fluid, brush it on each joint, and go back over the system checking for bubbles, which indicate a leak. Normally the gas is turned on for this test, so you need some confidence in your work. A cheap substitute for leak detection fluid is dish washing soap diluted with some water to about 10-25% soap solution depending on the strength and foaminess of the soap. If any bubbles are found, that joint will need to be redone. Try tightening the fitting if you can and that may do the trick, otherwise turn off the gas, take the joint apart and inspect it to see what went wrong. Now with threaded pipe, you will not be able to tighten the leaking joint less you have a union nearby that you can open and main lines will require unions on all the branches to the main line so the main line can be rotated to tighten the leaky joint. To avoid leaks on threaded pipe use a thick pipe dope like TFE and you will have very few. I find most of my leaks are at unions, sometimes you can just tighten them up and they will seal, but sometimes not. The problem I have found is that the nut on a union will allow the female part of the union to be at a greater offset angle than what the union will seal at. The only way to correct these union leaks to open the union and adjust the pipes so the union halves line up straight and then reassemble the union. One trick is to open the pipe at another point and line up the union and close it up tight and straight, and then close the other joint. If that will not work, you will have to rerun part of the pipe after the union to get rid of the offset. Always be alert for the smell of gas when checking for leaks, since not every leak will be at a joint, sometimes there will be a fitting or pipe with a hole in it or some other manufacturing defect.

Installing a Natural Gas furnace

Gas forced air furnaces are a very popular and flexible heating system, available in updraft, downdraft and side draft models. An updraft can be installed in the basement to blow heat up into ductwork heating the house above. A downdraft can be installed in a first floor closet blowing heat into ductwork underneath the house. A side draft can be installed in the attic blowing heat through ductwork in the attic space with vents in the ceiling or routed down inside interior wall spaces, plus all three models work with air conditioning coils which can be added later. A gas forced air furnace is a lightweight sheet metal box with a stainless steel heat exchanger and a fan. The condensing high efficiency models exhaust through one and half-inch diameter sized PVC pipe, so no chimney is required. The furnaces can often be located in a closet converted into a furnace room or in the basement or crawl space. There are three classes of efficiency of gas furnaces on the market, the 80% mid-efficiency that require class B metal gas pipe chimneys that should no longer be installed due to their low efficiency. Then there are the about 90% high efficiency condensing gas furnaces, which vent with PVC, theses are the models to buy having the most bang for the buck. Last, there are the very high efficiency gas furnaces with efficiencies in the 92-98% range and have multi stage heating and variable speed fan motors. These top end furnaces are over priced and have some parts that are expensive if you ever have to replace them. These models will probably be unable to pay off the cost difference (about $1000 or more) between them and the high efficiency models. In shopping for which furnace to buy, you should be aware that many furnaces are built by the same company and different names are stuck on identical furnaces. The furnace boxes often have a hole in the front so that the name brand label can be applied after the furnace is already in the box. So if a large rush order for a certain model of furnace comes in, a warehouse employee literally grabs a box of the desired furnace labels and reaches in through the hole in the box front and labels the furnaces as they ship them. One of the big heating manufactures is ICP, International Comfort Products owned by Carrier. ICP makes Arocaire, Clare, Comfortmaker, Dettson, Heil, KeepRite, Lincoln and Tempstar heating products. Gas furnaces sold under any of these names and others, could be identical or may have significant differences. In general if the BTU rating and efficiency rating is the same, it is probably is the same furnace.

The PVC exhaust for high efficiency gas furnaces can be vented much like a clothes dryer exhaust. The exhaust line must slope downwards towards the furnace one-quarter inch per foot so that any condensate will drain back to the condensate drain. A drain will need to be provided for the condensate, which is acidic water. The codes in some areas require the condensate to be drained through a neutralizer filter that removes the acid from the water. The PVC exhaust often is routed out through the basement sill board between the floor joists. It is recommended that the exhaust be located at least four feet away from any window or other opening including soffit vents. Since few homes have over eight feet of outside wall space without any windows or vents, this requirement is often ignored. The danger is if the exhaust is placed underneath a window and the furnace is running when the window is open, the exhaust may enter the house through the open window. The danger is minimal since it is unlikely that the windows would be open with the heat on. The correct solution for the problem of not having a proper venting location on the outside wall is to vent through the roof. The problem with roof venting is the fear of acidic water dripping on the roof, discoloring, and damaging the roofing material, which is why sill venting is often preferred. In either case the vent line needs to have a elbow or two on the end, to keep out rain and a metal screen is included in the last elbow to keep out large insects like bees or wasps that could build a nest and block the exhaust. Sill vents also need a riser to raise the exhaust outlet above the highest expected snow level.

Gas furnaces have a front panel that is removable for servicing the controls inside the furnace, so you need to allow space in front of the furnace for someone to stand and work on this panel, 2 or 3 feet of space. The walls on the other three sides can be pretty tight around the furnace if need be, but two or three feet is nice all the way around for getting at wiring or adding AC later on.

On a updraft furnace the cold air return duct will connect to the bottom of the furnace, most will accept the duct on either side or the back of the furnace. At the point where the cold air duct connects to the furnace is where it is common practice to box in a space for the air filter. The most common air filter size is 16 by 25 by 1 and if possible, you should make yours this size. This way it will be easy to get air filters and the large size will give a longer filter life, where smaller filters clog up quickly. Always use quality pleated filters; they will last much longer and will give better service while removing much more dust. The cheap fiberglass type that you can see through are a waste of money. The cheap ones should be changed every month while an extended life pleated filter can last entire heating season or more. Filters need to be changed before they start to bow or clog. Write the date on the side of the filter when installing it, so you know how old it is.

Installing a Natural Gas Boiler

Gas boilers while heavy are still very lightweight for a boiler. Like gas furnaces, gas boilers can be located just about anywhere, but unlike furnaces, they cannot be located in the attic since there is too great a risk of freezing the water in the boiler and piping. Hot water piping has the advantage of being very flexible and needs far less space than ductwork to carry the heat to where it needs to go. Once again, a basement location is preferred so that heat can flow upward in the pipes and you will still have some heat even if the pumps are not working. Now while a gas boiler will not heat without electricity, a secondary boiler like wood or coal can, and having a good piping set up will allow the back up boiler to possibly heat the house without electrical power. The boiler can also be located in a furnace room on the first floor with the piping running underneath the house to reach the radiators located along the outside walls. The piping will need to be well insulated if the space under the floor is not heated (boilers with lines in unheated spaces should use a water/antifreeze mixture). It is desirable to insulate the walls of the space underneath the floor so any heat lost from the pipe remains inside the heated part of the building. Even if the basement is well insulated, the hot water piping should still be insulated to prevent the area from being overheated. The waste heat coming off the boiler should be more than enough to heat a well-insulated basement. By keeping the heat in the pipes, the basement is not overly warm and less heat will be needed to heat the house.

Boilers need to have a drain for the pressure safety relief valve and for draining the boiler. Boilers tend be messy, small leaks, oil from the pump coupler bearings, so a boiler room should have a smooth easy to clean floor with good lighting.

Installing a Natural Gas Heater

Gas heaters are a rare breed, since gas furnaces have become so common, however they are still used in small homes in warmer parts of the country where it is felt that too little heat is needed to justify installing a furnace. Furnaces are often installed even in very warm climates since forced air is needed for most central air conditioning, so gas heaters do not have much of a market. Normally having a fan but no air filter or ductwork, gas heaters will heat a large room but like other space heaters will do a poor job of heating other parts of the house. A simple gas heat source used by many in warm climates when heat is needed, is to just turn on the kitchen oven and maybe do some baking.

Vent less natural gas heaters from Europe are now available in the USA, with prices from about $99 for a bathroom heater, to $220 for a model that will heat up 1000 sq ft. These space heaters sometimes have a fan, however they will also work without electricity, but without the fan. The heaters can be mounted to a wall or floor mounted with an optional feet kit. The units only require a gas line and an electrical outlet for the fan if they have one. No chimney or venting is used; the exhaust, which is carbon dioxide and water, is discharged into the room air. Some models (hopefully all) have a built in low oxygen sensor that shuts the heater down if the oxygen level in the room drops. This safety feature will prevent the heater from operating in a low oxygen atmosphere and will prevent the creation of deadly carbon monoxide gas. It is easy to see why these units are very popular in Europe. Space heaters come in two types, one that mostly heats the air, the blue models with blue gas flames visible behind glass like a futuristic fireplace and the orange models that run hotter, designed to radiate heat like an open fireplace. With the blue ones, you heat the air in the room to the desired room temperature while the orange models heat the things in the room and the room air is left at a colder temperature. The orange radiant heaters work nice for drafty rooms where the air is only passing through so there is no point in trying to heat it. If you currently do not have a heating system like ductwork or radiators, natural gas space heaters can be a very economical way of switching to gas heat. With a cost of only $99 for small models to heat a bathroom to $220 for larger rooms, it is reasonable to install a heater in every room. A gas line would need to be routed to each location and an electrical outlet would be needed for models with fans. However, the cost for a small home would also be small, each room would have its own thermostat, and each could be heated to its own set temperature.

The downside, is that while natural gas space heaters work very well for average homes, there is some water produced in burning NG and that moisture in a tightly sealed house in a cold climate may be too much moisture and result in steamed up windows and possible mold problems. Very airtight homes may also have a problem with carbon dioxide gas accumulating to high enough levels in the home, to trip the oxygen sensors on the heaters, which would shut them down. A tightly sealed but poorly insulated home in a cold climate may not be able to maintain temperature if it needs more heat than there is fresh air leaking in. Few homes are well sealed enough for this to be a problem, and most that are, need so little heat that the heaters will not run long enough for them to be a problem. A fresh air heat exchanger can also fix the problem by bring in fresh air without bring in the cold.

Operating a Natural Gas Heating System

The first thing you should know about operating a gas heating system is where the shut off valve on meter is located and where a wrench is, to use to turn it off. In case there is ever an emergency such as an earthquake or anything that causes a strong smell of gas in the house, so you can quickly turn the gas off.

Natural gas heating appliances are so reliable and trouble free, that people tend to forget to do the little maintenance that is required and just expect the house to be warm. Natural gas furnaces should be checked once a year for how they look inside. Like what does the heat exchanger look like, how rusty is it? The thin stainless steel heat exchangers are the weak point and will eventually develop a hole and the furnace will have to be replaced. One way of checking is to see if the blower fan cycling on and off has any effect on the gas burner flames. A hole may blow air at the flames effecting how they look. If you think you may have a hole, you can aim a bright light in the burner area, remove the fan, and look for the light shining through any holes in the heat exchanger. The simplest method is to put some peppermint oil in the burner area and see if you can smell it at any of the heating registers. Other than an annual inspection, changing the air filter is about the only maintenance a newer gas furnace requires.

Gas furnaces have a quick recovery time so they work well with setback thermostats so the temperature in the home can be set at a lower setting at night and brought back up to temperature quickly in the morning.

Natural Gas boilers require far more maintenance than forced air furnaces but Boilers with their heavy heat exchanger can far out last a thin walled furnace. Most of the maintenance on boilers involves the waterside of things. It is necessary to maintain a water treatment in the boiler water that prevents corrosion. These treatment products are normally added once a year. Pumps and valves need to be checked and pump bearings may need annual lubrication, a few drops of oil per bearing. On most pumps there will be an oil tube with a flip up cover, the oil runs down the tube and soaks a pad that wicks oil to the bearing. Radiators should be cleaned of dust so the airflow is not blocked. The pump couplings should be checked for wear once a year and replaced if heavily worn. The burner assembly and heat exchanger can be inspected and cleaned by using a vacuum cleaner to suck up any metal flakes and grime. Since natural gas is so clean burning, the heat exchanger will probably not need cleaning. If it looks like it is getting dirty, the access plates can be removed and the heat exchanger can be brushed to remove any dust or other dirt.

Boilers do not respond as quickly as to forced air furnaces, but most hydronic heating systems can work well with a setback thermostat if the setbacks are not too large or too short and time is allowed for the boiler to bring the temperature back up. Hydronic heating systems with a lot of thermal mass such as piping in a concrete floor for radiant floor systems, are not designed for sudden swings in temperature and will not work well with a setback thermostat. Such systems are best used to maintain a constant temperature. The savings if any from operating a radiant heat floor system comes from the warm floor allowing a feeling of being warm at a lower air temperature, if the room air temperature is heated to normal temperatures like 68 or higher, there is no savings in energy. The room air temperature needs to be maintained at a setting below 68 F perhaps as low as 62 F for a radiant floor system to work as it was designed to work.

Gas heating systems can be turned on at the end of the air conditioning season in the early fall and left on until late spring. The thermostat will bring on the system almost invisibly to take the morning chill out without you even noticing. Gradually as the days grow colder, the system will run more each day until the coldest days of winter it will run nearly all the time. Then in the spring, the furnace will run less and less each day until it does not run at all for the summer. So smooth is a gas heating system in operation that a chill breeze on a summer day with the windows open will surprise people when the heat kicks on, since they had forgotten to turn it off in the spring. That is the seductive thing about gas heat, you just take it for granted that it is always going to be there, like houses are just suppose to be warm on their own.

Chapter 10

Propane/LP

Propane or LP is a recent discovery. In the year 1910, someone noticed that gas was disappearing from his model T gas tank and asked Dr. Walter O. Snelling to investigate. Snelling discovered that the gas was giving off a volatile vapor. By the year 1911, he had isolated the gases propane and butane and created a way of refining them from the natural gasoline, which was then in use and contained lighter hydrocarbon gases that were vaporizing out as noticed by the upset model T owner. In 1912, Snelling and friends created the first company to sell propane and the first gas range was developed. Cleaner burning Propane replaced the use of acetylene gas, which was more expensive and can be sooty and has more safety problems than propane. In 1928, the first propane refrigerator was sold. Finally, in the year 1933 a scent was added to propane so leaks could be detected before a fire occurred. At times, it is hard to conceptualize the great risks earlier generations took in their everyday lives.

Today LP or LPG (Liquefied Petroleum Gas), is a mixture of propane and butane with a few impurities. Propane and butane burn very similar and are interchangeable, the differences are that butane burns hotter than propane while propane vaporizes more readily, which is important in the wintertime. The scent ethanethiol is added so leaks can be smelled since LP is odorless without it. The mix of gases in LP varies; propane can be from 100% to less than 50% with butane making up the difference. This ratio of the two gases is varied seasonally in colder areas to allow for the fact that butane boils at 30 F. Which means at outside temperatures below the boiling point, once the tank has cooled down to 30 F, butane will not vaporize and will stay as a liquid in the tank outside, and no vapors will be present in the gas lines for heating. In areas where the temperatures can be expected to drop below 30F the butane is reduced or even eliminated and is replaced by using more propane, which boils at -43 F. Even with a pure propane LP mix, there are still many places where outside temperatures can make drawing propane vapors from an LP tank nearly impossible. Customers wishing to save money by buying enough LP at cheaper summer rates to last through the winter need to check with their supplier that they are buying his winter mix and not a summer mix. Another option is to install an underground LP tank, which is not exposed to colder air temperatures and the tank is also protected from physical damage. Underground LP tanks have Cathodic Protection to prevent corrosion and are designed so that the tank fittings are all accessible through a hatch cover that projects above the ground surface. It is not legal to bury a standard LP tank since it is not designed for the more corrosive environment of being in contact with ground moisture. LP tanks should never be covered with insulation since vaporization absorbs energy and chills the tank as the LP turns into a gas. An insulated LP tank in use would soon drop to temperature of boiling or vaporization and then very little vapor would be produced. No air pockets can be allowed in the ground around the tank since LP is heaver than air and will collect in low places and could be ignited. The underground LP tank should be back filled with sand or other rock free material to prevent stones from scraping the paint on the tank. The tank will also need to be anchored in the ground to prevent it from bobbing or floating to the surface in waterlogged soils. The two standard methods of anchoring are to lower the tank legs into freshly poured cement or to use metal strapping connected to anchors. The line from the tank to the house can be buried to protect it as well, but the line will need to be rated for underground LP use.

LP tanks cannot explode, since they contain a fuel but no oxygen. The danger is that they can be ruptured by impact or by being overheated in a fire. LP tanks have safety pressure relief valves that vent gas if the pressure rises too high. If a LP leak is ignited near the tank or a fire from another source is burning near the tank, the LP will be heated and the LP may start to boil. The pressure relief valve will vent LP vapors to prevent the tank from bursting but this may feed the fire and increase the heat, which in turn can cause the LP to boil faster than the relief valve can vent and the pressure may rise to the point where the tank will burst. The tank may simply split a seam and dump more LP into the growing fire or it may burst violently such as blowing off an end cap or a long tank splitting into two halves that fly apart with the energy imparted from the internal pressure being released, which can launch the tank halves like LP propelled rockets with enough speed, weight and heat behind them to punch through block walls. This is why LP tanks should not be near the house nor should a long tank be pointing towards the house. The relief vents release the LP upwards so an LP tank should never be located underneath anything. Since the liquid in the fill line from the LP truck maybe vented when the hose is disconnected after filling the tank, the fill point has to be at least 10 feet away from any potential ignition points such as a outdoor grill or a intake vent for a furnace. The larger the size, the farther a LP tank must be located away from any structure, with most residential tank sizes needing to be at least 10 feet away. While many LP tanks are located right next to the house wall, that is not a safe location since if the house was to catch fire the heat would cause the LP tank to vent which would feed the fire and the tank may over heat enough to burst probably destroying the home entirely. The LP tank should also be located where is unlikely to be hit by a car or truck, if such a location is not available at least move the tank far enough from the home so if it is ever hit, the resulting fire will be far enough from the home that the fire will only cause one tragedy instead of two.

Another consideration in placing an LP tank is that LP is lighter than water and floats on water, which means an LP tank will float in water if the water rises above the level of LP in the tank. In floods LP tanks float away down stream, some recommend taking a picture of the tank and recording the serial number, but that does sound ridiculous when the sensible thing to do is to prevent the tank from floating away by anchoring it. The first step is not to locate the tank in an area that can be flooded, but rather located it on higher ground if possible. The other option is to anchor the tank by chaining it to mobile home anchors secured in the ground or chaining it to a tree. Now I know that many people have no choice but to live in areas that can flood. However, you do not have to let the water into your house. The common sense thing to do is to raise the house above the level of flooding that can occur and back filling with earth around the house to create a small island in times of flooding. Just make the raised island big enough to include space for the LP tank so it will not be flooded and still anchor it just in case. When building a home in low laying areas, don't follow the standard of having the home floor or top of the basement walls just above ground level, but rather only dig any basement half way or less and have the basement walls stick up above the existing ground level and use the earth that was removed from the hole to back fill for the island. Existing homes can be jacked up and foundations below them extended upward. While raising a house may not eliminate the possibility of being flooded, it will reduce the frequently since there are far more small floods than there are big ones.

An LP tank also has to be located within one hundred feet of the driveway or road so that the hose from the LP truck can reach it. LP is produced from the refining of oil and gas and is stored in tank, sent through pipelines to truck terminals and trucked to local supplier's storage tanks. The local supplier is the one from whom you buy the LP from and who delivers it to your tank. The local supplier could be a regional gas company or a small business. The distribution of LP in the United States is dependent on the pipeline system, which is undersized for meeting the needs in winter when more LP is needed. LP suppliers in general do not have enough tank storage to weather occasional winter supply shortages and often have to pay to have LP trucked long distances instead of piped which is more expensive. This is what results in the wintertime spike in LP prices that often occurs. LP users do have the advantage of having a number of suppliers in their area to buy from, and hopefully one of them will have the foresight to have adequate LP storage and will be able to sell LP at a cheaper rate. Many LP users end up locked to only one supplier by getting a "free" tank installation. There is no such thing as a "free lunch" the cost of the tank and installation is simply added to the price charged for the LP so that over a period of time the customer pays for the tank. The problem is that even after the cost of the tank has been covered there is no reduction in the price charged for LP. If you can afford it, you are better off paying for the tank and installation so you will be free to buy LP from whom ever you want. While those who did not pay for their tank will be forced into paying whatever their supplier chooses to charge, even if other suppliers are much cheaper.

Other factors affecting the price of LP is that LP is a by-product made from refining natural gas and oil, there are no wells drilled for LP or vast deposits of LP. LP or propane and butane are minor gases found with oil, their supply is small and limited by nature. The production of LP occurs as propane and butane are removed from oil and wet natural gas, the refining of oil and gas goes on year round and the LP produced is stored. LP for the residential heating market is used mostly in the wintertime and results in a surge in demand, which can sometimes exceed what local suppliers have on hand and what the pipeline system can carry to some areas. Improving the pipeline system would help to reduce the wintertime price spikes in some areas, but would do nothing for price spikes caused when a cold winter simply depletes the stored LP gas in the United States. This occurs because LP is a by-product and oil production cannot be increased simply to produce more LP. Shortages of LP in the U.S. have to be met by imports. Currently 10% of LP used in the U.S. is imported. Seven percent is from Canada and the remaining 3% comes by ship from other countries. Since in petroleum pricing it is the tail that wags the dog, the price of LP when supplies are short will be heavily affected by the cost of imported LP. For in a cold winter when the LP is running out and suppliers are in a bidding war with each other to get their hands on what's left before their competitors do, the upward explosive rise in price is only slowed by the docking of an LP tanker ship. It is the price and availability of the overseas shipped LP that has the greatest effect on pricing in a shortage. The problem with getting extra LP tanker ships to come to the U.S. is that they normally would have gone somewhere else and have to be diverted by the prospect of getting a higher price for their cargo. For these reasons, the LP market will always be prone to cold winter price spikes whether new pipelines are built or not. The smart thing for LP users to do is to have sufficient LP in their tank or tanks to last the winter.

Since LP is not competitive with NG, LP tanks disappear from neighborhood backyards rapidly when NG becomes available. This restricts LP for home heating mainly to areas not served by NG lines.

The typical LP user will tend to live in isolated areas or other less populated country areas. LP does have a far lower heating cost than oil or electricity in nearly all areas of the country.

Installing a LP Furnace

Most Natural Gas appliances are available in a LP version, so there are plenty of high efficiency low maintenance furnaces to consider. One key difference between LP and NG is that LP is heaver than air and any leaks will tend to collect in low places. This makes crawl spaces particularly dangerous places for an LP furnace to be located since a leak could occur and the heavy gas would not rise up into the house above and a furnace drawing combustion air from the crawl space would ignite the air/gas mixture causing an explosion, sending the house above high into the sky to rain back down over the neighborhood. For this reason it is no longer legal to install a LP furnace in a crawl space. In some areas even basements may be illegal for LP furnaces. The crawl space restrictions can be handled by installing a down draft furnace on the first floor with the ductwork running in the crawl space. The furnace cannot use crawl space air for combustion and will need a fresh air intake either from the attic or outside the house. LP furnaces can be equipped with a sniffer valve that shuts off the LP gas line if LP is detected in the air. Some furnace rooms for LP furnaces have a pan with a one and half inch PVC drain line designed to drain the heavy fumes of any LP leak to the outside. Due to the nature of LP leaks, furnaces with sealed combustion cambers in which the combustion air is drawn in from outside by means of an intake line, are an excellent choice. Attention should also be given to the water heater, since the standing pilot light would ignite any LP gases and most water heaters draw their combustion air from right off the floor.

Like with NG forced air furnaces, the best furnaces for LP are the condensing high efficiency furnaces that vent through PVC. The sealed combustion condensing furnaces that have a second PVC line for intake air are the best choice. The very high efficiency furnaces with efficiencies in the 92-98% range with multi stage heating and variable speed fan motors may not be worth their extra cost for NG, but with the higher cost of LP over NG they may be worth it for LP use. While their marginally better efficiency may not pay with NG, the cost savings in LP usage will be larger and when faced with wintertime LP rates you will want the most efficient furnace you can afford.

Installing a LP Boiler

With the restrictions in some areas on LP use in crawl spaces, boilers have to be located in a basement if allowed or on the first floor in a furnace room. The hot water piping of course can be routed through the crawl space. LP boilers are of course modified NG boilers, so there is a wide selection of fine boilers available. Condensing boilers that exhaust through PVC piping are available.

Installing a LP Heater

The vent-less NG wall heaters are available for use with LP. These heaters have a glass front like a fireplace so the blue flames of the burning LP is visible. There is no chimney or exhaust venting. These heaters are vent-less and vent right in the room they are heating. The exhaust is mostly just carbon dioxide and a low oxygen sensor turns the heater off if the oxygen level in the room drops, which prevents the heater from burning LP in a low oxygen atmosphere, which would create deadly carbon monoxide. Infrared models are also available which radiate heat like a warm fireplace. These wall or floor mounted units sell for about $100 to $240 and only need a gas line and an electrical line for a fan if they have one. These units will run without electricity, minus the fan of course. It is possible to heat entire house with these heaters by installing one in each room. The heaters can be controlled by a programmable thermostat, which would allow for programming the heat in each room of the house for when and where it is needed.

Operating a LP Heating System

Operating an LP heating system is nearly identical to operating a NG system. The key difference is keeping an eye on the level of LP in the tank. The level of LP in an above ground LP tank can often be seen on the outside of the tank by watching the dew line or frost line on the tank. The liquid LP as it vaporizes into a gas cools the liquid in the tank, which chills the outside walls of the tank from the liquid level down. This chilling can cause dew to form on the lower part of the tank when the upper part is too warm, and the same can happen with frost on the tank. A glance out the window on damp mornings can tell you exactly how much LP is in the tank. You should know how much your tank can hold, tanks can only be filled about 80% to allow for expansion and for gas vaporization. You should also know how much LP you use in cold weather so you know how long what you have in the tank will last. Most tanks also have an internal float gauge that reads in percentage of fill or in fractions of tank fill like a gas gauge. It is recommended that you call for a tank refill when the level drops to 40% or 20% so there will still be enough LP to last until the delivery can be made. Many LP suppliers keep track of your LP usage and calculate what is called the K-factor which is the number of degree days it takes your house to use one gallon of LP. Then by monitoring the degrees days or how cold it is, they can calculate how much LP you have probably been using and how much is left in your tank and when you will need a refill. The reason that they do this is so that they can schedule a route for their truck in advance so they can fill the most tanks with the least amount of driving. The advantage is that the supplier can keep your tank filled without you having to worry about it or having to call them to schedule a fill up. The customers on the automatic service may also pay ten cents less a gallon than call in customers.

Another key difference with LP from NG is lighting pilot lights. Lighting an NG pilot light is no big deal, but with LP due to the way it can collect in low spots, the danger of flash back is much greater. There is also the danger that you may not smell LP gas as easy as NG because the LP gas may be literally under your nose down on the floor. Before lighting an LP pilot light, get your nose down low and check for LP smells. Be careful about the smell of LP being masked by other odors particularly musty smells. Keep your furnace area clean and dry so such odors are not present. An LP furnace room should also have fresh air venting with a vent at the floor level for venting out any LP gas vapors to the outside. If there is a smell of LP, if it is strong turn off the LP and have the system checked, if it is weak try and track it down with your nose, it may be just a trace from the pilot flame being blown out. Leave the door open and let the air out to see if it will dissipate, if it does not air out you have a leak that is feeding it and will need to turn off the LP and call a repairman. If the smell seems to be coming away from the furnace such as the LP line feeding the furnace, you could do a bubble test with soapy water to check for leaks and tighten or replace any leaky fittings. Once the room has been carefully checked for any LP smell, and is clear, you can light the pilot. Pilot lighting is done by turning the gas valve inside the furnace to the pilot setting and pressing down on the dial while holding a lit match over the pilot. It will take a minute or so for the gas to reach the match flame and be lighted. You have to keep holding the dial down for as much as two minutes while the pilot flame heats up the thermocouple, which sends an electrical voltage that, keeps the valve to the pilot open. The pilot valve closes if this voltage is lost. If the pilot goes out as soon as you release the button after holding it down for two minutes, the thermocouple is bad and will need to be replaced. Thermocouples are about ten dollars and are a very common part with the only difference being in the length of the line. You can replace a short thermocouple with a long one, but you cannot replace a long one with a short one since it will not reach from the gas valve to the pilot. On my service truck, I only carry the longs ones to save space. Once the thermocouple is replaced, try lighting the pilot again and it should work fine, if it does not check the pilot gas line for kinks, if there are none the problem is with the gas valve and it will need to be replaced. About the only place you are still going to see pilot lights is on water heaters since nearly every thing else has gone to pilot less ignition systems in which the gas is ignited by an electric arc or a hot surface igniter.

Nearly all LP heating systems will be controlled by a thermostat and will heat as needed. Even most vent-less wall heaters can be controlled by a thermostat or will have one built in. Some models may only have a heat output setting and maybe as simple as On and Off, which in that case you are the thermostat and will need to turn the heat on and off as required to maintain your desired temperature. Due to the high cost of LP, setback thermostats for most systems can save an enormous amount of money as will any insulation you add as will reducing any drafts. LP can be one of the more expensive heating methods so any improvements in efficiency and reducing heat losses will have major savings.

Chapter 11

Fuel Oil

Heating oil as hydrocarbons goes, is a rather heavy fuel and needs to be heated above 140 F degrees before it burns. Oil was not used much for heating until M.A. Fessler invented the oil burner. In 1915, he installed the first oil burner in Boston and in 1920 opened a factory in Stamford, CT to manufacture oil burners. With oil burners being built in large numbers, in the 1920s oil begin to replace heating with coal. At the time, oil was cheaper than coal, oil was also far cleaner than coal and there was no soot or ashes or coal to shovel. Oil heat was also the first automatic heat controlled by a thermostat, you could set the desired temperature and when you came back days later the house was still at the temperature you had set, while with coal, if no one was around to keep the home fires burning, the house got cold.

Oil heat replaced coal heat, and coal chutes and bins became things of the past. Oil remained the main preferred heating method until natural gas heating came along, but oil remained the main stay until the mid 1970s when the oil embargo caused oil prices to shoot to unbelievable heights and people began to switch en mass to the now much cheaper gas heat. Gas heat has continued to cut into the oil heating market in the decades following the 1970's until the upswings of oil prices in the early 2000s finished oil as a competitive heating fuel. Oil is now so expensive that it is cheaper to heat with LP and in some areas, at times electricity can be cheaper than oil. Oil heat still finds a market in the northeastern part of the United States where about 70% of oil heating units are located. Even this traditional market for oil is being eroded by increased availability of natural gas and LP. Even if oil was as cheap as gas, oil burners tend to be more expensive, have lower efficiency and require far more maintenance. While there have been many large improvements in oil burning technology and design, oil burners remain user unfriendly and expensive to have serviced. More than a few people would rather call the dentist than their oil repairman. Oil does make sense for truly remote situations like where you need to operate a diesel generator for electrical power where it makes sense to use the same fuel for heating as well; otherwise, in general my advice would be to avoid oil burners at nearly all costs.

Oil does have advantages, it is still normally more economical than electric resistance heat and oil is a stored heat. Once the oil is in the tank, you know where your heat is coming from this winter. Oil is the most energy dense fuel used in heating; it takes up less space than any other fuel. Oil being a heavy liquid pretty much has no risk of explosion like is the case with both NG and LP. Burning oil is also a simple well-developed technology that has proved itself for a very long time and oil burners can last for decades.

Heating oil is commonly known as No. 2 heating oil and is also sold as diesel oil for use in trucks and diesel cars. Since diesel is used in vehicles that drive on public roads, diesel is taxed like gasoline is, to pay for the cost of building and maintaining the roads. The problem is that the taxes make diesel more expensive than the untaxed heating oil, and people with diesel vehicles are known at times to use heating oil in place of diesel oil. Since heating oil and diesel are the same product, some countries now add a dye to heating oil to identify it and identify any heating oil that has been diverted into the diesel market by unscrupulous fuel sellers. In the United Kingdom, a red dye is added and there heating oil is now known as red diesel and in the European Union a yellow die is used creating yellow diesel. In the U.S., there are no plans at the moment to add a dye to fuel oil, but if a dye is added, it will probably be blue or green so we can claim we are not copying anyone.

Oil can now also be green in the sense of being a renewable fuel made from plant oils. Soybean oil has been used in place of heating oil and diesel fuel with successful results. Various heating oil/plant oil blends are also on the market, such as Bioheat, which is 80% low sulfur oil with 20% plant oil such as soybean oil. There is also B5, which has 5% plant oil along with other blends on the market. Plant oils tend to be more expensive than heating oil, which is why various blends are on the market since pure plant oil would be a good bit more expensive than regular heating oil and may require some changes in handling and combustion.

Options in Heating with Oil

Oil heat options include hot air furnaces, boilers supplying hot water to radiators or radiant heating systems. The better option of course with the high price of oil is just about anything else other than oil heat.

Fuel Oil Tanks

Heating oil is delivered by truck and a hose is used to pump the oil into heating oil tank that can be located underground, sitting at ground level outside, in an out building like a garage or can be located in the basement. The tank will have a fill line normally a one and half-inch size threaded pipe and a smaller air vent line. In the case of basement oil tanks the lines extend out through the basement wall so the tank can be filled from outside without having to enter the home. The vent line has a whistle or level alarm that alerts the oil delivery person when the tank is nearly full. The lines on underground tanks extend above ground for filling and venting. Most tanks also have gauges, which show how much oil is in the tank often in terms of fractions of fill like a gas gauge in a car. Like a car parked outside in cold weather, oil tanks can collect water as condensate from moisture in the air. Oil is lighter than water, so the water will collect at the bottom of the tank. Some tanks are equipped with a bottom drain valve for draining off any sediments and water from the bottom of the tank. A clear container is held below the valve and water is drained off until oil starts to come out. Tanks that are buried underground do not have drain valves since it is not possible to drain them unless you are a gopher since you would have to tunnel under the tank to reach such a valve. The water in underground oil tanks can be removed by lowering in special water absorbing socks or using additives that get the water to mix into the oil so it will be evaporated off as the oil is burned. Due to water in the bottom of the tank, most underground oil tanks rust from the inside out. If an underground oil tank gets a hole, the oil will begin to soak into the ground. Leaks can be detected by noticing that you are buying more oil than normal and are "using" oil in warm weather as if it was wintertime. Underground oil leaks can also be detected by noticing an oily film on water puddles near the tank, since oil floats on water; it can rise to the top of water-saturated ground. If the underground oil tank leaks; you are suppose to report it, which will result in having to have the tank removed and having all the oil soaked soil removed as well. The costs of this type of clean up can exceed $20,000 and your insurance policy may not cover it. Underground steel oil tanks are a huge finical risk and are best avoided entirely. The expected life span of a steel underground oil tank before it springs a leak is as little as 10 years, while the same tank in a basement can last 30 years. The trend has been away from underground steel tanks, today underground tanks should be fiberglass or plastic with a double wall design so any leaks can be detected before any soil contamination occurs.

Oil tanks are now more commonly placed above ground outside or in an out building to avoid possible soil contamination problems and clean up costs. An above ground tank when filled is very heavy, the typical oval shaped 275-gallon tank weighs about a ton when filled with 260 gallons of oil and needs to be well supported. Tanks with legs should be placed on concrete. It is much easier to spot any leaks with an above ground tank than it is with underground tank and a catch pan can be placed underneath the tank to catch any leaking oil but will also tend to fill with rainwater so such pans are probably only workable underneath tanks in sheltered locations. Another safe guard is to build an earthen berm around the tank to contain any spills to prevent the oil from running down hill, which can spread the spilled oil over a larger area. By localizing the spill to the berm area, the amount of contaminated soil that will have to be removed can be greatly reduced. The big problem with above ground tanks is exposure to cold temperatures. Fuel oil begins to form wax crystals and get cloudy at 15 degrees F and these crystals will collect in fuel line filters or nozzles and clog the fuel line. This is why fuel oil tanks were placed underground to begin with, to keep the tank warm to reduce the risks of the fuel jelling and clogging the line. The cure for a cold jelled tank of fuel oil is to add a gallon of kerosene for each 20 gallons of fuel oil, if the temperature is below -20 degrees F add one gallon of kerosene for each 10 gallons of fuel oil. It will take a few hours for the kerosene to disperse through out the tank and dissolve the wax crystals. The other trick is to heat the fuel line oil filter to melt the wax crystals, such as by placing a pail of hot water so the filter is submerged in the hot water. This will take maybe 20 minutes to work but it is only a temporary fix since more crystals from the tank will probably soon clog the filter again. There are also a number of fuel oil additives that depress the pour point (the lowest temperature oil will pour at) by inhibiting the formation of wax crystals. Most fuel oil suppliers sell a summer oil bend (straight No. 2 oil) and a winter blend oil (No. 2 with 10-20% No. 1 oil which is basically kerosene). If you are filling up the tank for the winter, be sure that you get the winter blend if you have an exposed tank or fuel line. The biofuels jell at higher temperatures, soybean based biofuels can jell at 32 F and some biofuel oils jell in the 50 F degree range. Blending the biofuel oils with No. 2 fuel oil, No. 1 or other additives can lower the temperature the blended fuel jells at (standard fuel additives may not work with Biofuel mixes since the chemistry is different). It is wise to remember that cold temperatures can be a problem with biofuel blends so check the stated pour point temperature for the fuel mix you are thinking of using.

Another point to consider with above ground tanks in exposed locations, is the fuel line and filter need to be protected from damage and vandalism. Some filter housings are glass, which is handy for checking for water, but could easily be broken by a rock kicked up by a lawn mower. If the filter housing is broken or the fuel line cut, the entire tank will drain out on the ground. Metal filter housings are stronger, but the filter should still be located indoors where it is protected from damage and freezing temperatures. The fuel line should be robust and resistant to damage or vandalism, for the outdoor section, threaded pipe with no unions or drain valves that can be opened, maybe a good choice. Considering that fuel oil is diesel and diesel was selling for four dollars a gallon recently, a filled fuel oil tank can be quite the temptation for anyone with anything that uses diesel and has questionable morals. For these reasons, a fuel tank should not be visible from the road and should be concealed. Plastic covers are available for hiding tanks, or the tank can be located in an out building. Fuel thieves will attempt to open the fuel line from the tank and drain oil into a container, they may cut the line and take what they want and leave the fuel to drain on the ground. Such a spill can result in a $20,000 clean up bill. It makes sense to secure the fuel line and any drain valves on the tank as much as possible. One option would be to build a small enclosure over the tank with the fill and vent lines extending out the top or side. The fill line can also be fitted with an anti-siphon device like a coil spring to prevent a hose from being inserted into the tank to siphon or pump out the oil. The vent cap should be secured and the fill cap fitted with a lock to prevent oil theft and to prevent a vandal from pouring any thing harmful into the tank.

A tank located in a basement with a secure vent cap and a locked fill cap, has the advantages of being very secure and the tank is protected from the cold and jelling of the fuel oil is not a problem in a heated basement. Some new tanks for basement installations come with a double wall construction of galvanized steel with a plastic polyethylene liner will last a long time and the double wall design will prevent leaks.

Venting Requirements for Oil heat

Oil furnaces and boilers have normally always required a class "A" venting system like wood and coal. A class "A" venting system consists of 24-gauge stovepipe with 6-inch clearance to combustibles, can be vented out as a "tin chimney", or connected to a masonry or insulated metal chimney. Oil cannot share a chimney with any solid fueled appliance like a wood or coal stove. You can however have multiple non-solid fueled appliances on one chimney if the venting system is sized large enough to handle it.

Newer mid and high efficient oil burners do not require class "A" venting and some may be vented through plastic venting systems, which sometimes includes PVC piping. The manufactures instructions on venting requirements will state what can be used for venting. All vents should have a minimum of a quarter inch slope back towards the heating unit to allow any condensate to drain back to the unit rather than collecting in the flue and leaking out or flooding and blocking the vent.

Fuel Oil System Operation

When the thermostat calls for heat, the valve in the fuel line opens and the fuel pump draws oil from the tank through a filter and pumps it at about 100-120 PSI to the nozzle, which sprays the oil into the whirling cyclone of air created by the burner blower. A spark is jumped across the arc rods and the oil is ignited. The bright flame is detected by the flame sensor and the fuel valve is kept open. The hot flame heats the heat exchanger and the hot gases pass through the heat exchanger and exits out the chimney. Once the desired temperature is reached in the house, the pump and burner fan motor shut down and the valve in the fuel line closes.

Installing an Oil Boiler

The massive giants of the past have been replaced by much smaller lightweight oil boilers that run circles around their ancient brethren. Modern furnaces have less thermal mass and heat up quicker making the boiler system much more responsive to temperature swings. Old boilers had efficiencies of 56–70% while new boilers can have efficiencies of 81- 95%. Installing a new oil boiler is quite a bit different from installing the huge behemoths of decades past. While old boilers often had to be brought in pieces and assembled on site or required special heavy duty moving, newer home boilers are smaller and lighter and many will fit through a doorway on an appliance dolly.

A boiler is most often located in a basement or on the first floor, which allows the heat to rise and for a taller chimney with a better draft. Oil boilers of course require combustion air; older homes tend to have plenty of drafts, so often no special provision for letting in combustion air was needed. However, in new better-sealed homes and older homes that have been properly weatherized, an intake vent for combustion air should be provided. The best set up is to have a boiler with a direct connection for combustion air so the intake air is directly ducted into the boiler. If the boiler is not designed for a direct connection, the second best set up is to duct the fresh air right up to the boiler, so there is no cold draft blowing across the room, which can freeze pipes in the boiler room in cold weather. If the boiler is to be installed in a small furnace room, it should be placed in the room with the front of the boiler facing the doorway, so the controls are directly and easily accessible. There will also normally need to be clearance on all sides around the boiler to allow for access and room for running the piping. The main line is piped from the boiler to the pump or to pumps, which feed the branches that supply the radiators. Each branch line should be valved at both ends so it can be isolated in the event of a leak. If the piping system will be done in PEX be sure to use tubing with an oxygen barrier, otherwise oxygen can defuse through the PEX into the water and will rust the boiler out. For PEX piping, the pump or each pump, feeds a manifold with the valves for each PEX branch. The pumps unless connected to threaded pipes, will need to be supported.

The lines if possible should be routed uphill going out from the boiler and down hill on the way back to encourage thermo siphoning in case you need to operate the boiler without pumps. It is not possible to operate an oil boiler without electricity since you need electric power to operate the oil pump, the burner fan motor and the spark ignition and the safety control system.

The fuel line from the tank can be run across the basement ceiling and then routed down to the pump next to the boiler. For oil tanks located in a basement, the line is normally placed in the basement floor before the cement is poured. The line enters the cement floor by the oil tank and exits by the boiler. Oil lines installed later can be cemented in a cut or groove made in the cement floor and then cemented over. The other option is to route the fuel line in threaded pipe along the block walls so the line needs no priming and flows freely to the pump. The line should be protected from possible damage by routing the pipe out of harm's way or by using strong piping where the pipe can be stepped on or kicked. Lines routed above the level of oil in the tank will need to be primed so oil can be siphoned through them by the pump.

The area where the boiler is located should be designed for easy cleaning and handling of any oil spills. While it may be legal to install some oil boilers or furnaces in an unfinished closet like room with an unfinished wood floor as is done in mobile homes. It makes sense to seal the floor so spilled oil cannot soak in and to drywall the walls to help contain a fire should there ever be one and to help sound proof the walls to reduce noise from the furnace room.

One of the most important steps in installing an oil boiler is selecting the correct boiler to install. The boiler has to be matched to the load, a boiler that is too small will not be able to keep the house warm and one that is too large will cost more than what you need to pay. Other points to consider are efficiency; with the high cost of oil, it makes sense to buy a boiler that will not waste oil.

Installing an Oil Furnace

Modern oil furnaces look like gas furnaces and some have zero clearance requirements to combustibles. The key difference between a boiler and a furnace is the ductwork. If you are replacing an existing furnace, you will need to connect the furnace to the existing ductwork. I know this sounds so easy, but if you are replacing a lowboy, (old short wide furnace design) with a highboy (newer standard tall design); you will have to make changes to the ductwork. With an oil furnace, you particularly want to keep the ductwork on the cold air return tight. Since the furnace blower is drawing air from the return ductwork, it has negative air pressure like a soda straw and any air leaks in the furnace room will draw in the smell of any spilled oil or oil smoke blow back. The return cold air duct can be sealed by taping all joints and seams with duct tape or foil tape. Most furnaces are designed so that the cold air return can enter on either side or some times on the back, this will give some flexibility in how you do the installation. The front of the furnace should ideally face the door in a small furnace room, or at least not face a close wall with little clearance to work on the furnace. Remember to install a large air filter in the cold air return duct just before the furnace, 16 by 25 is the most common size and the easiest to find. Always put in a large air filter, small filters often end up with too much air pressure across them to work effectively and clog quickly.

Operating an Oil Burner

Oil heat is not like gas or electric heat; oil burners require regular care and attention. Once the heating season is over, the oil burner should be opened up and cleaned thoroughly. The basic cleaning method is to first spread a small tarp or drop cloth in front of the burner, remove the burner assembly, and remove the panels from the heat exchanger so that it can be cleaned using long wire brushes. After the heat exchanger has been brushed down, a shop vacuum the wet/dry type, is used to vacuum out the firebox and to vacuum up all the soot. After being used for this job, the vacuum will be too dirty to use for much of anything else. The burner will also need to be cleaned. The nozzle may need to be replaced. Nozzles come in many different sizes for different rates of oil sprayed per hours and you need the exact one that you have, there should be a number stamped on the nozzle to identity it, otherwise take it with you and they should be able to identify it for you at the parts counter where you buy furnace parts. The electrodes will need to be cleaned and adjusted or replaced. Any firebrick should be inspected and repaired if needed. The chimney or exhaust piping should be checked and any fresh air inlet as well. The fuel system should be checked for any leaks or any spots that could leak in the future. It is better to repair any weak sections before they leak in the summer when you have time and good weather rather than after a leak in the middle of the winter when you need to get the heat back on and don't have time to spare for cleaning up an oil spill. The oil pump will also need to be checked over, the strainer will need to be cleaned or if a filter is used in place of a strainer, it should be replaced.

Inspect your oil burner when cleaning it, a well-tuned unit should not be clogged with soot or have oily ash in the bottom of the firebox. Soot can indicate a lack of air getting to the fire, as can ash in firebox, oil in the firebox can be from ignition problems like dirty or maladjusted electrodes. Now if your furnace is clean with only a light dusting of a light colored ash, your furnace is running clean. Carbon is black, any black soot or ash is unburned wasted carbon that should have been burned and turned into CO_2 and vented out the chimney. Some boilers, due to the coldness of water returning to the boiler, cause the surface of the heat exchanger to be excessively cold and this chills the fire causing sooting, due to incomplete combustion. This can be corrected by installing a bypass line, so the heating system water goes in a loop with its own pump and the boiler's pump moves only some of the water through the boiler at a time instead of all of it. This way the boiler stays hotter and does not soot due to an overly cold firebox.

The key to knowing how to service your newly installed oil burner is to read the instructions that the manufacture sent with it. Included with each oil boiler/furnace shipped, are normally installation directions and operation/service instructions. Often the homeowner never sees this information because the installer keeps it, yet you paid for it, it belongs to you. Always insist on getting all the paper work that came with any appliance that you have installed. If the installer insists on keeping it for himself for his own reference, tell him he can photo copy it. If the installer still refuses to turn over the information, probably for reasons of job security, you maybe able to locate a website for the manufacturer and download a copy of the instructions. If they are not available on line, you can request a copy by E-mail or by regular mail by writing a letter to the manufacture. Once you have the service instructions, read them over and see how hard or easy the maintenance procedures are and if you could do them.

Selecting an Oil Burner

Oil furnaces and boilers come in a number of sizes and you will have to determine which one will best heat your house. This can be as simple as checking the BTU rating on your existing heating system and getting a new system with an equal heat output or you may need to do a heat load calculation to determine how much heat it will take to heat your home. Checking similar homes for what size of heating unit they use can be helpful as well as simply asking someone who works in the heating trade for what they think you need.

The other factor is whose furnace or boiler to buy. Beware of cheap junk made in China, look for produces made in the USA, not because of keeping Americans working, but simply so you will able to get parts when you need them and with oil heat you will need them. The big reliable brands in oil heat are Lennox, Carrier, Goodman, Trane, Bryant, Coleman, York, Rheem, Amana and

Armstrong. This list is not all-inclusive, there are other reliable brands, and some of them may give you a reliable produce without having to pay for a big name. Do not forget Sears and their Kennmore line of products, Sears has products built to their specifications or sells a major brand name model with a Kenmore label on it and sells it with extended warranty as well as having their own service system. Now don't you think that if you were having products built to your specs, which you have to service under warranties that you offer, that you would have the product built to be very reliable so you could make out like a bandit on the warranties? While the extended warranties are a rip off, (check consumer reports if you don't believe Me.), products made to be low maintenance are a bargain if sold at a competitive price.

When shopping for an oil burner, look for high efficiency and low maintenance. With better designs, a new oil burner should perform far above the old standard of service provided by oil heat. New heating units should burn oil cleanly, efficiently and require less servicing and be far easier to service and easier to install.

Chapter 12

Wood

Heating with wood is as old as mankind, for long have we gathered about the flickering flames of a bright wood fire and long have we coughed on the smoke. Open campfires are really lousy for heating or cooking as anyone who has gone camping knows. Well into the middles ages the wood fire for heating and cooking was located in an open hearth on the floor with a smoke hole in the roof, which resulted in a very smoky atmosphere in the home with a lot of the heat going right out the hole in the roof. Over time, people learned to build a stone or brick wall around the open hearth to enclose it to try to funnel the smoke up and out. These early smoky fireplaces partly cleared the air but did little for heating efficiency since the fireplace and chimney openings were huge, the amount of air drafted out of the house was also huge. Benjamin Thompson known as Count Rumford in 1796 published his designs he had developed for improving fireplaces, which greatly improved the draft and finally cleared the smoke out of the house while reducing the amount of air going up the chimney and increased the amount of heat retained inside. Even a Rumford fireplace is a poor heating device; true heating came with the development of the cast iron wood stove. The first cast iron wood stoves were made in Alasce, France in 1490, probably were designed to sit in the opening of a fireplace, vented the smoke freely into the fireplace opening, and as a result probably failed to reduce the excessive hot air exiting through the chimney. Ben Franklin invented his Franklin stove in 1742, but it was not until David Rittenhouse improved the design in 1772 that the Franklin stove became really usable. The Franklin stove was not really a stove but rather a freestanding cast iron fireplace box with an open front.

The huge advantage of the Franklin stove was that the flue pipe restricted the air going up the chimney to only the smoke from the fire and the hot cast iron warmed air that stayed in the room rather than being vented outdoors. Enclosed cast iron wood stoves begin to appear in 1752 and were mass manufactured starting in 1760. These early "six-plate stoves" had six plates of cast iron bolted together to form a metal box with a loading door and a chimney hole. By enclosing the fire, the draft could be controlled and the hot air stayed in the room rather than being vented out the fireplace chimney. Cast iron wood stoves remained the preferred choice for heating until wood was replaced by more convenient coal in the late 1800's which in turn was replaced by oil in the 1900's that was in turn replaced by natural gas in the late 1900's. Today natural gas is the most common home heating fuel, but as consumption is over taking supply, it is becoming more expensive and may soon be ever more expensive and increasingly harder to get. Since oil heat was abandoned due to high cost, and coal is becoming expensive if it is even available locally at all, many are turning back the clock to wood heat. Since the oil embargo in the 1970's there has been a resurgence in old kitchen wood stoves and potbelly cast iron wood stoves. In the time since the 1970's wood stoves have under gone a rapid evolution from primitive dinosaurs Ben Franklin may have used, to the high tech fuel efficient clean burning EPA approved wood stoves that are available today.

In areas where it is plentiful, wood is set to become the clean burning renewable "green" fuel of tomorrow. While to some it may seem like a ridiculous idea that burning wood can be "green" or clean, the new EPA certified wood stoves are clean green wood burning machines. While wood burners have traditionally emitted clouds of dark sooty smoke with a high particulate count, EPA certified wood stoves reduce particulate counts by 90% and increase efficiency by about a third over old wood stoves so a third less wood is burned to provide the same amount of heat. How EPA certified wood stoves reduce particulates and increase efficiency is by burning the creosote and soot that otherwise would go up the chimney. Other than at start up, these stoves generally operate smoke free. On cold damp days, only the white puffy clouds of steam are seen and on dry cold days a keen eye can only see the heat distortion of the hot air coming out of the chimney mixing with the cold air outside, even the smell of wood burning is greatly reduced. These stoves ideally emit only carbon dioxide and water vapor and the carbon is from wood and would have been emitted anyway when the logs otherwise would have rotted on the forest floor and will be reabsorbed by the next generation of growing trees. If you cut trees on your own land and cut sustainably, cutting at or below the replacement rate which for many areas is one cord per acre per year. You are not adding to the amount of carbon dioxide in the air since the trees are taking the carbon back out of the air as fast as you are putting it in. By cutting and burning fallen trees and dead trees, you clean the forest of debris and reduce the risk of damaging forest fires as well as using recycled carbon. Burning wood cleanly and responsibly can be as much a harmoniously part of the cycle of life on this planet, as when we breath oxygen and emit carbon dioxide that the plants use in turn and give off oxygen.

The Three Main Choices in Wood Burning Methods

In Ben Franklin's day, choosing a way to heat your home with wood was simple, while today we have an endless variety of choices. The best options however do boil down to three main categories; a wood stove or insert, a furnace or boiler or an outdoor boiler. There are other opinions which I am not going to consider, either because they tend not to be clean burning and efficient or they are not readily available or practical to install, such as the Koran heated floor system, which uses a sub floor space as part of the chimney flue. While the Koran heated floor system inspired Frank Lloyd Right to invent hydronic-heated floors, it is a system that is tricky to build and has to be a chimney sweep's nightmare. Choosing from the main three choices depends on your situation and what you are tying to heat, how you want to heat and whether you wish to heat with wood all the time to save money or just occasionally for firelight in the evening or as backup heat for emergencies.

For the occasional wood burner, the huge investment of furnaces or boilers indoor or out does not make any sense. For occasional use, a wood stove makes the most sense since the cost is much lower and the installation is much easier. If you want a fire to watch, a wood stove with a glass window is the only choice since even if the furnace or boiler has a glass door, it is unlikely that you are going to sit into the basement and watch it. If you have a fireplace, a fireplace insert can be your best choice since you will be able to continue enjoying fires in the fireplace and installation will be very straightforward.

For those wishing to heat with wood full time, a furnace or boiler is the only choice. While wood stoves are nice for supplemental heat, or for emergency heating, they do not perform as well for heating a whole home, as does a furnace or boiler. Wood stoves only heat the part of the home in which they are located while rooms at the other end of a large house can receive little or no heat at all, while furnaces and boilers due to having a heating distribution system can evenly heat every room in the house. Small homes with an open layout can be heated by a single wood stove while a larger home may need several. Traditionally old homes used wood stoves the same way we use large space heaters today. Such a system with wood having to be fed to a number of stoves all over the house and ashes to be carried out with a number of flues and chimneys to clean is inefficient and labor intensive. It is far more efficient in both energy and labor to have one furnace to feed and tend, then a whole herd of wood stoves. Furnaces can be located in a basement or furnace room so that wood and ashes do not have to be hauled in the living spaces and hot surfaces are located away from exploring little hands. Furnaces are safer than wood stoves due to having double walls, which enclose most of the hot surfaces, and due to the furnace being located outside of the living space, which reduces the odds of something burnable accidentally coming in contact with a hot surface.

A friend of mine had a wood stove but his wife was so terrified that it would start a fire when she was sleeping that each night before she went to bed she would pour a bucket of water over the fire. For those who are overly worried about the risk of fire or have an insurance company who is, or just prefer to keep the mess of wood burning outside the house, there are outdoor water boilers. OWBs remove nearly all risk of fire by locating the wood burning boiler outside the home. They also remove the smoke, ashes, and wood mess as well. OWBs are not for the occasional wood burner due to their high cost and the large inefficiencies occasional use would cause. A typical outdoor boiler holds hundreds of gallons of water, if allowed to cool the water will reach outdoor air temperature which could be well below freezing, so a single use firing, may have to raise the water temperature in the OWB by over a hundred degrees before being able to supply heat to the home. Even with the huge firebox many OWBs have, this may take more than one load of wood. Operation of an OWB only makes sense if the unit is used constantly; otherwise, the massive losses in having to reheat a large boiler from possibly sub-zero temperatures are extremely wasteful. Since OWBs are located outside, you need to be outside to load them and operate them, so you need to be willing to go outside in the worst weather to keep the house warm. These units appear to be more suited for areas where one would not have to trudge through deep snow in arctic temperatures to reach them. OWBs appear to be nearly ideal for farmers who have an endless supply of wood, have more than one building to heat and are outside frequently during the day.

Installing a Chimney

The first step in installing a wood stove is locating where the chimney will go, the second step is deciding where the stove will go. The reason for this is that the chimney location will determine where the wood stove can go. The connection between the stove and the chimney needs to be kept as reasonably short as possible. I have seen installations where the flue pipe rises from the stove and then crosses the room to the far side of the room or even runs into another room. But I bet that the person's local fire inspector and their insurance agent hasn't seen it, for while such installations are possible, and more heat is extracted from the exhaust due to the long flue pipe, it is an inherently more dangerous set up. Overly long runs of flue pipe result in too much heat being extracted from the wood smoke and the creosote will coat the inside of the flue pipe and chimney resulting in a high risk of a chimney fire. Newer wood stoves are designed to extract all the heat you should while leaving enough heat in the exhaust gases to exit the chimney without condensing out much creosote. The trick is to keep the temperature in the chimney above 250 F; you need to maintain this temperature or above, all the way out to the chimney cap. I was careful to do this, but I forgot about the chimney cap itself, what happened was the creosote cooled enough in the outside air to condense on the cap, then one night I saw a flickering light in the backyard. I ran outside in the snow in my boots and pajamas and looked back at the house to see my chimney cap on fire. I got the ladder, climbed up on the roof, and checked out my chimney. I did not have a chimney fire; just the chimney cap was burning. A thick layer of creosote which had built up on the cap, had caught fire, and was burning off. I let it burn and after about half an hour, which that at the time seemed much longer, the fire burned itself out. I had a funny little adventure standing in the snow on my roof in the middle of winter in my pajamas, but if I had cooled the exhaust gases to below 250 F and had a chimney and flue lined with creosote, my adventure would have been much bigger and down right disastrous. There is a tremendous amount of heat in creosote; it is like coal, imagine a hot coal fire burning in your flue pipe. A hot creosote fire can get a flue pipe bright orange and can be even hotter in the chimney. Such excessive high heat will cause the flue pipe to fail and drop the hot burning liquid creosote in the room. In the chimney, the tiles will overheat, crack, and suffer heat erosion. The hot burning creosote will flow like burning oil and will soak into every crack and crevice taking the fire with it. Often in chimney fires, the hot burning creosote will find a way out of the chimney and will drip out onto the wooden structure of the house and start the house on fire. Flaming droplets of burning creosote can be blown out the top of the chimney to land on and light on fire anything nearby, even asphalt roofs will burn if given enough of an incendiary incentive. This is the main reason why you do not want a long flue pipe, some others are that a long flue pipe will make turning down the heat of the wood stove nearly impossible, since even if you reduce the fire in the wood stove, the long flue will still give off an enormous amount of heat. You should also not have more than two elbows in your flue pipe or the draft will be reduced too much for most chimneys to draft effectively.

Since the flue pipe needs to be kept short, the wood stove needs to be near the chimney, ideally just in front of it. If you have an existing chimney that you wish to use, it cannot be used by anything else. It is common for older homes to have a tile lined brick chimney that was once used by an old low efficiency gas furnace that has been replaced by a high efficiency-condensing furnace that is now vented in PVC. Such chimneys of course are well suited for wood burning, but they can only be used for one wood burner and nothing else. The reason for this is that any unburned soot and creosote can coat the chimney and block other openings of any other flue pipe entering the chimney. The most common problem is with a gas water heater, when the homeowner has installed a high efficiency gas furnace and decides to add a wood stove to save even more on his gas bill. The trouble is that his gas water heater is still vented through the chimney. The homeowner uses the wood stove for a while and gets a light coating of soot that builds up in the flue connection for the water heater, eventually blocking the small flue pipe. The water heater is now no longer vented, and the exhaust gases now back up and exit from under the draft hood at the top of the heater. The level of carbon dioxide gas increases in the basement or room where the water heater is, and as the level increases there is less and less oxygen available for combustion. Eventually the flame in the water heater burner becomes so starved for oxygen that incomplete combustion occurs and deadly carbon dioxide is now produced. The homeowner and his family die in their sleep and the resulting investigation places the blame on a "malfunctioning" gas water heater. This is why nothing else can be vented through a chimney serving a wood burning appliance. The solution is to vent the water heater with a gas approved metal chimney, which comes in standard round or an oval cross section, which is designed to fit inside a standard 2 by 4 wall.

An existing chimney will need to be thoroughly inspected to see if it is suitable for venting a wood stove, furnace or boiler. The chimney will need to be built of bricks or cement blocks and will need to have a clay tile liner. If the chimney does not have a liner, a flexible stainless steel liner can be installed, which is done by lowering it in from the top. The liner will also need to be connected to the flue thimble in some manner. One method is to turn the liner like an elbow and pull it out through an enlarged thimble hole, attach the thimble and slide the thimble back in place and cement the thimble in place. This set up has the disadvantage of not having an ash pit and any accumulation will quickly block the chimney. A second method is to stop the liner just above the thimble and install a collar or plate around the liner to prevent the smoke from leaking between the liner and the chimney, with this system the ash pit is still used. The other way of doing this is to attach a stainless steel tee with a length of pipe or flexible flue on the bottom end of the tee. The tee is lowered in and connected to the thimble and the extension on the tee bottom is collared just above the ash pit door. In this method, the collar is below where the smoke enters the chimney and the ash pit is still used. A word on flexible flue liners, since they are flexible, they have an accordion like surface and are not smooth and are difficult to sweep. Do not use a flexible flue liner unless you are using them on a very clean burning unit that is EPA approved, anything less will plug up a flexible flue for sure and even an EPA rated unit will plug a flue if incorrectly fired. More expensive rigid flue piping liners are available which sweep much better, but are trickier to install. Since the sections will need to be connected together and lowered into the chimney like pipe sections in a well. To replace a single piece, the entire liner will need to be raised up and dissembled piece by piece until you the reach the piece needing replacement. So measure more than once and plan carefully, and you can still figure on doing it more than once to get it right. Once the flue liner is installed correctly, the space between the liner and the chimney was some times filled with vermiculite insulation which was poured into the space. Today however, the chimney is sealed at the top by cap to keep the warm air in the chimney as an air gap, or fiberglass insulation jackets are fitted over the flue liner. The airspace between the liner and the chimney will act as insulation as long as the top of the space is sealed by the liner's chimney cap to keep the warm air from venting out.

Before attempting to install a liner, look down the inside of the chimney from the top and lower a light like a trouble light down inside to inspect the inside of the chimney. A chimney can look great from the outside and be a total disaster on the inside. You may need to stand a stepladder on the roof peak next to the chimney or even erect scaffolding to be able to reach the top of the chimney. You may also be wish to wear coveralls, gloves and a good dust mask as you lower the light down the chimney. Watch the chimney walls as the light descends and you can twist the cord to turn the light if needed to see all sides of the inside of the chimney. If the cord is too short on your light, knot it to an extension cord to prevent dropping the light in the chimney. Check for old creosote or soot buildups, cracked or missing flue sections, projecting bricks in unlined chimneys, and any old thimbles that maybe hidden behind walls but not properly sealed. Using a light lowered on a cord, you will be able to do a great inspection on the top few feet of the chimney, but as the light gets lower and lower in the chimney, you will be able to see less and less until the light may be only a dim glow below a bend in the flue. To really see everything, an inspection camera would have to be lowered inside the chimney; some chimney sweeps offer this service. A professional chimney inspection by a good chimney sweep can be a wise investment since he or she may be able to spot potentially dangerous flaws that could slip by someone inspecting a chimney for the first time.

If the chimney looks good, you may still have problems since if the chimney was installed for gas or oil furnace, for the chimney may not clear the roof high enough to get rid of the smoke of a wood burner. The problem with better oil burners and gas furnaces is that the exhaust is normally so clean that the chimney is often only designed to get the smoke outside and not to get it away from the house. These short chimneys vent the smoke just above the roof peak and the wind coming up over the house roof and down the other side pulls the smoke down with it. The wind causes the smoke roll in an eddy on the down wind side of the home, and some of this smoky air is drawn back inside the home through drafts in the walls creating a smoky smell in the house. Often times in order to break the smoke clear of this down draft, the chimney needs to be extended about 2 feet higher. It is also helpful if the chimney is narrow, a broad chimney acts as wall that the wind flows over and down instead of around. The trick is to have a narrow chimney with the clay flue extending out above the chimney top as much as can safely be done.

Extending a chimney can be done in a number of ways, the most conventional is to set a clay flue section on top of the top existing section and to brick and mortar up around it and make a new cap. Not every chimney is strong enough to support the additional weight of bricks and mortar for extending it higher and not every one is a mason. A solution some have come up with is to place a clay tile flue on top of their existing flue and clamp it in place with some galvanized sheet metal and some stainless steel hose clamps. The basic method is to cut a sheet metal band that over laps the old flue and the new, each about four or six inches and a hose clamp is placed over each and tightened. Be very careful when tightening the hose clamps, clay tile is not compressible and will crack if you try, however most hose clamps will strip and break before they can exert that much force. The concept here is to create a sheet metal pocket that the extension flue sits in and the clamps hold it to keep the wind from tipping it out.

Another way of extending an existing chimney is to use a section of manufactured Stainless Steel Class "A" Insulated Chimney as an extension. The insulated chimney section can be attached to top of a masonry chimney by using an adapter for insulated chimney to stovepipe and attach a section of stovepipe on the bottom end. A six-inch stovepipe will fit inside a six-inch square flue tile, and an eight-inch pipe will fit inside an eight-inch square tile. Then use a fire stop plate used for insulated chimneys that has a hole that will fit over the stove pipe but not the thicker insulated chimney section, place the plate on the chimney top and lower the stove pipe down through the hole into the chimney. The stovepipe should fit snugly inside the chimney and will hold one section of insulated chimney in place in all kinds of weather. I have used up to two three-foot long sections of insulated chimney this way, but did put a crack in my flue, which I had to patch with cement. One section is usually enough to get the smoke clear of the down draft caused by the wind blowing over the house. The insulated chimney manufactures also sell a chimney cap adapter plate, which is anchored with four concrete anchors into the mortar of the chimney cap. The plate has to be mounted flush on the cap, which means that it does not work for chimneys with a clay flue liner that extends above the cap, as is the case with most chimneys. The plate is also rated for securing only one three foot long section from tipping over in the wind, anything more requires the use of guy wires, but considering the strength of the weathered cement found in most chimney caps I wouldn't trust the anchors to hold even one section. You can of course cement up the chimney cap until it is flush with the top of the flue liner and install the mounting plate in new cement and with the use of guy wires; you can extend the chimney as high as you can run guy wires. I do not recommend guy wired tall chimney extensions for a simple reason, how are you going to sweep it?

The next problem in chimney design is even after you get the smoke clear of the house; the wind can blow over the top of a high nearby object like a tree and blow the smoke back down your chimney in what is called Down Drafting. Ideally, a chimney should be two feet taller than anything else; this is not often possible so we settle for two feet taller than anything within 25 feet. This lets the smoke get out of the chimney, most of the time. The trouble is that when the wind blows across the top of taller objects that can be over a hundred feet away or even farther away, the wind rolls like a crashing wave on the beach in the still air pocket behind the tall object. When the downward moving part of this invisible wave of air passes over the chimney, it creates a downward movement of air in the chimney, which can cause back puffing of smoke. Metal chimney rain caps reduce this effect but do not eliminate it entirely and even with a cap, there will still be some down drafting. If the top of the chimney were raised above the height of the offending object, it will probably solve the problem, but the chimney top will still probably be lower than another tall object like a hill that is just a bit farther away. I have trees around my house and some of them reach to heights of perhaps over 100 feet and even a twenty-foot temporary extension wasn't tall enough to raise my chimney above them and even if it did, the nearby hill is far taller, so in the end I had to put up with some down drafting.

If an existing useable chimney is not located where you wish to locate your wood stove or your home does not have a suitable chimney, you can install a prefabricated Stainless Steel Class "A" Insulated Chimney. These are excellent in a number of ways. Since they are insulated, and have low thermal mass, they heat up quickly and draft very well. Since they tend to run hot, they tend to collect less soot and creosote in the chimney and since they are stainless, there is little chance of deterioration and they clean up well when swept and are available in sizes ranging from 5 inch inside diameter up to 16 inch. These chimneys come in sections that are connected together to form the chimney. Tees, elbows, adjustable elbows, adapters, thimbles, fire stops, heat shields and straight pipe are some of the different pieces available. Putting the chimney up is like building with Legos, the different sized pieces are put together with different lengths of straight pipe so that everything ends up where it should be. Common lengths of pipe are 6, 12, 18, 24, 36, 48 inches long but the available lengths will vary by manufacture with other lengths being common, and no, you cannot interchange insulated chimney sections from different manufactures. Many newer stoves now have the chimney thimble on the top of the stove rather than the back, which allows for a direct venting up from the stove out through the roof above. Such direct drafting improves the strength of the draft by eliminating the two elbows that would normally be used in a conventional flue pipe installation. That also simplifies and shortens the needed chimney, which is good because insulated chimney sections are expensive with the cost running from about $3 to $10 per foot.

Chimneys if at all possible should be placed in the center of the house and never in an outside wall. Chimneys need to be warm to work, and cold chimneys have to be warmed up before they will draft and this can be a big problem with outside chimneys. The inside routing of a Stainless Steel Class "A" Insulated Chimney is not much more difficult than mounting it on the outside of the house and will give much better performance. The steps in installing a stainless steel insulated chimney are fairly simple, the first step is once the location has been chosen for the wood burner; locate the route for the chimney. On wood burning units with a top mounted chimney connection, the chimney is run straight up and out through the ceiling and roof above. While with units with a flue connection on the back, the chimney is located behind the unit with enough backset to allow for two elbows and some pipe, about 18 to 24 inches from the back to the center of the pipe for 6 inch size flue pipe. Locate the ceiling joists above and check inside the attic and roof above for the chimney routing. If there is another floor above, the chimney will need to be framed in by walls with two-inch clearance between the chimney and any wood. Fire stop plates will need to be installed at each floor or ceiling that is penetrated by the chimney. Most insulated chimney manufactures make a ceiling piece for mounting in the ceiling between two ceiling joists. You will need to cut a square or round hole sized for the size of ceiling piece you are installing. You will also need to frame the hole by nailing a two by four on each side of the hole between the ceiling joists and two more between the first two to box in the hole so you have wood on all four sides to anchor the ceiling piece to. On the bottom side of the ceiling piece, you can install an adapter and run flue pipe down to the wood burner, but you may need to run at least one section of insulated chimney to keep the stove pipe far enough away from the ceiling to maintain the required clearances for stove pipe. I would recommend that you run insulated chimney sections down as close to the wood burner as possible and if you can, mount a stove pipe to insulated chimney adapter right on the wood burner's flue connection. With insulated chimney sections you will lose much less heat compared to stove pipe which will keep the chimney hotter while at the same time will reduce the amount of heat given off and reduce any overheating problems. If you have to run the chimney through a second floor or floors, plan on where the chimney will be located upstairs, to avoid having a boxed in pillar like chimney in the middle of a room or hallway. If necessary, move the chimney installation over a bit, so the chimney when it is walled in will be in a corner, a closet or part of an existing wall. Insulated chimney pieces include 45 degree pieces, which can be used to route the chimney around obstacles. Use any bends sparingly since they will add resistance to the draft.

Insulated chimney sections fit on top of each other with the top section having a flange on the inside and the outside that fits over the bottom piece. This over lap is necessary to keep any condensate inside the chimney or rain outside the chimney, from entering the joints. Once two chimney sections are nested together, a twist locks the pieces together and a band clamp is placed over the joint and tightened. I find that these metal to metal joints are not always smoke proof. I recommend either taping the joint with foil tape before installing the clamp, or putting a continuous bead of high temperature (550 F) red silicone sealant around the outside edge of the metal seal before the two sections are put together. Since the chimney is rated for 1000 degrees and red silicone is only rated for 550 degrees, keep it away from the center and only use it along the outside edge of the flat part of the joint where it will be cooler due to the insulation blocking the heat.

Cutting the roof hole can be done by drilling a small hole from below in the exact center of where the chimney will go, and lining up the flashing piece on the roof as a template for cutting the hole in the roof. The small pilot hole will be much easier to find on the roof if you stick a piece of bright colored wire up through the hole to act as a flag. The flashing can be installed and a chimney section lowered down through it and clamped in place. A "storm collar" is fitted around the chimney and is pushed down on top of the flashing and silicon caulk is applied around the top edge. The caulk breaks the path of water running down the side of the chimney and deflects it out over the flashing. The reason a separate rain collar is needed above the flashing, is that as the chimney heats up it expands and gets taller which would tend to pull apart a caulked flashing-chimney joint. The chimney can reach four feet above the roof line before guy wires will be needed for support, and with guy wires, the chimney can be run very high but will be hard to sweep. To sweep the chimney you or your chimney sweep will need to be able to reach the top of the chimney to put the brush down inside or you will need to sweep the chimney from the bottom which can be far messier. Tall guy wired insulated chimneys otherwise often need to be disassembled and lowered for access for cleaning which makes sweeping labor intensive and expensive if you pay to have it done.

While a chimney rain cap is not necessary, it reduces down drafting, keeps rain and other foreign objects out of the chimney and it looks better. There are also heat shields for keeping insulation back from the hot chimney surfaces, support brackets, roof brackets and other details that will vary according to manufacturer and type of installation. I suggest picking up an installation guide at your local building supply store, which will show pictures of common installations and the necessary pieces and how to put them together to do the job.

Installing the Flue Pipe

The flue pipe or stove pipe is normally a sheet metal pipe that connects the wood burner to the chimney. The standard set up was a flue connection located on the back side of the wood burner to which a stove pipe elbow was attached that pointed up into another elbow that pointed back into the thimble in the chimney wall. The reason for this zigzag set up was simple, if you just had a straight pipe between the wood burner and a thimble directly behind it, there would be no way of removing the pipe for cleaning short of dragging the stove forward to get the pipe out and moving it back again when done. The other reason is, it would be very difficult to perfectly line up the flue connection on the wood burner with the thimble. The practical solution was to locate the thimble well above the expected height of the flue connection on the stove and just pipe up to it. Today we now have available telescoping flue pipe sections that have a tube inside of tube, so a flue pipe can be adjusted to fit in between the wood burner and the chimney and can be shortened for removal. Of course, if you build a set up with a thimble that matches the height of the flue connector on your wood burner, what will you do if your next new stove does not match it? For wood burners with a top mounted flue connector, the first elbow is eliminated and only one elbow is used that points back to the thimble and in the case of an overhead insulated chimney, a straight up connection with no elbows at all is possible.

Traditionally a damper and draft regulator or barometric damper was installed in the flue pipe. For old stoves and furnaces, which were not air tight, they were necessary to control the large draft that could occur even with the air intakes closed, or otherwise this excessive draft would result in over firing and overheating the stove or furnace. I can remember seeing wood stoves so over fired that you could see the logs inside through the steel side walls, the logs were visible as bright orange shapes in the steel sides while the surrounding fire was merely red hot. Obviously, it is dangerous to operate a wood stove or any wood burner at such high temperatures, which is why dampers are used to restrict the draft to prevent this. Excessive draft is like a blacksmith bellows blowing air into the fire to get it hot enough to melt iron, and a strong enough draft can melt steel and iron, causing destructive failure in the flue pipe, stove or chimney. Old drafty wood burners with tall chimneys need dampers, newer air tight wood burners do not need dampers or draft regulators since the draft can be reduced by closing the air inlet dampers on the wood burner. I would recommend not installing a damper or draft regulator on air tight units and just keep on eye on how drafty your installation is, as the weather gets colder. The draft in a chimney is created by hot air having expanded in size making it lighter than cold dense air, and the colder it is outside the greater is the difference in density and the greater is your potential draft. If the fire gets too hot on cold days even with the inlet air damper closed all the way, then you need a damper or draft regulator. Barometric draft regulators are fitted in the open side of a tee and consist of a weighted damper plate that excessive draft will pull open allowing cooler room air into the flue reducing the pull on the flue connected to the wood burner, because the cool air reduces the temperature of the air in the chimney and thus reduces the draft. Barometric draft regulators however are notorious for back puffing smoke when down drafting occurs. If you have a problem with down drafts, you should use a regular stove pipe damper instead. A damper is a paddle like plate that mounts on a rod that is punched through the flue pipe and can be rotated like a butterfly valve to open or close the flue pipe. Even when closed most dampers are designed to allow about 20% of normal flow by either being smaller than the inside of the flue pipe or having holes in the plate. The trouble with flue pipe dampers is soot plugs them up fairly quickly, since it will plug the plate holes and line the flue pipe so the plate closes nearly air tight on the lining of soot. If you have a soot problem, you are better off with a Barometric draft regulator. The key point here is not to use dampers or regulators unless you need to.

It is very important to remember to run a flue pipe like a drain line that drains from the chimney to the wood burner. By running the flue pipe up hill to the chimney, the hot gases will flow smoothly up and into the chimney with a negative draft air pressure at each stove pipe joint, while any downward bends in a flue pipe on the way to the chimney can create a high pressure spot where smoke may back out through a joint in the stove pipe. The downward slope back towards the wood burner is also needed for draining any creosote that collects in the pipe back into the wood burner where it can be burned, rather than draining into the chimney where it could collect and cause a chimney fire. Draining creosote is also the reason why each stove pipe joint has to fit inside the fitting towards the stove and over the next piece towards the chimney.

Flue pipes need to be hot to work right, or else creosote and soot will collect at cold spots. When you clean your flue pipe, you will find it clean by the stove and dirtier by the chimney. Just as the soot and creosote collects at the cold end of the flue pipe, it will do the same if the chimney is cold. The trick is to keep the flue and chimney hot enough to keep the creosote from condensing. With older stoves most soot and creosote problems can be mostly eliminated by eliminating low firing and instead simply burning hot and clean and burning only when needed rather than continuously. While newer EPA approved units burn clean even at low firing rates, even with the cleanest wood burner in the world, there is still some creosote and soot mainly from starting, and these will coat the flue pipe and chimney if these surfaces are not hot enough. The problem is that stove pipe is just a single layer of sheet metal and an enormous amount of heat is given off through it. Just six feet of horizontal pipe can give off as much heat as the wood stove it is connected to. It may sound great to pull all that extra heat off the fire, but an installation where half the heat comes off the stovepipe can never be fired at less than half. Overly long flue pipe runs takes away control of the heat output and results in over heating and over firing in an effort to keep the chimney hot enough to prevent creosote build up, which is why the length of the flue pipe needs to be kept as short as possible. In straight up venting the insulated chimney can be run down practically right to the connector on the wood burner, and will insure a hot chimney that will stay hot even with a very small fire. When the flue connector is on the back of the stove, the insulated chimney can be run down behind the wood burner and a short flue pipe section can be connected to the bottom of the insulated chimney or a short two elbow connection into an insulated chimney tee. For connections to masonry chimneys, keep the distance short as possible with as few elbows as possible. For installations where you are stuck with a longer flue pipe run, and even for shorter ones, double walled flue pipe works wonders. Double walled flue pipe reduces the clearance requirement for flue pipe from 18 inches to six and greatly reduces the amount of heat given off by the flue pipe. I have a fairly long horizontal run on my flue pipe that was collecting soot, but once I switched to double walled pipe, the problem disappeared and the chimney stayed cleaner too.

Stove pipe traditionally is put together with three sheet metal screws at each fitting. The reason is that it takes three screws at a minimum to prevent wobbling, just as a three legged stool will not wobble. The screws should not project more than quarter inch into the pipe or they will act as a point for soot to collect on and will reduce air flow. Furnace cement can be used to help seal the joints and is recommended, it can however make disassembling the flue pipe for cleaning difficult. Foil furnace tape can be used to tape the joints, but high temperatures can cause the adhesive to fail. My trick is to use one long piece of tape so it wraps all the way around the pipe with the end of the tape coming over the top of the pipe and ending at the three o-clock position, so if the adhesive fails, gravity will keep the tape from falling off the pipe. A compromise is to use furnace cement at all the flue pipe connections except for two and use tape on those. The idea is that you take the flue apart at those two fittings and carry it outside for cleaning.

You may have noticed that I have not described how to install a stove flue pipe in a fireplace chimney, the reason for that is simple, if you want to use the fire place chimney for your stove, you should install a fireplace insert instead.

Installing a Thimble

It is only with masonry chimneys that thimbles are an issue since with insulated chimneys the thimble is a stove pipe adapter. Inspect an old thimble before you use it, check for rust and flushness with the inside of the chimney. Use a light, reach your hand inside, and feel the inside edge of the thimble and feel if it projects into the chimney flue space. If the thimble is too long, you can remove it and shorten it with a tin snips or a hacksaw if need be. Old thimbles can be removed by twisting them to break to cement bond. If the thimble will not twist, and careful hammering on the metal has not released it, you can remove it by collapsing it. Remove any collar, use a punch, and hammer to pound in a fold working from the outside of thimble toward the inside. Pound in the edge in one spot, slip the punch between the metal and the cement, and bend the metal inwards, which will reduce the diameter of the thimble making it smaller than the hole it is mounted in. Once the thimble is out, the cement hole can be enlarged if needed to fit in a new thimble. A male end piece of stove pipe can also be cut to length and cemented in place to use as a thimble, just leave the male fitting sticking out from the chimney with the other end flush with the inside of the chimney flue.

Installing a Wood Stove

With wood stoves the location is critical since there will normally be no heat distribution system other than the normal air movement in the house so a central location in the middle of the house from which the warm air can spread out to the rest of the house is the best choice. Wood stoves are normally installed in a living room or den, but there are other locations to consider as well, the kitchen can be a good location if it is more centrally located and if there is enough space for a wood stove. A kitchen location can also work well if a wood stove is chosen that includes options for cooking like a flat top that can be used like a stove top. Another factor to consider is the need to haul wood in to the stove daily and the mess of removing that ashes and the need to clean the stove and chimney from time to time. Some people have put wood stoves in basements and have attempted to heat the house by heating through the floor, which never worked well in the past because they couldn't get enough heat through the floor to make up for what they were losing through the walls without seriously over heating the basement. However, if you have a well insulated house with R-20 walls and a well insulated attic R-40 or better, your heat loses may be small enough that a basement wood stove may be able to heat the house very nicely. While a furnace would be the more logical choice for heating from the basement, a basement wood stove has the advantage of not needing a furnace fan to move the heat and may be the better choice for emergency back up heating.

Locating a wood stove in the living space of the house is by nature risky since the floors are generally wood and most homes are filled with things that can burn. Great care needs to be exercised in installing the wood stove with adequate clearances from anything that can burn and in keeping burnable things away from the stove after it is installed. It is easier to maintain this separation if the wood stove is located well away from where things tend to collect and if clutter in the home is kept to a minimum. The wood stove needs a good location so it maybe necessary to alter the layout of the home by changing the layout of the furniture. Move furniture back away from the wood stove, a fire should be admired from across the room and not from within arm's reach. You really need a wide space around the wood stove to allow for the necessary clearances that most stoves require from anything that can burn, which is often three feet, and you will need space in which to load and operate the stove. The open space around the wood stove also aids in allowing freer movement of air and helps spread the heat more evenly in the home. In tight situations, a wood stove can be placed closer to a combustible wall by installing a heat shield with an air space behind it. Heat shields can be sheet metal or brick installed with a one inch air gap behind it. The drywall or brick on a wood farmed wall does not act as a heat shield since they are touching the wall and are good conductors of heat and will transfer the heat to the wood. A number of wood stoves have a built in metal heat shield on the back side to allow for closer placement to the wall. It is wise to check the clearance requirements on a wood stove before you buy it; some stoves can be placed as close as 6 inches on the back and sides to combustibles.

Wood stoves are made of metal, and metal is a great conductor of heat, which is why wood stoves normally can not be placed directly on wood floors unless the manufactures states that the stove can be installed directly on a wood floor without any floor protection like a hearth pad or stove board. In the old days, wood stoves with long cast iron legs were often set on hardwood floors and many operated for years without any problems. I know of one case where this was true, and then one day they came home to find that the wood stove had burned a hole in the floor and had dropped into the basement, fortunately the house did not burn down. What had happen was, over time the wood stove dries out wood beneath it and once the wood is very dry, a hot fire that otherwise would not have been a problem, is now hot enough to start the wood floor burning, a temperature as low as 212 F can over time eventually ignite wood. It will be necessary to check in the manual for the wood stove for the requirements on what it can be placed on, and the type and size of hearth pad needed. Even if your wood stove were rated for placement on a wood floor, you still would be wise to have at least a hearth pad or a fireproof hearthrug in front of the stove for any sparks or hot coals that pop out the door when you are putting more wood in the fire. A smooth surface like a hearth pad works much better than a hearthrug for sweeping up small pieces of wood and bark and any fallen ashes. If you have an older stove and do not know, what the recommendations are for what it can be placed on; the general guidelines are that stoves with less than 6 inches of ventilated space between the bottom of the fire box and the floor, can be set on hollow four inch thick concrete blocks laid on their sides with the holes lined up for air flow and covered with 24 gauge sheet metal. The floor covering should also extend out from the stove at least 18 inches on all sides. For stoves with 6 to 18 inch long legs, a standard hearth pad will do. For stoves with legs more than 18 inches long, a piece of 24-gauge sheet metal is enough protection for wood floors.

A wise feature to include is a fresh air intake. For most wood stoves, a four-inch diameter dryer type vent will provide more than enough air. Some stoves include provisions for directly connecting a fresh air intake duct to the stove. The intake vent can be routed beneath the floor and routed up to the stove or connected to a floor vent with a damper in the floor near the stove. If your stove requires a hearth pad, the air intake duct cannot be routed through the pad. Another routing option is to put the intake vent in the wall behind the stove, or route it up into the wall from below and run a duct straight to a connection on the stove. However you run the intake duct, be careful not to create a cold draft that will be present when the stove is not operating. For example it is possible to simply put a through the wall vent in an outside wall behind the stove, but then you simply have a hole in the wall with a grill on it and the cold air will blow right in. Heat rises, and cold doesn't, which is why putting the intake vent below the floor level in the outside wall and routing the duct up through the floor, will help keep the cold air out unless the wood stove is running and drafting in fresh air. Another trick is to use flexible metal ducting which having a corrugated inside surface will help restrict unwanted drafting as will having the duct several feet long. A strong wind blowing against the side of the home that the intake vent is on, will create a higher air pressure on that side of the home and will push cold air in through the duct. To keep out the cold, a damper in a floor grill will help or simply having a thick rug that can be placed over the vent will help keep out the draft. It is also wise to insulate the intake duct so it does not act as a hole in your house insulation.

On installing your wood stove, follow the installation directions from the manufacture, if you do not have the directions you may be able to download them from the manufacture's website. If you do not have internet at home, most libraries these days have free internet access available in the library. If you are unable to get any installation directions for your stove, follow the general guidelines outlined here in this chapter and be sure to check and follow any local codes in your area. Be sure to install an EPA approved wood stove which will need less wood to heat and will burn it cleanly which will help to keep your chimney clean and will reduce the risk of a chimney fire.

Installing a Fireplace Insert

Fireplace inserts are the better wood stove. The fireplace is already the focal point of the room, and being set into the wall it requires less floor space than a freestanding wood stove. The fireplace also acts as a heat shield on all sides but the front, making inserts less of a hazard for burns and accidentally starting fires by contact with flammable items and you are able to use an existing chimney that is bigger than what you need.

Disadvantages of fireplace inserts are having to fit them into an existing fireplace opening can make the firebox rather small and being recessed into the fireplace can restrict the natural air flow of rising hot air. Many inserts have electric powered fans to blow hot air into the room, these units will still heat without electricity but they will give off less heat into the room without the fan.

Fireplaces are the blast furnaces of home heating, with the open design, fires burn large and fast with a ton of hot gases and excess air flowing up the chimney and the fire burns hot and short compared to fires in an airtight wood stove. This is why fireplace chimneys normally do not have much creosote and often are not designed with creosote in mind. While a fireplace insert, is just the opposite with a firebox that has limited air intake to carefully control the rate of burn for maximum efficiency and there is little if any excess air going up the chimney. Since a fireplace often has a large flue, it is necessary to install a smaller flue liner for the insert. Otherwise, the insert will not draft properly since the amount of hot gases it vents will not be enough to keep the chimney hot and the exhaust gases will cool in the oversized chimney and creosote will collect on the chimney walls and on the smoke shelf. Smoke shelves are designed to catch and hold rainwater and this depression above and behind the damper will tend to collect a large amount creosote than tends to go unnoticed until it catches fire one day. It is now code in most areas for fireplace inserts to be installed with a flue liner sized for the insert. This is why inserts are shipped with a collar for attaching a stainless steel flexible flue liner.

To install a stainless steel class "A" flexible flue liner, you will need to check the installation directions for your fireplace insert and check the size of the flue connector on the insert and inspect and measure your fireplace chimney. It is recommended that you have your fireplace chimney cleaned and inspected before installing an insert. Your chimney may need repairs before an insert can be installed. You may decide to do the work yourself, which will involve sweeping the chimney and inspecting it by lowering a trouble light down it to check the flue. You should also inspect as much of the outside of the chimney as you can for gaps in the mortar or cracking by going up on the roof, into the attic, looking up through the damper and down into the crawl space or basement to check the foundation. You will need to check to see that all wood is at least two inches way from the chimney and that non-combustible fire stops are in place at each floor or ceiling. The two-inch rule is the code, but if you have a smaller space, you would nearly have to rebuild the house to increase the clearance. I only have an inch and half clearance and do not worry about it. If you have used the fireplace for years, the smaller amount of heat an insert will put up the chimney will be less of a potential problem anyway. Flexible flue liners are often used as the cure for the problem of cracked or missing clay flue tiles for chimneys that do not have a clay flue liner, so the fireplace chimney does not have to perfect. But the chimney does have to be sound and without any cracks that will allow gas to flow out through the sides of the chimney, any such gaps will need to be repaired by being filled with cement or the chimney will need to be rebuilt or replaced. If the chimney is a real mess and needs replacement, you should consider installing an EPA approved prefabricated fireplace unit instead of a fireplace insert. The prefabricated EPA approved fireplace units are larger and can take longer pieces of wood and will hold more wood for longer burn times than will the smaller fireplace inserts. Quatrafire's 7100 can take 24-inch long logs and can achieve an efficiency of 78 percent and burn for 16 hours and is installed as a prefabricated chimney and can efficiently heat a home with wood. ($4,441.00 for the fireplace unit) For inserts Quatrafire has some excellent products, a friend of mine has the 3100i and it is quite something, a lot of heat from very little wood and very little smoke.

If your fireplace chimney is in adequate shape for installing a fireplace insert, measure or estimate the length the flexible flue will need to be to reach from the cap to the insert with an allowance for error. Also be sure to order a class A stainless steel flexible flue and not a class B stainless steel flexible flue, class B flues are rated for natural gas and are not rated for wood. Flexible flues are often installed in fireplace chimneys by using a pulling nose cone that is pulled with a rope up the chimney. For most fireplace chimneys, the fireplace damper will not be wide enough to allow the flue to fit, if the damper cannot be reasonably removed and is not overly narrow, the flue can be lowered in from above with the last foot or so of the bottom end flattened into an oval to fit through the damper opening. The top of the chimney will need a cap plate to support the flexible flue in the chimney to keep it straight and to keep the warmed air between the flexible flue and the inside of the chimney from exiting out the top of the chimney. This warm air acts as the insulation for the flexible flue. If this air is allowed to convect up and out of the chimney, the flue will be chilled by the cold air that replaces it and the flexible flue will tend to collect creosote. For fireplaces with huge flues where the flexible flue will probably not give off enough heat to keep air inside the chimney hot enough, insulate the flexible flue with flue liner insulation jackets that fit over the outside of the flexible flue. There is also a cap that fits over the end of the flexible flue to keep out rain and foreign objects like squirrels and bird nests as well as reducing down drafting. Once the flexible flue is threaded down through the damper, the end of the flexible flue is rounded back into shape to fit on to the connector on the insert. After the flue is attached, the damper will need to be sealed with noncombustible material to prevent airflow or the chimney can be sealed by the insert trim. The insert will also have a provision for a fresh air intake from outside the building, which you are wise to install. The blower motor will also need to be wired or at least plugged in; a cord is routed from a front corner of the insert and plugged into an outlet next to the fireplace. The insert is then pushed back into place and after a quick check is ready for your first fire.

Installing a Wood Furnace

Selecting which wood furnace to buy is simple, as of early 2009 there is only one EPA approved wood furnace on the market, the Caddy E.P.A. wood Add-on furnace that is also available in a mini version made by PSG. (http://www.psg-distribution.com/index.aspx) The Caddy EPA approved furnace is also sold by US Stove

Company under the name Hotblast EPA Furnace 1950 (http://usstove.com/) The price is $3,042.00 for the USSC version.

Wood furnaces and boilers are wonderful, they heat the whole house evenly and they heat it well. All the mess of burning wood is removed from the living space and is located in the basement or a furnace room. The risks of fire are greatly reduced compared to wood stoves and are about the same as conventionally fueled furnaces and boilers. The safety risks of accidental burns associated with stoves is also largely eliminated by being located out of the living space and due to furnaces and boilers having an enclosed firebox with far less exposed hot surfaces. Insurance coverage is sometimes less of a problem for wood furnaces and boilers than it is for wood stoves. Generally being located in a basement rather than upstairs results in a taller chimney and a better draft and a fresh air intake duct does not result in any cold air drafts in the living space. A hot air furnace if it is being installed as an add-on furnace to your already existing system, for the best set up will need to be installed next to your existing furnace for series airflow. In which the blower in your existing furnace is used to blow air through the existing furnace and then through the wood furnace and then into the ductwork. Your existing furnace has a plenum duct that rises up to connect to the main duct. The wood furnace will need to sit beneath the main duct and be connected to it with its own plenum. The top of the existing furnace's plenum is blocked off with sheet metal and then a large duct or ducts with a cross section equal to the plenum is routed from below the block and is connected to the intake on the bottom of the wood furnace. So the air will be blown up through the existing furnace into the blocked plenum and then down through the connecting duct into the base of the wood furnace and then up through the wood furnace and into the duct system.

The wood furnace will need to be connected to the main duct, the existing furnace plenum and the chimney. In locating where to place the wood furnace you will need to consider the need for all three connections. If you are not able to find a location that will allow for making the three connections, you may have to consider other installation set-ups other than installing the wood furnace in series with the existing furnace. There are other installation methods such as various parallel set ups in which the wood stove has its own blower and blows hot air into the duct system on its own without any direct connection to the existing furnace aside from the main duct. To prevent the existing furnace from blowing hot air backwards through the wood furnace and wasting it in the basement, in parallel set ups both furnace fans are run together to prevent back flowing heat out through the other furnace. Of course this set up depends on both blowers developing about the same amount of air pressure in the ductwork so one doesn't overpower the other, plus this method wastes electricity by running two blowers when only one is needed. To over come some of these problems, dampers can be used, but air dampers are expensive and dampers under fan pressure will leak a lot of air. Therefore, while parallel installations can be made to work, they are inherently less efficient and tend to be more complicated than a series installation. Another possibility that can work better than a parallel set up is a separate installation. In a small home with a basement, it is possible to run a small second ductwork system for the wood furnace, that way each system can run independently of the other, of course you do end up with a lot of ducting and extra grills and heat vents.

Since wood furnaces can deliver much hotter air than a gas furnace, some changes may need to be made to the ductwork. Metal ductwork is often mounted with inch or two of space between the top of the duct and the wood framing above to prevent the hot ductwork from drying out the wood and possibly lighting it on fire. The thought is if the heat exchanger in the furnace were to fail, the hot combustion gases would enter the ductwork above the furnace. Since with a wood furnace, if the heat exchanger failed there potentially would be the flames and smoke from a hot wood fire entering the ductwork. To contain this amount of heat without lighting the wood framing on fire, the ductwork within six feet of the wood furnace, should it be six inches below the wood framing above and the rest of the main duct should be mounted one or two inches below the wood framing above. The main duct can be lowered by shortening the plenum on the existing furnace and releasing the duct hangers on the main duct and supporting the duct with pipe strap. Since the branch ducts will nearly all be run out to the outside walls, lowering the main duct will give them some slope, which will help for natural heat flow if you need to heat without a fan blower. If you have a long main branch, you may be able to just lower the sections over the wood furnace.

You don't have to worry about the cold air return duct system since the connection will be to the bottom of the wood furnace and natural convection of heat will take the heat from any fire that breaches the heat exchanger, up the plenum and not down into the cold air return. If lowering the duct over the wood furnace is impractical, and if you already have one or 2 inches of space, installing insulation on the top of the duct such as a nonflammable insulation like foil backed fiberglass will reduce heat the duct can give off and will reduce the clearance needed.

A major disadvantage with wood furnaces is that when the power is out, there is nothing to run the blower fan to move the heat up into the house. Hot air rises and a well-designed hot air wood furnace installation can heat fairly well without electricity. How this is done is by making sure that the wood furnace is connected to the main duct with a large as plenum as possible. In old gravity systems, the plenum is the motor that moves the air, the taller and the wider it is, the more push it will have from the flow of rising hot air. To feed the rising hot air in the wood furnace, cold air has to be able to freely flow into the bottom of the furnace. There are two way of doing this, one is when the power goes out, to open large panels on the sides of the wood furnace to allow basement air to flow in. The other is to have a large duct connected to the cold air return on the existing furnace that connects to the bottom of the wood furnace, for bypassing the existing non-wood furnace. This duct is normally kept closed by a sheet metal slide, which is a piece of sheet metal that slides into the duct like a wall to block the duct, to prevent the flow of air from the furnace fan from being short-circuited. When there is a power failure, the slide is pulled out and cold air descends down the cold air return and flows through the bypass duct into the base of the wood furnace where it is heated and rises up through the wood furnace into the house. This setup creates a gravity heating system that while not as efficient as a forced air system, will heat your home without electricity. I have this set up on my wood stove and I find that it works well, though only about half as well as using the furnace fan.

Wood furnaces can be fitted with a pipe running through the firebox that is connected to the water heater that will heat hot water. The one problem with this water heating systems is they lack a way of turning them off. So if you need heat but don't need any more hot water, you will still be heating water anyway which is why these systems tend to over heat the water so a tempering valve is needed on the hot water outlet line of the water heater to prevent scalding hot water from coming out of the taps. While the tempering valve will prevent scalding, your water heater may still be overheated and the high temperature relief valve may open and discharge water. Once enough cold water has entered the water heater to drop the temperature a few degrees, the valve should reclose. If you install one of these systems, have a way of draining away any hot discharge water from the water heater so that you do not end up with any water damage or flooding.

Not all furnaces are in basements, if the furnace room is on the first floor there are a number of problems that will need to be solved. First and foremost is if the furnace room has a combustible floor which will require the wood furnace to be placed on hollow four inch thick concrete blocks laid on their sides with the holes lined up for air flow and covered with a piece of 24 gauge sheet metal. This metal covered pad will need to extend out from underneath the furnace by 18 inches on the front and 8 to 18 inches on the back and sides depending on the design of the wood furnace. The furnace will also have to be kept away from combustible walls by as much as four feet on the front and three feet on the back and sides. Some wood furnaces have reduced clearance requirements due to better design. Also, remember the stovepipe clearance to combustibles requirements of 18 inches for single wall stove pipe and 6 inches for double walled stovepipe. The weight of the wood furnace and the concrete block pad may require that the floor be reinforced to support the additional weight. This can be done by placing adjustable steel columns underneath the floor below the furnace. A set of four steel columns can be used with one underneath each corner of the wood furnace with two steel or wood beams crossing bottom of the floor joists.

If you have a down draft furnace in which the hot air comes out of the bottom end of the furnace and is blown down into ductwork below the floor. A blocking piece can be placed below the bottom of the heat exchanger allowing enough room for a connecting duct or ducts to transfer the air to the bottom of the wood furnace. Then from the top of the wood furnace, a duct is run down through the floor and into the main duct. If the duct from the top of the wood furnace is too large to route between the floor joists to reach the main duct below, it can be split into two or more smaller ducts, which can fit between the joists and connect each one to the main duct. Obviously since the heat leaving the wood furnace is ducted downward, there is no provision for supplying heat to the house without the furnace fan to move the air. Frankly, this type of installation is a bad idea, you are far better off if you can get the wood furnace below the ductwork, even if you have to dig a basement furnace room to do it. If wood heat is desired for back up heat for power outages, and it is not possible to install the furnace below the ductwork, a wood stove or fireplace insert should be considered instead or in addition to a down-ducted wood furnace.

Installing a Wood Boiler

With wood boilers, you have much greater flexibility in where to put the boiler since you can run the piping wherever you want it. The HUGE advantage of boilers over furnaces is that a boiler can store heat in the water. By having a large secondary tank or a boiler with a large water volume, the heat of a fire can be stored and used later. A fire in a boiler can be a hot clean quick fire in the morning that heats up the water in the system, which is kept in the insulated boiler or tank until needed and then is pumped to where ever heat is wanted throughout the rest of the day. The downside of boilers of course, is that without electricity to operate the circulation pumps in a power outage, the heat will remain trapped in the tank or boiler and you will not be able to heat the house. Some systems with the boiler down in a basement with the pipes rising up to the radiators, if piped just right, will have some heat due to hot water rising in the pipes and cold-water flowing back down to the boiler. The systems with a better pipe layout for thermal heat convection will be the old steam systems that were converted to hydronic heating or a hydronic system that was piped by pipe fitters who still run their pipes the way they should be run. Newer systems however are often piped with no regard for heat flow convection, so without electricity they will supply little if any heat.

A wood boiler can be piped in parallel with the existing boiler with check valves to prevent back flow or in series with it. With series piping, you do not need another pump, while with parallel flow you do not have to pump hot water through an unheated boiler. Ideally, a wood boiler should be piped to make maximum use of thermo siphoning so the system can provide at least minimal heat during a power outage, otherwise a wood stove is needed as well for backup heating. A large water volume in the wood boiler is ideal for use with brief hot firing, or a large tank can be used for hot water storage to increase the system heat storage capacity. The boiler can be piped to the tank with a circulation pump controlled by a differential control that will turn the pump on whenever the boiler is hotter than the tank. The system circulating pumps that pump water from the tank to the radiators when needed are each controlled by a wall thermostat.

Unfortunately, at this time (2009) there appears to be only one residential indoor wood boiler that is EPA approved. Many manufactures do not list efficiency ratings for their boilers and even the ones that do are listing the results of tests that they paid for. To illustrate the problem one manufacture claims that their boiler is "*the most modern, efficient heating appliances possible*" and yet sports a primitive steel firebox without any firebrick. Of course with wood to achieve a clean efficient burn you have to have a hot fire and a bare steel water-cooled box is as bad as it gets. With the absence of government standards and independent testing, the manufactures are free to lie to their hearts content; they want your money and will tell you anything to get it. Some general guidelines in looking for a good boiler are to first eliminate the boilers without any efficiency rating from consideration; there is a reason why they do not tell you. Second, remember that the efficiency ratings that are given should be taken with a grain of salt, so look at the design of the boilers for some clues as to performance. Generally the more firebrick the better, since a hot fire is an efficient fire and there is plenty of time to extract heat from the fire after combustion is complete. Other marks of better efficiency are secondary burn chambers, secondary heat exchangers and most importantly, secondary air or post combustion air, which is added to burn off unburned gases. The very best boilers at the moment are gasification boilers that have a heavily insulated chamber in which the wood is burned under a forced draft that exits the chamber at the bottom where the fire is the hottest. The superheated exhaust gases are burned off in a second chamber normally below the first. The hot gases then pass through the water cooled heat exchanger and are cooled down to as low as 300 to 350 degrees Fahrenheit. The hot gases sometimes exit through a centrifugal ash separator, which is important since with the gases being blown out the bottom of the fire chamber, most of the ash is blown out with the exhaust gases. A good gasification boiler can have an efficiency rating as high as 80 to 85%. However, they are expensive starting at about $7,000 just for the boiler and most have the disadvantage of requiring electric power to operate the blower to drive the exhaust gases out the bottom of the fire chamber. The best wood boiler is probably the Greenwood Hydronic Wood Furnace model 100 indoor boiler, which at this time to the best of my knowledge is the only indoor boiler with an EPA approval and has a Phase 1 Orange Tag "Year Round" rating with an efficiency rating of 84.6% and costs about $7000. (http://www.greenwoodusa.com/) This boiler also has the advantage of having a natural draft so it can operate without electrical power and if your piping is right, you may able to get some heat even in a power outage. A problem with this boiler is it exhausts at only 300 F and needs a very short and hot venting with a good draft. In my opinion, it really needs an insulated chimney since if the temperature drops below 250 F before the gases clear the chimney cap, you will have creosote and soot problems, you will also need a good draft, which includes having a fresh air vent. The best venting option is to have an insulated stainless steel insulated chimney connected to the boilers flue connector with a stovepipe adapter and have the chimney vent straight up with no bends. The chimneys on gasification boilers need to be kept warm, which means they should be in the center of the house where they will stay warm and not run outside the house or in an outside wall where the chimney will get cold when not used for a while. The other key point with gasification boilers is that with only 300-350 F exhaust gases, it will take a long time to heat up a cold chimney; during that time water, creosote and soot will be deposited in the chimney. It is very important that the chimney venting is designed so that all condensates will drain back to the boiler where they can be vaporized or burned off. If you have a chimney with an ash pit or trap, it may fill up with a mixture of black sooty water that may drain out and make a mess. Since this unit is a boiler and has a marginal exhaust temperature like most gasification boilers do, it makes sense to run it hot and keep the exhaust temperature hot and store the heat in the water rather than trying to keep a small fire running all day.

Installing a Wood Outdoor Water Boiler

Outdoor Water Boilers, OWBs are very easy to install. A concrete pad with a notch for the water lines is poured and insulated lines are buried in a trench running from the pad to the buildings that are to be heated. The OWB should be located downwind of the house if possible or at least not upwind so the smoke is not blown to the house. (In the USA the common prevailing wind direction is from the west) All homes have drafts and if the house is in the OWB smoke plume, the house will be filled with smoky air. OWBs are sold with a very short stack, which tends to release the smoke so close to the ground that if there is a wind blowing the wind will tend to hold the smoke to the ground. The reason for this is that the chimney of the OWB is often shorter than other things nearby which results in the wind blowing over them and down towards the OWB pushing the smoke towards the ground. This is why many OWBs operate in a cloud of smoke. The trick to fix this is simple; a OWB needs a chimney that is at least 2 feet taller than anything within 100 feet. Of course it is often impractical to have a chimney taller than tall trees, which can be over a 100 feet tall or nearby hills that can be even taller, but the smoking problems, can be reduced by having a chimney as reasonably tall as possible. In some areas such as northeastern part of the United States, a number of states and counties are enacting regulations for OWBs that are following the NESCAUM (Northeast Center for a Clean Air Future model) for OWB regulations. The NESCAUM rules for OWB chimneys are that they must be five feet higher than the peak of any roof within 150 feet. Most OWBs are not designed to operate with very tall chimneys, and such chimneys will clog up with creosote and soot. A chimney has to be kept above 250 F to work right and not collect creosote. A short extension of insulated stainless steel class "A" chimney to bring the chimney height to 15 to 22 feet above the ground will help to get the smoke up away from the ground and with the insulation; it should be short enough for the OWB to keep the stack hot. If creosote begins to collect in the chimney, a section at a time can be removed until the chimney stays relatively clean between chimney cleanings. However if you live in an area that has chimney height rules, to avoid having a requirement for a chimney height that may not work for your OBW, and that would be a problem to clean, locate your OWB outside of the distance from a structure that would require a higher chimney, often 150 feet. Locating a OWB 150 feet away from any structure may be difficult, if not impossible, if it is impossible you should look for an OWB that can handle tall chimneys or reconsider getting an OWB.

OWBs are also restricted in some areas in how close they can be to the house that they are heating (50 feet, Massachusetts) and how close they can be to a property border (50-250 feet depending on emissions in Maine, 200 feet in Ohio,) and how close they can be to a neighbor's house. (75 feet Massachusetts, 200 feet Vermont, 200 feet Connecticut) The offset distance for the state of Washington is the OWB has to be located in another state, since Washington has banned all OWBs. Washington State is not alone in banning OWBs, some townships, cities and counties have banned or severely restricted OWBs. Every year there are new rules against OWBs and it is to be expected that more states and local governments will ban OWBs, so you would be wise to check on what the local rules are in your area for OWBs before you consider installing one. You can check for state regulations by going to the EPA website at this address epa.gov/woodheaters/whereyoulive.htm and selecting for your state and the link will take you to the site for your state's regulations on OWBs. The Vermont Department of Environmental Conservation Air Pollution Control Division website at anr.state.vt.us/dec/air/owb/regl-other.html has a listing and links to all states with regulations on OWBs and those that are moving towards regulation. At the moment (Feb 2009), the site lists states with regulations or moving towards regulations as Connecticut, Illinois, Indiana, Maine, Maryland, Massachusetts, Michigan, Minnesota, Montana, New Hampshire, New Jersey, New York, North Carolina, Ohio, Pennsylvania, Rhode Island, Virginia, Washington and Wisconsin. If you live in any of the proceeding states, you will certainly need to check for state and local regulations. The above website does include a listing of some local regulations.

OWBs are facing an increasing amount of emissions regulations. The designs of OWBs are unregulated unlike wood stoves, which have had to meet EPA emission standards since 1990. Due to this lack of regulation many OWB manufactures have used cheap inefficient designs that create enormous amounts of very nasty smoke. The typical OWB produces as much soot as 22 EPA approved wood stoves or four diesel semi-trucks. OWBs produce about four times the soot of even old non-EPA approved wood stoves. Due to the lack of regulation on OWB emissions, OWB manufactures are free to market OWBs that are highly polluting and local governments have had to deal with the inevitable fallout. This lack of regulation on OWB emissions has resulted in a huge backlash against OWBs that is in many cases an over reaction, and has resulted in some cases in a complete ban on OWBs, even including OWBs that are clean burning and EPA approved. While in comparison EPA approved wood stoves have far less restrictions and are more accepted than OWBs. Part of this difference is because EPA wood stoves are less polluting than EPA approved OWBs and a wood stove needs to burn less wood than an OWB to supply the same amount of heating due to the outdoor location of an OWB. Wood stoves are also of course only used when heat is needed in the house while OWB are sometimes operated year round to supply hot water. The minimal heat load for supplying hot water results in OWBs in warm weather spending nearly all their time in idle mode with no load which is when they give off the most smoke, and warm weather is when most people are more likely to be outside and to be bothered by the smoke. It is all too easy to imagine the irritation of being down wind of an idling OWB in hot humid weather. Which is why some areas are restricting the time in the year when an OWB can be fired like from October 15 to April 15 (Monson, Mass.) or September 13 to April 15(Ohio). A solar hot water system can complement an OWB by supplying hot water in the summer time when the OWB is too big to operate efficiently and the OWB can supply the heat and hot water when there is too little sun for the solar system to effectively supply much heat. If the solar system is over sized compared to the hot water needs, it may be able to heat the home in the early fall and late spring when it is still kind of warm for using an OWB and local regulations may prohibit firing up the OWB.

The states and local governments are modeling their regulations after the model regulation provided by NESCAUM who in turn is assisted by the EPA. In terms of states, only the state of Washington has gone with a higher standard than the EPA, which has resulted in the complete ban of OWBs in the state of Washington. There are some local governments that have also banned OWBs outright, but for the most part due to the way nearly all the regulations are directly or indirectly following EPA guidelines, EPA approved OWBs should meet the requirements in most areas if the required setbacks are observed.

The future for OWBs is decidedly dark, while they will no doubt continue to be used by people out in the country outside of townships with no close neighbors, the days maybe numbered for use in townships, subdivisions and cities. NESCAUM has a document titled "OUTDOOR WOOD BOILER FACT SHEET" that discusses what to do about existing OWBs.

"What are the options for existing OWBs?

Limits on use – The strategy restricts or limits the use of existing OWBs to certain periods of time, such as limiting use to the heating season only and/or limiting use based upon air quality conditions, such as when high ambient particulate pollution levels are likely to occur. This strategy would address high emission events but would not address the day-to-day contribution of pollution from OWBs to the ambient air or where an OWB causes nuisance conditions for neighbors.

Zoning requirement – This strategy would require that existing OWBs meet a setback requirement. If the OWB cannot meet the requirement, removal of the unit would be required. The same factors regarding stack height and enforcement as described above for new OWBs apply to this approach.

Stack height requirements – While increasing stack heights would not reduce the total amount of pollution emitted from an OWB, it may assist in dispersing smoke. However, no testing has been done to determine how raising the stack height will affect stack emissions. Discussions with combustion experts indicate that a height change will likely affect air flow rates, which could increase overall emissions from the OWB. In addition, this strategy would not address broader regional pollution caused by OWBs.

Ban on use of polluting units – *This strategy would ban the use [of] all OWBs that do not meet an emission requirement by a certain date.*

Change-out upon transfer of property – *Another strategy would require a certification prior to the completion of a sale or transfer of any real property on or after a certain date that states all wood burning appliances not meeting an applicable emission requirement have been replaced, removed, or rendered permanently inoperable."* nescaum.org/documents/owbfactsheetfinal.pdf/

While the above NESCAUM document is only a list of possible ways of dealing with existing OWBs, it does show what the future may bring for OWBs. If you are planning to install an OWB, you would be wise to buy an OWB that is on the EPA Phase 2 White Tag list and to observe all the setback requirements that may become law in the future. Such as installing the OWB at least 50 feet from your house, 200 feet from your lot line and 500 feet away from anyone else's house. For the chimney height requirement, you may have to install the OWB 150 feet away from any building including your own home. I hope that if you follow these general guidelines you will not have any problem, but remember that since they are always making up new regulations it is not always possible to avoid all future legal entanglements.

The EPA tested and approved the following OWBs giving them three classifications of approval. The White Tag Phase 2 has a maximum of 0.32 lbs of particle pollution per million BTU heat input. The Orange Tag Phase 1 all year have a maximum of 0.60 lbs of particle pollution per million BTU heat input and Phase 1 Orange Tag "Heating Season Only" Models which meet the 0.60 lbs requirement under heating type load conditions and not necessarily under light heating loads. Some boilers are on more than one list and may have a different rating on each.

EPA Phase 2 White Tag Models

Central Boiler; *Maxim M250*, 0.06 lbs/million BTU output

Central Boiler; *E - Classic 2300*, 0.37 lbs/million BTU output

Greenwood Technologies, LLC; *Aspen 175*, 0.27 lbs/million BTU output

Hardy Manufacturing Co., Inc; *KBP 270*; 0.20 lbs/million BTU output

Northwest Manufacturing, Inc. (Woodmaster); *AFS 900*, 0.20 lbs/million BTU output

Silverwinds Metals (Wood Doctor); *WD-HE8000*, 0.26 lbs/million BTU output

EPA Phase 1 Orange Tag "Year Round" Models

Greenwood Technologies; *Aspen 175*, 0.27 lbs/million BTU heat output

Central Boiler; *E - Classic 2300*, 0.37 lbs/million BTU output

Central Boiler; *E - Classic 1200*, 0.59 lbs/million BTU heat output

Heatmor; *200 SSR*, 0.76 lbs/million BTU heat output

Heatmor; *SSR 400*, 0.68 lbs/million BTU heat output

Bioheat Resources; *BH500 Eco Energy*, 0.77 lbs/million BTU heat output

Sequoyah Paradise; *E3400*, 2.37 lbs/million BTU heat output

Hardy; *KB175*, 0.87 lbs/million BTU heat output

Greenwood Technologies; *100*, 2.046 lbs/million BTU heat output (note this model is an indoor boiler, the only one on the EPA approved list.)

EPA Phase 1 Orange Tag "Heating Season Only" Models

Greenwood Technologies; *Aspen 175*, 0.28 lbs/million BTU heat output

Central Boiler; *E - Classic 2300*, 0.32 lbs/million BTU heat output

Central Boiler; *E - Classic 1200*, 0.51 lbs/million BTU heat output

Sequoyah Paradise; *E3400*, 2.37 lbs/million BTU heat output

Greenwood Technologies; *100*, 1.362 lbs/million BTU heat output

Alternative Fuel Boilers; *EBW150,* 0.80 lbs/million BTU heat output

Bioheat Resources; *BH500 Eco Energy*, 0.90 lbs/million BTU heat output

Aqua-Therm; *Omega 100*, 1.17 lbs/million BTU heat output

In the above lists notice that the top two boilers on the Phase 1 Orange Tag "Year Round" list are also on the Phase 2 White tag list, and that all the boilers on the Orange Tag "Year round" list are also on the Orange Tag "Heating Season Only" list with lower emission levels, except for the Hardy KB175 boiler, which for some strange reason is missing. The point to learn from the "Year round" and "Heating Season Only" tests is that even the cleanest OWBs are cleaner yet if not operated in warm weather. The other point to remember is that the EPA test is an emissions test and is not a quality test in terms of construction, though a low emission rating is an indication of good design.

The second most costly investment after the cost of the OWB is the cost of the insulated lines that will carry the hot water to and from the buildings that are to be heated by the OWB. The number one choice in the market is ThermoPEX, which is a black plastic polyethylene tube about 5 or 6 inches in diameter filled with high-density urethane foam with two oxygen barrier PEX lines.

ThermoPEX is sold by the foot and costs about $12/ft. For even a minimal distance of 50 feet ThermoPEX would cost $600 and for 150 feet the cost would be $1,800. INSUL-SEAL is an even higher priced product consisting of thick PVC pipe with high-density urethane foam covering with a plastic cover over the foam. INSUL-SEAL comes in 10-foot lengths and has to be joined together by gluing the PVC, caulking the foam and taping the plastic cover. INSUL-SEAL is also rigid and needs careful support and back filling to avoid cracking the PVC. There is also the difficulty of sealing the joints in a trench and many people who do their own installation have ground water leaks from either joint failure or cracked PVC due to improper back filling. A simpler and better way of installing the lines is to install two oxygen barrier PEX lines in a trench and hire a foam insulation company to spray 4 to 5 inches of urethane foam over the pipes. How this is done is the worker with the foam spray gun walks in the trench and lifts the PEX lines with his foot and sprays foam under the lines to hold them in place. The foam starts to harden in seconds and will support the lines as the worker sprays foam on the sides and top as he works his way backwards in the trench. Urethane foam holds up well underground and underwater which is why it is used in ThermoPEX. The cost for the spray insulation can run about $7 a foot, and one-inch oxygen barrier PEX lines cost about a dollar a foot and you need two lines, which brings the cost to about $9 per foot. While the cost is only a bit lower than the cost of ThermoPEX, you will have several times the insulation value and will lose far less heat. Heat loss with even ThermoPEX is considerable and in some installations with it have a strip of unfrozen snow free ground between the OWB and the buildings that are heated. With the recommended setbacks of 50-150 feet from the house, insulation on the OWB water lines is critical since this is where many OWBs lose most of the heat they produce.

The PEX lines are connected to the OWB and at the other end are routed into the building that they are heating through a hole in the basement wall and piped to a heat exchanger in a tank or in the furnace plenum or connected to a main line or directly into the existing boiler. A heat exchanger allows only the boiler and ground lines to be filled with anti-freeze. Not using anti-freeze requires that the OWB to be kept hot all winter long to prevent freezing. If it is not practical to keep burning wood in the OWB, it can be kept warm by pumping heated water from the existing boiler, of course at a huge heating loss. I recommend that the entry point for the PEX lines be well sealed to prevent water entry, in the event that the covering over the lines develops a leak, the water will follow the lines and will tend to drain into the basement.

OWB heating for homes with forced air is accomplished by installing a water to air heat exchanger in the furnace plenum. A fan switch or heat switch on the line will turn on the furnace fan when the exchanger is hot and the thermostat is calling for heat. An OWB with automatic controls is wired to maintain a set hot water temperature and as heat is lost through the heat exchanger the OWB will increase its firing rate to keep the water at the set temperature.

How to Light a Wood Fire

For all of our high tech modern wood burning appliances, it still comes down to the ancient art of starting a fire. While with our matches and lighters it is easy for us today to light a flame, we still have trouble with the kindling stage needed to get the wood burning. Of course, the official way to start a fire is very straight forward and simple. You take two split pieces of firewood and lay them with the split sides towards each other with a hand space in between. Then take some newspaper and make balls using one sheet each, and place them in between the split pieces. Next, lay smaller split pieces at right angles across the two split pieces with gaps in between them and lay more wood on top. Use a match to light the paper, which should burn hot enough to light the wood. Fire burns hottest when it the heat is reflected back on itself and has a ceiling above it to burn. Bark is fire resistant and hard to get started, and the larger a piece of wood is, the harder it can be to burn. The surface of split wood is normally covered with ragged pieces, which will light easier. Flames like to travel up with the gases that their heat drives out of the wood, by having smaller pieces of wood above in the path of the rising flames; they will be in the best place to light and add to the strength of the flames to light the larger pieces above.

Traditionally a wood furnace was fired up in the fall and the fire was kept going until spring. If that is your situation you do not need to light many fires and do not need much kindling. With today's well-insulated homes, far less heat is needed, so a continuous fire would overheat the house and waste wood. For proper heating and saving wood, fires are lighted daily and allowed to burn out. With having to light anywhere from one to three or more fires a day, a much larger amount of kindling is needed than has been the case before. This is why I have a woodpile and a kindling pile. I also stack kindling in with the woodpile in the spaces between the larger pieces. That way when I take a load of wood into the house, I should also have enough kindling to light the fire. When I cut wood, I also cut the branches for kindling, making more efficient use of the wood, leaving less waste.

To make it easier to start a fire, split your wood into fist-sized pieces when possible. I burn a lot of elm and that wood tends to go in whole since it does not split well, while the easier to split stuff is split into nice little pieces. It is good to have a mix of different sized pieces on the woodpile, little stuff for kindling and small fires in warmer weather and big pieces for colder weather. The most important point is that your firewood has to be dry. The old pioneer method of stacking the wood bark side up with a top layer laid like wood shingles to shed the rain, does not work very well. The wind blows the rain into the pile and gets the wood wet and the water as it runs over the cut ends, soaks into the wood. I know. I have tried it. Put a tarp over the pile to keep the rain off, but leave the sides open a bit so the ground moisture is not trapped underneath the tarp and to allow the wood moisture out. A wood shed works best if you have one. I know one old fellow who always stacked his wood out in the open, of course how he got his fires started was he had a pail of old oil that he soaked both ends in before he put the wood in the stove, otherwise he couldn't get his wood to burn.

Most of the time the wood you will be trying to burn will be less than ideal and you may have few if any small kindling pieces. For extra kindling I keep a paper bag next to the trash in the kitchen and all the paper trash goes into the paper bag. I save all cardboard boxes. Keep your old phone books; if you live near a large city your phone book will be huge. Save old newspapers also. Paper and cardboard are smoky so you want to use them only for kindling and not as your main fuel. You own a wood burner; it is not designed to burn paper or cardboard, at least not cleanly. The trick for using cardboard as kindling is to flatten a box and stand it against one side in the firebox and put the wood in next to it. Then take about a 1/8 to a 1/4 inch thickness of pages out of an old phone book or newspapers, and rip into narrow strips and place against the front of the cardboard in a pile. Light the paper with a match and the paper will light the cardboard, which will light the smaller pieces of wood next to it, which in turn will light the bigger pieces of wood. A fire is a chain reaction that builds on itself, but if any of the links fail, the fire will go out. Each link in the chain has to burn hot enough to light the next. Paper and cardboard kindling has to be standing on end to burn hot, to stand a better chance of lighting the smaller wood pieces. If you lay paper or cardboard flat on the bottom or middle, and put wood on top. The paper is pressed together and is not getting enough air inside to burn; it is like trying to burn a closed book. Despite being made of paper, books do not burn well and tend to just get scorched on the outside edges unless subjected to intense heat. However, if the book is standing on end and the pages are open, the flames will race up between the pages and the book burns readily. It is the same with cardboard and paper, if they are on edge the flames will shoot upwards between the pieces and the kindling goes up in a quick hot fire, and that intense heat, is what will light the smaller pieces of wood.

If you have enough small twigs, you do not need cardboard or much paper to start a fire. Just pile in a lot of twigs and then place small pieces of wood on top, and if there is enough room, maybe a large piece on top. Then rip in narrow strips some paper and place a handful down into the front of the twigs and light with a match. The paper will be hot enough to light the twigs if they are dry, and the rising flames from the twigs will heat and light the larger wood above. Twigs make great kindling, the problem is that they are so bulky and take up a lot space both in the firebox and in the brush pile. A twig fire is great for when it is too warm for a wood fire but you need some heat but not too much. The only problem with twig fires is that they are smoky since there is bark on each twig.

Once you have your kindling in the firebox, you have to put in the wood. The best way is to put in the smaller pieces on top of the kindling or next to the kindling if it is on the side. The trick is to lay the wood so that there are spaces in between the pieces that rise to the top of the wood in a maze like pattern, so that the flames will flow over the edges of one piece of wood and up against the bottom of another piece of wood. However, you do not want to block the flow, always try to leave a path for the flames. Then the big pieces go on top or to the other side from the kindling. If there is no room for big pieces, light the fire and then once it has burned down to hot coals, throw in the larger stuff.

Most wood burners have a grate at the bottom of the firebox, and I have written my fire lighting directions for that type of design. If you do not have a grate, you may have to modify the procedures. In some cases such as for a gasification boiler with a forced down draft, you can pretty much turn the whole thing upside down and put the kindling on top of the small wood with the big stuff on the bottom. So as the kindling burns in the down draft the fire will follow the downdraft down into and through the wood below it. For fire boxes without grates, place the kindling towards where the air hits the fire so the fire when lit will have plenty of air and will flow into the rest of the wood. Before you light the fire, open the draft up all the way, if the firebox has a grate, open the ash pit door. A strong flow of air will feed the flames and the fire will burn hotter, and heat is what is needed to get the wood burning. Once the fire is burning hotly, you will generally need to close the ash pit door and perhaps dial down the draft a bit, so the fire does not burn too hot and overheat the firebox.

Lighting Difficult or Wet Wood Fires

There will always be those days when the fire does not light, maybe you did not have enough kindling or maybe the wood is a bit damp. You should always have a backup plan for these kinds of things like keeping jumper cables in the trunk for when the car does not start. The first thing to do is to look inside the firebox and see if you can identify the problem. Often times it is because a log got hung up and failed to fall down into the kindling so it do not get hot enough to burn. If the coals are still hot below it, you can just use your poker and push the log free so it drops down into the fire. If the fire is gone, reload the kindling and push the log free so it will drop into the coals this time and relight the fire. Sometimes with grates, a log will block the grate and smother the fire, in this case use a poker to move the log to one side or lift it up and throw a small piece of wood under it to keep it up off the grate so the air can flow, then reload the kindling and relight the fire. Of course, sometimes the wood is just sitting there, where it should be, and is just blackened by the flames and does not burn. Large pieces of wood with the bark on can be very hard to start, or it maybe that the wood is just to wet to burn easily. One trick is to take a lot of small pieces of wood that you know are dry and build a pile on top or next to the damp wood, light your kindling and let the fire burn really hot. The heat will hopefully drive out the excess moisture from the damp wood and get it burning. Damp wood burns cold and smoky and is what gives wood burning a bad name. If you find you have damp wood, check your woodpile, perhaps rain or snow has been getting on the wood. Maybe you have a leak in your wood shed roof or your tarp has a hole in it. If you find a wet section in your woodpile, work around it and just use the dry wood. Maybe the wet wood will dry enough to be usable before the end of the season or save it for next year.

Lighting the Impossible Wood Fire

First off, you should not be burning wood that is really too wet to burn cleanly. There are only two reasons for doing so, one is if you have a load of half burned wood in the firebox and you have to get rid of it or you only have wet wood and are freezing. Smoking wood that did not burn can relight and burn on its own hours later. I think we have all at one point or another poured water over a camp fire until the wood was soaking wet and went to sleep only to be awakened hours later by a roaring fire. Once a piece of wood has been exposed to fire there is a chance that there is a smoldering ember inside it that may later burst into flame. It would be foolish to take smoky pieces of wood and put them back on the woodpile, for if they were to relight later your whole woodpile would go up, in one huge fire that would take anything nearby with it. To get rid of wood that would not burn, you would need a metal tub that you could transfer it to from the firebox and then place the tub outside away from anything that can burn. Embers can smolder inside wood for days, the only way to be really sure is wait a good week or more, or fill the tub with water. Since wood that refused to burn when you wanted it to, can be such an unpredictable problem, it is often better to burn it in the firebox to get rid of it. If there is not enough room to build a dry wood fire in the firebox or you do not have any dry wood, here are a few tricks. What you need of course is a good bed of hot coals, one way of getting this is to use charcoal. Shovel in some charcoal that can be lit with a match and work it down between the wood pieces towards the grate if you have one. Light the fire and let it burn hot, hopefully it will be hot enough to burn off the wet wood. You may have to repeat the process a few times to burn off really wet wood. If you do not have any charcoal, I know the temptation is to use an accelerant, which is a fancy word for gasoline, oil or lighter fluid or anything else that burns quickly and hotly. Flammable liquids are very dangerous if used in anything that burns a solid fuel for the simple reason that a solid fuel burner is not designed to burn liquids. If you were to take a can of lighter fluid and squirt it into a fire that was not burning well, the fluid if encounters a hot coal will flash. A flash over in an enclosed firebox will send a flame out the loading door if it is open, and if you are standing in front of the door spraying lighter fluid, you maybe will have much bigger problems than trying to light a fire. Even if the firebox is empty a flammable liquid can run down into the ash pan and encounter a buried hot ember, and flash back, or the flammable liquid may not find anything hot and you might light the fire just fine. However, if some of the liquid ran down into the ash pan and leaked out the ash door, and ran down on the floor and then later a spark or hot coal gets kicked out and whoosh, you suddenly have a fire that could burn down your house. There are safe ways of using liquid fuels in a wood burner, the simplest way to buy Fire Starters. Fire Starters are generally a compressed sawdust product that has been soaked in a liquid fuel or wax. These products come with directions on how to use them which is generally to place them in with the wood and light with a match. The larger sized ones can have quite a kick for jump-starting a fire since they burn hot and long (20-30 Minutes). While Fire Starters are good for getting stubborn wood to burn, at a cost as much as a dollar a use, they are simply too expensive for everyday use. Some people make their own Fire Starters by soaking a piece of wood in oil or mixing some oil with sawdust and packing it in a small cardboard box. A reusable Fire Starter is the Woodfield Cast-Iron Fire Starter ($25-30) which is sold mainly for fireplaces, also works well for wood burners that have a grate. To use the Woodfield Fire Starter you take kerosene or lighter fluid and pour it on the stone, which is mounted inside of a cast-iron tray. Once the stone has soaked up the liquid, you place it in the ash drawer towards the front, light it with a match and slide the drawer in. Leave the ash pit door open for a while. The flames from the Fire Starter should create a draft in a few minutes that will fan the flames and pull them up through the grate and into the wood. The Woodfield is the nuclear option for fire starting, it really works well and if the fire does not start, you can pull the Woodfield out and once it has cooled, reload it and use it again. A good trick with the Woodfield is to reload the kindling when using it to increase the amount of heat you are applying to the wood that does not want to burn. When putting the kerosene or lighter fluid on the Woodfield stone, be sure to do so in a safe place for handing flammable liquids like outside or in the garage, do not use flammable liquids near a wood stove or in your living room.

For those of us with our wood burners located outside or in areas outside the living areas which have a noncombustible floor where handling flammable liquids is safer to do, I do have a trick. Even in these locations simply pouring or squirting flammable liquids into a firebox is too dangerous to do. There are however safe ways of using flammable liquids in a wood burner. One way is to have a dual fuel wood burner that can burn oil as well. In some designs the oil burner can be used as a fire starter. If you have a grate, my little secret method is to take the Woodfield Fire Starter, remove the stone and use the cast-iron tray for oil. What I do is to place the empty tray in the front of the ash drawer and pour about a quarter to a third of a quart of old motor oil into the tray. I then take a square of paper toweling, fold it into thirds, lay it across the top and pat lightly into place so the bottom layer of the paper is touching the oil but not soaking in it. I then light a corner of the paper toweling with a match and gently slide the drawer closed. The paper toweling burns off and the oil will start to burn very weakly, then in several minutes after the heat of the burning paper and oil has heated the oil and created a draft, the draft will fan the oil flames and the oil will burn briskly with flames over a foot tall for about 20 minutes. The heat of the oil flames are incredible and will start just about anything to burning. Since oil does not ignite very easily, if the fire fails to take, you can pull out the drawer and pour another shot of oil into the tray, replace the paper toweling and relight it for another try. Even if the wood does not burn, the oil itself gives off some noticeable heat by itself.

While probably one of the most primitive ways of burning oil for heat, it does work.

Getting the Firewood

Firewood for use as backup fuel is very different than wood for fuel for everyday heating. For everyday use wood needs to be affordable or using it for heating is not going to be. While fuel for backup heat is an investment in the future and can be worth paying more for. Fuel that you are going to store for future use should store well so you do not have to keep using it and replacing it. Rotten buggy wood can heat a home but is not going to last long if it is not used soon. Ideally, wood put away for possible emergency use should be good quality wood free of rot or bugs so it will store well for years. Manufactured firewood such as pressed sawdust logs and wood briquettes or even bags of charcoal are excellent for backup emergency use. They are designed so if they do not sell, they can sit for years on store shelves any out any problem. A stack or pallet of manufactured firewood can be stored indoors without making a mess since there is no problem with insects coming out of the wood and no bark mess. Having an emergency fuel supply stored indoors can be convenient even if you are burning wood everyday, as an emergency alternative when you can't use wood from your wood pile like in the middle of a blizzard or if the tarp blew off and the whole pile got soaking wet.

Wood for everyday heating of course needs to be inexpensive. In many areas you can pay to have cut dried firewood delivered and sometimes even stacked where you want it. However, it will cost you. In hard times, people selling firewood are often selling for less, so we may see prices drop for firewood. Firewood is sold by the Cord, which is a pile of stacked wood eight feet long, four feet high and four feet deep, which is a volume of 128 cubit feet, containing about 85 to 110 cubit feet of solid wood, the rest being the air between the stacked pieces of wood. A face cord is firewood stacked four feet high and eight feet long but with no depth measure measurement, so depending on how long the pieces are, a face cord can be anything from a half cord to next to nothing. Never buy face cords, unless you can see the wood and can accurately gauge what you are paying for. The national average price for firewood I recently heard was about $250 a cord, which would put the cost of heating with wood, close to current cost of heating with natural gas. However, with times being what they are, the price per cord will probably drop closer to $100. A wet cord can weigh four tons and a dry cord weighs about two tons for oak. A cord is equal to 4 and 3/4 cubit yards, but if it is dumped into a truck bed instead of stacked, it will be about 175 cubic feet or six and half cubit yards. A pickup truck will hold about a fifth to a half of a cord of stacked wood, if just thrown in, a good bit less. If you are buying wood by volume ether by cords or truck loads, you will get more wood if it is unsplit since a lot of little pieces will take up more space than a few larges ones and unsplit wood will also generally be cheaper. The best deals on delivered firewood are generally a full truckload of random length logs, of course then you will have to cut to length, split and stack.

Firewood is cheaper the more work you are willing to do yourself rather than paying to have it done for you. The cheapest wood is wood you cut yourself, if you do not spend too much doing it. Some people buy a truck for cutting and hauling wood home, which is ludicrous since the truck will rust away before you could save enough money to pay for it. If you need to haul wood, and have a mid-size car or larger, install a hitch and buy a trailer for hauling wood. A trailer is far cheaper than a truck and should last far longer. A trailer that is 4 by 8 feet with two-foot high sides with a two-ton capacity could carry half a cord. A wheelbarrow for carrying out the wood is very handy since you will seldom be able to drive up to the tree you are cutting and you would probably drop it on the car any way, and the wheelbarrow should fit mounted to the front wall of the trailer above the hitch. In the trunk, you can carry your gas chain saw, gas, oil, wedges, splitting maul, hardhat-face shield-earmuffs, leather gloves and files for sharpening the saw, plus spare chains.

If you live on wooded land, you may not even need a trailer. You maybe able to cut all the wood you need right at home. Temperate forests produce firewood at the rate of one cord per year per acre. Trees don't live forever, so every woods has some dead trees, by clearing out the dead trees you can clean up the woods and reduce the amount of potential fuel for forest fires. Forest fires are much more destructive if the forest is loaded with dead wood; dead wood feeds a fire and makes it burn hotter. Many live trees can sometimes survive a small fire, but will be burned to ash in a larger one. Selective clearing of dead wood reduces the risk of fire and improves a forest. Dead trees are where the animals live, so leave the dead ones without branches that have holes in trunk, for each hole is somebody's home. The first wood to take is the fallen logs, trees rot faster when they are on the ground, so you want to take this wood first before it is too rotten to burn. Just kick the log with your heel, if it breaks apart or mashes it is pretty much gone. Rotten wood cuts and splits easy, but has a lot less heat in it than good wood. After the logs, clean up dead branches, this way you will have cleared out the debris and will have room to work in the woods. Now locate the dead trees and size them up. Some dead trees will be dangerous, in that they maybe leaning towards power wires or a building. If you are new to cutting trees, you may want to start with easy trees and work up to the hard ones.

I will talk you through the basic steps in cutting down trees, but you will probably want to read some books on woodcutting with some well-illustrated step-by-step pictures and a good video on it. The basic premise is to make a horizontal cut into the tree about two thirds of the way through so that the center of balance of the tree is forward of the back of the cut. The center of balance is the point that if tree was cut all the way through, and a steel pin was put there, the tree would balance on it without tipping over. For a prefect tree, this point is the exact center of the tree trunk. Most trees are not perfect; they grow towards the light, are shaded unequally by other trees and lose branches unequally. Often times the center of balance is located several feet outside of the tree trunk, as is the case with a leaning tree. To balance a tree you need to look up at it from all sides and mentally weigh the branches and estimate where the balance point is, for where the balance point is; is where the tree wants to fall. Ideally, you want to cut a leaning tree to drop the way it is leaning, but often they are leaning over something. The really bad ones are best dropped in pieces, which means working up in the air. Trees that have been dead for a while are not safe to climb; sometimes you can stand a ladder against them and reach what you need. Another trick is to climb a good tree next to the dead one and reach over with a tree trimmer and saw and nip off the branches one by one. If the tree is not too big, you can even cut the trunk down in sections with a tree trimmer from a neighboring tree. I had to take down a dead elm this way that was by the house and leaning over the power line, it works but it is not easy. If you are able to remove the upper branches, controlling the drop of the tree is much easier since you have lowered the center of gravity.

My big trick for controlling the drop of a tree is to put an extension ladder up against the tree and tie a heavy rope on the tree as high as I can get it and tie the other end to a car. I have a 100-foot rope so the car can be far from the tree and I can route the rope around another tree so I can pull the tree I am cutting in the direction I want it to go which is not always toward the car. Once I have the rope tied in the tree I put the ladder away and route the rope to the car. Then I make the first cut normally two thirds of the way through the tree and cut a second cut just above it angled down to meet it at the back of the cut, cutting free a wedge of wood. This wedge cut is what will allow the tree to fall. Next, I move the car to put some tension on the rope. I believe that I can put about 500 -1000 pounds tension on the rope before it breaks which I have done a few times. Now comes the fun part, back cutting the tree. Back cutting is making a second horizontal cut starting on the backside of the tree a few inches above the wedge cut. The amount of distance above the wedge cut is your hinge. You normally do not want to cut into the back of the wedge cut or the tree will drop on the saw and bind it, and pivot on it as the tree falls. With no raised lip from a raised back-cut there is nothing to keep the tree trunk from kicking back as the tree falls, and the worst part is that you would be standing right there holding the saw. By cutting the back-cut 2 to 10 inches above the wedge cut, you leave some wood to hold the tree, so when it is ready to go, you have time to back away from the tree and the raised shelf formed by the back cut gives the falling tree something to push against as it falls. The depth of back-cut usually needs to be cut just past the top of the wedge cut or close to it. If the wood grain in between the two cuts is not severed by one of the cuts, the tree will have to bend and then tear the wood fibers in half. While a small amount of uncut hinge fibers, can nicely anchor the tree trunk while the tree is falling on its branches, if it is too thick, the tree will close the wedge cut and stop at that angle when the hinge wood fibers do not tear. The fix is to take a saw and carefully and evenly slowly cut the hinge while standing to one side, and watch the tree. She will start to move, as the fibers start giving way and that is when you back away from the tree.

Once the tree is on the ground, nip off the small twigs, and use a hand bow saw to cut up the branches into lengths that will fit in your firebox for kindling. If you do not want kindling, cut the branches off with a hand or chainsaw, at the point where you feel that they are too small for firewood; throw the branches on a brush pile. A brush pile is very handy to have, great place to throw tree trimmings too small for kindling or that you just do not have time to cut up right now, and is a great place for small animals. I have a family of woodchucks living in my brush pile, now if they would just stay out of the garden. What you have to watch for when cutting branches is that when the tree fell, some of the branches were compressed like springs and will spring back as soon as the weight is light enough for them to do so. Which is why I start with the branches first. The ones underneath the tree are the ones you have to watch out for. Always cut a spring-loaded branch on the outside of the bend, for if you try to cut on the inside, the wood as it moves will bind the saw. Stand clear of the path the branch will take when you cut the bend, for the two ends will kick out. Some of the branches will be unreachable underneath the tree and you will have to deal with them later. Once the branches are cleared up, then you can cut the tree trunk into sections short enough to fit in your firebox. Greenwood is harder to split, so you may want to wait until the wood is dry; but I usually give it a try. The splitting maul to have is the Friskars splitting maul; it has a cutting edge like a knife and runs circles around everything else. A wood grenade-splitting wedge is handy as well. Then stack the cut wood or load it into a wheelbarrow and walk it to your woodpile or trailer.

Cutting dead trees is a lot easier than cutting green living trees. The small branches will often have fallen off and the tree when it falls will be far less likely to become entangled in other trees. Once the tree is on the ground, there are a lot less branches to clean up and the branches are dry and break rather than bend so there are no spring-loaded branches and the wood splits a lot easier and is often nearly dry already. Dead elms are particularly good once they have been dead two or three years, they still have most of the heat left in the wood and the wood has weaken enough that it actually splits fairly well. If you have a tree that dies and needs to be removed, but is just about impossible to do so, sometimes you can leave the tree to rot and let the branches drop off. Then when the tree is not so top heavy, it will be easier to handle and less work to cut and saw.

Handling Wood Cutting Disasters

If you just cut a tree and it got hung up in another tree, here is what you do. If the tree is not too heavy, you may be able to pull it with a rope. If you pulled it over with a rope you may be able to reroute the rope and try pulling the tree off the tree is hung up on, by pulling towards the side or even backwards if there is room for it to fall that way. When a tree falls into another it often drops into a valley between two branches and the only way it can come out is to pull it back up and the tree is normally way too heavy to do that. Therefore, you can try pulling with a rope on the cut end of the tree trunk, if the tree is over far enough and you are pulling with a car, you may get it clear. If you cannot, there is another way, it is tricky but can be done. What you do is cut the tree trunk most of the way through from the bottom side as high up as you can comfortably reach with the saw. The tree should keep the cut open and not bind the saw, so you should be able to cut nearly all the way through, but leave a little bit that you can break. Now with a rope tied just above the cut, pull the trunk forward toward the tree it is hung up in. When the trunk breaks at the cut, it will swing forward and drop towards the ground. If it hits the ground, you will have to cut off another section. Once the tree is close enough to the other tree, it maybe vertical enough for you to pull it back if you have a rope up on the top, or you can pull the tree towards the other tree even more by cutting the trunk nearly through once more. When the cut breaks, the trunk will pass underneath the tree and while you keep pulling it forward with the car maybe 5 or 10 feet before the end hits the ground. The tree will now be leaning the other way, away from the tree it was hung up in, and will now fall back from where you cut it. If you have shortened the trunk enough, it will fall short of whatever was on the other side of the tree you were trying to avoid hitting in the first place.

A Few Safety Points on Cutting Trees

Cutting trees is dangerous and some of the things I have described doing are quite dangerous and you should be extremely cautious if you value your life. Learn how to use your saw, read the manual cover to cover and follow the safety precautions. Always wear a hard hat when dropping trees, dead branches high up are called "widow makers" for a reason. Wear eye and ear protection as well, a chip in the eye at the wrong time could cost you more than just an eye. Wear leather gloves to protect your hands and good leather work shoes to protect your feet and to give you good traction when you need it. Clear the brush where you are cutting so you can move freely, so if you have to move quickly, you can. Watch out for what is overhead; keep an eye out for power lines, dead branches or anything else that could fall on you. As the tree starts to fall, keep your eye on the branches in case something breaks loose and springs out. Cut your hinges well and carefully back away from the tree so you are a good distance way, so if the trunk kicks out it does not hit you. If working alone, always try to let someone know where you are going and what you are doing, and carry a cell phone if you have one, so you can call for help if you get pinned. Always always, think about what you are doing, if you are getting fuzzy with fatigue, it is time to put the saw away.

Operation of a Wood Stove or Fireplace Insert

There is a lot more to operating a wood stove or a fireplace insert than lighting a fire, with any new wood burner there is a teething process. It will take awhile for you to get a feel for the amount of heat a given fire will give off and how much heat your house needs at different outside temperatures. A roaring fire that is just right for January may cook you out of the house in April. When building fires, check the temperature in the house and note how many degrees you wish to raise the temperature, and look to check the outside temperature so you can see how much cold you are working against and you may even have to consider the wind, for some homes lose much more heat due to drafts on windy days. Even the wind direction can have an effect since your house maybe sheltered from the wind in some directions and not in others. If you check these things each time you make a fire, you will begin to develop some general guidelines for yourself on how much wood to throw in the firebox. Today's EPA approved wood stoves and inserts are incredible. The flexibility in heat output while maintaining a clean burn is just plain great. However, even with these new wonders, you can only turn them down so low, so even if the house is hot, you are still going to get heat until the wood is burned up and the stove has cooled down. The heat from a stove or insert is going to be concentrated right around it; even with a stove fan, the heat will be largely confined to the room where the stove or insert is located. Moving heat to other parts of the house is a problem that some try to solve with fans mounted in door ways and leaving doors open. The real way to move the heat around the house if you have a forced air system, is to turn the furnace blower fan on. Many thermostats have a fan switch, just slide the fan switch to "On" and the blower will run until you slide the switch back to "auto". To increase the furnace blower moving the heated air, insure that the hot air is free to flow to the cold air return grill. If you have central AC you may have a warm air return up by the ceiling, which you can open, to pull hot air into the ductwork so it can be spread throughout the house.

In larger homes or poorly insulated homes, one wood stove or insert is not going to be able to maintain temperature in cold winters no matter how much wood you throw in it. You should find out what it can keep warm by itself, so if the power goes off, you will know what it can do, and what it cannot. If one stove or insert cannot keep the place warm, consider insulating rather than just adding more stoves.

One teething problem with wood stoves is smoke, you are probably going to notice smoke in the house when you first start burning wood. Smoke will be less of a problem with inserts due to the fact that inserts are never installed with smoke pipe dampers and generally have well drafting chimneys. Wood stoves are often installed with stovepipe barometric dampers, which are often not needed and can be a real problem with releasing smoke inside the house. My advice is to install an EPA wood stove without any stovepipe dampers and use the inlet dampers on the stove to control the draft and see how the stove operates. If the stove tends to overheat because the chimney is very tall and the draft is excessive, then install a barometric damper to reduce the draft. On shorter chimneys the stovepipe dampers are not needed and with weak drafts, down drafting will blow a puff of smoke right out through the opening on the barometric damper. Despite what you may have seen on TV or with other wood stoves, do not expect to be able to open the loading door on a roaring fire and not expect to get smoke in the house. Unless you have a really good draft, smoke will tend to spill out the door if it is opened when the fire is smoky. One way of improving the draft is to add a 4-inch fresh air inlet near the stove or insert, which helps with smoking by eliminating any vacuum in the house caused by the stove draft pulling air out of the house. The draft can also be improved by increasing the height of the chimney or installing a chimney cap with an inducer fan to pull the smoke out. Regular chimney caps can help by reducing down drafting caused by the wind spilling over objects nearby that are higher than your chimney. The real trick to keeping the smoke in the stove, is to keep the door closed. Load the wood, light the fire, close the door and keep it closed until you need to add more wood. If you do not have a window in the door to see the fire, put a stovepipe magnetic thermometer over the door. Magnets only work up to about 1000 degrees F because the heat causes the molecules to vibrate so vigorously that the alignment of the crystals is disrupted and the magnetic field collapses. You want the thermometer over the door, so if you get the stove really hot and the magnet gets weak and the now 1000 degree magnet falls, it will rest on the top of the door rather than falling to the floor and maybe rolling off the stove pad and ending up laying on something that could burn. The idea here with the thermometer is the temperature will tell you what the firing is doing and you will not have to open the door as much to check.

If the smoke is not getting out of the stove and you can still smell it, start sniffing around and see if you can find where it is coming from. Check each stovepipe joint. Smokey joints can be sealed with furnace cement or foil tape. Check your chimney for leaks as well. The most probably source for smoke in the house is reentry from outside. If the smoke coming out the chimney top is being down drafted next to the house, extending the chimney is the traditional answer and is probably your best bet on fixing the problem.

Operating a Wood Furnace or an Indoor Boiler

While a furnace is basically just a stove in a metal ductwork box, the two are really totally different animals all together. While stoves are for a nice fire in the evening, furnaces & boilers are for heating the house 24-7. Stoves are fun, furnaces & boilers are workhorses. The average stove owner makes a fire now and then, but even if he makes a fire "all the time" he really is not heating that much. Starting with an already warm house, an evening fire does not take much wood and even heating all day on the weekend is still only 2 days out of seven. Furnaces take the whole load and carry it. The average wood furnace owner heats 100% with wood and only uses other heat for backup. The difference in usage means that the typical stove or insert owner only needs a cord or two for "heating" his house with wood, since most of this heat is still coming from the gas company. A wood furnace owner is going to need cords and cords of wood to make it through the winter. Here in Wisconsin, with a very well insulated modest home, you will need 3 to 4 cords for the winter, while a house with average insulation will need 6-10 cords. Therefore, to operate a wood furnace you are going to need tons of wood. Boilers will still need tons of wood as well, but not as much as a furnace, and sometimes as little as half. The huge advantage boilers have, is of being able to store heat in hot water. The heat that is wasted when a furnace over heats the house because of putting too much wood in, a boiler can store for latter use. By including a large hot water tank in the system, wood boilers can be fired once a day with a hot clean burning efficient fire and the heat is stored in the system to be drawn on as needed and delivered to where it is needed in the home. This flexibility gives boilers an enormous advantage.

Since you will be moving tons of firewood, it makes sense to have a good plan for doing so. In my case, I have a wood furnace in the basement and have a garage door in the basement wall, which allows me to walk in a wheelbarrow of wood and park it a few feet away from the furnace. I have the woodpile 20 or 30 feet out the door, so bringing in wood is easy. Moreover, by keeping the wood in the wheelbarrow until it goes in the furnace, I keep the wood off the floor and reduce the mess. With furnaces and boilers, you need some kind of direct access for firewood. Other options some people use are to make a wood chute with a locking door at the top and a wood bin at the bottom. One way to install a wood chute door is to use a basement window and if necessary deepen the window opening and install a deep window well. The door swings out and downward and rests on the lip of the window well acting as an extension of the chute. The chute is made of plywood covered in galvanized sheet metal with a two by four wood frame, as is the wood bin. Another option is if you have outside cellar steps is to lay a narrow ramp with a lip on each side for walking a wheelbarrow up and down the steps. The last thing you want to do is to have to carry every piece of wood in a firewood carry by hand to the house, in through the door, down the stairs and over to the wood bin.

Now with actually heating your house with wood rather than just supplementing, if you try to keep the house warm all the time you are going to burn a lot more wood. It makes sense to let the temperature drop at night when every one is warm in bed and it is coldest outside, and would otherwise burn the most wood. Let the house temperature drop down to about 50-60 F at night, and make a large fire in the morning. This will be the big fire for the day, you are going to try to raise the house temperature by about ten to twenty degrees working against the coldest part of the morning, unless you are a late riser. I light my fire at 5 AM as soon as I wake up. I loaded it the night before and need only light the kindling. Then I get ready for work and at 5:30 AM, and I check the fire on the way out. I close the ash door, which I leave open for lighting, and I head off to work. The fire will take two to three hours to bring the house up to about 72 degrees. Then the house will slowly begin to cool and in cold weather, a second fire will be needed in the afternoon. Once the temperature has dropped to 68, I light a fire with enough wood to bring the temperature back up to 72. Sometimes I fall short and have to add more wood to the hot coals and sometimes I overshoot and the house temperature goes up into the high seventies. If it is really freezing outdoors, I may even need a third fire in the evening, but I do not like to burn in the evening, so that I have time to clean and load the stove for the morning fire before I go to bed. I am able to space out my fires because I have insulated the house and now have R-20 walls and R-99 attic insulation. Before I increased the insulation, I had to keep a fire going constantly to keep the house warm. Back then, in the morning I checked to see if I had any hot coals left and I just threw more wood in or I started a new fire, which I tried to keep going all day. The problem was constant firing always ended up overheating the house and wasting a lot of wood. I find I have much better control now and use far less wood and my burns are much more efficient. Some wood furnace owners have old drafty homes and like it that way, since they lose enough heat that control is just a matter of throwing in the wood as fast as you can. Of course, they need to have just about an endless supply of wood and if the fire goes out the house gets cold very fast. Boiler owners rise above all these petty little problems of furnace owners since they merely have to keep the water hot and let the system heat the house. Boiler owners will probably need to make a fire in the morning unless they have enough heat storage in the system to handle bringing the house back up to temperature as they come off the nighttime setback. The morning fire will heat the system back up and there will hopefully be enough heat stored in the system and in the house to make it through the day until the next morning. If later in the day the system water temperature has dropped, a fire is made to bring it back up. By allowing the system temperature, to drop from a high temperature like 180 F to a low one like 110, a sizable fire can be made that will burn hot and clean to bring it back up. With the system back up to about 180 again and the house warmed up, the system can idle along for hours until the water has cooled off again. By insulating the house to reduce heat loss and having enough water in the system to store heat, you may only need to make one fire a day if that. While many claims have been made for how long an outdoor boiler can go between fires and ease of use, the indoor boilers are the real performers.

In power outages, wood furnaces can normally supply some heat if the ductwork rises from the furnace to the living spaces above. Read your manual on power outage heating procedures and follow the directions. Now if you have improved the natural heat flow by adding furnace bypass ducts or oversized ductwork, you may be able to safely make bigger fires than what the manual states. But keep an eye on things so you do not overheat anything. With boilers you can heat up the water if you can operate with a natural draft, and with hot water in the pipes you will hopefully get some heat upstairs and at the very least, the pipes cannot freeze if you keep them hot. I would suggest that you turn off the power to your furnace or boiler some cold winter day, and see how your system works without power. That way if your system does not perform as well as you would like, you will have a chance to improve it or add a wood stove before you really need it.

Operating an Outdoor Water Boiler

Though OWBs have been pretty thoroughly demonized, they can be an idea heating system for some. I have one about 500 feet up wind of my house and I really cannot complain much. My one and only complaint would be that I can smell the smoke because my neighbor has a short chimney and the exhaust gases follows the ground. If my neighbor had a taller stack I mite not even have noticed that the OWB was there. Now if my neighbor starts burning wet green wood or plastic trash, my attitude could become decidedly more negative. That is the most important thing with OWBs, getting a clean burn so you are not smoking up the neighborhood. Hopefully you have an EPA approved OWB which if used correctly will produce little visible smoke. Old non-EPA approved OWBs can be operated in ways to greatly reduce amount of smoke that they vent. We have already discussed how to improve the efficiency of an OWB by improving its design but even the best designs are all for naught if an OWB is not used right. An OWB is not a trash incinerator nor despite some manufactures claims to the contrary, you cannot burn wet wood efficiently or cleanly. Wood burning OWBs are designed to burn dry clean wood, burning anything else can make for a very smoky OWB. You can cleanly burn old wood like pallets, if the wood is dried before it is burned. Cut and stack the wood in a woodshed or under a vented tarp and let it air dry a few months before burning.

Now even burning dry clean wood, OWBs will make more smoke if they idle. Do not run an OWB in the non-heating season, if you need an alternative summer time water heater put in a solar hot water system. Do not overload the OWB with too much wood, if you over shoot on the wood, the OWB will of course go into the idle mode and the non-EPA models will pump out a lot of smoke. If your OWB smokes badly with good wood even when running hot, you have a problem and really need to improve the efficiency as was discussed, or you need to replace it. Some OWBs have a huge water capacity and store a lot of heat, if the heating load isn't too large, the OWB can be fired and the water brought up to temperature perhaps one or twice a day and the fire allowed to burn out. This way idling is avoided. You can also do your burning after dark or before sunrise if the start up smoke is a problem. With smaller capacity OWBs or

OWBs with large heating loads, large tanks can be installed in the building to be heated. The idea is to fully load the OWB so it is running hot and clean, and then store the heat so the OWB does not even have a fire burning most of the time. Due to the time lag of having to heat up large amounts of water before any real heating takes place, the OWB should be fired up when the temperature of the water is getting low in the tank, before heat is needed in the house. Otherwise there will be a considerable time lag before the house begins to feel warm again.

If an OWB is sized correctly, in cold weather it will be fully loaded and a hot fire will be burning constantly, just do not overload the firebox with wood. Some OWBs have vastly oversized fireboxes in which most of the wood smokes rather than burns because there simply is not enough air flowing through to feed a large enough fire and if there was, it would damage the OWB. This problem can be overcome simply by limiting the amount of wood that is loaded into the firebox. Through trial and error find out how much wood you can load without excessive smoking, and keep your wood load at or below that amount.

Monitoring the operation of an OWB can be tricky since it is outside. Checking the hot water line from the unit is one way, a remote digital temperature sensor mounted on the OWB with a display unit right in the house would be very convenient. But so far no one seems to make a thermometer that would work well for an OWB. What some OWB owners do is to mount a remote wireless smoker or barbecue thermometer on the hot water supply pipe from the OWB where it enters the house. Just strap the probe to the PEX line and cover with insulation so the probe is warmed to the water temperature. The remote unit often has a 100 foot range and some models can be set with high and low alarms to let you know if the OWB water temperature has dropped because the fire is out or is going too high because the OWB is overheating. Maybe you left the ash door open? But the simplest method is to watch the chimney, with most OWBs the fire is out, if you cannot see any smoke.

Chimney Sweeping

Some occupations require long apprenticeships or many years of college to learn, chimney sweeping is not one of them. Do not get me wrong, chimney sweeping is a skilled trade, a good sweep is invaluable. But sweeping a simple home chimney is not rocket science and is easy to learn how to do. The two areas where you can really need the skills of a good chimney sweep are chimney inspection and repair. I would suggest that if in doubt, have your chimney cleaned, inspected and repaired if needed. But learn to do the routine cleaning. Unfortunately there are a fair number of crooks in the chimney sweeping business as well. The standard tactic is cold calling and offering low prices for an inspection and then telling you that you need to have some expensive repair work done. If you need a chimney sweep, ask around if anyone knows a good one, or look one up in the phone book and check with the Better Business Bureau. (http://www.bbb.org/) Expect to pay about $100 - 200 for cleaning a chimney. Many chimney sweeps now also clean dryer vents to remove lint buildup to prevent fires and charge about $100 for this. This should clue you in on chimney sweeps. They often charge big bucks for simple jobs that you could do yourself in less than an hour.

A chimney can be swept from the top or sometimes from the bottom. Cleaning from the top is far easier if you can safely reach the top of the chimney. You will need a ladder to reach the roof, and will hopefully be able to walk up to the chimney and look down inside while standing on the roof. If the chimney is at the peak, and the roof is too steep to walk up, a ladder with hooks can be pushed up the roof so the hooks catch on the other side of the peak. If the chimney is at the peak and is too tall, a stepladder can sometimes be placed next to the chimney and opened to stand level with one side resting on one side of the roof and the other on the other side of the roof. Ladders should not be leaned against tall narrow chimneys as the sideways pressure of the ladder and the weight of the person on the ladder, maybe enough to push the chimney over. A chimney is a stack of bricks or stones with cement between the stones. If there are any cracks in the cement, the only thing holding the chimney pieces together is gravity. Cement is not known for its tensile strength, a sideways force on a tall chimney is lifting the side towards the ladder apart as the chimney tries to tip over, and the taller the chimney the more leverage there is on the joints. Carefully judge the weight and strength of any chimney you are thinking of putting a ladder up against. To reach the top of tall chimneys that are located at outside walls, a tall step ladder standing on the ground may be the best bet or scaffolding may need to be set up. If you do not have a ladder that will do the job, you should consider buying one since you will need it regularly for cleaning your chimney.

To clean the chimney from the top, you will need a steel bristled chimney sweeping brush the size and shape of your flue. (Chimneys with stainless steel flues are cleaned with nylon brushes.) Square flues need square brushes and round flues need round brushes. The brush will have a threaded fitting on the top for attaching fiberglass threaded rods to the brush. You will need enough threaded rods to reach from the top of your chimney cap to the bottom of the ash pit in the basement. You will also need a good quality dust mask and coveralls or clothes you don't mind getting dirty and can thrown into an empty washer to wash as soon as you are done since they will be too dirty to go into the regular laundry. To clean your chimney, the fire has to be out, not even warm ashes or the warm draft will lift dust into your face while you sweep. The loading door, ash door and all openings must be closed. Barometric dampers should be sealed and the chimney ash pit door should be closed. To clean, put on the coveralls, mask and screw a section of rod on the brush and grab the rods together in one hand. This does leave you only one hand to climb the ladder with, if you have much of a climb, you may want to consider making or buying a bag like holder for the rods that can go over your shoulder like a quiver for arrows. Climb to the chimney top and insert the brush down inside the flue. The brush should fit tightly and it should take some pressure to push it down, if it is loose in the chimney it is too small for the flue and will not clean the chimney. Push the rod down half way, screw on the next rod and push down again, repeat for the next section of rod. Keep doing this until the brush hits the bottom. The brush will go down with the same resistance until you hit an obstruction. You may hit a protruding mortar joint, a build up of creosote, brick or cement chunk. Work the brush up and down over any obstructions to see if you can gently knock them down, but do not hit them too hard in case they turn out to be something that should stay. You may discover old cemented over thimbles from old stoves that used to be on an upper floor or old chimney repairs. The first expected obstruction you should encounter is the thimble that you are using.

Push the brush pass the thimble down towards the ash pit. Your chimney may not have an ash pit and the flue may simply end just below the thimble, and even when there is an ash pit it is often unlined. The open space may be narrower than the flue and it may not be possible or wise to force the brush into the pit. Once the brush has gone as far as it will go, you may want to remove the stove pipe from the thimble and look in with a light to see if the brush has indeed passed the thimble or if it has hit something above it. If you have a problem, use a large size inspection mirror and a light to look up or down the chimney from the thimble to see what it is. Once you have the brush down to the thimble, start pulling it back out. You may want to take the rod apart as you pull it out, but always be very careful to firmly hold the rod below as you unscrew the rod above, otherwise you may unwittingly unscrew the rod at a fitting down inside the chimney and you will have to fish for the brush to get it back out. When moving the brush always keep some clockwise twisting pressure on the rod to keep it from being unscrewed. Now if the chimney is not too tall and if nothing much is nearby, you may be able to leave the sections screwed together as you pull them out. Once the brush reaches the top, send it back down to the bottom and repeat a few times until little dust comes out of the chimney top when the brush is coming up. If you find that you have to take the brush apart, to avoid having to constantly keep taking it apart and putting it back together again, clean by brushing up and down with each section as you add it until that part of the chimney is clean before you put the next section on. So by the time the brush is at the bottom of the chimney, the entire chimney is clean. I find pulling the brush up and down the entire length of the chimney easier than sweeping bit by bit; the reason for this is it is hard to reverse the brush, as the wires have to flex the other way.

Once the chimney is clean, put the brush way and get ready to clean the stove pipe. The best way of cleaning stove pipe is to remove it from the chimney thimble and the outlet connector on the stove in one piece and carefully carry it outside. You may need to cover the floor with a drop cloth or tarp and may need to cover the ends of the stove pipe as well so soot doesn't spill out on the floor on the way out. Once outside, inspect the inside of the pipe. You will probably find a thick layer of black soot. The fastest way of getting rid of soot, is to take a hose and flush it out with water. If there is any creosote buildup in the stove pipe, you will have to disassemble the stove pipe into sections so you can put a round steel wire brush through or so you can reach in with a wire hand brush. A putty knife can be handy for prying out thick deposits. A trick here is to flex the pipe, since thin sheet metal is flexible and creosote is not. Flexing will cause the creosote to fall off the inside of the pipe in large pieces. The straight sections will flex clean very well, the elbows will not flex as well and it will be tricky chipping out the creosote from the folds in the elbows. While cleaning, inspect the stove pipe for rust and holes, there is no point to struggling with a hard to clean stove pipe that has to be replaced anyway.

After the stove pipe is clean, clean the thimble and inspect the chimney flue by looking in through the thimble with a light and mirror. If you have an ash pit with a door, you can open the door and shovel out the soot and creosote. What works nice is to place a dust pan against the chimney on the floor and use an ash shovel or large putty knife to shovel the ash out on to the dust pan. Have a trash can handy with a heavy duty plastic trash bag to dump the dust pan into. Lower the pan down inside the trash can so you are making as little dust as possible. Keep air currents down inside the house so you are not blowing soot around and keep the kids and pets away. I left the glass doors open on my fireplace one time and my white cat decided to check it out, at least he was white when he went in and he was white again after a bath. Soot is not just messy it is also unhealthy so be careful when handling it.

If you do not have an ash pit door, but have an ash pit, you can clean it out from the thimble. If it is shallow, you can shovel it out with a spoon if need be, but if it is deep you will need a shop vac. A good shop vac is fantastic for cleaning out ash pits and fireboxes and ash drawers. The problem is once you have used a shop vac this way, you will probably not want to use it for anything else. The vac will get so dirty it will be fit for little else. By feeding the hose in through the thimble and down into the ash pit you can vacuum the pit clean.

Give the stove a good cleaning, clean the flue connector with a brush and putty knife if need be and clean out the firebox and ash drawer if you have one. Remove any access plates and clean any secondary heat exchangers or other hard to reach areas. Once the stove is clean put the stove pipe back, reconnect it, and seal any lose joints.

What did you find? If the chimney and stove pipe had only some fine ash you are doing great. Soot collects at any cold spots; you may have found some at the end of the stove pipe just before the chimney and maybe at the top of the chimney. To keep soot from collecting you need to try burning hotter and cleaner, so there is less soot in the exhaust and the exhaust gases are hotter, so the pipe and chimney are hotter and so any soot in the exhaust gases does not find a cold spot to collect in. Low firing creates more soot, and non-EPA approved wood burners on low fire with reduced air intake, soot up really bad and can pack a stove pipe nearly solid with soot in as little as two or three months. Even EPA approved wood burners produce some soot and will produce more on low firings. It is best to run hot and size the wood load to run out when you are up to temperature. Another common soot pattern is the stove pipe is clean from the stove to the barometric damper and sooty from it to the chimney. What is happening is the damper is letting in too much cold room air and the exhaust gases are being chilled and with the temperature drop, the soot drops out. The cure is to adjust the damper so less air gets in, or get rid of the damper. This will increase the draft on the wood burner, which could result in over firing, so you will have to either leave it in and just clean the stove pipe more often, or take it out and just keep the air inlet dampers on the wood burner adjusted to allow less air in compensating for the increased draft.

If you found creosote in the chimney, you can clean a thin layer by making a scraper if you have a square tile flue. Take some sheet metal and cut a piece narrow enough to fit in the flue but about a half inch longer than the flue is wide. Drill a hole in the middle of the piece and bolt it on to the threaded fitting on the end of one of the rods for the chimney sweeping brush. Push the rod down into the chimney from the top, the thin sheet metal will flex and the ends will scrape the flue. Push down to the thimble and pull back up; to come back up, the metal will have to flex from being bent one way to the other, so the metal can't be too thick or it will get stuck. Next, turn the metal scraper and do the other two sides of the square flue. Scraping only takes off thin layers and loose projections of creosote. To remove the creosote, the simplest and most effective way is to use Creosote Remover, which is a powder that once a week you sprinkle a spoon full on the wood before you light the fire. The powder chemically reacts with the creosote and turns it into a gray powder that falls into the ash pit. If you have a heavy creosote build up, use the Creosote Remover daily and check the chimney again in a month and the creosote should be gone. I use this produce regularly and it works wonders, I highly recommend that you use it to prevent creosote deposits from forming and thus greatly reducing any risk of having a chimney fire.

You can clean from the bottom of the chimney, which is sometimes the only way of reaching the insides of tall inaccessible chimneys. The cleaning is done through the thimble or ash pit door. It is not normally possible to use standard chimney sweeping brushes and rods through such small openings. Instead a chimney cleaning brush system is used that looks like a plumbing snake. Instead of rods there is a long flexible snake that comes in a coil, like the Wohler Handy Viper (http://www.wohlerusa.com) that costs about $550 and needs a brush for about another $40. The brush is put on the end and it is pushed up the chimney. Sweeping from the bottom of the chimney means that you are on the receiving end of a soot falls. Every black and sooty thing in the chimney is coming your way and you have the chimney open, which is why you will need a large drop cloth and maybe some hanging cloths to block the soot dust that may come rolling out. Bottom sweeping is very messy and while working from the top, a mask and coveralls are hardly needed, they are real necessities when working from the bottom. As you feed the brush up the chimney, you will feel a pop as the brush clears the chimney top, or feel a stop as it hits the chimney cap. Just do not push the cap up and off the chimney, caps often do not have much holding them down, a hard push with a brush will probably lift most caps right off. Once the brush is at the top, pull it back down and work it up and down as needed to knock the soot down. When the soot stops falling, that section is clean, move the brush down to do the next section.

Wood Ashes

I wanted to end this chapter with ashes since it is the logical end subject for wood burning. When a tree grows, it uses carbon dioxide from the air to bind with minerals from the soil to create wood. When you burn wood you return the carbon back to the air, and you can return the ashes to the ground. Wood ashes can be spread in gardens, on lawns and in woodlands to return the minerals back to where they came from.

Check your ashes each time you empty them from your wood burner, the color tells you how well the fire burned. A good clean fire only leaves fine white ashes as all the black carbon has been burned off. Grey ashes still have some carbon in them showing that the fire was not hot enough because there was not enough air or the wood was damp. Black ashes show a cold fire with too little air and maybe wet wood. Ashes with black lumps of charcoal is signs of hot coals falling through the grate, which can be reduced by not shaking the grate as much so the coals are not knocked into the ash drawer before they can burn.

Ash is a great insulator and a hot coal can smolder for days buried in ashes, which is why ashes should always be kept in a metal container. Many a fire has been started because someone put "cold" ashes in a cardboard box. Never stick your hand into ashes, or a hot buried coal can give you a very nasty burn. If you have been burning pallets or other wood with nails in it, remove the nails by using a large magnet, the magnets in a can with a release handle work very nice. Run the magnet through the ashes to pick up the nails and then release the nails into a pail. It best to keep ashes in a metal container with a cover to keep any embers from getting air to prevent smoke in the house and to keep the kids from getting into the ashes. The old stories about using ashes for traction on ice are true, it really works. I have a driveway on a hill and one winter I was using ashes for traction on the ice and did not notice that the driveway was wet from an earlier light rain, my car shot down the drive and flew off and hit a tree. Ashes only work on ice when dry, when wet they do not work at all, as I discovered. It took me two days to pound the dents out of the car with a sledge hammer.

Chapter 13

Coal

In 1833, Jordan Mott developed the first usable coal stove, and the age of coal began. Coal was the energy that powered the industrial revolution and heated the Victorian age. Coal steam boilers where the technological wonders of their day, supplying steam heat and high pressure steam that drove steam powered machinery of all sorts from steam powered ships to steam turbines for electrical generation which is still where largest share of our electrical power comes from today (U.S. 48.4% Jan 2009). In the US, each person uses an average of 3.8 tons of coal every year by using electricity generated by coal and by using products produced from coal or with energy from coal. The coal age never really ended, coal began the industrial age and if we ever run out of coal, it will be the end of the industrial age.

While coal remains the major industrial power source, home heating use has largely disappeared, even in coal mining areas. In many areas, coal for home use is simply not for sale. Here in Wisconsin, coal is not for sale at any retail store that I know of, and this is true for many parts of the United States as well. While home heating with coal has waned, coal-burning technology has advanced, but with residential coal burning exempt from EPA rules, evaluating the claims of different manufactures can be difficult. There are also now more ways of burning coal for home heating than ever before.

An Assortment of Coal Home Heating Methods

Coal can be burned in an open fireplace on a coal grate, which is like a large cast iron pan like grate designed to keep the coal from falling through or rolling off. Of course, with 15% efficiency, fireplaces make lousy heaters. A far better option for burning coal in a fireplace is a fireplace coal burning insert with an efficiency of about 50-65% which means about four times as much heat from the same amount of coal. Free standing coal stoves, furnaces, boilers both indoor and out are other coal heating options. Coal fired ranges and cook stoves are still sold as well. Coal heating units can be hand fed or fed automatically by a stoker mechanism that feeds a fine grade of coal to the fire from a bin.

Types of Available Coal

It does not matter if there was free green coal on the moon that burned hot and totally smoke free, since you can not get your hands on any. Just as you cannot heat your house with my imaginary moon coal, you cannot heat your house with coal if it is not available in your area. The same goes for different types of coal; some are only available at reasonable prices in limited areas. Though considering coal prices of late, I am not sure just where that limited area is anymore. Coals stoves and other coal-heating units are often built for the type of coal that is available locally where the manufacturer is located and not necessary where you are located. Therefore, it is possible to buy a coal stove only to find out that it works best on a type of coal that is not sold locally. There are five types of coal available and each type of coal is available in a range of sizes, like the different size grades of gravel. Like mined gravel, coal is a rock that is dug from the earth and broken into small usable size pieces.

Anthracite Coal

Anthracite coal is nearly pure carbon, rock hard, hard to light and burns nearly smoke free. This is the Cadillac of coals, the cleanest and hottest. Mined mainly in Pennsylvania, it is very popular in the Northeast and most stove manufacturers there and nearly all manufacturers everywhere build their stoves to burn it. Though hard to light, Anthracite is by far the best coal for heating and is particularly well suited in small grade sizes for automatic stoker coal burners. Moisture content is generally less than 15 % and being 86-98% carbon with low sulfur content, it has about 15,000 BTU per pound and with an ignition temperature of 925 F.

Bituminous Coal

An anthracite want-to-be, Bituminous coal is similar to anthracite but softer and a bit smoky but still nearly smoke free if burned correctly and a bit easier to light. This is the majority of the coal located in the United States and is the most widely available coal with the largest reserves located in wide areas from Appalachians through the Mississippi valley area, and is found in Colorado and Alaska. Bituminous coals have a range of quality with the better ones being very nearly equal to anthracite, and the lesser ones being of less quality, but of better grade than Sub-bituminous coal. The Bituminous coals with high volatile content swell or increase in size when burned and can fuse together which is called caking. Caking coal can form a bridge, which can prevent the coal from falling down towards the grate and is more of a problem in fireboxes with sloped firebrick sides and less of a problem in fireboxes with vertical firebrick walls. The moisture content is less than 20%. Bituminous coal is 45-85% carbon with high sulfur content, and produces 10,500-15,500 BTU per pound and has an ignition temperature of 765-870 F.

Sub-Bituminous Coal

Sub-bituminous coal when mined has excessive moisture and needs to be dried before burning to increase efficiency but has the advantage of having very low sulfur content in the majority of deposits in the US. The coal is widely found along the east side of the Rocky Mountains from Montana down to Arizona and east out into Colorado and Utah. Sub-bituminous is mainly mined for use as low sulfur coal for power plants and is not widely sold for home heating use. It is a bit smokier than Bituminous coal, but not nearly as smoky as lignite. Sub-bituminous has about 20-30% moisture and is 35-45% carbon with a very low sulfur content, and produces 8300 - 13000 BTU per pound and has an ignition temperature of about 750 F.

Lignite Coal

Lignite is the bottom end of coal, being only a step up from peat, even having a color that ranges from brown to black. Think of it as black compressed peat. Like peat, Lignite can hold a lot of water, about 45% or more and should be air dried down to about 20% or less before it is used as fuel. Lignite has low energy content per pound, which makes it expensive to transport, and it is susceptible to spontaneous combustion, which is why it is recommended not to pile it higher than 10 feet deep to reduce the chance of a spontaneous fire starting in the pile. Due to these problems, lignite is mostly used by power plants constructed near a lignite mine to reduce the transportation costs. Lignite also creates a lot of smoke when it burns and is very soft and breaks apart easily. Lignite is mined mainly in North Dakota and Montana. Having only 25-35% carbon, it produces 4,000-8,300 BTU per pound and has an ignition temperature of 600 F. Lignite burns more like wood than coal.

Cannel Coal

Cannel coal is an odd coal that for the most part is not even available any more if at all. It has a very high content of volatiles and is a kin to burning chunks of tar. This stuff burns like gas powered fireworks, tons of sparks and lots of bright flaming out gassing. The original use for it was burning in fireplaces for a flashy fire more like a wood fire rather than the dull glow of a coal fire. Cannel coal is not safe for use in an enclosed firebox due to the large amount of volatile gases it gives off. Cannel coal is prone to explosive flash overs and the large amounts of burning gas creates a very tall flame that reaches up the stove pipe and into the chimney and can ignite coal soot resulting in a chimney fire. It is not unusual for cannel coal to heat a stove and stovepipe to bright red heat. The strong draft created by the intensity with which cannel coal burns, will carry the many sparks it gives off, up and out the chimney. If a chimney fire is started by the Cannel coal, the high heat creates a stronger draft that fans the cannel coal into burning faster with even higher flames that pumps even more heat into the chimney fire turning your chimney into a blast furnace.

Coke and Other Coal Fuels

Coke is a produce made from coal, most often from Bituminous coal in which it is heated to a high temperature but not allowed to burn, which drives off the volatile "coal gas" which is used as a gas fuel and a chemical feedstock just as natural gas is. The resulting coke is much like a spongy version of Anthracite coal, since coke is also nearly pure carbon with ash of course. Coke can be just as hard to get a fire started as with Anthracite but will burn more readily due to its porous nature. Coke is nearly smoke free as Anthracite and can have high heat content as well. Cokes made from coals with high ash contents however will have high ash content. Petroleum cokes made from oil residues like "Petcoke" have a high acid content and have little ash, so are doubly hard on grates. Oviods and Briquettes are compressed chunks of solid fuel and can be made from coal, peat, woods, sawdust, etc, such fuel products burn very well with great consistency, generally with little smoke or ash. The coal-based products will burn like coal or charcoal, while the wood-based products will burn like wood and may not burn as well in a pure coal burner. Any processed fuel product will have a higher cost since some one has to pay for the cost of the processing. While such fuels can be very convenient, in terms of keeping heating costs down, it makes sense to use fuels in their cheapest form.

NewEarth ECO Clean Coal or E-Coal

E-coal is not really coal but is a coal substitute made from "bio-fuels" like wood and other plant material, which have been carbonized which means everything but the carbon has been removed. The company New Earth (http://newearth1.net/) sells E-Coal in four BTU/lb ratings designed to match and replace lignite, sub-bituminous, bituminous and anthracite coal. The heat output range is from 9,500 to14,500 BTU/lb at a cost of $125-210 a ton and has 2% or less ash. The low ash content could be a problem with over heating the grates on hand fired coal stoves, but otherwise this product is a "green coal" that is carbon neutral in that the carbon is not fossil carbon. While not yet available at your local store, E-coal is not the only coal replacement product out there. There are a number of products, some made with some coal as a bio-fuel & coal mix and others that like E-coal do not contain any coal at all. Just as wood pellets have entered the wood heating market, replacement coal products may soon take over part of the coal market.

Coal Grades

Coal is found in the ground in thick flat layers like limestone, and is broken up into pieces and removed from the mine. The coal then is broken into smaller pieces at a "breaker" and the pieces are sorted by size and sold under different names for the different sizes. Each size of coal chunks has its best use, and some coal burners can only use one type of coal in only one size. It pays to know what is available in your area before you buy a coal heater. All though coal is technically a stone, coal sizes are not written in stove and can vary from one suppler to the next with variation in size names and in the size range of pieces of coal in a given size. The smaller sizes used in automatic stokers are pretty consistent since if the size varied too much, it would not work in the stokers and they could not sell it.

Anthracite Sizes

Broken over 3 inches

Egg	2 5/16" - 3"
Stove	1 5/8"-2 5/16"
Nut	13/16"-1 5/8"
Pea	9/16"-13/16"
Buckwheat	5/16"-9/16"
Rice	3/16"-5/16"
Barley	3/32"-3/16"

Bituminous Sizes

Egg	2"-5"
Nut	1 1/4"-2"
Stoker	3/4"-1 ¼"
Slack	0-3/4"

Notice that Anthracite and Bituminous sizes have very little relationship to each other, the reason for the difference is Anthracite is hard coal and Bituminous is soft coal. Hard coal breaks into sharp well-defined pieces, and can be graded rather finely, while soft coal crumbles more, and is not so well defined. Just pouring a size of soft coal back and forth a few times between two containers could reduce it by a size. The reason grade sizes are only listed for Anthracite and bituminous coals is that these are the only coal types commonly sold on the retail market. Sub-bituminous and Lignite coal is normally only sold to large commercial users such as coal fired power plants. Large users do not need sized coal since they process the coal themselves; coal power plants powderize the coal into a fine dust that is blown into the furnace for a maximum efficiency burn. Any Sub-bituminous coal that makes it into the retail coal market would probably be sold as Bituminous coal, if you see any low sulfur bituminous coal for sale it is probably sub-bituminous since bituminous normally has a high sulfur level. Sub-bituminous coal is also smokier than bituminous coal and has a larger amount of volatile gases, which will require more secondary air above the fire to burn off, otherwise the gases can exit the chimney unburned and their heat value is lost. Lignite coal is more like wood than coal and most coal stoves would not burn it well, if at all, with its high volatile gas content Lignite may burn better in a wood stove that has a grate. Lignite if burned at a high rate of fire may overheat a wood grate, so the best stove for lignite maybe a wood/coal stove, which will have enough secondary air to burn off the coal gases and a coal grate that will take the heat of coal. Cannel coal is still around but is so rare that it is a specially coal. Some hand fired coal burners like cannel coal for rescuing a fading coal fire; a few pieces of cannel coal will flash into a hot flaming fire to which more coal can be added to continue the burn. The trick in burning coal is to never let the fire go out.

Installing a Chimney

Burning coal requires a class "A" chimney as does burning wood. See the previous chapter on Wood burning for chimney installation procedures.

Installing the Stove Piping

Coal stovepipe is identical as installing stovepipe for burning wood, so I will once again refer to the previous chapter on wood burning for stovepipe installation procedures. Some will argue that stove pipe for coal burning does not have to have the section joints lapped so that creosote can drain back to the firebox. However, this is not wise, since the traditional way of starting a coal fire is with a wood fire, so creosote is potentially present at times in coal stove piping.

How to Light a Coal Fire

What will light one coal fire may not light another. The harder a coal is, the higher is its ignition temperature, and the harder it is to get a fire started. Also the larger the pieces of coal are, the harder they are to light. Large chunks of Anthracite are the hardest to light and Slack sized Bituminous is the easiest.

The traditional method is to build a wood fire or at least a kindling fire and add coal to the hot wood coals. (See previous chapter for section on how to light a wood fire.) Open the draft up all the way and you will probably need to leave the ash door open as well. Once the wood fire is down to hot coals start adding the coal is slowly a bit at a time and allow it to light before more coal is added to the fire. The other method is to lay a thin layer of coal on the wood before it is lit. In either method, once the coal is burning well the firebox is then loaded with coal. Coal burns best when the firebox is filled with coal up to the base of the loading door or even higher.

Another "traditional" method is to use a "coal mouse" which is very similar to a small road flare. The stove is filled with coal and the coal mouse is buried in the coal with the tail sticking out, the tail is lit with a match and the door is closed. The coal mouse burns hot enough to light even an anthracite coal fire. This product is the better mousetrap, and is the cat's meow for starting coal fires. The downside of the product is that due to its solid flammable chemical makeup, it is classified as an explosive and is limited in the ways that it can be shipped, so there are no coal mouse mail order houses. The product is however often carried by coal stove dealers and coal sellers.

Newer Ways of Lighting a Coal Fire

The simplest way to start a coal fire is to lay a layer of match light charcoal in the front end of the firebox and then load in the coal and light the charcoal with a long match from underneath the grate. The draft is strongest in the front area of most fireboxes, if your draft is weak you may need to leave the charcoal uncovered by any coal and wait until the charcoal is burning well and then rake the coal forward from a pile in the back to cover the charcoal.

For those of us too cheap to buy match light charcoal, regular charcoal can be used by placing some balled up newspaper on the grate underneath the charcoal and lighting the paper with a match. Another method is to put some charcoal in a pail, pour on some lighter fluid, and toss the charcoal in the pail like tossing a salad until the lighter fluid has coated all the charcoal and has been fully absorbed. Then dump the charcoal on the front of the grate and cover with some coal and light. Lighting from below the grate with a match is easier if a ball of newspaper is placed in the ash drawer under the grate and the match is used to light the paper, which in turn will light the paper or charcoal above the grate.

Some other ways of starting a coal fire are to use solid charcoal starters, or wood fire starters. These starters are blocks of pressed sawdust, or other material often soaked with a wax or oil, and can be lit with a match. One or more of the starters are placed on the front section of the grate with a pile of coal on the back section, the starters are lighted with a match and then the coal is raked forward over them. A safer way of lighting the starters is to place them on the grate and cover them with some coal and light them through the grate. This way you do not have to reach over the flaming starters to rake the coal forward.

Once the coal fire is burning well, more coal can be added to fill the firebox for a long burn. One of the big advantages of coal over wood is the long predicable burns coal can provide. Coal has about four times the heat energy content of wood, so a load of coal can burn four times as long as a same sized load of wood. A properly sized coal burner will only need to be tended to once or twice a day. Coal is always added to the previous fire before it goes out.

Some newer coal stoves, generally top end stoker models, are available with a coal igniter for starting coal fires at the push of a button. The igniter is an electric heating element that gets hot enough to light the small coal pieces used in stokers.

Stokers use such a fine grade of coal that the small pieces can be lit on fire with a propane torch or a small fire starter used for starting wood fires. Some crumble two pieces of charcoal on top of coal and light the charcoal with some burning paper.

Now for Some Ways on How Not to Start a Coal Fire.

Not only is trying to light a coal fire by spraying it with lighter fluid or gasoline dangerous, it will probably fail to work. You stand a better chance of lighting yourself on fire than the coal, since when you light it, it will probably flash over and if you are lighting from above with the door open, you may catch the wall of flame, right in the face. While lighter fluid and other flammable liquids may burn hot enough to light coal, the problem is that they don't burn long enough to achieve ignition, since unless the coal has been well coated or soaked in it, there is not enough on each piece of coal to get it hot enough to ignite. The coal has to be heated to its ignition temperature to ignite. A brief exposure to even very high temperatures does not heat things up instantly, it takes a while for the heat to 'soak in' and bring things up to that temperature. Propane burns at a temperature more than hot enough to melt solder, yet it can take quite some time to heat up copper pipe hot enough to solder a joint, and the larger the pipe, the longer it takes to heat it up. The same is true with coal, the larger the pieces, the longer it can take to heat them up to ignition temperature. That is why lighting coal with a dosing of flammable liquids often does not work; it tends to burn off before the coal is hot enough to burn, unless the liquid has been soaked into the coal in large enough amounts so the coal is heated to ignition before the liquid is burned off. However, most hard coals simply are not porous enough to soak up enough flammable liquid for this trick to work. If you are faced with having to try to light a coal fire with a flammable liquid, the safe way is to use the Woodfield Cast-Iron Fire Starter ($25-30) which is made for starting wood fires in fireplaces using kerosene or lighter fluid, that is poured on the stone in the cast iron tray. Once the liquid has soaked in, the tray is placed below the grate and lit with match. Once draft gets going, it will pull the flames up through the grate, and if the flames are hot enough and burn long enough, it may light the coal fire. In the section on starting wood fires in the chapter on heating with wood, I go into more detail and explain how you can use oil in the tray, which may work better for starting coal fires since oil burns hotter.

Believe or not, some people get so desperate to start a coal fire going, they resort to using explosives such as gunpowder. A firebox is an enclosed metal box and setting off an explosive inside can turn the firebox into a bomb with metal pieces flying through the air at high speeds. Like trying to light coal with flammable liquids, explosives are even less likely to light a coal fire since the heat is so short lived that the coal will probably not be heated to the ignition temperature.

Maintaining a Coal Fire

Once you are over the mountain and have the coal fire going, the next trick is to keep it going. In stoker models, the new coal pushes the ash off the edge of the funnel operating much like a conveyor belt moving the coal through the fire, but if the stoker feed breaks the fire will die once the coal is burned up or if the ashes back up and smother the fire. A hand fired coal fire is also a continuous fire that burns its way up through the coal that is added to the top of the fire as the ashes are shaken out through the gate in the bottom. A coal fire is always burning up through the coal, leaving ash below it as it climbs. Maintaining a coal fire involves adding enough coal regularly enough to keep the fire fed, but not overloading it and removing the ashes as needed, but always leaving a thin layer of ashes to protect the grate from the high heat of burning coal. When shaking ashes, use only short sudden shakes, because large shakes will tip the grate too much allowing coals to drop through. Only shake until you may see a glow in the ash drawer from the hot fire above or you start seeing small hot embers dropping. On some coal burners with a strong draft, a thicker bed of ashes is kept to restrict airflow to reduce the rate the fire burns at, but in most cases, the ash door damper will be adequate for controlling the draft.

Always remember that nearly all coal has some volatile gases in it and many coal burners do not supply secondary air above the fire to burn off these gases. Therefore, if you open the door suddenly you are letting in a surge of oxygen that will cause these gases to flash burn in a gas explosion that may send a wall of flame out the loading door. If you can, allow extra air above the fire before opening the loading door by opening up the draft as much as you can and open the loading door very slowly to allow the gases to burn off and if they do flash, the nearly closed door will block the flash. The best rule of course is not to open the door for a while after adding fresh coal to allow time for the gases to burn off. Keep the loading door closed as much as possible. The fumes from coal burning are hazardous to your health and particularly so for young children and the unborn. The way these fumes normally get inside the house, other than leaks, is back smoking out the loading door. Many stoves have windows in the loading door to reduce having to open the door to check on the fire, the other trick is to put a stovepipe thermometer on the front of the stove above the loading door or on the stovepipe and monitor the fire by the heat it is putting out. The temperature will begin to drop as the size of the fire shrinks as there is less coal to burn and the ashes are starting to block the draft. A temperature reading will tell you more about the condition of the coal fire than looking at the top of the coal bed will, for you can only see the top of the fire while the temperature reflects the total over heat output.

The procedure for managing a coal fire is as follows, once the coal fire is started; wait until blue or yellow flames are visible at the top before adding more coal. If the fire was started with a thin layer of coal, this should only take a few minutes for the coal to reach this stage. Once the coal is burning well, add more coal and repeat the process to build a full depth of coal in the firebox. On coal burners with a strong draft that can pull well through a full load of coal, once the starter coal is burning well, the entire load can be shoveled in. Leave the ash door or damper open as needed to fully establish a hot fire with blue or yellow flames visible at the top. By visible I mean through a glass window in the loading door since you should not be opening the door at this point. If you do not have a window use a thermometer to watch for when the fire is hot and then dial down the damper to the desired setting for the amount of heat wanted or set the automatic controls at this point if you have any.

The fire will burn for hours or longer, after all this is what coal is all about, so leave it alone and don't fiddle with it too much. Poking the fire is a bad idea since mixing hot coals with the ashes below tends to make clinkers, which are unburned lumps that can form in coal fires, and poking may knock unburned coal into the ash drawer. The fire will need to have the ashes shaken down one to four times a day depending on how fast the fire is burning. The need for shaken is evident by a drop in temperature when there is still plenty of coal as the ash begins to restrict the draft and slows the fire. Open up the draft fully and shake the fire but only until a glow is seen in the ash drawer or hot coals start dropping. Check to see if you need to add more coal then dial the draft back down once any added new coal is burning well.

Always remove and dump the ashes when you shake down the fire. Coal has an amazing amount of ash in it compared to wood and will required far more frequent ash removal. You should have a covered metal ash pail with a well fitted lid to keep in the smoke from any still burning coals in the ashes, a few hot coals in the ashes can smoke up a house with the smell of coal smoke and isn't healthy. You have to keep the ash drawer empty because as the fire burns, more ash will fall between the grates and will build up in the ash drawer. If the ash fills the drawer, it will block the airflow entering underneath the grate, and it is this flow of air that cools the grates and prevents them from overheating. If grates are insulated on the underside by ashes, the fire above may warp the grates and greatly shorten their lifespan.

Keep an eye on your ashes, they tell you how efficiently or inefficiently you are burning your coal. Some people shift their ashes through a wood frame with a bottom of hardware cloth to catch any unburned coal so they can recycle it back into the fire. Of course if they would learn not to over shake the fire maybe they would not have to do that.

Installing Coal Stoves and Inserts

Coal stoves and inserts are installation wise, interchangeable with wood stoves and inserts which were covered in the previous chapter. The difference with coal is that wood mess is not a problem and far less coal will need to be carried in than is the case with wood. However far more ashes will need to be carried out with coal than with wood. A coal stove can be located on a second floor and the coal carried up as needed, but I would not care to do the same with a wood stove. Coal is carried in a coal bucket called a bid, which has a spout with which to pour the coal in through the firebox loading door. The coal bucket can be kept near the stove, but not too near, it should be kept outside the range for combustibles, which is normally the size of the stove mat underneath the stove. The ashes are also kept in a covered metal container that is often a coal bucket; just do not get the two mixed up. A rack of fire tools will also be needed as well. The main tool needed is a rake or shovel for moving coal in the firebox, and sometimes a poker.

Some small coal stoves have the loading door located on the top of the stove, this design should be avoided since opening the door to refuel will result in exhaust gases entering the living space. The goal in using any stove is to keep smoke out of the house, which is after all, why you have a chimney.

Coal stoves come in two basic types, hand loading and stoker. Hand loaded stoves are filled with coal by hand and you have the flexibility of being able to burn any coal grade large enough not to fall through the grate and you may be able to burn wood as well. Stokers have a feed mechanism, generally a screw feed in a tube that draws coal from a bin mounted on the side of the stove and the tube ends in a broad funnel in the firebox. Fresh coal is forced at a constant slow rate up the tube into the base of the funnel and this feeds coal to the fire burning on the funnel. The fire burns the coal in the center of the pile on the cone and continues to burn as the coal is pushed towards the edges of the cone with the ashes falling off the edges of the cone. A beautiful system that is simple and works very well, but it is dependent on using a stoker grade coal. The coal has to be fine enough to be pushed through the feed tube and in small enough pieces that they have time to burn to ash before falling off the edge of the cone. Most stokers can only burn one or two grades of coal and some will only burn Anthracite but not Bituminous.

With the total lack of EPA testing and efficiency ratings, it is difficult to tell if one coal stove is more efficient than another is. With such a lack of reliable information manufacturers claims of better efficiency have to be taken with a lot of skepticism. Quality manufacturers will tend to not only have better built products but are more efficient as well. The generally recognized quality coal heating manufacturers are A/A, AHS, Alaska, EFM, Harman, Harmon, Hitzer, Keystroker and Leisure line. The lower quality brands are companies like U. S. Stove, Vozelgang and the cheap models sold in some building supply stores. A quality coal stove will pay for itself by lasting longer, burning less coal to supply the same amount of heat and having fewer mechanical problems like broken grates or jammed stokers.

Installing Coal Furnaces and Boilers

See the section on wood furnaces and boilers in the proceeding chapter for installation details. Coal furnaces and boilers like their wood counterparts will normally be located in a basement or furnace room, which serves to keep the coal and ashes out of the living space. Coal furnaces are very traditional and work very well, the one problem with them is that coal fires are continuous affairs that burn all the time and the demand for heat is not constant. In cold weather the coal furnace can be fired with a bigger fire for when more heat is needed like in the morning and low fired for at night. The trouble comes with warmer weather when heat is only needed part of the day and a continuously running coal furnace will overheat the house. This is where coal boilers shine, for they can be low fired with the heat being stored in the hot water, which is only pumped to the radiators as needed. A well insulated coal boiler can be fired all summer long to supply hot water and not overheat the house since the circulating pumps are not turned on unless the thermostat calls for heat. Coal boilers also tend to be more efficient than furnaces due more efficient heat transfer. The Coal Gun Coal Stoker Boiler by AHS (http://alternateheatingsystems.com/) has a stack temperature of only 350 F, which for a coal burner is remarkably low and is the sign of a very efficient coal burner (84%).

Installing Coal Outdoor Boilers

See the OWB section in the preceding chapter on heating with wood for how to install an OWB. Coal outdoor water boilers have some distinct advantages over OWB that run on other fuels. The better grades of Coal unlike wood, does not absorb water and does not need to be kept dry. The coal for an OWB can simply be dumped in a pile on the ground and shoveled into the OWB as needed. With its higher energy content of about four to one over wood, a coal fired OWB will have much better burn times and will burn cleaner than non-EPA approved OWBs. Where wood fires do not idle well and smoke a lot, coal fires idle very well and produce little smoke. Automatic stoker feeds are available for coal fired OWBs making them nearly entirely automatic. There is no EPA approved coal burning OWBs and the OWBs that burn coal look pretty crude. Most OWBs have oversized grates and do not even have any firebrick, indicating a poorly thought out design built with extensive corner cutting as a basic design element. OWBs are notoriously inefficient and waste most of the heat that they produce. A typically installed coal burning OWB will burn 4 to 10 times as much coal as a high quality efficient indoor coal boiler like the coal gun boiler. Increasing the normal coal chimney exhaust by a factor of 4 or even 10, and then emitting it out of a short stack only 8 to 12 feet off the ground, may very well make you quite unpopular with your neighbors. The oversized grates in coal burning OWBs are very likely to require far more coal be loaded on the grate, to block the air flow so the draft will flow through the coal rather than around it, which will result in coal loads far larger than what is actually needed. While a large coal load can give a long burn, that is only true for the depth of the coal bed, an overly large grate provides an overly large burning area. Restricting this large grate area from burning at too high a rate will require restricting the draft coming up through the grate. Restricting the inlet draft will result in a cold sooty coal fire, if there is too little secondary air supplied above the coal to burn off the volatile gases contained in coal. Anthracite coal contains only small amounts of volatile gases if any and will create little or no smoke, but Bituminous coal, which has more volatile gases can smoke badly if, burned under these conditions which could create a real nuisance problem with black coal smoke. If you want to burn coal in hand loaded OWB, plan to burn anthracite coal to avoid smoke problems. The coal stoker OWBs eliminate the problems with the oversized grate and have better control, but can not burn wood of course. The huge efficiency problems remain however for OWBs, which typically lose half their heat in the ground loop. This problem can be addressed by insulating the lines with spray foam insulation as detailed in the section on wood burning OWBs in the chapter on wood heat. Most OWB also lose a lot of heat due to being placed outside with little insulation. The manufacturer's claims of being well insulated are nearly universally lies. A well-insulated OWB will have 4 to 8 inches of foam insulation, few if any have that much.

The covering of the OWB can be removed and cheap thin fiberglass type installation removed and replaced with sprayed on foam insulation. The mounting brackets for the OWB cover can be extended so that they will be above the foam once it is sprayed on, and the covering panels can be reinstalled with added pieces at the corners and top to make up for any increase in size due to the thickness of the added insulation.

By far the best coal OWB is a high quality coal boiler like the Coal Gun installed in an out building. By using a well-built efficient coal boiler with well-insulated ground lines, it is possible to create a coal burning OWB with an efficiency very close to an indoor coal boiler. By locating a coal boiler in its own building, the boiler will be much easier to care for and the coal can be indoors and warm which will eliminate frozen coal pile problems. A tall-insulated chimney will help create the necessary draft for the boiler and lift the exhaust up and way from being a noticeable problem. The trick to not having any problems with neighbors with having a coal fired OWB, is to have invisible exhaust that is vented too high for any one to smell the distinctive scent of coal.

Operating a Coal Insert or Stove

The basic operating problem with inserts is that because they have to fit inside of a fireplace opening, they have a firebox that does not hold very much coal. While wood burning inserts work great for occasional fires to take the chill out of the room, coal fires are hard to light and work best as constant sources of reliable heat. Trying to maintain a season long coal fire in a fireplace insert can be tricky, Harman's Harman Magnafire Series Coal Stove Elite Insert is stated to hold enough coal for 24 hours but I would guess that is more of an ideal figure for low firing and high firing will require more frequent reloading. The other insert on the market is Hitzer's model 983 Fireplace Insert and seems very similar to the Harman model. Neither has a stoker option since there is not enough room for one inside the limited confines of a fireplace opening. Both models take Nut and stove size coal. Operating a coal insert will take more frequent loadings than with a freestanding coal stove with a larger firebox that holds more coal. An insert will particularly run through the coal fast if you are trying to heat the whole house with it. The other problem with inserts is most of the heat is very local, the Harmon and Hitzer both have hot air fans to move the air so they will easily heat even a large room, but moving the heat to other rooms will still be a problem. In a power outage of course the fans will not work, though these units will still run and produce heat.

Freestanding coal stoves distribute the heat better than an insert simply by not being stuck in a hole in the wall. With larger fireboxes, they can hold more coal and stoker attachments and stoker models are available as is push button fire starting. The non-stoker models will work without electrical power, but without any fans of course.

Daily operation normally consists of checking the fire early in the morning and opening the draft, shaking down the ashes and filling up with coal. Once the fire is going well, the damper is set to warm up the house or the automatic controls are set. The fire brings the temperature up to a nice cozy setting and you or the automatic control reduces the draft to maintain temperature without over heating the house. If it is cold outside you may have to shake down the ashes and remove them at lunch and dinnertime, or even more frequently depending on the percentage of ash in the coal and how much coal you need to burn to stay warm. Then before going to bed you check the fire again, shake and remove ashes, add coal if needed and dial down the damper for the night. By slowing the rate of burn and allowing the temperature to fall at night, you save coal. In the morning, you start over again.

Operating a Coal Furnace or Boiler

Coal hot air furnaces work well with a automatic damper controlled by a room thermostat. The control works as follows; the room cools and the thermostat calls for heat opening the damper wider, which allows more air into the fire increasing the size and temperature of the fire. The increase in temperature warms the air in the plenum and turns on the fan switch, which runs the furnace blower moving the warm air through the ductwork up into the rooms. If you do not have a automatic thermostatic control, you have to adjust the damper yourself for the amount of heat you think you will need. Basically, if it is cold in the house, you open it a bit more and if it is too hot, you close it a bit. Over time, you will get to be pretty good at predicting where to set the damper for the day. If you lose electrical power the blower fan will not run of course, but you can still get some heat if the warm air from the furnace is free to rise through the ductwork and up into the rooms above. The amount of heat you can get will depend on how well your ductwork is set up for the free upward movement of rising hot air and the sinking of returning cold air. This movement can be added by removing any air filters or opening an access door to let air enter the furnace and rise in the ductwork. Opening wide all heat registers and any other restrictions will also help.

The daily pattern of operation of coal furnaces is the same as for coal stoves, with the exception that coal furnaces have larger fireboxes and may be able to hold a larger coal load for longer burns. Stokers are very common on coal furnaces, and the rate of feed can be controlled by a thermostat. The thermostat can slow the rate of coal feed for a lower temperature at night and then ramp it up to a warmer setting for the day. Stoker furnaces will feed automatically from a hopper or bin and may have coal enough to last for a week or more. The ashes may also be automatically dumped into a hopper able to hold ashes from perhaps a week of operation or more.

Coal boilers like furnaces can be hand fed or stoker fed. The key difference between furnaces and boilers is that with a boiler, the rate of firing is controlled by the boiler water temperature, not the room temperature. The boiler stores its heat in the hot water, which is used as needed by the heating needs of the house. Due to this storage capacity, the boiler does not have to immediately increase its firing rate to meet a sudden increase in a call for heat. The circulation pumps will pump hot water to where it is needed, and the cooler returning water will gradually cool the water in the boiler. Once the water drops below a preset temperature, the fire will be increased to warm the water back up and once the water is raised to the high point cut out temperature, the fire is reduced. With the boiler heating the water instead of the house, this allows for sudden increases in room temperature that other coal burners cannot match. While with a coal furnace or stove, increasing the damper setting will increase the rate the fire is burning at, it will take time for a coal fire to respond, and more time for this increased heat to be given off to the areas needing heat. While with a coal boilers, the hot water is always ready to be pumped at once, to where it is needed.

Coal boilers tend to have large fireboxes and fire like a coal furnace or stove, except for that feeding the fire is less tied to swings in daily heat load. The morning increase in temperature maybe able to be handled by the stored heat in the hot water and the firebox may not need filling until a more convent hour of the day. Stoker boilers are very automatic in their operation and the constant feed of a stoker works particularly well combined with the load smoothing effect of a boiler and results in stoker boilers having the highest efficiencies of all home coal heating systems.

Operating an Outdoor Coal Boiler

Most OWBs that burn coal also burn wood and tend to have vastly over sized grates. It may be practical to block off some of the back area of the grate area with plate steel, perhaps with the front edge folded up, to keep the coal from spilling back over the plate. This would force the under grate draft air to flow up through the grate area covered with coal and would have the effect of reducing the size of the grate area allowing smaller coal fires that will not overheat the water in the boiler. A deep pile of coal on a reduced grate area will burn longer and better than the same amount of coal spread out over the whole grate. The coal burning can be further improved by making a vertical box out of firebrick to burn the coal in on the reduced grate area. A metal rack to hold the firebrick in place can be welded together from steel angle iron and flat stock. Weld the rack so that the fire bricks can be lifted out for replacement when they break and make the sides as tall as will work in your firebox, 12 to 24 inches would work nice. If the rack is going to be be too big to fit in through the loading door, it can be made in two pieces and bolted or pinned together inside the firebox. The coal bed should be at least 6 or 8 inches thick for a proper burn, and much thicker for longer burns. Once the fire is going well, fill the coal box in the firebox up to the top. If you are burning anthracite coal, you will want nearly all the air directed underneath the grate while if you are burning bituminous coal directing about 10% combustion air above the grate can help burn off the volatile gases and reduce sooting and black smoking. Some OWB operators have reported that when burning or trying to burn bituminous coal, that they have had a problem with the overly large OWB firebox filling up with unburned volatile coal gas and then exploding with enough force to blow the soot out of the chimney like someone sneezing, or even blowing the chimney off like a soot propelled rocket. If smoking is a problem with bituminous coal, you can try increasing the air above the grate, or increasing the temperature of the fire by increasing air below the grate to increase the rate of burn. If you do not have a blower and are working with a natural draft, the draft can be increased by increasing the height of the chimney or adding a draft inducing chimney cap, which has a powered fan to suck out the exhaust.

Even with the modifications to burn coal, wood can still be burned, just cut it short enough to fit in the coal bin in the firebox, but be careful when loading not to break the fire bricks by tossing logs at them. For wood burning you will want to redirect some air (20%) above the grate for burning off the creosote.

The stoker models do not require any modification to burn coal, and will have automatic controls to regulate the rate of coal feed. Stoker models will only burn coal sizes that will work with the feed mechanism, normally the fine coal grades made for stokers and will not able to burn wood unless the stoker can be removed and wood burned in the firebox with it out of the way. This maybe possible in wood OWBs that were converted to burn coal by installing a stoker.

Monitoring a OWB is often a matter of watching the smoke coming from the chimney, though if you are burning clean burning anthracite coal, the lack of visible smoke may make this more difficult. The other method is installing a remote temperature monitor on the heat supply line as it enters the house. (See the section on wood burning OWBs for details on this) The monitor has a remote that can be set with a low limit alarm that will sound if the temperature drops below a set temperature. Then if the alarm goes off, you dash outside, open the draft and check the fire. Shake down the ashes and add coal if the fire has not gone out.

__What to do with Coal Ashes__

Coal ashes could some day be classified as hazardous waste;

containing sulfur, arsenic lead and mercury, yet fly coal ash is used as a soil amendment to improve agriculture yields. Tests have revealed that at high concentrations of fly ash in the soil, (5% and higher) significant accumulations of dangerous elements occur in produce making it unsafe to eat, while at lower levels (1% or lower) the amounts of dangerous elements in produce remained low and safe to eat. Obviously coal ashes are dangerous and should be placed in plastic bags and put in the trash for proper disposal, since dumping them on the ground can create dangerous levels of hazardous elements in things grown nearby and can leach into ground water.

Some coal burners have come up with some uses for coal ashes. One is to use coal ashes as pothole filler for gravel and asphalt driveways, presumably away from the garden and well. Just fill the hole and compact by driving over it. Of course this driveway patch will have high levels of some nasty elements in it, but then so does asphalt, so this one idea to use with discretion. Another use is as an additive to concrete. The Romans built the coliseum and many other structures using a volcanic ash based lime mix that has proved to be very lasting and stronger than a standard concrete mix. Using fly ash can reduce the amount of cement needed by up to 50% without weakening the strength of the concrete. The fly ash can also improve the chemical resistance, reduces efflorescence and acts as a plasticizer improving the flow of concrete when poured, making working with concrete easier and reduces voids and improves finishing. Wal-Mart now requires all interior steel-troweled concrete floors to contain 15% to 20% fly ash to reduce the amount of cement needed in the concrete mix and to reduce CO_2 emissions from the manufacturing of the cement. (I will confess that I have not done the math to see if the amount of CO_2 reduced by using fly ash equals the amount of CO_2 created in making the fly ash.) The "Wal-Mart" mix has a reduction in the cement normally used by 15-20% by replacing it with fly ash. The basic non-"Wal-Mart" mix using fly ash is a up to 50% replacement of cement by an equal amount of fly ash. Obviously any ashes from your coal burner are probably going to contain a high level of impurities in the form of non-fly ash, the heavy clunky ash the doesn't blow out the chimney and unburned coal pieces, so I would not expect top grade results or super strong concrete. However, if you are pouring a sidewalk or a patio, it could make it an interesting conversation piece and an interesting experiment.

Chimney Sweeping and Maintenance

Chimney sweeping details are covered in the previous chapter on wood heating. The difference between sweeping a chimney for a wood burner and one for coal burning is coal chimneys will be much cleaner and will require far less sweeping. The absence of creosote in coal tends to lull coal burners into ignoring their chimney until they wake up dead one morning. Coal burning will produce some soot and fly ash, of which some will settle in the stovepipe and chimney. Soot and ash can collect in stovepipe elbows and in chimney bases until they form a pile big enough to block the stovepipe or chimney. With a blocked chimney or stovepipe, the smoke will back up into the firebox and deprive the fire of oxygen causing it to produce carbon monoxide. The blocked draft will cause the backed up fumes to exit back out through the inlet dampers and any other opening on the stove. So while coal chimneys need far less sweeping than chimneys for wood stoves, they still need sweeping. Many coal systems are very efficient, clean burning, and will only need a sweeping in the spring at the end of the heating season. Coal systems need to have all the soot and ashes removed before summer to prevent summer humidity or rainwater from damping the coal ashes or soot and forming a corrosive mix that will eat just about any thing including some stainless steels. The chimney needs to be thoroughly cleaned, the stovepipe disassembled and cleaned and the firebox cleaned and vacuumed out so all the ash is removed. The firebox should also be sprayed with a light spray can type of oil that will leave a protective oil film to prevent rusting.

When cleaning, inspect everything for wear and tear so any replacements or repairs can be done before the start of the next heating season. Check the coal grates as they may be corroded or starting to warp and may need replacement soon. It is wise to keep a replacement grate on hand, so if a grate breaks you can replace it at once, instead of having to order it and wait for a replacement to be delivered. A spare grate is handy in another way, for if they stop making parts for your coal burner, a spare grate will let you keep it running far longer than otherwise.

Chapter 14

Wood pellets

Sometimes dark storm clouds really do have silver linings. Back in the 1970's when the Oil Embargo created the energy crisis in the United States, a lot of people jumped into burning wood for home heating that didn't have a clue about wood heat and who didn't even have a wood supply. This odd situation created a need for a wood stove that could operate itself and use a wood source that did not need special handling. In 1984, Whitfield sold the first pellet stove for residential use. The pellet stove was the perfect solution for the problem; being fully automatic with wood pellets in 40 lb plastic bags available at local stores selling for less than a buck a bag, you could heat your house for a fraction of the cost of heating with oil or gas. The huge bargain heating with wood pellets once was, can be quickly grasped by considering that 40 lb bags of pellets that once sold for as little as 19 to 89 cents a bag, now sell for over $5 and lately over $6 and seems to be heading only higher in price. Heating with wood pellets was once a fantastic bargain. However, with the recent surge in pellet prices and the fall in gas futures, it appears that wood pellets are becoming too expensive to compete with natural gas and now are only worth the costs of installation if your fuel choices are limited to high cost heat sources like electricity, oil and perhaps propane.

Pellet stoves aside from the rising price of pellets are simply fantastic. Pellet stoves have efficiencies ranging from 78 to 85% making them one of the most efficient ways of burning wood. The high combustion efficiency also results in very low emissions, so low in fact that pellet stoves are exempt from EPA smoke testing rules and can be used in many places where wood stoves are restricted or banned. The secret behind how pellet stoves burn so efficiently and cleanly, is the burn pot. The burn pot is like a firebrick lined metal cup, that the small wood pellets are dropped into, where the pellets are burned in a mini controlled fire. The airflow is controlled by a fan and fresh pellets are added to the fire, with ashes removed automatically (in some designs). The result is a small perfect hot fire that is fed nearly ash free very dry pellets that burn hot and clean. Once and a while you can get a wood stove to burn this cleanly, but soon the fire over heats the house and heat is wasted, while the pellet stove fire is so small that at low fire, the heat output is small enough not to over heat the house. The pellet stove is the gas furnace of wood burning; self igniting models can turn on and off the fire as easily as a gas furnace can turn the gas on and off as needed. The controlled feed mechanism in Pellet stoves over comes the problem of matching the heat output of a wood fire to the heating load, with the burn rate being matched to the heat load, the fire always burns wood "hot" in an intense fire.

The downside of pellet stoves is that they can only burn pellets, and they are complicated and require electricity to run (about $9 a month), the guy with a pellet stove freezes just as fast as the guy without one in a power outage. The pellet problem has been addressed by stoves that can also burn corn and multi fuel stoves that can burn anything from pellets to cherry pits. Back up battery power source systems are available for about $500 that will power a pellet stove for about 10-13 hours (Surefire Stove Sentry by SEC America [P.O. Box 2266 South Burlington, Vermont 05407 - Phone:(802) 865-8388)   (http://www.secamerica.com/ss_sentry.html)   Despite these improvements, the pellet stove still has its limitations; the battery backup only lasts about a day, and the multi fuel units are limited in what they can burn and how many people have a few tons of dried cherry pits sitting around?

Wood pellet stoves are now available as freestanding stoves, fireplace inserts, hot air furnaces and boilers. The freestanding stoves are the traditional pellet stove and have been around the longest and are still the most common type sold. Like freestanding wood stoves, a pellet stove is a space heater and will only heat the room it is in. Fireplace inserts likewise only heat a limited area, while a pellet furnace will heat the entire house. Pellet boilers are a newer option and are a bit of a strange animal since the advantage of a pellet burner is the ability to control the fire to match the load and the advantage of a boiler is the ability to store heat from a large fire for later use. Therefore, a pellet boiler seems to be a way of heating water with an over priced fuel. Wood pellets have become too expensive for a pellet boiler to make much sense, since it would be much simpler to burn wood since the boiler can store the heat of a hot wood fire for efficient use and wood is much cheaper than pellets and works just as well in a boiler.

Wood Pellets

Wood pellets are compressed sawdust. Originally making wood pellets was a neat way of getting rid of a waste product and making some money while doing it. Now the demand for wood pellets has far out stripped the available supply as a waste by product of wood manufacturing and has pushed prices to levels where using pellets is often only marginally economical to do so. Wood pellets are in such demand that they are now sometimes made directly from felled trees. The complete equipment set up for such is now available on line at a single web site and can be ordered with a click of a computer mouse, so it is to be expected that the wood pellet supply will increase with time as more people jump into this expanding market to make a buck.

Wood pellets come in two grades, Premium and Standard; the Premium grade has less than 1% ash while the Standard grade has less than 3%, but before you get too excited, remember that the manufacturer grades his own product. Therefore, the ash content can be higher than advertised with some pellets. Wood pellets also come in two types, hardwood and softwood, which is less important than the BTU rating, the cheaper pellets are the better buy. The one concern, some have voiced is the possibility of softwood pellets made from pine having a lot of pitch that could clog the flue, which should not be a concern since a pellet stove should be too efficient to have unburned pitch in the exhaust. The other key factor is the percentage of "fines" or saw dust from broken pellets in each bag. Fines are a problem cause they can clog the feed mechanism on many pellet stoves. Some use a pellet sieve or screen to remove the fines before they load the pellets into the hopper on the stove, however some stove feed mechanisms have less trouble with fines and can handle them up to a point. Currently many pellet manufacturers seem to be having difficulty with quality control and pellet quality can vary widely from one pallet load of pellets to another. A 40 lb bag of pellets should have less than half a cup of fines at the bottom of the bag, and while the ash and dirt content should be less than 1% for premium or 3% for standard grades. Some bags of pellets are turning up with much higher levels of fines and higher ash levels requiring much more frequent emptying of the ash pan. Top fed pellet stoves tend to be designed for low ash content pellets while bottom fed pellet stoves can handle slightly higher ash contents as is found in standard grade pellets. Newer pellet stoves designs maybe more tolerant of higher ash content.

The high cost of wood pellets has spurred interest in cheaper pellets made from other things like waste paper, agricultural wastes and grass. Pellet stoves are designed to burn wood pellets that have very low ash contents, most of the possible substitutes have ash contents that are much higher and as a result, will not work in a wood pellet stove. A multi fuel or Wood/corn pellet stove may the wise choice so that you may be able to burn these cheaper pellet fuels. Some of the non-wood or bio-pellets are designed to be burned in regular wood pellet stoves and offer a cheaper alternative, but not all stoves can burn them, so it would be wise to try a bag before you buy a pallet.

Making Your own Pellets

The current high cost of wood pellets and the lack of cheaper alternatives has driven a market for equipment to make your own pellets at home, using anything from sawdust to leaves or grass. A pellet mill for home use with a three Hp 220 volt motor costs about $2,000 and will produce about 50 lbs of wood pellets in an hour. Larger pellet mills are also available but with larger price tags of course. The small three Hp model is a bit underpowered for making hardwood pellets, and still has a motor that has a considerable electric current draw. The larger models are all three phase or powered by gas or diesel engines and some can use the PTO on a farm tractor. To make pellets, a dampened mixture of sawdust at the correct moisture level is poured into the hopper, often with a cornstarch-based binder, and if every thing is just right the machine with a lot of straining and noise will start spitting out damp pellets which will need to air dry for a few hours. Very much like trying to potty train a toddler who does not like fruit, the pellet making process can strain your patience and tax your coaching skills. The trick is that the moisture content has to be in the correct range (about 10%-15%) for every bit of sawdust in the batch, the moisture has to be evenly distributed, a single dry handful, can plug the machine and a wet one, will make pasty pellets that can clump. Small pellet mills also fail to run as hot as large mills, which are hot enough for the wood fibers to fuse together without a binder, so small pellet mills require the use of a binder (1-5%) in the pellet mix. The pellets should come out of the machine steaming hot and will need to air dry for a few hours until the moisture is less then 8%, then they are dry enough to burn in most pellet stoves.

The smaller pellet mills are all made in China and the die and rollers are under extreme wear, one dealer only expects about 360 hours of use before they have to be replaced at a cost of $230-600. Since the smallest machines only produce about 50 lbs of pellets an hour, just the cost of replacing the die and rollers can add about a dollar to the cost of making each bag. The larger pellet mills since they produce far more pellets per hour of operation will have a lower operating cost, even if their parts did not last any longer than the cheapest pellet mills, making them more cost effective. The larger machines that cost about $6000 dollars like the TT75 by Pelletmasters, has dies that should last for 2000 hours instead of the 360 hours with the smaller mills, and it can make wood pellets without adding a binding agent. The mill will also produce about 110-200 lbs of pellets per hour which is about 2 to 4 times as much as the smaller pellet mills, which results in a much lower die cost in terms of wear per bag of pellets made. The TT75 like other pellet mills of its size has a three phase 220 volt, 7.5 horsepower motor. To run a three-phase motor at home, where you do not have 3 phase power will require the use of a phase converter.

Pellet mills also are only designed to make pellets from material that is less than 1/4 inch in size; larger pieces must be reduced by a hammer mill to this size or smaller. A "small" 15 Hp hammer mill costs $5000. A hammer mill will handle anything up to large wood chips, larger pieces of wood need to be reduced into chips by a chipper first. Wood chippers are large expensive pieces of equipment used to turn tree branches and sometimes even logs into wood chips. The companies that trim the trees back from around the power lines often use wood chippers, so you have probably seen these machines. These chippers cost about as much as a car. Therefore, once you cut down a tree, you feed it in a $15,000 chipper, then feed the wood chips into a $5,000 hammer mill and then feed the saw dust into a $2000 pellet mill to make pellets that sell for about $6 a bag. Even if everything else were free, you would need to sell 3,667 bags for $6 each just to cover the cost of the equipment. With the three Hp pellet mill, it would take you 3,667 hours to make the pellets, or nearly two years if you worked at just feeding the pellet mill 40 hours a week. It is really much worst than it sounds, since you will probably of had to replaced the die and rollers ten times at a added cost of $2,300 to 6,000. Once you start adding up the other costs, small pellet mills are not cost effective. With the larger $6000 pellet mill and a $150 phase converter, you would need to sell 4,358 bags at $6 to cover the equipment costs, but the machine will produce the pellets in as "little" as 800 hours or five months of 40 hour work weeks. In addition, the die will still be good and you will not have the cost of having to use a binder. While the idea of making your own wood pellets at home may sound very attractive, it is often not the bargain it may appear to be. It is far simpler and cheaper to simply cut the wood as firewood and burn it in a wood stove.

To be fair, you can save a lot of money by making your own pellets if you set it up the right way. First making pellets from trees or cut wood is not cost effective unless it is done on a large scale. If you are going to make wood pellets on a small scale you need to have a plentiful source of sawdust that can be fed right into a pellet mill, thereby avoiding the cost of equipment it isn't cost effective for use in a small operation. Even still, it is hard to see how the cost of a $2,000 pellet mill with a operating cost of over a dollar a bag can be cheaper than simply buying pellets or paying a gas heating bill. Since even at $6 a bag for pellets your savings would be less than $5 a bag so it would take over 400 bags of pellets to pay for buying the pellet mill before you would even begin to start saving any money. It would also take you 400 hours or ten 40 hour work weeks to make the pellets and with most homes only needing about a bag of pellets a day for heat in the winter, it would take several winters to even use that much. Therefore, it would take several years for a pellet mill to pay for itself, even if you have a free source of sawdust. While the larger pellet mills will produce pellets at a lower cost, it is hard to see a single home needing that many pellets, and it will take longer for you to use enough pellets to pay for the cost of the more expensive pellet mill, odds are that you would have the mortgage paid off first. In short, making wood pellets even from "free" sawdust may only make financial sense if you are planning to sell pellets as a side business or if you need enough heat that you would use enough pellets to cover the costs of the pellet mill in a reasonable period of time.

While making your own wood pellets may not be a home money saver unless you are planning to sell them on the side, another option that may make better financial sense is non-wood pellets made from paper, leaves or grass. The dies and rollers on the smaller pellet mills can last ten times longer when used with softer materials and the motor will have less stress on it. In theory, a hammer mill is still needed, but a mulcher may work just as well to chop the material to size and costs a lot less. A bagging lawn mower with a sharp blade will cut the grass into small enough pieces for use in a pellet mill. People with huge lawns (over an acre) could possibly pelletize their grass clippings and then burn them in the winter time in a corn or multi fuel stove to heat their homes. A similar operation may work for leaves as well, they could be chopped and bagged with a bagging mower and then pelletized. The trick to making pellets at a low cost is to use a free waste product that can be cheaply made suitable for pelleting and will not be too hard on the smaller pellet mills to handle. Non-wood pellets however tend to have much higher ash contents than wood, and will not work in most wood pellet stoves and may or may not work in corn or multi fuel stoves. Be sure to read the chapter on grass pellets. While it is possible to make pellets from almost anything, there is no guarantee that any stove currently available will be able to heat with it. You could invest a lot of money and time and end up producing pellets that are not usable. Assuming that you will be able to successfully heat with home made grass pellets, making the pellets will take longer since a larger volume of material will need to be fed into the pellet mill, because the grass clippings will be compressed more than sawdust would be in making pellets, while the die will last much longer. Since you would have to cut the grass anyway, the only major additional cost maybe just the price of the pellet mill and if you were to heat your home entirely, simply dividing the price of the pellet mill by your winter fuel bill could give you the number of years it would take to pay for the pellet mill. For a $2000 pellet mill and a $500 annual heating bill, it would take four years to pay for the pellet mill while with a $1000 annual heating bill it would take only two.

For more information on making your own pellets and sources for equipment see-
http://www.pelheat.com/
http://www.nighthawkmfg.com/

Venting a Pellet Stove

Pellet burners in general use special flue pipe called Pellet Vent Pipe or PL Vent Pipe (a double wall pipe, the inner pipe is stainless steel) made just for pellet stoves and it is illegal to use anything else in most cases. The manufacturer will state in the manual, the requirements for each model and situation. Local fire codes also have to be considered, but in general, the codes will state to follow the manufacture's recommendations as stated in the manual. Some codes will place some restrictions on what is allowed, such as requiring Pellet Vent Pipe inside masonry chimneys routed out the top with a cap rather than allowing the pellet stove to use the large masonry chimney as a vent. Due to its small output of exhaust gases, a pellet stove would probably not put out enough waste heat to keep a masonry chimney hot and the gases would cool and fail to vent properly and condensate could collect in the chimney, which is not designed to handle it.

The common requirements by the pellet stove makers is to use three inch size PL vent pipe for most smaller models, the larger stoves use the four inch size. The best way of venting a pellet stove is to run PL vent pipe straight up through the roof, the vent line stays warm and drafts well and the smoke is released above the roof. The second best is to route the PV vent pipe through the wall behind the pellet stove and then straight up above the roof, the vent does not stay warm but the smoke is released above the roof. The worst way of venting is to vent through the wall behind the pellet stove with a direct vent which dumps the smoke right outside the wall. Direct venting of pellet stoves often results in smoke stained siding and smoke reentering the house through windows, attic vents located in the overhang above the direct vent or an air intake located on the same outside wall.

Because pellet burners use a fan to blow air through the burn pot, the exhaust venting system is under positive air pressure unlike natural draft venting which are under negative air pressure. Where a loose seam on a natural draft wood stove pipe results in some room air being drawn into the pipe, a leak on a positive pressure pellet vent will result in smoke being blown out into the room. The pellet vent system has to be air tight; every joint has to be sealed perfectly to work. Most manufacture's recommend using high temperature silicone (the red stuff) in the joints and foil taping over the joints.
.

Installing a Pellet Stove

Installing a pellet stove is a bit different from installing a wood or coal stove. While the pellet stove still needs a non-combustible floor or pad under it, the clearance requirements to combustibles are greatly reduced. Where an old wood stove may need as much as 36 inches of distance from any combustibles on the sides and back, a pellet stove may only need as little as 1" clearance on the back and 6" on the sides (requirements will be stated on a label on stove or in manual). The reason for the reduced clearance requirements is that the back and side surfaces of a pellet stove do not even get hot enough to burn your hand on most models. The glass door on the front will however get hot enough to burn and more space is required in front of the stove since pellet stoves often direct most of the heat forward and room is needed for tending to the stove, such as filling the bin and maintenance. The trick here is that a free standing pellet stove is built more like a furnace than a stove, having a steel firebox that is covered with a metal box that has a fan to blow the heated air out the front towards the center of the room. By some strategic use of insulation and a fan, the surface of the pellet stove and the electronic controls, can be kept cool. Electronics and heat do not mix well; a home computer has a cooling fan for a reason. A key part of the design of any pellet stove is placing any electronics or any other heat sensitive parts away from the heat and directing the air flow the so that they stay cool. This is part of the reason why pellet stoves need electrical power to run, not only do they need power to operate the pellet feed system, they need a fan moving the hot air away from the control system or they could be badly damaged rendering the stove useless. Normally if a pellet stove has a vent that rises, at least three feet above the top of the stove, there will be enough natural draft to draw the smoke of any pellets burning in the fire pot when the power goes out, otherwise the smoke can back up into the room. Manually feeding pellets to a fire in a pellet stove without any power is not a good idea since without a fan to blow the heated air out, the controls can be damaged by being overheated and the smoke may fail to vent properly.

Like other wood stoves, pellet stoves need to be placed on a fireproof floor or a stove pad. But due to their much cooler surface temperatures, the pad or non-combustible flooring only may need to extend 6 inches in front of the stove, 2 inches to the side and be flush with the back and can be as little as a piece of 20 gauge thick metal. The exact requirements will vary from model to model and will be spelled out in the manual.

Due to the minimal clearance requirements, pellet stoves do not project as far out into the middle of the room and can be placed in areas too small for wood or coal stoves. The built in fan moves the air far more effectively than does natural convection does for stoves, which do not have a fan. While they still cannot be placed in tight corners or very small rooms, they can be placed in smaller areas than other solid fueled stoves can be. Pellet stoves come in a range of different heat outputs, the more heat a pellet stoves puts out the more room it will needed for the heat to spread out in, without soon over heating the area and causing the stove to turn off.

Installing a Pellet Burner in a Mobile Home

This has become a bit of a no no. The pellet stove may possibly be acceptable to inspectors if in addition to standard home installation requirements, the pellet stove is secured to the floor, is grounded to the mobile home frame and has a fresh air intake preferably directly attached to the stove. Check the manufacture's installation manual if the stove is approved for use in mobile homes and what the requirements are before buying.

Operating a Pellet Stove

A pellet stove or other type of pellet burner can be operated manually or by a thermostat, which can be mounted on the unit or can be mounted on the wall. To start or light a pellet burner, the thermostat has to be calling for heat or if operating manually the unit must be turned on. The fire is lighted in one of two ways, either automatically by an electric heating element or manually by putting some pellets in the fire cup and squeezing out a small amount of starter jell or placing a pellet starter on the pellets and lighting with a match. The trick is to light a handful of pellets on fire while they are sitting in the little mini firebox that they burn in, in a pinch a propane torch works nice. Once the pellets are burning well the stove should feed pellets at a rate to maintain the set heat output. Pellet burners commonly have a heat sensor, so if the fire goes out, they stop feeding pellets or else you could come home and find that the fire went out and the stove fed the entire bin full of pellets out onto the floor. The problem with this heat sensor is that if it takes too long to start the fire or if the fire smolders, the stove may think that the fire went out and may turn off the pellet feed. If this happens, you will just have to relight the fire and get it burning hotter quicker by using a little bit more starter or using more pellets so the fire is bigger, so the stove will sense the heat and will keep feeding the pellets to the fire.

Like any heating system, you will operate the pellet burner by its control system, either by setting a heat setting on the stove or by setting the thermostat to how warm you want it. In addition, you will need to keep the pellet bin full. Normally this will involve dumping in a 40 lb bag of pellets every day in the winter time. Stoves have small bins and will need daily filling, while pellet furnaces tend to have bins that can hold a week's worth of pellets. Pellets come in plastic bags stacked on pallets, and if you order your pellets in bulk before the season starts, you will probably have one to six pallets of pellets sitting in the garage or outside under a tarp. 40 lbs is light enough that you will probably just throw a bag over the shoulder and carry it in. If moving a 40 lb bag is too much for you, you should consider a different heating system.

Newer pellet stoves are more tolerant of "fines" and higher ash contents, so you should not have to sift your pellets with a sieve before pouring them into the bin. Pellet stoves have very small ash drawers, so check it often, especially if you are burning a high ash fuel. The weak spot in pellet burning is the feed mechanism. Keep the manual for reference when something breaks and you need to order parts. Some keep spare parts on hand so that they can quickly repair the feed mechanism if it breaks. While you can do without a stove, if you have a pellet furnace, you will probably want to think more seriously about keeping some key spare parts on hand, since unless you have another heat source, a breakdown will leave you without heat. Few if any furnace repair services are going to have pellet furnace parts on hand, and it can take days for parts ordered to arrive. It is wise to have more than one way of heating the house, so such unexpected events are not a big heating disaster.

Operating a Pellet Boiler or Furnace

Nearly all boilers and furnaces are operated by a thermostat that will control the rate that the pellets are burned at to match the demand for heat. The boiler pellet burner will attempt to maintain a set water temperature in the boiler while a furnace will try to keep the house at a set temperature. The boiler has it easy since the boiler holds a lot of heat and will dampen any sudden swings in demand for heat. If someone leaves the door open, and the temperature drops in the house, the circulating pumps will turn on and pump hot water through the radiators. The boiler will not even notice increased demand until enough cold water returns to the boiler to drop the water temperature, and if someone eventually remembers to close the door, the boiler may not even notice. While a furnace will go into a higher rate of firing as soon as the room temperature drops and will attempt to bring it back up. Once the door is closed the furnace will succeed in bringing the temperature up and will then reduce the firing rate and go back to idling along at low fire. While a furnace can respond quicker, the furnace has to change its heat output to match the load much more than a boiler does. While they will in theory end up using the same amount of fuel, the boiler has a smoother output without the sudden swings in output the furnace can experience. For operation, this means that the furnace ends to be flexible and any failure to match the load will be readily apparent by the house being either too cold or too hot until the furnace responds to the change in demand. While when the boiler messes up, the boiler water will be a bit colder or warmer than the setting, which unless it is really out of range, will have little effect on the temperature in the house. That is the beauty of hydronic heat, but this ability to smooth out irregular heat output is not needed with pellets since pellet burners have great heat output regulation and a good pellet furnace should easily be able to match the changes in heat demand and keep the house at the set temperature. Despite the flexibility of pellet burning, pellet burners that do not have automatic ignition, will need to maintain a small fire and even small fires put out heat. In very well insulated homes, on days when little heat is needed, the pellet furnace in low fire may put out more heat than what the house needs resulting in over heating on mild days. A boiler may have a problem with high boiler water temperatures that heats up the basement. The solution of course is to turn off the boiler or furnace in mild weather to avoid this problem and burn less pellets. However, if the weather turns cold and heat is needed, the system will have to turned back on and the fire lit. While pellet burners in general work very well, there are still a lot of moving pieces and even the best designed unit can be jammed by a bad batch of pellets, so it is to be expected that a pellet heating unit will fail to work now and then. If you have an automatic backup heat source, like a gas furnace or boiler, when the temperature drops below the setting on the thermostat the backup heat will take over. This way if you need to order a part from China for the pellet furnace, you will still have a warm house while you wait for the part to arrive.

Pellet Stove Maintenance

The specific maintenance requirements for your stove will be listed in the manual, the general maintenance steps for pellet stoves are daily removing the ashes. Depending on how messy what you are burning is, you will have to clean the burn pot perhaps once a week by cleaning it out and scraping out any build up and clearing any plugged holes. Many stoves need to be cleaned out inside with a vacuum to remove dusty ashes once a week or even daily. The fine dust may blow through most vacuum filters, so a HEPA vacuum may be required, or you can just use a dusty old shop vacuum with a long hose. Leave the vacuum outside and run the hose into through a window and vacuum away. With many pellet stoves needing to be vacuumed out weekly or daily, many owners vacuum the stove nearly immediately after turning it off, which can result in vacuuming up hot embers which can start a fire inside the vacuum cleaner. Only vacuum the stove after it is cold and the fire has been out for some time. There are also special vacuum cleaners that are designed for vacuuming the ash from fireplaces. These vacuums have special features like filters that will catch and hold fine ash and not allow it to blow through into the air, and the hose and filters are fire resistance so a hot ember will not set them on fire. Once such vacuum cleaner is the Cougar MU405 Ash Fireplace Vacuum, $239.95   (http://www.govacuum.com/coashfiva.html).   These vacuums are only designed for vacuuming ash, if used for general use; the bag will be full of flammable material that a hot ember can ignite. The vacuum is not designed for handling a large internal fire and will suffer damage and will probably not be able to contain the resulting fire. These vacuums are great for ash and are used by chimney sweeps and furnace repairmen.

Once a year use a special pellet stove flue brush to clean the flue, you may have to remove part of the pipe so the brush can be inserted into the pipe. Normally the elbow behind the stove will need to be removed so that the brush can be inserted up the chimney flue, be sure to use a drop cloth and wear coveralls and a dust mask. If you find a lot of ash, soot or creosote in the venting, you should have the stove checked for proper operation and sweep the venting more frequently. Insect the venting for wear and tear and replace any sections that are in bad shape. The stove will also need to be opened and cleaned, especially the feed mechanism, which may have a build up of fines in it, and may also require oiling and adjustment for wear. Inspect the parts in the feed mechanism and order replacements for any parts that appear to be well worn, so you have replacements on hand should they give out in the middle of the next heating season. Some of the parts of the stove, like the blower and the venting, can be cleaned outdoors to reduce making a mess indoors. The stove itself will also need to be thoroughly vacuumed out, including all the places that was not cleaned out in the normal cleaning. You may also have to inspect gaskets, check bearings and oil them. There can be a whole list of things that have to be done each year, and many of them can be specific to your pellet stove, check your manual for the annual maintenance procedure and go through it step by step.

Selecting a Pellet Stove or Furnace

The best pellets stoves are often considered to be the Harmans, which are thought by many to be the most reliable, and low maintenance out of all pellet appliances and are able to burn pellets with higher ash contents, which not all pellet appliances can do. The Harman model P68 Pellet Stove that sells for $2800 is particularly highly regarded. The Quadra-Fire pellet stoves are also considered to be very good but needing more minor maintenance than the Harman models, the Castile model that sells for $2200 is another top contender.

Richard Reed at HVAC-FOR-BEGINNERS.COM (http://www. hvac-for-beginners.com/pellet-stove-ratings.html) rates most brands of pellet stoves available today from a repair basis on a five star system and the above generally highly regarded models only received one star, the lowest rating. Only two pellet stoves received five stars, *Cumberland* (cumberlandstoveworks.com) and *Lennox* (Lennox hearthproducts.com).Three stoves where rated four star, *Archgard* (http://archgard.com/), *Hudson River* (hudsonriverstoves. com) and *Osburn* (http://www.osburn-mfg.com/index.aspx). There were none that received three stars and only one that had two stars, the rest were one star. Considering the complexity of most pellet stoves, the low ratings for repairs is understandable. Reed's ratings are based on how good the warranty is, the premise is that a better built product is more reliable and will have less problems so the manufacturer can afford to back an extensive warranty. While with a product that falls apart, the manufacturer can not afford to offer a good warranty since the repair costs would put him out of business. While there is certainly a lot of truth to this line of reasoning, it is not true in all cases. I bought a cheap made in China vinyl floor with a lifetime warranty that in less than three years, already needs to be replaced. Obviously not all warranties are even worth the paper that they are printed on, while some products are considered so reliable that a warranty is not considered necessary. So while Reed's rating system is not always correct in all cases, it probably is true in most cases and I would check and consider his ratings very seriously.

Chapter 15

Corn

In the Great Depression when corn prices crashed, many corn farmers burned corn for heat because they did not have the money to buy coal. Corn can be a really lousy fuel in a stove that is not designed for it. Corn still held great promise as a heating fuel since it has a heat content not all that much lower than wood and per BTU, corn in bulk is cheaper than just about any other fuel sold. The promise of cheap corn heat however remained as elusive as the leprechaun's gold at the end of the rainbow until 1969 when Carroll Buckner of Arden, NC invented the first corn stove, the Dove Corn Stove (now Amaizablaze). Buckner sold his Dove stoves mainly to a small market in the south and southwest with little interest until the energy crisis hit. The huge spike in energy costs moved corn stoves from an obscure niche market to the mainstream. In 1980, President Jimmy Carter had a Dove corn Stove installed in the White House. Other people began to take notice and by 1985, Mike Haefner (American Energy Systems Inc) and Dane Harmon (Harmon Stove Co.) both had also "invented" the corn stove and began selling to the expanding market. A number of other wood pellet stove manufacturers also begin modifying their pellet stoves to burn corn but with mixed results. Many of the corn stoves on the market today are modified pellet stoves, and were originally designed to burn wood pellets and have been modified so that they can burn corn, sort of. Not every corn stove burns corn well. The ash from corn is totally different than the ash from wood burning. Corn has a surprising amount of silicon dioxide in it, which is basically a glass and melts or at least fuses together at temperatures normally found in burning corn. Many corn stoves produce a clinker or pellet of fused corn ash everyday that has to be removed manually. Some stoves even come with a special poker and tongs for removing the corn clinker pellet.

Due to the tendency for corn to fuse or clump, most corn stoves have a stirring rod for breaking up clumping corn kernels. The hard ash pellet that forms from corn burning has even been known to break the stirring rod. The stirring rod trying to break up hard ash pellets is what causes some of the banging and shaking sometimes seen (and heard) when operating a corn burner. To reduce clumping and hard ash pellets, some manufacturers recommend adding a half pound of ground oyster shell with each bushel of corn. The ground oyster shell; also called chicken scratch, helps to prevent the corn ash from fusing together. Other stoves are designed not to need or use oyster shell with the corn, always check the manufacturer's instructions on how the stove is to be operated.

Corn and pellet stoves come in two basic types, top fed and bottom fed. In top fed stoves the pellets or corn comes down a chute that drops into a cup like burn pot. The corn ash collects in the pot as a glass pellet that has to be removed; some top fed stoves have an automatic method for dumping the ash. In bottom fed stoves, the burn pot has a tube that comes up in the bottom of the burn pot and new pellets or corn is pushed up the tube into the pot. The ash and clinkers are pushed up and over the edges of the burn pot and fall into an ash tray below. The tray can hold more ashes and clinkers than the burn pot can, and as a result can be emptied less frequently rather than daily and can be emptied even if the stove is running.

Corn Stoves Vs Ethanol

Currently in the United States, the gasoline at many stations contains 5 to 10% ethanol made from corn. The idea is to reduce use of imported oil, but it is really more a demonstration of the power of the corn growers lobby. For it takes the energy on average of nearly 1 gallon of gasoline to produce 1.4 gallons of ethanol which only has about 66% of energy of gasoline, so the 1.4 gallons of ethanol is equal to about a gallon of gasoline, so it is really just a way of turning gasoline into ethanol, with only small gains in energy. The energy return from ethanol production is improved if the by-product Distillers Grain which still contains a third of the heat energy in corn, is either burned as a fuel or used as an animal feed.

It took half a bushel of corn to make that 1.4 gallons of ethanol. However, if you burned the corn directly it will produce about three and half times as much energy as burning the ethanol, and you did not have to burn nearly as much energy to make it (planting, fertilizing and transporting the corn still takes energy). Burning a bushel of corn can replace 2.8 gallons of fuel oil, or 4.3 gallons of LP, or 114 KWh of electricity, or 4 CCF of natural gas, or 3.4 gallons of gasoline. Therefore, to sum up the math, making ethanol from a bushel of corn will take the energy of nearly 2 gallons of gasoline and will produce 2.8 gallons of ethanol, which will be equal to about two gallons of gasoline, while burning the corn for heating will yield the heat equivalent of 3.4 gallons of gasoline or 4.6 gallons of ethanol. While ethanol is at best a marginal energy source, corn stoves can save far more energy and corn is currently one of the more economical fuels on the market (in bulk). To include the energy from Distillers Grain in the above results, remember that two thirds of the energy from the corn is in the ethanol, so add half to include the third part in the Distillers Grain. So if you have 1.4 gallons of ethanol, add half or 0.7 to include the energy in the By-product. However, since that extra energy is in the form of a By-product, it's energy may not be directly available and converting it to a more usable form will reduce the available energy. Distiller Grain can be dried and used as an energy source in making ethanol which can reduce the energy costs of making ethanol, minus the energy of drying the wet by-product so it can be burned as fuel. However with current technology, drying Distillers Grain and then burning it for energy would be about a break even process, which is why it is instead often sold as an animal feed at a price above the cost of the energy it took to dry it. Newer drying methods may lower the energy costs of drying and may make it cost effective to use Distillers Grain as part of the energy to produce ethanol which would lower the energy costs to produce ethanol. In theory if drying costs where cut in half, it could reduce Ethanol productions costs by one sixth, and by half if the dried By-product was used as fuel.

If you drive your car 20,000 miles a year, and got 20 mpg while burning gas that is 10% ethanol, you would burn100 gallons of ethanol made from 36 bushels of corn each year. That amount of corn could heat a home for one to two months. If you ran your car on E85, you would in a year, burn more corn as ethanol than you would heating your home all year with a corn stove. A good part of the corn crop in the United States is grown for the ethanol market, if it was not for this use, much of this corn would not be planted. Corn ethanol production however has definitely contributed to the rise in corn prices, and corn stoves must take a small part of the blame as well. But while ethanol use does cause a minor reduction in oil use, corn stoves can have a far greater effect on reducing oil use and can in turn lower corn prices by reducing the energy costs it takes grow and bring corn to market, if it is used to replace oil used in home heating.

 Of the homes in the USA, 7.6 percent use fuel oil for heating, using about 5 billion gallons of fuel oil in a year, making up about 1.6% of the total oil used in the USA. In 2008, 9 billion gallons of ethanol was produced from 3.2 billion bushels of corn. If 1.7 of 3.2 billion bushels used for ethanol had instead been used to heat all the currently oil heated homes, the USA could reduce its oil use by 1.6 percent. Such a reduction would result in lower oil prices, lower gasoline prices, and lower costs for corn production.

Where to get Corn and What it Costs

There are three basic types of corn in the world. Sweet corn is type you eat off the cob roasted at the state fair and is the vegetable served at the dinner table. Popcorn is the popping variety of corn that costs too much at the movie theater. Field corn is the corn that corn flour is made from, is fed to animals and is burned in corn stoves or is made into ethanol. Corn is all soft like sweet corn when it is growing and you can eat field corn just as you eat sweet corn, but since field corn has only half the sugar content that sweet corn does, field corn just does not taste as good and is rather bland. Field corn and popcorn are left out in the fields in the fall and the corn kernels dry and become hard seeds. If the Fall weather is dry, the corn will air dry down to the 15% moisture level or less needed for burning the corn efficiently for heating. If the weather is wet, the harvested corn will need to be dried by heated air blowers. The corn when harvested is husked; the leaves are removed from the ear of corn, and shelled; the kernels are removed from the cob. The corn kernels also need to be cleaned of cob pieces, leaves, rocks, etc, by screening and air separation. Corn in bulk is sold by the bushel, which is 52 lbs of dried corn, while bagged corn is often sold in 50 lb bags. Most field corn is grown in the Midwest. If you live in an area where field corn is grown, you can probably get it locally at a low price, while if you live in another part of the country, transportation costs may make burning corn less of a bargain.

Probably the most economical way to buy corn is from a local farmer, co-op or grain silo, in bulk. Be sure that the corn is dry enough to burn well, 15% moisture or less. Farmers have to sell dry corn so it does not mildew or get moldy in storage. Buying in bulk means that the corn is not bagged and you will have to be able to handle tons of loose corn kernels. Corn does not stack like firewood, and acts more like ball bearings. Take a bag of popcorn, pore it on a plate, and see what I mean. Field corn does not flow quite as freely as popcorn does, but it is similar. Field corn in bulk needs to be kept in a bin, one that rats and mice cannot get into. Corn is a highly sought after food source in the animal kingdom and any pest problem is like a tear in a sail in a strong wind. Either you fix it right away or you can lose the whole thing. Be careful about any spilled corn, since it may attract pests who will look for more and they will be able to smell tons of corn sitting in a garage or basement, and rats will chew their way in through wood or concrete to get to food. Every corn stove should probably be shipped with a free cat. Design your bulk storage with a mind to keeping rats and other pests out. In a garage, a metal bin raised above the floor with a metal feed pipe leading to the hopper on the stove may work well. In basements, a corn bin constructed using a corner with strong wood walls may work if you can keep the pests out of the basement, perhaps with a rat patrol staffed by one or more good mousers. However, you store your corn, set up a defensive parameter of traps and perhaps poisoned bait stations. The large windup live catch traps used by exterminator services work well, they can handle large rats and keep working even after they have caught some.

If you buy from a local farmer, he may be willing to deliver and how he will deliver the corn, will probably be with a bin that is a trailer with a gravity chute on the bottom. Open the chute and all the corn in the trailer will spill out on the ground. If you have a bin in the basement, the trailer can be parked next to a basement window and a chute placed under the trailer to direct the corn in through the window. Alternatively, the corn can be dumped on concrete or asphalt and vacuumed up with a corn vacuum system. How many corn users handle bulk corn, is to make or buy a system for blowing or vacuuming corn through pipes to move it to where they want it. Some systems are made using a large shop vacuum and some PVC pipe, while others are put together using pre-made components from companies like Cornvac Systems (http://cornvac.com/), such systems also use a shopvac and PVC pipe and can move a ton of corn in less than an hour. They also have a corn cleaner for $68 that used with a shopvac will clean cob pieces and other impurities from corn or fines from pellets. Considering the tons of corn, a corn stove or furnace can use in a year, a vacuum corn handling system makes good sense. If you have a pickup truck or a trailer that can hold corn without it spilling, you can pick corn up in bulk at a local grain silo. The loading is done by a chute that pours the corn into your trailer or truck, once home you use a corn vacuum system to unload, clean and transfer the corn to your corn bin. If you install a fitting with a slide valve for connecting a hose to, most of the corn can be sucked out of the truck or trailer without even having to get in with a shovel. The remaining corn can then be shoveled into the vacuum hose or a flexible hose can be used like a vacuum cleaner to vacuum out the corn.

The second most economical way of buying corn is get it in 50 or 100 lb bags at a local feed outlet that sells to farmers. While buying corn in bulk is cheaper in bulk, bags are only a bit more expensive at the wholesale level. The advantage of bagged corn is that the bags can be handled and stacked in trailer or truck and unloaded by hand and stacked where you want to store them. Course after an afternoon of hauling in a few tons of corn in 100 bags, you will probably be wishful of having a corn vacuum system. Rats and other animals readily chew through corn bags, so you will have to take the same pest precautions as you would for bulk corn.

The least economical way of buying corn is to buy it from pet stores or stores that sell bagged corn for feeding deer or birds. At times when corn is selling for $4.50 a bushel, the price for a 50 lb bag can run from $10.50 up to $30. Such inflated prices would take corn heat from being one of the cheapest forms of heat, to one of the most expensive. If you are considering heating with corn, first check on where locally you could buy it, and for how much.

Growing Your Own Corn

The average yield of corn per acre in the USA is normally over 150 bushels. Most homes can be heated with about a half bushel to a bushel a day, so as little as one to two acres of land maybe enough to grow all the corn you need to heat your house all year. To understand how fantastic this is, compare this with what growing your own firewood would entail. A cord of good hard wood can have about 25 million BTU, which is equal to the heat in 69 bushels of corn. So one acre of land can produce the equivalent of over two cords of firewood in the form of corn, the traditional amount of firewood a northern forest can produce sustainably each year is one cord. Corn can produce over twice as much fuel per year as a wood lot and you do not need to be a lumberjack. Part of this higher output is due to fertilizers, and corn requires weeding or herbicides, and maybe an electric fence to keep out the deer and raccoons. At a minimum you are going to need a good 10 HP rototiller or maybe a garden tractor with some attachments to plant an acre of corn or more every year. I have not seen a corn harvester attachment for garden tractors, so you will probably have to harvest the corn by hand. Once the corn has dried well enough in the late fall, you can pick and husk the ears in the field. Then the ears are fed into a hand cranked shelling machine that takes the kernels off the cobs and you store the kernels in your corn bin. Growing your own corn is tons of work and time, but it is probably easier and safer than harvesting your own firewood. There is little danger of being crushed by a falling corn plant, or having a rototiller accident. Though hitting a large rock while deep tilling when you are standing over one of the handles, can make for a rather eventful day, other than that, growing corn is far safer than wood cutting.

Heating Options in Corn

There are corn stoves, fireplace inserts, furnaces, boilers and outdoor boilers. Nearly all corn burners are modified wood pellet burners and many of them can burn wood pellets as well, and some can burn other biofuels like cherry pits or farm waste pellets.

Venting a Corn burner

Since corn stoves are so similar to wood pellet stoves with many of them able to burn pellets, corn burners use the same venting pipes as wood pellet stoves use. See the venting information in the preceding chapter on heating with wood pellets. The one big difference is that direct venting with an outlet vent mounted through the outside wall behind the corn stove is commonly used, but this kind of venting will stain and discolor the outside wall. In my opinion, direct venting should not be used, since it does not have any draft and is not good for your siding. Spend some extra money and vent it the right way, up and out through the roof. That way if the price of corn is higher than wood pellets next year, you can burn them without the wood smoke staining the outside of the house. Be sure to install a direct air intake for the stove to reduce drafts and ensure better stove operation.

Stoves or inserts vented through an existing chimney will require a PL Vent Pipe or a chimney liner the same size as the vent on the insert or stove, routed up through tiled chimneys or stainless steel chimneys since the corn insert or stove is not going to be able to keep the chimney hot enough for proper drafting.

Installing a Corn Stove or Fireplace Insert

Like any stove, to get the most out of it, a corn stove should be located where it can heat a large room rather than being stuck in a corner or small room. Corn stoves similar to pellet stoves have minimal clearance requirements, such as sometimes as little as 2 inches on the sides and even less on the back. Check the manufacturer's manual of course. The heat pad the stove sits on also only needs to extend out about two inches on the sides and front. Like a pellet stove, a nearby electrical outlet will be needed to plug the stove in. Read in the proceeding chapter, the details on pellet stove installation since pellet and corn stoves are so very similar.

While you will not be hauling in logs or loading buckets of coal, you will need room for daily hauling in a 50 lb bag of corn and pouring it into the bin. Plan on spilling some corn that will need to be cleaned up from time to time, so do not put the stove in a corner where cleaning up loose kernels would be difficult. Also, plan on how you are going to bring in the bags of corn, since you will be beating a path from your corn pile to the stove.

Installing a corn stove in a mobile home fails under the same rules as a wood pellet stove.

Installing a Corn Furnace or Boiler

If you wish to heat the whole house, a furnace or boiler is the best choice. Since furnaces and boilers are normally located outside the living spaces in a home, a direct filling method using a corn vacuum system can be set up. A vacuum filled hopper is installed above the corn bin on the furnace/boiler so that the hopper can be opened and the corn can flow down into the bin. The bins are also much larger than the small bins found on stoves and instead of a day's worth of corn they can often hold a week's worth. There are also secondary bins that stand next to the furnace and automatically keep the bin full so you can be gone for nearly a month and still come home to a warm house. Furnaces are a great application for the variable output of a corn burner, controlled by a thermostat the heat output is as well regulated as a gas furnace. While a corn boiler will also work just as well, the ability of a boiler to absorb wide swings in heat output and store heat is not needed with the steady and automatic control of burning corn. Like other boilers, corn boilers can also be used to supply hot water year round.

Outdoor corn boilers are also available, be sure to read the part in the wood heat chapter on outdoor boilers. Corn outdoor boilers due to burning nearly smoke free corn will not be a smoke problem like many wood OWB are, but because they are an OWB, they may fall under many of the same rules and restrictions that apply to OWBs.

Lighting and Maintaining a Corn Fire

While wood pellets can sometimes be lighted with as little as a match, corn is much harder to light. A corn fire is started by putting about a cup of wood pellets in the burn pot and pouring on some starting jell or adding a fire starter and lighting with a match, then close the door and start the stove. The wood pellets will burn creating a hot fire that will start the corn burning. The feed rate has to be set right so that corn is added fast enough to keep the fire burning, but not faster than the fire can burn. If the corn comes in too fast, it can bury the fire under a pile of unburned corn causing the fire to smolder and go out. Adding corn too slowly can cause the fire to starve and burn down to a fire too small to light the incoming corn, which will then bury the small fire and put it out. If you are not watching the fire, it can be hard to tell whether a fire went out because it smothered under too much fuel, or if it starved and burned out and then was buried under fuel, it was too cold to burn. One way to tell what happened is to check for partly burned corn kernels, a too fast feed will have a lot of them, while a too slow feed will have few if any.

More of the newer corn stoves have auto-igniters and can self-light a corn fire. Stoves with an igniter can be controlled by a thermostat and can fire themselves up as needed, unlike stoves that you may have to light every morning. An Auto-igniter is an electric heating element that gets hot and stays hot long enough to get a corn fire burning hotly.

Corn stoves are famous for failing to light well or even burn well after the stove is a few weeks old. What happens is the new corn stove owners often fail to properly clean and service the stove. Often they fail to clean and check that the intake holes that blow air into the burn pot are clear and working right. Ash build up inside the stove can adversely effect operation as can a dirty flue pipe. Normally a corn stove flue only needs cleaning once a year, but a bad batch of wet corn can soot it up in a hurry and a flue full of soot will interfere with getting a good burn. If any corn stove is to operate well, the maintenance steps outlined by manufacturer must be followed to the letter.

Selecting a Corn Stove Heating Appliance

Many corn stoves are a maintenance nightmare, with way too many motors, gears and other moving parts controlled by electronics or even a built in computer. It is not smart to combine heat and electronics, your lap top computer would not work for very long if you put it in an oven set at the temperatures that many corn stoves produce. The only way the more delicate parts of the corn or pellet stove can keep working is for the heat to be directed away from them, failure to do so can result in a breakdown. A number of corn stove manufacturers have at times come out with some very complicated models that their dealers have no clue how to fix. While the promise of some of these high tech corn stoves are impressive, their maintenance track record is not so inspiring. It is very common for parts for high tech corn stoves not to be available locally and need to be ordered from the factory. Even with over night express shipping, it can still take two or three days before the dealer can install the part only to find that another part is still needed. If the local dealer can even figure out what is wrong with the stove, it may take him days or a week or more to get the right parts and get the unit running right.

It makes much more sense to buy a corn stove that does not have a lot of bells and whistles that you do not really need, that are only going to break down on you. The Amaizablaze (http://cornstoves.info/) manufactured by Nesco doesn't have all the technology of the high tech stoves, but it works and is known for being low maintenance, trouble free and easy to operate. The Amaizablaze will require you to remove an ash pellet one or twice a day, and like all corn stoves, it will need to have the dust and ash brushed out of the unit monthly if not weekly.

An even more simple and trouble free way of burning corn are the Sedore multi-fuel stoves, (http://www.sedorestoves.com/) which are wood stoves that can burn corn and other things. How a Sedore burns corn is a wood fire is made and burned down to hot coals, then a basket is placed on the fire and a small amount of corn is poured into the basket. Once the corn is burning well another layer of corn is added and allowed to catch fire before the next layer is poured in until the basket is full or you have added as much corn as you think you will need for heating. Since there is no feed mechanism or blower fans, the Sedore does not need electricity to operate and will provide heat in a power outage. A Sedore is extremely low maintenance and there is next to nothing to break, but there is little control. The whole advantage of pellet and corn stoves of having a small controllable fire is gone, and you are back to wood stove heating methods. Now if you are a corn farmer and have a hard to heat farm house, the Sedore maybe just what you are looking for. It has a large heat output, while many of the corn stoves are rather limited, and it is simple and it works and it will keep working for a very long time. However, if you work away from home and want to come home to a warm house, or have a well-insulated house, the Sedore may not be the corn stove for you.

If you wish to heat the whole house and it is too large for heating with a stove, then you need a furnace, and the furnace with a reputation of low maintenance and great reliable is the Superior furnace. (http://ja-ran.com/superior.php) The Superior furnace can burn Corn, rye, wood pellets, cherry pits and switchgrass. It comes with a gravity fed side mounted bin that holds 12 bushels. The furnace produces 100,000 BTU ($3,850) and comes in a double burner model that produces 200,000 BTU ($7,500) for larger homes.

Information on Burning Corn for Heat

Heating with corn is still a relatively unknown technology in many parts of the country and some of the dealerships lack the support and or knowledge to repair the products that they sell and there are no books available on "How to burn corn" or "How to repair your corn burner". There is a goldmine of information available online at websites like http://www.iburncorn.com/ which has details on most major corn burners, including manuals. The site has a discussion board with a section devoted to each major corn burner in which people post problems and others post helpful advice on how to fix the problem. The only thing missing is a source for after-market parts.(Just joking of course, since unfortunately there are no sources for parts aside from the manufacturer and often only through a dealer.)

Corn/Pellet Blends

Corn can be tricky to burn and wood pellets are getting expensive, so some are turning to the logical conclusion of mixing the two to get a product that is cheaper than wood pellets and burns better than corn. One such product is Sunrise Agra Fuel's "Island Pellets" (http://www.sunriseagrafuels.com/) which is a corn/wood blend with some agricultural wastes thrown in. Sunrise Agra claims that their pellets don't form clinkers like corn does and has a higher heat value per pound than wood pellets or corn and is cheaper than wood pellets though still more expensive than corn.

It is also possible to mix corn kernels with wood pellets for better results, many pellet stoves have been able to burn up to a 50/50 of corn and wood pellets. A number of pellet stove owners have been know to mix in some corn to reduce fuel costs and to extend what pellets they have when pellets are hard to find. By using 50% or more wood pellets, the clinking problem with corn is reduced or avoided, and the settings on the stove work well enough, though with some stoves a lower percentage of corn needs to used like 25% corn to 75% wood pellets.

Operating a Corn Burner

Since corn stoves, boilers and furnaces are modified pellet stoves, be sure to read the proceeding chapter on them and see the section on operation. The key difference between pellet burners and corn burners, is with corn you often have to daily remove an ash pellet. Many corn heaters require daily maintenance due to corn ash build up and clinker formation. While some corn burners that have better ash handling systems can go a week or more without cleaning or ash removal.

Chapter 16

Grass pellets

Heating your home with a grass pellet stove is still largely hypothetical, for the future has yet to arrive. At this point in time (2009), grass pellets are not yet widely available and there are no grass pellet stoves on the market. There are a few multi-fuel pellet stoves that claim to be able to burn grass pellets, but their claims remain largely untried in the market place due to the lack of grass pellets. Despite this lack of both the horse and the cart, heating with grass pellets holds enormous promise. Grass will grow on land that you cannot grow food crops on and does not need fertilizers or cultivation, and can produce 40% more fuel per acre than corn, yielding 4 to 6 tons per acre. Switchgrass pellets sell for over $100 a ton and could sell for over $200 a ton and still be a bargain compared to wood pellets. Growing grass for pellet production could yield from $400 to over $1200 an acre. The United States has great prairies that are often too dry for growing agricultural crops without irrigation. The farms in these areas pump water from underground aquifers that are running dry. Soon the water will be gone and it will be impossible to grow crops there, and the land will revert back into grasslands. Grass pellet production would allow for these farms to switch from unsustainable crops to a natural grassland that would not require irrigation or fertilizers, and yet yield high profits.

Grass pellets are very similar to wood pellets and if pellet stoves were built that were designed to burn them, they would no doubt be even more popular for home heating than wood pellets, since grass pellets would probably sell for about half the cost of wood pellets. Grass pellets have 3-4% ash content, which is about twice what wood pellets normally have. Many pellet stoves could handle the higher ash content, but what they are unable to deal with is, that grass ash, like corn ash, has a lower melting point than wood ash and fuses together to form clinkers. Corn stoves have a stirrer to break up the clinkers, which is why some corn stoves are able to burn grass pellets with some success. Some newer multi-fuel pellet stoves that burn corn are also rated to burn grass pellets.

Another problem with burning grass pellets is that corrosive gases (chlorine, potassium and sulfur) are given off that may corrode even stainless steel heat exchangers . Some manufactures coat or paint the heat exchanger with a protective finish, another possible fix is to include some lime in the pellet mix to neutralize the acidic fumes that otherwise would be given off in combustion. It is of course possible to add about a half cup of lime per 40 lbs of grass pellets to reduce corrosion, but with grass pellet burning being such unexplored territory, this may not be a good idea for some future grass pellet stoves or maybe unneeded for some grass pellet brands.

Heating Appliances That Will Burn Grass Pellets Today

When I wrote this (2009), the Harman PC45 corn stove (http://www.harmanstoves.com/features.asp?id=26), was considered the best available stove for burning grass pellets. The PC45 is a wonder stove, wonderful technology and so complicated it is a wonder it works. I did not recommend this corn stove in the chapter on corn, because it is so complicated that it can be a real headache when it breaks and the support is often poor when it does. However, since there are so very few stoves that will burn grass pellets and this model is the very best for grass pellets, I decided to list it for grass pellets.

What sets the Harman PC45 apart from other stoves, is its "Sidewinder" burn pot with a horizontal stirring rod that is an extension of the feed auger. Whenever the stove adds fuel, it also stirs the fire breaking up the ashes preventing the formation of large clinkers. This stove successfully burned high ash grass pellets with no trouble. In the test they found that the ash drawer needed to be emptied every 2-3 days and the heat exchanger needed to be cleaned weekly.

The Harman P61A wood pellet stove (http://harmanstoves.com/), was also able to burn grass pellets, which is surprising because it does not have a stirring rod for breaking up clinkers, but instead is a bottom feeder. The pellets are forced in from the back and the ashes are forced up and over the lip of the burn pot and fall into the ash drawer. However after a day or two, a build up occurs on the burning pot surface and this eventually blocks the ashes from falling over the pot edge into the ash drawer, which smothers the fire with ash. To burn grass pellets, the accumulating ashes would need to be removed from off the top of the fire pot daily.

The Bixby biomass stove (http://www.bixbyenergy.com/) is actually two different stoves, a small cute 50,000 Btu model and a larger ugly box called the "Big Ugly Box" that produces 70,000 Btu. The Bixby stoves like the Harman PC 45 are wonder stoves, and Bixby also is known for poor support which is also why I didn't list Bixby in the chapter on corn. The technology is fantastic, with a self-cleaning burn pot that bottom dumps and a nearly unjammable feed system. In the test the university worked with Bixby engineers to change the software that operates the stove, to burn grass pellets, so whether or not these software upgrades are included in the current stoves would be a key point to check before buying. The Bixby is known for being one of the cleanest and most efficient stoves on the market, with a claimed efficiency of 97% compared with 80-85% for nearly all other pellet and corn stoves. This high efficiency combined with the neat way that a plug of ashes is dropped into the ash drawer, results in a stove that requires very little cleaning. Most other stoves spread a fine layer of ash all over the inside that needs to cleaned out weekly. Bixby is however well known for refusing to help customers and referring everyone to their local dealer, some of whom are very good and some are of no help. There is very good information at the "I burn corn" website-
http://forum.iburncorn.com/wiki/index.php/Bixby
that can be of great help for Bixby stove owners and those thinking of becoming one.

The Country Flame Harvester stove can burn grass pellets, a corn stove with a stirring rod that works much like the Harman PC45. The stove is even messier than the PC45, coating the inside of the stove with ashes everywhere but getting very little actually in the ash drawer. The ashes that do make it into the ash drawer tend to pile up and block the combustion air flow, so the ash drawer needs to emptied daily to keep the stove burning right. The feed rate is also slow for feeding in grass pellets and even at the highest setting the stove is under fired with a reduced heat output.

The above test results were produced by Cornell University Grass Bio-energy org and posted at;
http://grassbioenergy.org/res/pellet_stove_demo.asp

A furnace that probably should have been tested by Cornell is the Superior furnace by Ja-Ran enterprises Inc in Lexington Michigan (http://www.ja-ran.com/superior.php). The Superior furnace was listed in both the pellet and corn chapters, and will be listed in the chapter on other bio-fuels as well. The furnace is listed as being able to burn all grades of wood pellets, corn, rye, cherry pits and switch grass pellets. I have been unable to find any test results for this furnace, but it has been used commercially on grass pellets to heat buildings and is highly recommended by those who have used it.

Obtaining Grass Pellets

While in most places there are no grass pellets for sale at the moment (I have heard rumors of some pellet stove dealers starting to sell them), that will surely change since there are manufactures in China selling turn key set ups for making grass pellets. Considering the potential demand, I am sure that while I am writing these words, there are a number of enterprising business persons unpacking crates from China and setting up machinery to make grass pellets. The easy way of burning grass pellets for the moment, maybe to buy a heating unit that can burn grass pellets, but burn corn until grass pellets are available locally, or you could consider making your own.

In the chapter on wood pellets, we discussed making your own pellets and the conclusion was that unless you wanted to sell them on the side, the pellet making equipment was too expensive for home use. The smallest pellet mill (http://www.yankeepelletmill.com/) on the market costs $2000 dollars and can only make about 50 lbs of wood pellets per hour. Grass clippings however can be fed right into the pellet mill to make grass pellets, here is a video of a fellow doing just that. http://www.youtube.com/watch?v=4Cq63ak0Fmw (now if you are reading this book on the internet, you can just click on the link and see the video, while the rest of us holding this book in our hands will have to type the web address into a web browser program on a computer to see it.) Now if you need 5 tons of grass pellets to heat your house for the year, it will take a small pellet mill 200 hours or five 40 hour work weeks to make them. If you watched the video the guy did not exactly make a ton of pellets in the short video. I hope that you can see that this is way too labor intensive to be practical, or else you really have too much time on your hands. What may work better is a larger pellet mill that is powered by a PTO of a tractor, so you can make pellets in a more reasonable period of time. As little as two acres of lawn may supply enough grass clippings to produce enough grass pellets to heat a home year round. In theory a mower with a bagger could be used, and then the clippings could be fed into a pellet mill and the pellets stored once they are dry. Perhaps some day large riding mowers will come with a pellet mill attachment so you could cut your lawn and then make pellets to heat your home, which would make owning a lawn tractor much more attractive.

Any type of grass or weed can be used make pellets. Corn stocks, straw, leaves, paper, junk mail, just about anything that burns can be made into pellets. Most things will need to be chopped up into very small pieces before they can be run into a pellet mill however. Grass clippings will work, but fibrous weeds and other plants may need to be finely chopped before they can be put into a pellet mill. Chopping weeds up with the mower may work just as well as it does for grass, as long as the clippings are well cut.

The preferred grass for pelleting is switchgrass, but other varieties are being used as well and a mixed planting of locally native grass varieties may work best. Such a mix should become so well established that it will require no care at all. There are already seed companies selling the preferred bio-fuel grass seeds such as Applewood Seed Company (http://www.applewoodseed.com/). However, an existing pasturage or weedy field should produce acceptable grass pellets even if the quality varies a bit from pellet to pellet as it does with wood pellets.

While grass pellets for heating are hard to find, many animal feeds are available pelletized, including timothy grass and alfalfa. When bagged these feeds often sell for 11 to 14 dollars for a 40 or 50lb bag, which is currently over twice the price for corn. While not priced low enough to be an economical heating fuel, burning some will allow you to see how well or how badly your pellet burner can handle grass pellets.

Perhaps someday soon, grass pellet heating will be common and people with large lawns will be heating independent, and bags of grass pellets will be available at the grocery store right next to the water softener salt.

Chapter 17

Biofuels

In this chapter we will be discussing the other biofuels, things like wheat, rye, oats, peas, beans, cherry pits, olive pits, nut shells, nuts plus a number of animal feeds and agricultural byproducts that can be burned in a multi-fuel pellet stove or a corn stove, and some that may even be burned reasonably well in a regular pellet stove. The first potential fuels to consider are the grains. Corn is the most commonly burned grain, but all the grains can be burned though not all multi-fuel pellet stoves will be able to burn every type of grain. I would not recommend buying several tons of oats or some other grain without first trying a few test burns to see if your stove can be adjusted to handle burning oats and the same is true of any other grain or biofuel. Most grains can be purchased in small amounts at the grocery stove or in fifty-pound bags at a local feed mill. However, even just 50 lbs can be a lot of grain, that is an awful lot of oatmeal to have for breakfast if the stove cannot handle it. So if you would still like to have eggs occasionally, maybe just try a few one-pound bags from the grocery stove first, to see if your stove can burn it. Grains are bulky and expensive to ship, which results in a range of prices, with the grains being cheapest where there are grown and more expensive in distant areas where they are not commonly grown. Transportation costs can add two dollars or more to the price per bushel, if the grain is available locally at all. Grains are also "commodities" with investors buying and selling trying to make money on price swings in the market. This results in some sudden large increases and occasional decreases in price. Corn just a few years ago sold for less than $2 now currently (2009) sells for nearly $5 a bushel. Remember that a grain that is a cheap fuel today could be too expensive to burn next winter. Due to these swings in prices, it is not wise to commit to being able to burn only one biofuel as a heating source.

Here is what the grains were selling for in 2009, in dollars per bushel and the cost per pound, listed in order by increasing cost per pound. Notice that the measurement of "bushel" is a volume measurement, which results in a "bushel" of each type of grain having a different weight.

Grains   Price/Bushel, Weight of Bushel in Pounds   Price/Pound

Grains	Price/Bushel	Weight of Bushel in Pounds	Price/Pound
Oats	$2.38	32lbs	7.4 cents/pound
Corn	$4.78	56lbs	8.5 cents/pound
Wheat	$5.84	60lbs	9.7 cents/pound
Peas	$6.00	60lbs	10 cents/pound
Rye	$6.32	56lbs	11.3 cents/pound
Flax	$7.25	60lbs	12 cents/pound
Sorghum, grain	$7.24	56lbs	13 cents/pound
Soybeans	$10.77	60lbs	18 cents/pound
Sunflower seeds	$6.25	24-32lbs,	26-19.5 cents/pound
Rice	$12.71	45lbs	28 cents/pound
Barley	$16.32	48lbs	34 cents/pound

The above prices are bulk prices in areas where the grain is grown and some require a 20-ton minimum purchase to get the price listed. If you do not live, where a particular grain is grown or plan on buying less than 20 tons, expect to pay a higher price. Now what matters more than how many pounds you get for your dollar, is how many BTU you get. Here is a listing of BTU per pound for common grains and the resulting cost per million BTU, listed by order of increasing cost.

Grains		**BTU per Pound**	**Price per Million BTU**
Oats,	7.4 cents/lb,	8,242 BTU/lb,	$8.98 per MBTU
Corn,	8.5 cents/lb,	8,100 BTU/lb,	$10.49 per MBTU
Wheat,	9.7 cents/lb.	8,063 BTU/lb,	$12.03 per MBTU
Flax,	12 cents/lb,	9,615 BTU/lb,	$12.48 per MBTU
Rye,	11.3 cents/lb,	8,416 BTU/lb,	$13.43 per MBTU
Peas,	10 cents/lb,	6,255 BTU/lb,	$15.99 per MBTU
Rice	10 cents/lb,	5,479 BTU/lb,	$18.25 per MBTU
Soybeans,	18 cents/lb,	8,780 BTU/lb,	$17.60 per MBTU
Sunflower,	19.5 cents/lb,	8,800 BTU/lb,	$22.16 per MBTU
Sorghum,	13 cents/lb,	5,027 BTU/lb,	$25.86 per MBTU
Barley,	34 cents/lb,	6,800 BTU/lb,	$50.00 per MBTU
Hominy,	72.5 cents/lb,	8,075 BTU/lb,	$89.78 per MBTU

The BTU amounts for each grain are not as solid as they may appear since the quality of grain varies and different varieties of a type of grain can have different BTU/lb values. The BTU amounts are also dependent on how dry the grain is, if the grain has a higher moisture content than is normal, the BTU output will be less, since the excess moisture will have to be steamed off when the grain is burned. In general, the grains run about 8,000 BTU per pound, which is about the same as wood pellets. The price per million BTU will vary with the price for the gain of course, to figure the current price per MBTU, take the number for BTU/lb for the grain, divide it into one million, and multiply the result by the price per pound, which will give you the price per MBTU.

Natural Gas can cost about $14.50/MBTU, which is cheaper to heat with than most of the grains even if bought in bulk, and transportation was free. Even the cheaper grains will probably cost more to heat with than Natural Gas, once the cost of delivery is included. To find the current cost/MBTU for NG, multiply the cost per Therm by 10. If you were using an 80% efficient multi-fuel stove, compared to a NG furnace with an efficiency rating in the 90s, heating with wheat would be more expensive than NG. Most of us of course do not have the option of buying grains in bulk at a local feed mill, and have to pay the price for 50lb bags, which can be much higher, priced.

50lbs Bags   Price per Bag   Price per MBTU

Corn	$7/bag	$17.28/MBTU
Wheat	$9/bag	$22.32/MBTU
Barley	$12.26/bag	$31.00/MBTU
Oats	$13.40/bag	$32.76/MBTU
Sunflower	$34.50/bag	$78.40/MBTU
Rice	$25/bag,	$91.25/MBTU

At the above prices per 50lb bag, all of the listed grains are more expensive to use than natural gas, without even deducting for the lower efficiency of many grain stoves compared to high efficiency natural gas furnaces. The prices above are also the lowest prices I could find online in 2009 and are for local areas where the grains are grown. Today when you read this, the prices maybe even higher and shipping costs will increase the price even more. Frankly burning grains is often not economical at current prices, unless you are growing them yourself or can buy locally in bulk.

There are however cheaper agricultural products on the market that have lower prices than grains and are often used as cheap animal feeds. Many of these products are by products produced when grain is milled and the unwanted brain or hulls are sold off as scraps. A new by-product is distiller's grain, which is what is left over from making ethanol from corn.

Animal Feeds & Agricultural By-Products by the Ton

Rice Hulls	$11.50	0.58 cents/lb	6,575 BTU/lb	$0.88/MBTU
Rice Mill Feed	$32.50	1.7 cents/lb	6,000 BTU/lb	$2.83/MBTU
Oat Hulls	$70.00	3.5 cents/lb	7,000 BTU/lb	$5.00/MBTU
Soy hulls	$82.00	4.1 cents/lb	6,660 BTU/lb	$6.16/MBTU
Rice Bran	$82.50	4.1 cents/lb	4,372 BTU/lb	$9.38/MBTU
Distillers grain	$162.00	13 cents/lb	8,400 BTU/lb	$15.47/MBTU

The costs per MBTU for most of the above by-products are fantastic bargains with a cost that is a small fraction of the cost of heating with natural gas, (1/16 for rice hulls). These bargain basement prices are once again local bulk prices sometimes with a 5-ton minimum which most of us will never be able to get, so if you can even buy these by-products in your area, it will be at a much higher price. Most of these by-products are "fluffy" as I like to call them, meaning that they are lightweight and coarse flowing and will tend to jam in feed systems (think wood shavings instead of sawdust). Check carefully if a particular multi-fuel pellet stove will be able to burn it before buying a truckload. Nearly all of the disadvantages disappear with pelletization and bagging. Many of these potential low cost heating fuels are becoming available as pellets in 50 lb bags. The pelleting reduces the bulkiness, reduces feed jamming problems, and reduces shipping costs and bagging makes for easier handling. The big advantage of pelleting is it compresses a fluffy and tricky to burn fuel like saw dust or grass, into a fuel with better combustion properties than unpelletized wood.

Pellets in 50lb bags

Dry gluten	$2.50	9,600 BTU/lb	$5.21/MBTU
Distillers dried grains & solubles	$2.50	9,600 BTU/lb	$5.21/MBTU
Walnut shell	$2.50	9,200 BTU/lb	$5.43/MBTU
Wheat midds	$2.20	8,200 BTU/lb	$5.57/MBTU
Soy hulls	$2.00	6,660 BTU/lb	$6.00/MBTU
Peanut hull	$2.50	7,950 BTU/lb	$6.29/MBTU
Corn cob	$2.50	7,900 BTU /lb	$6.33/MBTU
Corn gluten feed	$2.50	7,199 BTU/lb	$6.95/MBTU
Bamboo	$2.50	6,500 BTU/lb	$7.69/MBTU
Cottonseed Hull	$7.25	9,200 BTU/lb	$15.17/MBTU
Gluten Feed	$6.98	7,199 BTU/lb	$19.39/MBTU
Linseed	$9.95	9,615 BTU/lb	$20.70/MBTU
Alfalfa	$11.19	7,729 BTU/lb	$28.96/MBTU
Beet Pulp	$11.50	7,345 BTU/lb	$31.31/MBTU

I have adjusted the prices for some items, which are sold in 40 lb bag to prices for 50lbs by adding 25% to the original price. Some items are not sold in bags in the USA at this time; those prices are based on dividing the price per ton by 40, (all the $2.50 and less prices) which results in unrealistically low prices. It is more reasonable to expect the price to triple to about $7.50 for a 50lb bag, which would make the cheapest cost per MBTU about $15, or about the cost of Natural Gas.

I checked at my local feel mill, pellet stove store and places where wood pellets are normally sold, and nobody had any of the above pelleted items and I was unable to even find some of them for sale on the internet. Even many of the ones I was able to find prices for, are very hard to find and maybe unattainable at the retail level. These things are beginning to show up at the import level and wholesale bulk, so it maybe only a matter of time before they are available. Some of these products may represent a real opportunity as a cheaper alternative than wood pellets, if you bought them by the ton in bulk and some can be burned in a regular pellet stove. Some problems with non-wood pellets are fusing ash as is found with corn and excessive ash levels, as is the case with some pellets in the above list and for the grains as well. Wood pellet stoves are designed to burn either premium grade pellets that have 0.5% ash, or standard grade pellets that can have up to 3% ash. Many pellets stoves can only handle low ash premium grade pellets and are unable even handle the ash levels associated with standard grade wood pellets. Some of the non-wood pellets on the list are low enough in ash that they may work in such stoves. Peat pellets have up to 9000 BTU/lb and have only 0.5% ash and may work well (peat pellets are not on the above list because I was unable to find a price for them, since they are not sold at this time.). Pellet stoves that can handle standard grade pellets may be able to burn corncob pellets, which have 7900 BTU/lb and 1.5% ash, or distillers dried grain without solubles, which has 2% ash, but be aware that dried distillers grain with the solubles has 4.15% ash, which is a much higher ash level. Walnut shell pellets (Eco-Burn which actually contains walnut shelling by products which includes more than just shells); with 1.5% ash and about 9000 BTU/lb may also work as well. Bamboo pellets also have 1.5% ash and may work in many wood pellet stoves as well. Wheat pellets can work in standard pellet stove, at times, various bio-pellet mixes have been sold for use in normal pellets stoves and most stoves have been able to burn them. Pellet stoves that can burn standard pellets should be able to burn peanut shell pellets, which have 3% ash, or sunflower hull pellets, which also have 3% ash. Many wood pellets sold today contain less than ideal quality wood, which results in standard grade wood pellets at times having an ash level above the 3% level, some wood pellet stoves like the Harmon stoves are known for being able to handle wood pellets with higher ash levels. However the rest of the pellets in the above list have ash levels that will probably overwhelm most wood pellet stoves, which is why someone invented the multi-fuel pellet stove that can be adjusted or programmed to deal with higher ash levels and different heat output level.

Now there are even cheaper fuels available in pellet form, a "pellet to pellet fuel". This new fuel of the future is animal droppings and not just animal manure. Animal waste and even municipal sewerage sludge can be, and has been, pelletized and burned in pellet stoves. Most animal droppings contain large amounts of undigested cellulose and other plant fibers that are quite burnable. In countries with a lack of readily available firewood, dried animal dung cakes have been used for heating and cooking since ancient times. The energy content per pound is only about half to a fourth of that found in wood, but the low energy density is more than made up for by the even lower cost of the fuel source.

BTU/lb for some common Types of Manure

Hen manure	2,500 BTU/lb
Pullet litter	5,700 BTU/lb
Turkey litter	4,350 BTU/lb
Spent mushroom compost	4,000 BTU/lb
Municipal waste ton	4,500 BTU/lb
Cow Manure	6,500 BTU/lb

Manure is normally burned for heat in one of three ways; combustion of dried manure directly like firewood, burned as pellets in a suitable stove or furnace, or the manure is digested or fermented to produce methane gas, which is used in natural gas appliances.

Manure can simply be dried and burned in a wood stove or furnace, or even coal or peat stoves and furnaces may work well enough. A number of farmers, heat animal buildings such as chicken houses with the animals droppings and find doing so is about 30% cheaper than heating with natural gas. In dry climates, drying manure is simple while in wet climates it will be far more difficult, requiring the use of covered structures to keep the rain off, and screens for airflow through thin layers of spread manure. Solar green houses can also be used to heat the air to accelerate drying. If you are reading between the lines here, you can see that burning dried manure is labor intensive and requires a lot of handling of manure. On the plus side, once the manure is dried, the odor is greatly reduced and the manure is a lightweight material that is more like dark clumps of sawdust than manure. Once the moisture level is below 15%, the manure is dry enough not to compost in storage and will burn well.

While burning manure can be rather odorific, burning manure pellets is odor free since the heat of pelletizing removes most of the odor and any minor traces of odor that could occur when burning the pellets, are exhausted out the pellet stove chimney. People who heat their homes with manure pellets report no odor problems at all. The only noticeable difference compared to using wood pellets for heating, is the lower heat output from the stove. To heat with manure pellets will require an oversized pellet stove or furnace since the heat output will be reduced. While the process of pelletizing manure can be less than fun, since everything in the manure itself has already been finely "processed" by the animal, a chipper and hammer mill are not needed. Manure at a suitable moisture level can be fed directly into the pellet mill and the resulting pellets will need to be air dried just as wood pellets are. The finished pellets look and burn like wood pellets, only with a lower heat output and they are gray in color rather than the light straw color of most wood pellets.

Composting manure to make usable methane gas is done in a biodigester, which is a sealed container into which manure and water is added, in which the manure is broken down by microorganisms. The biodigester can be a black plastic bag heated by the sun, which also holds the methane until used, or it can be a metal or concrete tank like structure with different compartments and design features for maximizing methane production, while reducing handling of the manure. The simple bag like biodigesters are often used in poor countries in warm places to produce methane gas for cooking needs, while the complex expensive systems are used on large farms in developed countries where the methane is often used on the farm in place of natural gas and may be used to generate electric power which is sold back to the power company as a sort of cash crop.

While burning manure for heat, requires that it be dry, bio-digesters work wet since the microorganisms that break down the manure need water to work, which eliminates having to dry the manure. If you have a ready supply of large amounts of manure, a bio-digester set up, is worth considering since you could power all your natural gas appliances; including water heaters, clothes driers, kitchen stoves and your furnace rather than just using the manure as a heating fuel. Methane gas can also be used to power internal combustion engines such as NG powered electrical generators, car engines, tractors, pump motors etc. Gasoline engines can be converted to run on NG, which is mostly methane. Stationary engines such a generators can be connected to a pressure regulated methane gas line, while mobile engines will require methane stored in pressurized tanks, which will need to filled, by a filling system that compresses the methane so enough can be carried to give the vehicle sufficient range to be useful in operation. A car that needs to refilled every 20 miles is not very handy. It should be remembered that methane is an odorless gas and is highly explosive if mixed with air. Bio-digester created methane gas has a trace of hydrogen sulfide that acts as a scent in the methane gas just as the gas company adds "sunk oil" to make leaks detectible long before enough can leak to form an explosive gas/air mix. Biodigester created "bio-gas" is 50-80% methane with the remainder being made up of mostly carbon dioxide. Since carbon dioxide is what you get when you burn anything, it being present in the bio-gas isn't a safety issue other than the fact that if the methane is only 50% of the mix, twice as much bio gas will be needed for the same amount of heat as produced by NG and twice as much carbon dioxide will be released. For indoor unvented uses like kitchen stoves, carbon dioxide could accumulate to unhealthy levels in well-sealed homes. Since the ratio of carbon dioxide gas in home generated bio-gas can vary widely, it would be wise to use a carbon dioxide detector to warn of any build up of the gas, and if high levels do occur it would show the need for improved ventilation, which can be as simple as turning on a stove top exhaust fan when using the stove.

While making your own natural gas from a biodigester may sound very attractive, it is wise to look before you leap and understand scale of the project. The average home uses 2 to 4 therms per day for cooking and heating over the entire year while winter time heating on average uses 10 therms per day. For Homes in warm climates, gas usage will be about two therms or less per day, while homes with average insulation in colder climates will be at four therms per day or higher. To provide heat equal to two therms of NG/day from biogas generated from animal manure would require the services of about 40 pigs, 5 cows or 700 chickens. For four therms per day, double the number of animals. Manure powered biodigesters usefulness is largely limited to farmers with enough livestock to provide enough manure to make using one worthwhile. Here are links and addresses to three companies that sell biodigesters for farmers.

http://www.rcmdigesters.com/
RCM Digesters
PO Box 4716
Berkeley, CA 94704

http://dialspace.dial.pipex.com/town/terrace/ae198/Catalogue1.htm
Solar House, Magherafelt, Co.
Londonderry, BT45 6HW,
Northern Ireland

http://www.bioplex.co.uk/index.shtml
Bioplex Technologies Ltd, Unit 5, The Cobden Centre,
Folly Brook Road, Emerald Park,
Emersons Green, Bristol BS16 7FQ.

An alternative to manure fueled biodigesters are biodigesters using plant material or a humus pile with a heat exchanger. Jean Pain developed a method of supplying all of his home's energy needs including his car with the energy from a large pile of composting wood chips. It has been calculated that he gained 20% more energy by composting the wood chips than he would have gotten if he burned them, and he produced tons of compost instead of wood ashes. Any one who composts will tell you that wood does not compost well and that is true. What Jean Pain did was to shred the wood into very small pieces only an inch long and with a thickness of only 1/16th of an inch. Such thin pieces of wood are more like wood shavings than wood chips, with the result that water and microorganisms can more readily soak into the wood. Even with such small pieces, it still takes 18-24 months for the wood to break down into compost. What Jean Pain would do was clear unwanted brush from a forested area taking trees up to four inches in diameter and feeding the wood, branches and leaves into a chipper and then running the resulting wood chips back through his home made chipper a second time to get them down to a small enough size. The finely shredded wood is laid in layers and soaked with water to form a round flat-topped humus pile. Heat is extracted from the pile by water pumped through 1-inch plastic pipe that is routed through the center of the pile in coil pattern. In the very center of the pile is a 1000-gallon steel or plastic sealed tank that is filled 3/4ths of the way full with shredded wood chips that have been presoaked in water for two months. This biodigester will be heated by the surrounding humus pile and will produce an average of 50 CUFT of biogas each day, (a Therm of NG is 100 CUFT). A thermometer is mounted in the top of the biodigester, so the temperature can be monitored and kept at about 95 F for maximum methane production. Water is run through the plastic pipe for hot water heating, hydronic home heating and for keeping the biodigester from getting too hot. The energy is extracted from the humus pile in two ways. The first is the biogas from the digester, which is used for cooking, plus other NG uses and can be compressed and used to fuel a NG converted car. The second is the water pumped through the pile that is heated up to 140 F which is used for hot water and home heating.

Making a Humus Pile with the Jean Pain Method

The site for the humus pile needs to be fairly close to the building that the hot water will be used to heat, to reduce losing too much heat in the hot water lines before it reaches the building. The 1,000 gallon biodigester tank needs to be in the center of the pile location and will need a solid foundation. I would recommend considering using a four inch thick concrete pad poured over a layer of 2 to 4 inches of high density foam board, possibly with the plastic pipe laid in the cement rather than building the humus pile on the ground which will draw away some of the heat of the pile. Size the concrete pad so that the pile will cover it completely or the exposed concrete will conduct heat out from under the pile and expose it to the cold air. You can have a larger pad by installing a foam board divider in the cement to insulate the cement under the pile from the cement that extends outside of the base of the humus pile. By extending, the cement out beyond the pile will allow for the needed encircling trench to be made of concrete. The humus pile could also be insulated on the sides by locating the pile in a pit with foam insulated concrete walls and using loose foam boards laid on top for more insulation. Remember that once the pile is done composting, the compost will have to be hauled out to where you are going to use it, so allow for an easy way of removing the compost. Once the wood chips are broken down, the resulting humus should be in a liquid state and could be drained or even pumped by a pump that can handle a thick liquid with wood chips in it. By insulating the pile in cold climates, there will be far less heat lost to the outdoors and more heat will be usable for heating the house. This will allow for getting more heat out of a smaller humus pile, which is important since Jean Pain's humus piles tended to use from 14 to 40 tons of brush. The humus pile can be sized for your expected energy needs, and with practice and experience, you will be able to build a pile that will supply what you need for 18-24 months without wasting a lot of unused material.

Once the wood and leaves have been shredded to size, the bottom layer is put down 2.5-4 inches thick and is then soaked with water. Each additional layer is spread on top and soaked with water until the pile is complete, which can be nine feet tall and 18 feet in diameter. As the pile is being built and soaked with water, the water will drain into the surrounding ditch and is redirected back over the top of the pile by pumping and spraying or using buckets for three days after the pile is competed, until the wood chips are completely saturated with water. If the pile is located in hole or an insulated concrete vat, the sidewalls will retain the water and will eliminate having to pump the water back on top of the pile. The pile needs to be high enough to completely cover the digester tank in the middle, so that the tank is kept warm. For free standing piles, the pile is shaped by building a central tower five feet in diameter by using chicken wire wrapped around the tower, forming a cylinder of wood chips five feet in diameter or larger built around the center tank, covering the tank with at least two feet of wood chips on the sides. The plastic water pipe is then spiraled wrapped around this tower with a six-inch spacing between coils in the spiral, using 200-400 feet of pipe. The rest of the pile is built by piling the chips in layers up against the tower. A tower is not needed for piles in a pit and the water pipe can be spiraled upward progressively as the layers are laid. The water lines of course have to be run out of the pile, and the tank will need a gas line running to a flexible gas storage that will expand as the generated gas flows into it. Jean Pain used 24 truck tire inner tubes for gas storage, but now that tubeless tires are common, inner tubes have pretty much disappeared. When was the last time you saw one being used for floating in the water? Today there are quite a number of heavy plastic storage bags or bladders that can be used instead. The top of the tower and tank is covered by two feet of wood chips on top to insulate and keep the tank warm. The thermometer in tank will need to reach from the liquid in the tank to the top of the pile, but today it makes sense to use a remote thermometer with a sensor or bulb in the tank, and have the thermometer mounted inside the house so the tank temperature is easily monitored and the water flow adjusted as needed to control the temperature of the tank.

If you would like to know more about how to do this, search on the web using the term "Jean Pain Method" or see if you can get one of his books, which unfortunately are all out of print. His book "*Another Kind of Garden*" is available in English as an E-book at this link http://www.jean-pain.com/mjp.htm for 15 Euros.

Stoves & Furnaces for Burning Bio-fuels

While organic bio-fuel material can be "burned" for heat by composting, most of the bio-fuels covered in this chapter will need a good stove or furnace for heating use. Most of the pellet multi-fuel stoves rated for bio-fuels can be programmed for nearly all of them including manure pellets. Dried manure that has not been pelletized can be burned in wood or coal stoves. Since even dried manure is not very housekeeper friendly, the manure burner should be located outside of the living spaces of the home. You really do not want to be hauling buckets of "chips" into your living room and dumping them into a stove. It is far better to use a furnace located in a basement with an outside access or located in a outside room with an outside door. This is one of the few times an outdoor boiler could be a good choice, though a boiler located in an out building would probably be a better choice since outdoor boilers tend to be more expensive and have lower quality than other boilers.

Grains can be burned by Grain stoves and by some multi-fuel pellet stoves, though oats and barley can be hard to burn in grain stoves and may jam in pellet stoves. Check that the stove is stated to be able to burn the fuel you want to use before buying it. The different bio-fuel pellets can be burned in many of the multi-fuel pellet stoves. Multi-fuel bio-fuel rated pellet stoves are extremely complicated and prone to breaking down and it is very hard to find service people who know how to fix them or to get parts for, while grain stoves are less complicated and more reliable.

Multi Fuel Furnaces and Stoves that can Burn Bio-Fuels

Superior furnace by
Ja-Ran enterprises Inc,
3541 Babcock Rd., Lexington MI 48450
(1 (810) 359-7985) (http://www.ja-ran.com/superior.php).
The Superior furnace comes as a 100,000 BTU single burner model ($3,850) and a 200,000 BTU Double Burner model ($7,500). The Superior can burn wood pellets, corn, rye cherry pits, switch grass pellets and will probably be able to burn many of the other fuels listed in this chapter. Built by a small company, but seems to be a simple and reliable product.

Genesis 108 & **Genesis 206** stove models by
Seraph Industries,
LLC, 1175 Krupke Road,
Caledonia IL 61011
(815-222-9686) (http://www.seraph-industries.com/index.html)
Can burn wood pellets, corn and can be programmed to burn "any" of the other biofuels, which would include the grains and everything that comes as a pellet in theory. Price- $2395 & $3895 respectively.

Cumberland stoves **MF3700** and the **MF3800** with automatic ignition by Ardisam, Inc,
1690 Elm St, Cumberland, WI, 54829-9486
Phone: 715-822-2415 (http://www.cumberlandstoveworks.com/)
The Cumberland MF models can burn wood pellets, corn, cherry pits and a "*variety*" of biofuels. Quality unit with a good warranty. MF3700 and the MF3800 both cost about $3,200.

Magnum Country side models including the **Baby Countryside** and the **Winchester** burn corn, wood pellets and *"many other"* biofuels are made by
American Energy Systems Inc.
Phone 800-495-3196 (http://www.americanenergysystems.com/)
MagnuM Country Model: 3500P price $2,194.00 MagnuM furnace 6500 price $2,992.00 Comes with a rather limited warranty, which could be the sign of low reliability.

Dell-Point Europa 75 stove by
Dell-Point Technologies, Inc, phone 450-979-6212
(http://www.pelletstove.com/right.html)
A gasification pellet stove that can burn most biomass fuels. A very clean burning stove. Price $4,699 just a bit pricey.

American Harvest product line by
US Stove United States Stove Company,
227 Industrial Park Dr.,
South Pittsburg, TN 37380
phone 800-750-2723 (http://www.usstove.com)
Burns corn, wood pellets, soy beans, olive pits, cherry pits, grains, processed silage and other biomass fuels. Stove prices start at $2199.00, there is also an insert for $2300.00 and a furnace for $4500.00 US Stoves are often very competitively priced and many dealers will sell far below the suggested retail. The good news is the low price, the bad news is that US Stoves are not known for reliability or good design features.

Mt. Vernon AE stove by
Quadra-Fire, Hearth & Home Technologies, 1445 North Highway, Colville, WA 99114-2008
(http://www.quadrafire.com//Products/Pellet_Burning/Pellet_Model.
asp?f=sternson) Burns wood pellets, corn, sunflower seeds, wheat and many biomass fuels. Price $3,699.00 is also available as an insert. Very high tech and the Quadra-Fire stoves are an industry standard, but this stove has had its problems and many dealers have had problems being able to fix it.

Operating a Biomass Pellet Burner

Most of the Biomass pellets will burn like wood pellets and the stoves since they are pellet stoves, will operate nearly the same. See the chapter on wood pellets for information on lighting and operation. Now for the differences, many of the biomass pellets have much more ash than wood pellets and the BTU/lb can be higher or lower, which results in having to increase the ash-dumping rate and adjusting the feed rate. Since how this is done varies with each manufacturer and model, you will need to carefully read the manual. Most of the manuals are going to be incomplete on the specifics for the settings for burning specific bio-pellets so you will have to be creative and come up with a good guess through trail and error. You can also e-mail the manufacturer for the settings and there is a chance that they mite tell you what they are, but do not hold your breath on that one. The burning of some of these fuels as pellets in high tech pellet stoves is so new that we are still in the learning phase. Welcome to the future.

Chapter 18

Super Insulation Retro Fitting

The wisest course of action for the future is to retrofit your home into a super insulated passive solar home that needs little heat. A super insulated home uses less heat per year than does your average water heater. Image winter fuel bills nearly as low as summer fuel bills. As wild as this sounds, it can be done to a greater or lesser degree depending on how your home is built, and how much time and money you can afford to invest in insulation. It is very possible to greatly increase the insulation in an existing home, and it is possible to take advantage of the existing passive solar potential of the home's south facing windows or even add some windows to increase the passive solar gain. If the home is insulated to the point where little heat is needed and some passive solar heat is available, then the need for conventional heating is greatly reduced. Adding insulation to an existing home can be done and is a great investment for the future and here is how you do it.

For traditional wood framed homes with siding, the siding can be removed and foam sheathing can be installed on the outside walls of the home as described in chapter 4, which is a description of installing 2 inch thick foam sheets with an R-10 rating, which with the existing insulated wall has a total R-value of maybe R-20, which is pretty good. However if you wish to super insulate, R-40 is recommended for the walls and R-60 for the ceiling. Filling the attic with enough insulation to reach an insulation value of R-60 is not hard, you just blow more in. R-60 is 24 inches of fiberglass insulation. Obviously, you are not going to have 24 inches of space at the edges of the attic, or even 12, so the insulation will be less along the outside walls.

Putting R-40 insulation on the outside walls is difficult, since it is only reasonably possible to nail through two inches of foam, for that is as long as they make siding nails and two inches of foam only has an R-10 rating. To attain a wall insulation value of R-40, even allowing for the existing wall having an insulation value of R-10, will take three layers of 2-inch thick foam. To install six inches of foam on the outside of your house, you will need to frame out around the windows and doors with boards wide enough to reach above the thickness of the foam plus the siding. To install more than two inches of foam, it is necessary to provide additional nailing surfaces. After the siding is removed, and the soffit space is insulated or opened so the foam sheeting can be run to the top of the wall, nail a three inch casing nail one half inch into the sheathing centered over each stud at the top and another just above bottom end of each stud. Then install the 2-inch thick foam over the nails so that they project above the foam. Once you have the first layer of foam installed, fill all gaps and cracks in the foam by cutting pieces of foam to fit in larger gaps and use cans of spray foam to fill in narrower gaps and any irregular gaps. Next, tape all joints in the foam and tape the foam edges to trim boards around the windows and doors. Be sure to fill all the gaps and tape all the joints on each of the three layers of foam or cold outside air will be able to infiltrate through the foam by flowing through the gaps. Start the second layer by cutting two by fours down to a two inch width and nailing them to the wall studs using the casing nails as guides. Nail the boards so that they are on edge, so they will be flush with the surface of the second layer of foam, they need to be long enough to reach from the soffit to the bottom of the rim or sill board that rests on the foundation wall. Nail the first one, being careful to get it centered on where it needs to be, and plumb, since you will be nailing through 2 inches of wood and then 2 inches of foam, so you will need a six inch nail to penetrate old sheathing and still have enough nail left to grab enough of the stud to hold on to. The best nails for this are 6-inch long ring shank pole barn nails. Due to the thick ring shank, these nails will tend to split the nailing boards, which can be avoided either by predrilling holes for the nails or by using a hammer to flatten the nail points. Yes it is counter intuitive but flattening the point on a nail does reduce splitting, because the point acts as a wedge pushing wood to the sides while a flatten point crushes it instead. Nail the boards about every sixteen inches, keeping the nails on the ends at about four inches away from the end of the board to avoid splitting. You will also need to nail boards around the windows and doors to provide a nailing surface for the siding that will abut against the extended trim nailed to the window and door casing moldings. A nailing surface will also be needed at the corners, inside and outside corners for nailing trim boards and siding. On outside corners since it is not possible to nail into the foam for support, there will be no nailing surfaces on outside corners on either side, for a distance equal to the thickness of the foam. That means if you have added six inches of foam, you will need an eight-inch wide trim board to lap the other corner trim board, and still be wide enough to reach back over to the nailing board. Once you are ready to install the trim, install the outside corner trim boards by ripping one to width so that when it is lapped by the other board, the total width is equal to the width of the wider board. Nail the boards together, place over the corner and nail along into the nailing boards to secure it. For nailing the siding, since with many types of siding it is necessary avoid nailing too close to the ends to avoid splitting, two nailing boards may be necessary on each side of outside corners, one on the corner for the trim boards and one back a few inches for the siding. On inside corners, keep the nailing boards out of the corner or they will not be reachable once the next layer of foam sheeting covers them. On inside corners, only one trim board is needed, but some like to install two. Place the nailing boards to that the trim board or boards can be nailed and provide nailing for the siding, so that it can be nailed without splitting.

The second layer of foam will need to be glued to the first, since there is not much to nail it to, since four inches of foam is too thick for the nails to reach. Use a adhesive for foam and use a caulk gun to apply it to the back of the foam pieces that have already been cut to size and test fitted, then press firmly in place, and if needed, press some foam sheathing nails through the foam and into the foam underneath to hold it while the glue sets. Cut the pieces of foam to match the spacing between your studs. Some studs will be out of place and you will have to cut foam to fit. Once the second layer of foam is glued between the nailing boards, once again fill all gaps with foam pieces or canned spray foam, and tape all joints and edges. Nail a three-inch casing nail in the center of the top end and bottom end of each nailing board. The third layer is pressed down over the nails, and is nailed to the nailing boards with the tops of the casing nails projecting out, marking the places for nailing the siding. Then once again after the third layer is all installed and all gaps are filled with foam, tape the joints and edges. However, since this is the last layer of foam, be careful only to apply the tape where the siding will cover it, so it does not stick out above the siding. House wrap is now installed over the third layer of foam and is nailed to the nailing boards as well; press the wrap down in place so the top of the casing nails pops through the wrap. Nail a row of plastic capped nails along the top of the nailing boards, then pull out any wrinkles and nail along the bottom casing nails. Nail the house wrap in place and tape the joints and edges of the house wrap making sure that you keep the tape back enough that it will not show above the siding. Next take a chalk line and hook it on each top casing nail and snap a line to the bottom casing nail over each nailing board. This will serve as the marking lines for nailing the siding. The siding is installed using siding nails designed for use over two-inch thick foam sheathing. These nails are normally about 4 inches long, and for lap siding will not provide enough length for nailing through two layers of siding as is done when face nailing. It will probably be necessary to blind nail along the upper edge of each siding board, where the nails will be hidden by the next siding board installed above it. Face nailing is designed to hold down the edge of warping boards, since most siding is no longer wood, having been replaced by cement board, vinyl or aluminum siding, it is not needed any more and blind nailing hides the nails which otherwise detract from the appearance of the siding.

A number of older homes are brick and while it is possible to install foam over the brickwork and then reside the house, it would be a shame to cover it up and many homes have stone or brick work that is too ill regular of a surface to cover with foam sheets. Putting foam over brick or stone is a bad idea anyway since the masonry will act as a thermal bridge conducting cold from the ground, around windows and doors, and from the top edge, behind the insulation thus greatly reducing its effectiveness. A better way of installing the insulation is to install it on the inside.

Brick homes that have block walls often have the drywall attached to firing strips with only a thin layer of less than two inches of fiberglass insulation between the firing strips. The heat loss is enormous with such minimal insulation. The drywall and firing strips should be removed. The painted drywall may act as a vapor barrier and trap out going water vapor and if cold enough, cause it to condense inside the wall, to prevent this it is recommended that vapor barriers not be located further out in the wall than one third of the insulated value of the wall. Since there is so little insulation on the outside of the drywall in a block built house with firing strips, the drywall should be removed or heavily "ventilated" with a hammer. It is best of course to remove the drywall, old insulation and firing strips.

Since the outside masonry wall has little insulation value, it makes sense to install eight inches of foam to achieve an R-40 insulation value. Four layers of two-inch thick foam sheets can be installed or eight inches of foam can be sprayed in the wall space or 16 inches of fiberglass or cellulose can be blown into the space behind the new inside wall. Spraying the foam in place has the advantage of being easy and does not take up a lot of space, but since you need to hire a contractor to install the foam, you pretty much need to do the whole house at once to keep the costs down. While with the foam sheets, if you are doing it yourself, you can do one room at a time, which is more reasonable, if you are living in the home. Fiberglass can be installed as loose blow in or in batts, but either way, you will need a thickness of 16 inches for an insulation value of R-40 and 16 inches is a lot of space to lose. Cellulose insulation is one of the least expensive, but settling can be a problem so it is important that every part of the wall cavity be completely filled. Since cellulose which is chopped up treated paper that is loose, it will fall out of the wall unless held in place. It will be necessary to install the drywall, drill a series of holes, and blow the cellulose in with a blower. Pay particular attention to spaces above doors, and above and below windows. Another way of installing cellulose is wet spraying in which the cellulose is blown in wet or at least damp enough to stick in place like a spitball. The wet cellulose will need time to dry out completely, before the vapor barrier can be installed.

The ceiling drywall should be cut back so as not to act as a cold thermal bridging point and the same should be done with interior walls. If there is loose fill insulation in the attic without a vapor barrier, it may be necessary to leave the drywall to keep the insulation from falling out. Cut the drywall in front of where the wood framing for the wall will be, allowing half the thickness of the new drywall for error. That way if you miss when cutting the drywall one way or the other, you will still have some margin to play with.

With the drywall cut back, check your nailing surfaces for installing the wood framing. Since you will be moving the corners of the room inward a few inches, you may need to install a two by four in the old interior walls to support the old drywall in the new wall corners. If the ceiling joists run parallel to the outside wall, you will need to install nailing blocks between the ceiling joists, so you have something to nail the top of your new wall to and for supporting the edge of the old drywall. Cut pieces of two by fours to fit in between the joists and nail them in on a spacing of 16 inches, and have a board at the ends in each room corner.

Once the drywall is vented or removed. The electrical will need to be moved forward and installed in the new wall surface, this can be often be done by removing the drywall around the outlets and switches and letting the wiring hang loose, and reattaching the boxes and cables to the new wall framing once it is in place. There will probable be enough slack in the cables to allow for moving the wiring six or eight inches forward. Heating vents can be moved forward by removing the registers and ductwork from the hole in the floor for the register and cutting a new hole in the new location in front of the new wall surface and shortening the branch duct and putting the ductwork back together. For hydronic heat, the radiators will need to be moved by removing them and removing the piping and drilling holes in the new location and repiping. Unless you are skilled at plumbing work, you will need a plumber for this, and an electrician for moving the electrical if there is not enough slack in the cables or if the wiring is in conduit. The trim around windows can be removed and the window frame extended by using wood cut to width so the new window frame edge will be flush with the new drywall surface. When trimming the windows, consider allowing for installing insulated interior shutters. The shutters are made out of plywood with two inches or more of foam insulation inside, that can be closed at night over the window opening. Since windows are where a home loses much of its heat, insulated window shutters can greatly reduce heat loss. Extending the walls in around the doors will have to allow for the door to swing inward and allow room for the latch, so it may be best to leave the door trim in place and start the new drywall next to it. Moving the inside wall in a few inches will present many challenges some of the greatest of which will be found in the bathroom where toilets and tubs may have to be moved. Kitchens will also be trouble some with cabinets and sinks that will need to be moved. Since it will be very difficult to move some things, it may be worth it to use high R-value insulation that will be thin enough to use in the existing space so that hard to move things do not have to be moved. Spray foam with its high R-value and ability to fill spaces, may allow you create a well-insulated wall without having to move the inside wall surface far enough inward that you have to move a toilet. There are other super high R-value insulation products like VIP or vacuum insulation panels which are only one inch thick and can have an R-value of 28-50 or even higher. The downside of VIP panels is that in addition to their high cost (about $24/sq ft); they have an expected lifespan of only about 15 to 25 years. These super insulating panels are normally used for large coolers and are not designed for being nailed through which would break the vacuum and render the panel nearly useless. In theory, these panels could be glued to the block wall and the drywall could be glued over them, but a single nail for hanging a picture would ruin an entire panel. The panels also cannot be cut and have to be ordered to size. In the long run, it is probably better to move the toilet.

If you are installing foam sheets, glue the first layer to the block wall, fill any gaps with foam, tape the joints, and tape the foam to the floor and the vapor barrier in the ceiling. Glue the second layer to the first, fill, tape again, and repeat for the third layer. Next, install the wood framing (probably best to cut wood framing to a two inch width to match the thickness of the last layer of foam) and electrical and cut the foam for the fourth layer to fit in between the framing pieces and glue in place. Fill the gaps with foam and tape the foam to the wood. Install a plastic vapor barrier and tape it all the way around, but not to the inside surface of the old drywall since it would be in the way of the plaster. Drywall the wall. The corner joints between the old and new drywall will be tricky, to do them use the self-adhesive fiberglass mesh tape and a corner plaster knife to create a joint that will not crack apart as can happen with the plaster paper tapes.

For insulating with spray foam, install the wood framing and the electrical and then have the foam sprayed in. With spray foam insulation you do not have to worry about gluing the foam to the outside wall or filling gaps between sheets or tapping joints and a good contractor will be able to neatly fill the wall cavity and trim the foam flush with inside wall surface of the wood farming. Spray foam is more expensive than foam sheets and has a lower R-value, but with spay foam, a vapor barrier is not needed. Finish the wall by installing the drywall.

With fiberglass batts, install the wood framing and electrical. Install fiberglass batts with a total thickness equal to the distance from the front of the wood framing to the block wall, which for R-40 would be 16 inches. The batts can be installed in a single layer which is cut on the front to fit over the studs, or two layers of batts can be installed with one sized to fit behind the wall and then another sized install to fit in the spaces between the studs. One the insulation is installed, the vapor barrier and drywall can be installed.

There are other types of building construction and there are different ways of adding insulation. With some thought and research you will probably be able to find ways of insulating your home, however it is put together, or you can hire a insulation contractor who will be happy to install as much insulation as you want to buy.

All this insulation will of course be largely wasted if you have drafts. To be effective, a super insulated home needs to be well weather-stripped. See section on weather stripping in the chapter on the Magic Furnace (insulation). If you successfully seal up your home, you will need a fresh air heat exchanger to bring in fresh air and to get rid of excess humidity. See the information on air exchangers in the Magic Furnace chapter.

Chapter 19

EMERGENCY HEATING TRICKS

If you just opened the book and flipped to this chapter, I will assume that either you have no heat or you can no longer afford to pay for your heat. First, here is what you can do if you have no heat.

If the outdoor temperature will be below freezing at night, the temperature inside your house tonight may drop low enough for your plumbing to freeze. If you still have water pressure such as from a city water supply, open all taps a small amount to allow for a fast steady drip to maintain water flow in the pipes to prevent freezing (be sure to have flow from both hot and cold water pipes). If you do not have water pressure, and your pipes are in danger of freezing, open the taps and let the water drain out, by opening a tap in the basement or opening the lowest pipe union, saving some water in containers for drinking water. Tanks such as pressure tanks and water heaters will have valves for draining. You will not have to drain the water heater if it is still working. If you decide to drain the water heater tank, remember to turn it off, so if the power comes back on, it will not heat an empty tank, which would ruin the tank.

If the furnace is broken down, while you try to fix it, for temporary heat if you have an electric clothes dryer, disconnect the exhaust vent and let the hot air vent inside the home for heat and run the dryer empty. You can do the same with a gas dryer, if you can take steps to prevent a build up of carbon dioxide and carbon monoxide gas from occurring inside the home. The first step is to use the dryer vent duct to vent the hot exhaust far enough away from the dryer so that the dryer will not be trying to run in its own exhaust, which is very bad. The second step is to open a window to insure that the dryer has fresh air, so it will not produce any carbon monoxide, which is deadly. The third step is to insure that the dryer exhaust does not fill the house with carbon dioxide gas by opening more windows if you feel sleepy or the air becomes stuffy or stale. Be sure to read the information on pages 325-9 about the dangers of carbon dioxide and carbon monoxide poisoning.

Emergency Furnace Repairs

If you still have electricity and fuel, here are some simple things you can do to possibly restart or repair your furnace. First, check your thermostat, is it set for the correct temperature, is it set in the heat mode and turned on? Many digital thermostats will not work without a good battery, if you have no display you may need to replace the battery or the transformer that powers the thermostat may not have power, check your circuit breakers or fuses. A quick check is, at the thermostat turn on the furnace fan by pressing the fan "On" button or switch; you should hear the fan start up. If the fan does not start, the furnace probably does not have power, the thermostat is broken or the fan control is not wired to the thermostat. If you have any doubts about the thermostat (and it is not a line voltage thermostat as is found in some resistance electric baseboard heating systems), remove it from the wall and jump or connect the red wire (Marked H or H1) to the white wire (marked C), and the furnace should start. If it does not the problem is not with the thermostat.

Check to see that there is power to the transformer that supplies power to the thermostat, this is a small doorbell type transformer and will normally be located on an electrical junction box in the basement and is often on a different circuit than the furnace. You can locate it by following the thermostat wires, or just looking for a second doorbell transformer that isn't connected to the doorbell wiring circuit. The normal voltage is 12 or 24 volts. If there is no voltage, then when the thermostat, closes its contacts, there will be no voltage to turn the heat on. To test for voltage, connect a 12-volt bulb (car tail light bulb) briefly across the terminals. If there is power, the bulb will light up brightly and may burn out if you connect if for more than a second if you have a 24-volt transformer. These small transformers are available at most hardware stores, since they are the same type used on door bell circuits, just be sure to get the same type and remember that the other side of the circuit is 110 volts and will need to be turned off before you replace the transformer. If you are not comfortable with electrical work, hire someone to do this for you.

If the furnace still does not fire up, check for power on the thermostat wires at the furnace, and at the thermostat, you may have a broken wire somewhere.

Check that you still have electricity on the circuit for the furnace by checking the fuse or circuit breaker. Check for power at furnaces by turning on the furnace fan by removing the front cover pressing the manual fan on button or switch on the fan control, a normally silver aluminum box mounted on the heat exchanger. You otherwise may be able to check for power to most types of heating units by turning the electrical switch on the side of the heating unit, on and off and listening for a soft clicking sound of one of the relays being pulled in when the power comes on, or even the sound of the arc in the switch as it is turned on if you have very good ears.

If the heating system is running and producing heat, but the house still seems cold, check for an open doors or windows since few heating systems can compete against an open window in the wintertime. I get quite a number of service calls where they cannot understand why the building is so cold, but when I ask around, it turns out that they had a door open for a long time before I came and just closed it before I got there. If something like this is the case, it is just going to take awhile for the heating system to catch up and you are just going to have to be patient.

On setback thermostats, an anticipation circuit starts the heat well enough in advance of a higher setting to bring the house up to temperature in time. These circuits remember how long it took to do so the day before and adjust accordingly. The problem is that they don't have an outdoor temperature sensor, so if the temperature suddenly drops outside, the thermostat doesn't know that and assumes it will take the same amount of time it did yesterday to bring the house back up to temperature. A sudden drop in outside temperature can result in a large lag in reaching a higher temperature setting. So occasionally, setback thermostats mess up and will sometimes be below where they should be, as long as they are calling for heat the thermostat is working properly.

If your heater is not running, to find what is wrong with your heating system and how to correct it, locate the type of heating system you have in the section headings below.

If you have a Gas or LP Furnace that has a Standing Pilot Light

Only older furnaces with stovepipe venting have standing pilot lights, all newer furnaces have spark ignition systems and do not have a standing or constant pilot light. Check to see that you still have gas by lighting a burner on the kitchen stove. If you have gas and power to the furnace, remove the front cover and try to relight the pilot light if it is not already lit. This is done by turning the gas valve inside the furnace, to the position marked "pilot" and pressing down on the valve handle. The handle should sink down about a quarter inch or more, there may be a red button you have to press as a release latch to do this on some gas valves. With the handle down, light the pilot. The pilot assembly has two tubes running from the gas valve to it, and you will need to hold a flame next to it while pressing the gas valve. The pilot light is often located too far back to reach with a match, so you may need to use a match holder which you can make by taking a coat hanger and cutting a length of wire long enough to reach the pilot and bending a tight loop on the end with a pliers. The loop should be tight so you can pinch a match between the wires, then light the match and reach in and place the lit match next to the pilot light assembly. It will take about 30 seconds for the gas to reach the pilot from the gas valve, and even once the pilot lights, you will need to hold the handle down on the gas valve until the pilot flame has heated up the thermocouple hot enough that it produces enough current to hold open the pilot valve, which can be 30 to about 90 seconds. My rule is to hold it for 2 minutes after the pilot is lit, and if the pilot goes out after I release the button, I tighten the nut holding down the thermocouple connection on the gas valve (the smaller tube) and if it still fails to stay lit, I replace the thermocouple. You should be able to get a new thermocouple at any decent hardware store, just be sure to get one long enough to reach from the gas valve to the pilot assembly. If the pilot still fails to stay lit or never lit at all (Be sure to check that ALL gas valves leading to the furnace are open.), the gas valve will need to be replaced which is probably a job you should leave to a service person.

If the pilot light is lit, make sure that the gas valve is set to "main" and that the thermostat is calling for heat. If you have thermostat voltage at the gas valve and the gas valve still is not opening to feed gas to the main burner, the gas valve will need to be replaced. If you do not have thermostat voltage at the gas valve, a switch is open in the safety circuit. The safety circuit is a series of various switches like high temperature limit switches, which are wired in series with the gas valve, and will not allow the main gas valve to open, unless all the switches in the safety circuit are closed. Some of these switches may have reset buttons, but otherwise the only way of really checking the safety circuit is by using a multi-meter for doing voltage and resistance tests to locate the switch that is open. All newer heating units will have a safety circuit, and newer units will tend to have more switches in the circuit.

Now if the main burner is lighting but not staying lit, is the furnace fan turning on? If the fan fails to come on, the heat exchanger will get too hot and the high temperature limit will shut the furnace down by opening the safety circuit breaking the call for heat. The high temperature limit is located inside the fan control, which is often an aluminum box with a snap off cover with a white plastic button sticking out. If you remove the cover, there will be a round dial with temperature markings stamped in it and two or more metal markers set at certain temperature settings on the dial. First, do not move the markers or try to rotate the dial, which can break it. Turn on the furnace and as the heat exchanger warms up, the dial will turn, and as the lower setting passes the indicator, the furnace fan should come on, if the temperature of the heat exchanger gets too hot, the dial will rotate until the high temperature-setting hits the indicator, which will turn off the gas valve. If the fan control is turning off the gas before hitting the high temperature setting, it is bad and will need to be replaced. If it reaches the high setting before turning off, the fan control is not the problem, you are not moving enough air through the heat exchanger to keep it from over heating. If the fan motor did not turn on, it could be bad, check it visually for blacken wires in the motor windings (don't be fooled by dust, check for sooty blackness by rubbing with your finger). These fan motors normally have vent holes and by looking in you can see the winding wires, any blackening is a sure sign of a burned out motor, and if you cannot see any blackening, you will able smell it by getting your nose up next to one of the vent holes. To be sure that the motor is bad, if you cannot see or smell any burned wires, someone has to do a continuity check with a multi meter. Normal readings will be a few ohms, while a bad motor is an open circuit or a short circuit to the motor shell. To get a replacement motor, take the old one to Johnstone Supply or a similar appliance parts supplier, put it on the counter, and ask for another one. They may ask for make and model of your furnace, which should be listed on an aluminum tag on the front of the furnace or on the inside of the furnace door.

If the fan runs for a while and then the furnace shuts down only to start up again and then shut down again (high limit turning the gas off, and then turning back on once the heat exchanger has cooled down), you have a restriction in the air flow, probably a dirty air filter. If the filter is clean, check the cold air return grills and registers, if they are clean then the restriction is possibly a dirty heat exchanger. The heat exchanger can be cleaned by flushing with water on the airside by opening an access plate or opening the ductwork above the furnace. Think twice before you try this one, it is not a common problem unless the furnace has been run a long time without an air filter and the water has to go somewhere and you don't want anything electrical getting wet, this maybe a job better done by a service person.

Gas or LP Furnaces Without a Standing Pilot Light

The basic design for these units is like the old standing pilot light units only with some extra bells and whistles. On the inside of the furnace front cover, there will or should be a circuit diagram showing how the furnace is wired. The diagram will probably be hard to understand, but what they are attempting to show is the furnace "safety circuit". What you have is instead of the thermostat wire just being just routed through a fan control switch to the gas valve, it is routed through a bunch of new of things to an ignition control module, which is a plastic box with a red spark plug wire running to the pilot assembly. In order for the gas valve to open the pilot gas valve and the ignition module to start sparking or for a carbon igniter to glow hot, every switch in the safety circuit has to be closed. If a single switch is open, the ignition control will not even start to light the pilot. In condensing furnaces, the ones vented with plastic PVC pipe, there is a draft inducing fan that is the first thing to start on a call for heat, which pulls air through the fire side of the heat exchanger and exhausts it through the PVC. If the fan fails to start on a call for heat, it is probably bad, but since this is about a $200 part, check for voltage at the fan wiring and for a good neutral wire and check the motor for continuity. A simple test is to connect the fan to 110 volts and see if it runs. (This is done with jumpers and is not a job for everyone) If the fan runs but is not running fast enough to pull in the vacuum switch on the heat exchange, the problem maybe that sometimes these fans develop mechanical problems, in that the plastic impeller inside the housing can fall off the motor shaft and drag on the housing. To fix, open the snap latches, open the housing and check it. If it has fallen off, glue it back on the shaft with super glue, reassemble, and test for operation.

The second step is for the draft-inducing fan to create enough of a partial vacuum or low pressure in the heat exchanger to close the vacuum or air pressure switch, this switch looks like a round flat sliver can with a two or three terminal switch mounted on top of it. The switch can be checked to see if it is closing, with a volt/ohm meter. If the other switches are all closed, the pilot gas valve opens and the ignition module will begin sparking or the carbon igniter will glow. With some spark modules, you can hear the circuit "pulse" even if no spark occurs at the pilot assembly; this is the number one problem and is easily fixed. What is happening is the spark is failing to jump the gap at the pilot assembly because the pilot assembly is rusty or has a coating that has built up on it. All you need to do is clean the pilot assembly by using a file, sandpaper, steel wool or in a pinch, even a knife blade will do. Clean the flame rod, a narrow metal rod, which some furnaces have and some do not. Also, clean the edges of the flame guide and the spark rod. If this fails to do the trick, reclean it, sometimes it takes a few attempts to get the assembly clean enough to work. If it still fails to fire and you can hear the spark module pulsing, you have a bad spark module but it is very unusual for a spark module to pulse and still not work, normally a bad module does not do anything. If the draft inducer fan runs and the air pressure switch is closing, and nothing else is open in the safety circuit, with voltage across the terminals on the spark igniter module, and the module is not sparking, you have a bad spark module. Spark modules are about $100 and there are quite a lot of different modules out there, but you can buy a universal model that will replace about 90% of them. You will once again need the make, model and serial number of the furnace, plus the spark module, and you can get a replacement at any where furnace parts are sold.

Carbon igniters will glow orange to ignite the gas, if the carbon is not glowing it may not be getting power or there maybe a crack in it. A crack opens the circuit and no current will flow, so the carbon does not glow. You can often see the crack if there is one. The big common problem with carbon igniters is that with age they begin to fail. What happens is as part of the carbon is burned away or begins to crack, the carbon conducts less current, and many ignition circuits use the carbon igniter current flow to pull in a relay to turn on the gas valve. Therefore, you can have a hot glowing carbon igniter that just is not drawing enough current to pull in the relay. The only fix is to replace the igniter, which can cost about $100 or more. When installing the new one, do not touch the carbon, so it stays clean of oil from your skin and be very careful about breaking the carbon. I dropped one once, and it broke so I had to go buy another one for another hundred dollars. The only thing worse than having to pay for an over priced part, is having to pay for it twice. The problem with carbon igniters is that if they glow, you cannot tell if they are not drawing enough current or if they are and it is the gas valve that is bad. You just have to replace the igniter to find out. The carbon igniter, it is probably the problem, since they tend to only last a few years while gas valves normally last for the lifetime of the heating unit.

Oil Furnaces

Check to see if the furnace is warm, if it is hot, the fan may not be working to move the hot air into the house. If the furnace is cold, turn the power switch off then back on again, you may able to hear a relay click or a hum which means the furnace has electrical power, otherwise check the circuit breaker or fuses. Oil furnaces and boilers are wonderful in that burners have reset buttons, one located on the ignition module and often times also one on the blower motor. GENTLY press the red plastic buttons, don't mash them, if pressing them once doesn't do anything, pressing them repeatedly harder and harder is not going to do anything other than flood the firebox with oil which may leak out and will need to be cleaned out before the burner can safely be restarted. Often times these reset buttons are crushed flat by desperate homeowners anxious to get the heat back on. How you really get the heat back on, is to start checking for possible problems. Pressing the ignition module (older units have a transformer) reset button should start the pilot cycle, the burner fan should start, and after a delay of about a minute the fuel pump should start and the fuel oil should be sprayed through the nozzle and the ignition module or a transformer (which started earlier when the pump started or earlier) should throw an arc across the arc rods igniting the flame. The flame sensor or Cat's Eye which is a type of photo sensor, sees the flame and keeps the fuel valve open and then the furnace fan comes on once the heat exchanger is hot enough and the furnace is running (older units may have a heat sensor in the vent pipe instead with a reset button on it). You need to watch this series of events and see what is failing to happen. The fuel pump may fail to work, you can check with a multi meter to see if it is getting power. You can often disconnect the fuel line after the pump and use a rubber hose to run the line into a clear glass or plastic container and turn the furnace switch on briefly to see if the pump is pumping the fuel or if the fuel filter is clogged or the fuel line is blocked or sucking air from a nearly empty oil tank. Hold the container up to the light and check for water in the fuel. If you have water in the fuel, you may be able to pump off the water into a bucket until you are just getting fuel oil and no water. To get rid of the stuff in the bucket, carefully pour off just the oil which can be poured back into the oil tank, and the mostly water part should be properly disposed of (we have laws about these things, maybe use an oil absorber like cat litter and throw it away in the trash). If the fuel oil barely trickles out of the line, the filter is probably clogged, but also check for kinks in the fuel line. The line may have been damaged by being hit and bent by something. Alternatively, if the pump is pumping well, the nozzle may be clogged and needs to be replaced or possibly cleaned by carefully reaming with a sliver of wood, (you should keep a spare nozzle on hand). If the furnace is not arcing, but maybe you can hear a hum from the transformer or a pulse from an ignition module, check the flame rods and clean them up with a file. To reach the nozzle or the arc rods, you will probably have to remove the burner assembly from the furnace. If the furnace still is not arcing, check for power to the transformer if you did not hear it make a sound. If the transformer has power and will not arc, replace the transformer.

If the Cat's Eye is not seeing the flame and keeps shutting down the burner, remove the eye and clean the lens. If the Cat's Eye still isn't working, put a multi meter across it and cycle the furnace, if it works you will see a drop in voltage to about less than a volt across it as it turns "on". If there is no change in voltage, the Eye is probably bad. You can check the flame by looking through the empty mounting hole for the Eye, to make sure that the eye if adjustable, is looking at the flame. If you have a heat sensor instead of a Cat's Eye, you can check the heat sensor with a multi meter, the sensor is a heat sensitive bi-metal snap switch, that is normally open when cold and closed when hot. It should have voltage across it when open and none when it is hot and closed.

In an emergency, if you do not have a multi meter or other means to check for voltage across either a Cat's Eye or a heat senor, you can check them by touching the wires connected to them together at the correct point in the start up cycle and the furnace should run if that was the problem. You can run the furnace with the part jumped out, but only if you watch the furnace and are ready to quickly turn it off, if the flame goes out. Otherwise, if the flame fails, and the furnace control does not know that the flame is out, it will continue to spray oil into the furnace until the tank is empty. The oil will flood the furnace and drain out on the furnace room floor. Then if there is another attempt at starting, the oil spill may ignite and you would have quite a fire on your hands. Therefore, if you need to jump a senor, to run the furnace to get the house warmed up in an emergency, monitor the operation of the furnace closely. Then once the house is warm, turn off furnace and remove the jumper wire so no one else can turn it on while you are gone, grab the part and go get a replacement and install it.

Electric Heat

Check to see if you have electrical power coming into the house, there maybe a power failure, and remember that with 220 volts, you have two power feeds and you need both for things to work. If one of the feed lines is out, half the circuits in the home will be without power. Since the 220 circuits need both, they will all be out. You can check for power on the feed lines by plugging something in on the 110 circuits supplied by each feed line. In most circuit breaker panels, ever other single width 110-volt breaker in each row is wired to one of the feeds while the other breakers are wired to the other feed wire, which is why 220-volt breakers are double wide so they are connected to both feeds for 220 volts across the two feed wires. If one of the feed wires has no voltage, one of the fuses on the pole transformer is out and the power company will have to be called to come and replace it. If you have 220 electric power, check your breakers or fuses, and remember that your heating system may involve more than one breaker or fuse. There are the ones at the main panel, and there maybe a local disconnect panel by larger heating units and possibly even inside the unit as in the case of some electric furnaces. The common wiring set up is a small 20-amp 120-volt control circuit, which feeds a transformer for any low voltage controls and thermostats and a 220-volt large amperage circuits for the heating elements, and if you have a large system, there may be more than one. Baseboard heaters are often wired on separate breakers for each room, or even more than one for large rooms.

If you have an electric furnace, if it is warm and the house is cold, you may have a problem with the fan motor. Some fan motors have a red reset button located on the end away from the shaft. If the fan motor is running and the house is cold, you may have a broken belt, or a really dirty air filter that is blocking the airflow.

Heat Pumps

Check the circuit breakers and any fuses, also check the outside temperature, if it is less than 40 F degrees it maybe too cold and damp, the outside coil maybe freezing up. If you see an ice build up on the outside coil or it is cold and the unit just is not producing any heat, press the emergency heat button on the thermostat, which will turn on the electric back up heat. Using the electric heat for a while may allow some time for the ice to melt off the outside coil if it is above freezing. On units that switch to electric heat automatically, and you still do not have electric heat, check the breaker or fuses for the heating elements, which are often on a separate circuit. There maybe circuit beakers or fuses at your main panel, at a sub panel next to the unit or even inside the service panel on the heat pump.

Another possible problem on heat pumps is that the unit may have tripped out due to high head pressure caused by poor air flow over the indoor coil. There is often a manual reset lever located on the front of an often gray metal box with what looks like a narrow window with a pointer and some numbers, the box has a copper tube connected to the pipe coming out of the high pressure side of the compressor. Press the metal level, in like a button, and you may hear a click if it was tripped. If the high limit trips out again, you will have to check why it is doing so. High head pressure is normally the result, that the coil that is hot, is unable to dump enough heat and the pressure increases. This is often caused by too little air flow over the coil due to a dirty air filter, broken fan motor, broken fan belt or a dirty coil.

Boilers All Types

The first thing to check on a boiler is the temperature gauge, if the house is cold and the boiler is hot, the boiler is working, the problem is in moving the heat in the pipes. If this is the case, check the circulation pumps even if they appear to running, the couplers that connect the electric motor to the pump could be broken. Turn off the pump and remove the cover and look down into the space between the motor and the pump and check the coupler or you maybe able to hear the whoosh and swirl of water in the pump housing, try using a metal rod with one end against the pump and place the other end against the bone just in front of your ear. If the electric motor is not perfectly aligned, with its shaft in line with the pump shaft, the circulation pump will eat couplers quite regularly. A coupler in a properly aligned circulation pump should last for years. Replacing couplers on many circulators is a job for a service person. If you have a small circulator and it is not too hard to get to, or you are very mechanically inclined, you can do the job yourself. On many B&G pumps, you can sometimes even change the yoke type coupler without having to pull the motor. Reach in through the access plate with long hex keys and unscrew the hex screws in the coupler shafts and use a large flat blade screw driver to pry the coupler halves off the shafts. The new coupler is worked into place and the hex screws tightened. Sounds easy, but normally takes an hour or two to do and will probably need a good penetrating oil to get the old coupler off the shafts, and it is still even money that you will have to pull the motor to do the job.

If the pumps are spinning but the water still is not moving, check all valves to see if one in the line is closed. If the line is not blocked by a closed valve, it maybe blocked by a large air pocket. Check your boiler pressure and the pressure rating of the safety valve, if the pressure is well below the release pressure of the safety valve, you can use the bypass on the water supply make up valve, to raise the pressure up to near the safety release pressure. This will compress the air bubble in the line and may make it small enough to blow out and let any automatic air bleeds in the boiler room bleed it off. The next step is to go to the air bleed located on the high point in the system piping and open it and vent out any air. The bleed will be located under the cover of the highest radiator, or may be on a pipe, if the pipes are above the highest radiator. The valve on top of the radiator or pipe, is opened with a small screw driver or a small wrench that looks like an old time roller skate key. If you do not have a key for the square shaft type, you can reach the shaft with a fine needle nose pliers. Often these valves are connected to the high point by a long narrow tube and hang down, so they are more accessible, and if under a radiator, they can be lifted up and any vented water drained into a pail. Open the vent slowly and let the water spray out into a pail for maybe a minute and shut it off if you don't vent any air, otherwise continue venting until you get water for at least 15 to 30 seconds. If you vented a lot of air, you may have solved the problem, return to the boiler and check the pressure. If the pressure has dropped really low, you may need to raise it back up again and vent again. Once circulation is established, the pipes will get hot and then you know things are working.

If the boiler is cold, press the low water cut out reset switch. This is located in a pipe on the side of the boiler or just above, it is designed to shut the boiler down if the water level drops below the top of the boiler. You can check the water level by lifting the level on the safety pressure relief valve on the boiler and see if water comes out. If air comes out, hold the valve open until water comes out and then press the lower water cut out reset switch and the boiler should start. If that is not the problem and the boiler still does not start, remove the front cover on the boiler and check the controls as outlined in the sections above for the type of heat the boiler uses such as oil, gas or electricity.

If Heating System is not Repairable or you do not have Electricity.

Use what other heat sources you do have, turn on the kitchen stove. If you have electricity and have an electric range, turn on the oven and all the burners on the stove top. Since electric ranges do not create fumes, this is safe to do. With gas ranges, you can turn on both the oven and the burners if you have both gas and electricity. If you do not have electricity, you will not be able to use the oven since you will not be able to get it to light. You can however use the burners by lighting them with a match. Gas ranges of course create fumes, (CO_2) but this is no more dangerous than when you use the stove for cooking. A gas or electric range is not going to be able to adequately heat the average home, but should produce enough heat to keep the pipes from freezing. Using all four burners on the gas range for an extended period of time, may create more CO_2 or carbon dioxide than cooking would normally produce. Carbon dioxide is what you exhale and it is the rising levels of it, in your lungs that triggers the urge to breathe and a higher level of it in the house will cause the house to feel "stuffy" and create an urge to open a window to let in some air. While CO_2 is fairly harmless since it has to reach levels of 5 percent or greater to cause unconsciousness and death, and most people will be well aware of it's presence before then, while CO or carbon monoxide is deadly at concentrations of less than 1 percent and can reach a toxic level without many people even noticing. The early symptoms of carbon monoxide poisoning are headache, weakness, dizziness, impaired judgment and thinking abilities, nausea and passing out. IF YOU HAVE ANY OF THESE SYSTOMS GET FRESH AIR AT ONCE. Open some windows and go outside, if there are others in the home check on them and wake them up if they are "asleep". If you can not wake them, check to see if they are breathing. If they are not breathing move them to fresh air and perform CPR or Mouth-to-Mouth Resuscitation as we used to call it, and call 911.

The Myths and Realities of Carbon Monoxide Poisoning

You will often hear news reports of people dying from carbon monoxide poisoning due to trying to heat their home with a kitchen stove or space heaters and they will often tell you that those appliances produce carbon monoxide and should never be used to heat a home. This is not really true, for stoves and space heaters do not produce any carbon monoxide by design. Often times the carbon monoxide is blamed on a malfunctioning space heater or stove. The reality is that the appliance did not malfunction for they generally can't, yet there was carbon monoxide for a very simple reason. Carbon monoxide is the result of incomplete combustion, carbon "C" when burned or oxidized reacts and combines with two atoms of oxygen "O" to form "CO_2". The only reason carbon monoxide "CO" is formed with only one atom of oxygen instead of two, is that the second oxygen atom was not available. To produce CO there has to be a lack of oxygen. While this can happen in an enclosed combustion camber due to a blocked air intake, it can't happen with a open flame like on a stove burner or with open combustion type space heaters since they are surrounded by the oxygen in the air. Yet every year people are killed by carbon monoxide produced by these very appliances. What is happening is that in a well sealed room or house, as the appliance burns the fuel, it is turning oxygen "O" into carbon dioxide "CO_2" and unless fresh air is getting in from outside, the oxygen is being used up and replaced with carbon dioxide. The percentage of oxygen in the air in the house is dropping and as it drops, the fire is having a harder time getting oxygen. At some point once the available oxygen level has dropped low enough, the heater or stove will begin to produce carbon monoxide. So the appliance never malfunctioned, for there is nothing wrong with it, the problem is the lack of oxygen in the room. In Europe wall mounted vent less natural gas room heaters are common and yet nobody dies from carbon monoxide poisoning because the units automatically shut off if the oxygen level drops.   The secret to using any unvented heating source in a home is to ensure a source of fresh air. The best way of doing this is to use a carbon monoxide detector to warn you, if a build up is occurring. However most older homes are drafty enough that a kitchen gas stove can be used a round the clock without needing to open a window. I know of one fellow who is living proof of this, his furnace broke a few years back and he has been heating his duplex apartment ever since with his gas range. Therefore, in an emergency you can use your range as a heat source as long as your house is drafty enough. Though certainly not fool proof, one quick way of judging the air tightness of your home is whether the air in the house in the wintertime is dry or humid. Better air-sealed homes tend to have problems in the wintertime with excess humidly while drafty homes have dry air. But in the end it comes down to the amount of oxygen used compared to what is leaking in, without a CO detector, it maybe wise to open a window a half inch , near the stove to let in some air to ensure that there is enough oxygen for complete combustion.

One reason why some times people can safely use their gas range but are poisoned by carbon monoxide from using a space heater is the height of the range top. Carbon dioxide is a heavy gas and tends to fill a room from the floor up, and a space heater sitting on the floor will have less available oxygen than a range top at counter height. <u>Space heaters used indoors are safer if placed on a tabletop, rather than on the floor.</u> Another trick is to place the space heater in front of a window and open the window a small crack to allow for fresh air to the heater to prevent it from producing any carbon monoxide. The importance of avoiding carbon monoxide poisoning by ensuring fresh air for combustion is well illustrated by backpackers, who in cold weather sometimes heat their tent with a candle. What has happened is if the tent is covered by snow, the candle can use up the oxygen in the tent and as the level drops and the candle fame is starved for oxygen, it then produces carbon monoxide. People have died poisoned by the fumes from a mere candle in an enclosed space while in Europe rooms are safely heated by unvented natural gas heaters, and the only real difference is the availability of fresh air. As long as there is adequate oxygen for combustion, an open flame will not produce carbon monoxide.

Signs and Symptoms of CO2 and CO Poisoning

Since the production of carbon monoxide is often caused by a rise in carbon dioxide, the detection of carbon dioxide can be used to prevent the creation of carbon monoxide. The exception to this rule of course is enclosed heaters that can have a build up of carbon dioxide inside the unit, that you will not be able to notice.

Signs of increasing levels of carbon dioxide include headache, tiredness, shortness of breath, racing heartbeat and dizziness, which are all symptoms of a lack of oxygen like one gets at high altitudes with thin air.

The effects of Increasing Levels of Carbon Dioxide

At One Percent, carbon dioxide some people begin to feel sleepy.

At Two Percent, most people feel sleepy, a carbon dioxide smell is noticeable and you will start to breath more heavily.

At Three Percent, your rate of breathing doubles.

At Four Percent, your rate of breathing is four times normal.

At Five Percent, toxic levels are reached and people begin passing out and dying.

The symptoms of carbon monoxide poisoning are similar including headache, weakness, tiredness and confusion. Notice that a key difference is that carbon monoxide DOES NOT cause heavy breathing, that while carbon dioxide triggers our breathing response, carbon dioxide does not and this is why it is called the silent killer. With carbon monoxide, your body does not know that it is suffocating, for it does not detect it and respond to it, as it does to carbon dioxide. While with carbon dioxide, you would be desperately trying to breathe as fast as you can, with carbon monoxide your breathing slows as you slump into the sleep of death.

The effects of Increasing Levels of Carbon Monoxide

At 0.02 Percent, tiredness and nausea,

At 0.04 Percent, can be lethal in as little as three hours,

At 0.08 Percent, can be lethal is as little as two hours and can cause convulsions,

At 0.64 Percent, can be lethal in as little as a half hour and causes convulsions,

At 1.28 Percent, convulsions and death in as little as one minute.

These numbers above should really scare you if understand them. Carbon monoxide is lethal at levels that with carbon dioxide are harmless and are frequently reached. If carbon dioxide was as lethal as carbon monoxide, mankind never would have survived the invention of fire; in fact, our own respiratory exhalations would have done us in. While carbon dioxide is like a nearly harmless old toothless lion, carbon monoxide is a Velociraptor. Due to the lethalness of even low concentrations and the lack of detection by our respiratory system, carbon monoxide can sneak up on you, without you knowing it and spring at you suddenly with extreme deadly force. Survival depends on avoiding its attack by preventing it from being created, for a fire produces a lot of carbon dioxide and if this large volume of gas was carbon monoxide instead, you would be quickly dead. Even a small fire producing carbon monoxide can quickly fill a home to lethal levels. While the build up in carbon dioxide is a slow nuisance, if it is allowed to increase to a high enough level, it will result in a sudden burst of carbon monoxide that is a swift and silent killer. The good news is that fresh air quickly flushes carbon monoxide from the blood stream if the person is still breathing, and recovery is rapid.

You may have a built in carbon monoxide detector if you learn to pay attention to it. It has been noted that people exposed to carbon monoxide have chest pains or tightness in the chest and older middle-aged persons are more prone to this. I have noticed that merely driving in city traffic is enough to cause some tightness in my chest, and this is due to the carbon monoxide present in the air, and here all this time I had thought it was the frustration of driving in traffic that was doing it. So pay attention to any pain in your chest, it could be an early warning sign of carbon monoxide.

Portable Space heaters

You can heat a home with space heaters if you have enough of them. Remember the fellow that heated his duplex with a kitchen stove? The gal living upstairs in the other halve of the duplex with the broken furnace, heats her half to nearly 80 F degrees with a bunch of electric space heaters, so it can be done. (And you thought your electric bill was bad!) With electric space heaters, you do not have to worry about carbon dioxide or monoxide since there is no combustion or use of oxygen so you can keep the windows closed. The dangers of electric heaters are fire due to placing heaters to close to things that can catch fire or combustibles being placed on or over the heater. More than one fire has started because of an electric space heater being used in a bathroom and a towel falls off the towel rack or shower curtain and lands on the heater. Another cause is that the radiant heat can over time dry out wood or fabric, and then it can suddenly catch fire without warning. People are caught off guard because the hazard is not immediate, sort of a fire time bomb. The other big hazard with electric heaters is the cord and plug, which can overheat and catch fire. How this occurs is a loose or dirty electrical connection results in heat and sometimes even arcing. This can be avoided by feeling the cord after the heater has been running for a while to check for warm spots or soft plastic caused by heat, pay particular attention to the plug itself. The plug is the most frequent problem since it is the part exposed to the most wear due to plugging and unplugging. Sometimes the problem is the plug blades fail to make a firm connection with the outlet receptacle and this can be corrected often times by slightly bending the blades together slightly, so that when the plug is inserted into the receptacle, the blades press firmly against the conductors in the receptacle making a tight connection. The blades can also become blackened due to arcing or corroded which can be cleaned off with sandpaper, steel wool, a small file or an Emory nail file. The plug end can be replaced, as can the entire cord.

Non-electric space heaters like propane and kerosene get very hot, and are filled with a flammable liquid fuel and use oxygen and give off carbon dioxide. The biggest danger is fire, these heaters are even hotter than the electrical ones, but that is an obvious danger for, which most people have the sense to take precautions. It is the less obvious dangers such as failing to have adequate ventilation that sneaks up on people. While most homes are drafty enough, for safely using the kitchen stove for heat, a space heater can use a lot more oxygen than a stove, since it can be designed to burn fuel at a higher rate to produce a lot of heat quickly. The more heat a combustion heater produces, the more fuel and oxygen it is burning. Space heaters should be used with caution and attention should be paid to the amount of fresh air entering the house to keep carbon dioxide levels from rising too high. If any of the symptoms of carbon dioxide poisoning occur, which was discussed earlier in this chapter, ventilation should be increased by opening windows or doors to allow in more air. Also, the space heaters should be placed where they can receive fresh air like in front of a slightly opened window or anywhere the air can flow freely and not in closets or back corners where the air could become stale. For if the heater is running in a stagnant pool of its own exhaust of carbon dioxide, the reduction in available oxygen will result in the production of deadly carbon monoxide. Since carbon dioxide is a heavy gas and tends to collect on the floor, a space heater is safer if placed on a table in the middle of a room or in front of a window that is opened a crack rather than on the floor in a corner.

For obvious reasons portable space heaters should only be refueled outside the home and should be allowed to cool down first to avoid fuel vapors from being touched off by a hot surface.

The Use of Charcoal Grills Indoors

Don't.

Some people actually have been known to do this and here is the reason why you shouldn't. Charcoal like coal is a pile of closely fitting pieces of burning carbon, and due to the way it is packed together, there is often a lack of oxygen in some of these tight spaces in the pile, which results in the production of carbon monoxide. While in a vented coal furnace or an outdoor grill this not dangerous, inside a home the carbon monoxide can rapidly collect to lethal levels since it can kill at concentrations as low as 0.04 percent. If you are in a situation that you feel that you have to do this, set up an emergency wood stove as outlined below and use it to burn your charcoal or coal. Vent the exhaust gases at all costs, to avoid killing yourself. If you are really cold and don't have a way of venting the smoke, sit by your grill fire outside and live longer.

Other Sources of Emergency Heat

If you have a fireplace, you can get some heat by burning a fire, but with only 15% efficiency, you will need nearly an endless supply of wood to even attempt to heat this way.

If you have gas but no electricity, and you have a gas hot water heater that has a standing pilot light, (this type has no electrical power connected to it) and you have a city water supply instead of a well, your water heater will still work and you should still have water pressure, so you can fill the bath tub with hot water and sinks and containers as well. The hot water as it cools will give off some heat and may help to keep the house warm. Once the water cools to about air temperature, drain and refill with hot water.

If you have no electricity but have gas, and you have a heating unit with a standing pilot light, there is a trick you can do to get some heat. The blower on furnaces or the pumps on boilers need 110 volts to run, but the thermostat circuit only needs 12 or 24 volts to run. If you remove the transformer wires from the 110 volt supply wiring and connect them to a backup power supply outlet (these units have a battery that supplies 110 volts and is often used for computers so data is not lose when the power goes out), the heating unit will run. What will happen is that the voltage will open the gas valve and the main burner will run until the high temperature limit is reached which will turn the gas valve off until the temperature drops back down below the cut in temperature. This will result in heat in the heating unit, but no blower fan or pump to move it to where it is needed. If you remove the filter in furnaces and open any control valves on boilers, the heat will rise and supply some heat to the house. While not enough to keep the house as warm as what you would like, it still is better than nothing and may be enough to keep the pipes from freezing.

The Really Desperate Heating Tricks

These heat tricks are strictly the sort of emergency last resort that will probably do some damage and may burn your house down unless you are very careful. But if you are given the choice of either doing something dumb, or watching your family freeze to death, here is what you can do and how you can hopefully do it so you don't burn the place down.

Here in Milwaukee in the inter city are fine old homes built with a lot of decorative wood work and some renters who don't have gas heat due to not paying the bill, have been known to strip the wood work and burn it in the gas furnace. Shockingly you can burn wood in an old gas or oil furnace if the firebox is on a concrete floor. We are talking really old furnaces, with cast iron heat exchangers and natural draft. The burners and the front baffle plate are removed, the wood is placed on the concrete floor and a fire is lighted. The smoke goes up the natural draft stovepipe and chimney, and the air heated in a furnace or even water in a boiler, will rise because it is hot and will heat the rooms above to a degree, even if the electricity is off. The danger is that the furnace was never designed to burn wood and the wood fire may do great damage to the heat exchanger and other parts on the furnace. The chimney may not even be rated for the hotter exhaust gases from a wood fire, and may get hot enough to light something near it on fire or even fail all together. A better and much safer method is so install an emergency wood stove.

The Emergency Wood Stove

Many building supply stores sell wood stoves as a sideline and they often sell a cheap little cast iron stove for cabins for about $100 or $200 dollars or maybe you can find an old wood stove lying around. Place the stove on patio blocks or bricks in front of a window, and run stovepipe out the window and above the edge of the roof. Keep the stove at least two feet away from everything including the wall behind it. Close the hole in the open window with sheet metal, cut a hole for the pipe, or fit some old cookie sheets around the stove pipe and plug any gaps with unfaced fiberglass insulation. The stove pipe chimney can get very hot and needs to be at least 18 inches away from any wood or anything else that can burn and even greater clearances will be needed for anything that can melt like vinyl. Since few windows will be large enough to allow for such large clearances, use stove pipe that has reduced clearances like Double wall stove pipe that only needs 6 inches. To save on costs you only need one piece of reduced clearance pipe for going through the window opening, the rest can be run in regular single wall. Of course it is far better and safer to connect the stove flue pipe to a thimble in a chimney. If you have a heating unit with a metal flue pipe connected to chimney that can handle a wood stove, you can disconnect the flue and connect it to the emergency wood stove. Some of the small cabin stoves may have a flue pipe small enough to use the thimble for a gas water heater. Just remember to turn off the gas or fuel valve so someone else cannot turn it back on once the power or gas is back on. You can also sit the emergency stove in or in front of a fireplace and run the flue pipe up through the damper. Then close the damper against the flue pipe and block the damper opening on each side of the flue with sheet metal or unfaced fiberglass insulation. The stove will give off 3 to 4 times as much heat as the fireplace would from the same amount of wood.

A small cast iron stove with a hot fire in it can really put out a lot of heat and can heat a room or two and keep the pipes from freezing. Anything dry that burns can go in the stove in an emergency. Split fire wood is the first choice of course, but you can burn anything made of wood, wood chips, wood pellets, bark; plus peat, paper, cardboard, corn, dry agriculture waste like corn cobs and wheat straw, dry grass, autumn leaves, paper, junk mail and bill collection notices. If the stove has a grate you can burn charcoal and possibly coal, though coal will over heat a grate made only for wood burning. Check the chapter on wood burning for wood stove installation details and operation.

The Emergency Heat Shelter

Assuming that you are trapped in a freezing cold home, this is what you can do. Pick an interior room with no outside walls if possible for your shelter and hang thick blankets or quilts over the doorways. If you have electricity, heat the room with an electric space heater or propane or kerosene if you don't have electricity, but be careful not to let the heater get too close to anything that can burn and allow for ventilation for fresh air to the heater to prevent a build up of carbon dioxide in the room. If you do not have space heaters, you can heat the room with body heat if you have enough bodies in a well enough insulated room, call the dog in for some extra heat. Lay rugs or carpet on the floor for insulation to keep the heat from escaping that way. You can also increase the insulation in the room by placing temporary insulation against the inside walls, such as by hanging blankets on the walls as they used to hang tapestries in drafty old castles for warmth. Other things can also be placed against the walls for insulation such as mattresses, which often have fairly good insulation qualities, while box springs, which are normally underneath mattresses, do not. If you are just one or two people and you are losing too much heat to keep the room warm, you can use mattresses to make a mini shelter. Lay one against an interior wall in the corner, and then place another on the floor against it. Then lay another one on edge on the other side, and place a fourth mattress on top for a roof. Hang blankets over the open end, and the other open end should be against the wall. Place a blanket like blocking a draft over the joint between the mattress and the wall. Two adults should be able to fit inside in a nest of blankets inside the shelter and stay warm even if it is below zero inside the home. At least you should be able to get a warm night's sleep. While this shelter fits two people, it takes four mattresses to make, you can cut it to three by using a box spring against the wall, but it will not be as insulating.

A more effective shelter is to make a box out of 4 by 8 foot sheets of foam. Make a 4-foot square box eight foot long lying on its side using four sheets of foam with one open end against the wall and the other covered with blankets. Tape the sheets together along the edges to hold them together and to seal out the cold air. You can use a half sheet at each end, but for air ventilation, do not tape the end you use as a door. If you have more sheets you can build a larger shelter, but keep it small enough and tight enough, that it can be heated by the body heat of the persons inside it, as sort of a mini super insulated house. If you have enough foam sheets, you could line the ceiling, walls and floor of your room with enough layers of foam to have a super insulated shelter room. If you wanted to set up something like this in advance for future possible use, by code the foam will need to be covered by half an inch of drywall or cement board to reduce the risk and rate of spread of any potential fire.

You may already have a sort of emergency heat shelter if you have a root cellar or a deep basement room. Once you get below the frost level, the ground never freezes and deeper down the ground is at a constant temperature year round. Caves often have year round temperatures in the range of 65 F in the south, to 55 in the north in the USA. A well-constructed root cellar will have the same temperature as a cave and while 55 F degrees is cold, it is a lot better than sub zero temperatures. With warm clothing and bedding, you could take shelter in a root cellar as long as you have enough air to breath. Root cellars are not designed for habitation and often have no provision for fresh air other than opening the door when you enter. While too much ventilation will turn the root cellar into a freezer, a small amount is all you need which can be gained by closing the door against a narrow piece of lumber or a small stick to keep open a small gap for air flow.

When you Cannot Afford to pay the Fuel Bill

If you cannot afford to pay the bill for the amount of heat you are using, you probably need to reduce your heating costs immediately while spending little or no money to do so. The first thing is to turn down the thermostat since about each degree of reduction is a 3% reduction in your bill. If you were to drop your thermostat from 70 to 50 F, would be about a 60% reduction in your bill, of course the house would be pretty cold. The compromise is to use a setback thermostat that reduces the temperature at night or when you are away. Setback thermostats are inexpensive with some costing less than $30, but if you cannot afford that, you can turn the heat down yourself at night and turn it back up in the morning and do the same when you leave and come back. The problem with doing it manually is that setback thermostats have an anticipation circuit that turns on the heat in advance of when the heat is needed so that by the set time, the house is back up to temperature, so in the morning when you get up the house is already warm. If you are doing it yourself, even after you turn up the heat, it may take a few hours for the temperature to rise to the desired setting.

There are other things you can do are to reduce your heat losses so you need less heat, look over the suggestions in chapter 4 about insulation and other energy saving tips. A cheap way of saving heat is to reduce heat loss through windows, by hanging blankets over the curtains to insulate the windows, especially at night when it is colder. You can gain some free passive solar heat by opening the curtains when the sun will shine in the window, but leaving curtains closed on windows in the shade. Then there is laying a folded towel across the bottom of the outside doors and on the inside of windows to block drafts.

Some people to reduce wintertime fuel bills stack straw bales outside against the house walls. My parents always used to put a couple of bales against the wall outside the kitchen sink to keep the drain from freezing. Some just stack the bales to cover the uninsulated basement walls; others stack them higher to cover the first floor walls as well. I don't have to tell you how dumb this looks and what rotting wet straw can do to wood siding, and what can happen if dry straw bales happen to be lit on fire. This old time trick, also only works if the bales are tight against the outside wall, if air can flow between the wall and the bales, it is as if the bales are not even there. You are certainly much better off to insulate the house, but in a pinch, straw bales can be a temporary short term fix to get you through a cold winter.

Aggressive Zone Heating

Turn off the heat to some rooms that do not have plumbing in them or in their walls that could freeze. The heat can be shut off by blocking heat vents, valving off hydronic branch lines (remember to drain the line), turning off electric baseboards or turning off fans in fan powered radiators. Move everyone into the living room and turn the heat off in the bedrooms, and only heat the "core" of the house such as one bathroom, living room and the kitchen. The plumbing in any unheated bathroom wall would need the water drained of course if the room will get cold enough to freeze. You need water in the toilet and sink drains as a water seal to keep sewer gases from entering the home, to keep a seal in sub-freezing room temperatures, use non-freezing liquids for the seal. After the lines and toilet tank are drained, empty the toilet bowl by pouring in a pail of water, which will flush most of the water out of the bowel. The last of the water can be removed by using a rag as a mop, to soak up the water and wring the rag cover a pail. Then fill the bowl with enough non-freezing liquid to cover the bowl exit. Some non-freezing liquids you can use are various cooking oils like vegetable oil or olive oil, which will jell but will not freeze and crack the bowl like water would. The traps in sink drains can be flushed of water by pouring in enough oil to displace the water from the trap.

Emergency Insulation

This is how to reduce your heating losses in a hurry. Insulate the attic with cellulose or fiberglass blown in insulation, cellulose is quite an inexpensive insulation and both types are quick and easy to do, and free rental of the blower is often included with the purchase of the insulation. Once the heat losses in the ceiling are reduced, insulate the walls. A quick and dirty way of doing this is to line the inside of the exterior walls with 2 inch thick foam sheeting boards. Press them up against as much of the outside walls as you can, secure with furniture, temporary trim board, a few foam board nails or some foam glue. Trim to fit around windows or go right over if you want. Use the foam sheeting temporally until you can do a proper installation job. Legally foam insulation, since it can burn, is required by be covered by a fire stop material like a half inch of drywall, if exposed in the living space. A more acceptable way of insulating wall, is if the wall has no insulation or has empty spaces in the wall due to having too little insulation, is that cellulose can be blown inside the walls through 2 inch diameter holes drilled from the outside or inside, with two holes for each space between walls studs.

Windows are where you lose a lot of heat, in a pinch; you can put foam sheeting plugs over windows. Doors also have little insulation, glue foam to the outside of doors to reduce heat loss or you can hang blankets over doors and windows. Is your basement or crawl space warm? Then you are losing heat, to save energy, line the inside of the basement outside walls with foam or insulate the house floor.

There are millions of little tricks you can use to save a bit of heat here and there, put your mind to it and you can probably come up with a few I missed. As good as these tricks can be in a pinch, it is better to have a well insulated and weather stripped home with a back up heat source so that you do not have to use them.

Chapter 20

Keeping Cool

While heat is a necessity, air conditioning is still regarded as a luxury and understandably so. While in many places the chill of winter is nothing less than deadly, even in the hottest places, cooling off can be as simple as opening the windows. Life however is not always as simple as that. While visiting my in-laws in San Jose who don't have air conditioning, it got into the nineties which is uncomfortable, but I noticed that inside the house even with the windows open, the temperature was hot enough to make you feel unwell. Every year people die in heat waves in temperatures that in themselves are not that dangerous. The problem is that many houses act like solar ovens that bake their occupants to death, unless constantly cooled by expensive air conditioning. While even a greenhouse on a hot sunny day could be air conditioned to a comfortable temperature, if equipped with a truly massive air conditioner, I would not want to have to pay the electric bill. While air conditioning does cool, it does so at a high cost in electricity, the trick is to reduce the amount of cooling needed so that either air conditioning is not needed or very little is needed to keep the indoor temperature in the comfort zone.

The first trick is to keep the house from getting hot in the first place is by having a cool roof. The common asphalt shingle roof gets as hot as an asphalt road on a hot sunny day, and that heat is conducted through the roof deck and is then radiated into the attic space below, which is why attics are so hot in the summer time. If another sort of roofing material is used such as wood, tile or a light colored metal roof, far less heat is absorbed by the roof since much more of the light is bounced off the roof rather than being absorbed as heat. Ample attic ventilation, particularly with large vents in gable ends that allows for cross ventilation, will let the heat be blown out of the attic instead of heating the rooms below. It should be remembered however that drafts in the attic in winter time could reduce the effectiveness of loose insulation by blowing the cold air through the insulation. Some homes also use an electric attic fan, that when the temperature in attic reaches a hot enough temperature turn on and blow the heat out of the attic. My Father-in-law has one so it is often times not enough in itself to keep the house cool and requires electricity to work. Having a good amount of attic insulation will reduce keep heat in the attic from heating the room below and will of course reduce your heating bills in the winter time as well, so good attic insulation pays for itself in summer time as well as winter time. Of course I just have to figure out how to convince my thrifty minded father-in-law who lives in California, that he should increase his attic insulation to stay cool in the summer time, his more economical solution to the problem, is to hang out at the local air conditioned library on hot days.

Proper landscaping to stay comfortable is a trick that most people miss these days. The ideal basic landscaping is to have a row of evergreen trees on the north side of the house to block the cold north winds in the winter and leafy trees on the other three sides. The way this works is that the leafy trees shade the house through the summer days and then when the leaves fall, the house is warmed by the sun in cold weather. Shading by trees makes an enormous difference, and a forest can even cool the air temperature by about 3 degrees F by the evaporation of water from the leaves. Windows are probably only second to the roof for heating up the house. Better designed homes have eaves on the south side of the house that shade the windows in the summer and let the sun in in winter. Homes that lack this feature can have it by installing aluminum awnings sized properly. Windows on the east and west where direct sunlight will shine in underneath an overhang can have a reflective film applied inside that will block the heat. Such films will reduce the amount of light entering and will block the heat from the sun in winter however as well as in the summer. Blocking the east and west sunlight from windows is really best done by leafy trees since they will block the hot sun in summer but let the warmth in when you need it. I once had a work shop with three large windows on the east side that had an overgrown tree that blocked most of the windows and stayed cool most of the day. Then someone over trimmed the tree and the windows had full sun for most of the morning, and the work shop got too hot to work in by 10 AM. Proper window treatments in terms of white backed curtains, shades and blinds can also do much to reduce window heat gain and help to keep cool air conditioned air away from glass that is heated by the hot outside air.

In the winter time you lose most of your heat through the ceiling while in the summer time you lose most of your cold air conditioned air through the walls, because while warm air rises, cold air sinks. At most, grocery stores they used to have open chest freezers that kept the cold air in them like water in a bucket. Like a bucket of water, an air conditioned house is filled with heavy cold air that will try to drain out the bottom of the house. While for heating, the attic door loses the most heat, with air conditioning the big loser can be the basement door. The cold air can flow down in the basement chilling it, instead of the rooms above. The cold air sinks to the floor and can flow underneath the basement door and outside doors as well, weather stripping is just as important in the summer for air conditioning as it is for heating in the winter time.

Natural air conditioning that does not require electricity is possible, to experience it take a tour of a local cave. The ground temperature a few feet below the surface remains cool even in the summer time. Before the wide spread use of refrigerators, people used root cellars to keep food in, the natural coolness of the ground extended the storage life of many foods. Basements are often cool refuges on hot summer days. Some people remove the access door on their furnace in the basement and tape down the door switch and run the blower fan so that cold basement air is drawn into the open access door and is blown through the heating ducts into the rooms upstairs. They leave the basement door open so the return air flow is through the basement back to the furnace. Neat trick, but there is only so much cold in a basement and most homes will have more heat upstairs than there is cold in the basement. However if the house is heavily insulated so that less cooling is needed, there maybe enough coolness in some basements for this trick to keep a home cool.

The coolness of a basement can be enhanced by some proper insulation to keep the summer heat out. Concrete and cement block walls act like heat sinks as they absorb heat and conduct it into the cooler ground below. If the outside surface of the basement walls is covered with two inches or more of foam insulation boards from the top of the wall down to a few feet below the ground surface, the basement wall will be insulated from the summer heat and will absorb most of its heat from the basement. I recently insulated the upper half of my house's basement walls like this, and the basement became noticeably cooler, so much cooler that we now sometimes have condensation on the basement floor, which we did not have before. Basement windows can be insulated by covering the glass with one-inch thick pieces of white foam board, which will insulate very well while still allowing a fair amount of light to enter. The spaces between the floor joists along the outside walls should be well insulated with fiberglass or some other insulation. Any outside basement doors should be weather stripped and insulated. By insulating the basement, it will stay cooler in the summer and warmer in the winter making you more comfortable all year round and saving energy.

For houses without basements that are built on concrete slabs, insulating the outside edge of the slab can prevent the summer heat from heating the slab below the house and prevent the heat in the winter from being drawn out through the slab and exiting below the insulation in the wall. Foam board insulation can be installed by digging a narrow trench along side the outside wall down to the top of the footing, or at least a foot below the ground surface. If there is no footing, just dig down to the lower edge of the slab, be careful not to undermine the slab by loosing any dirt or gravel beneath it.

For homes that are built above ground, the floor should be heavily insulated. A home with an elevated uninsulated wood floor deck where the air can flow underneath, will gain the most heat in the summer through the floor. The spaces between the floor joists should be filled with insulation and in most areas, additional insulation will need to be added below the floor joists for a sufficient R-value in the heating season.

The biggest cooling trick is to have a well-insulated house shaded from the sun that will stay cool for most of the day. Then in the evening when the temperature drops, open a window on one end of the house and place a fan to blow the air out, and open a window at the other end of the house to let cool air in. I do this one myself, and it works fantastic. I put a window fan in the kitchen window for blowing air out and then open a window in each bedroom where I want cool air to enter. This way the noisy fan is at the opposite end of the house from where you are trying to sleep, and cool night air is silently drawn in your bedroom window and as it flows over your bed, it being cooler than the room air will flow down on to the bed. Generally, I find myself pulling up the covers at some time during the night. The only problem with this trick is sometimes it stays hot at night, but it works most of the time.

When I was staying at my in-laws house without any air conditioning, we made good use of a ceiling fan to sleep at night. Even when the temperature was too warm for me to sleep, turning on the ceiling fan on, made it feel much cooler, so much so, that I generally slept with a blanket. Often times a fan can make hot temperatures bearable. The reason this trick works is that our bodies cool by radiating heat from our skins and by evaporation of water. A fan moving the air across the surface of your skin blows the heat off your skin like a fan on a car radiator and speeds the evaporation of water. However if the air is very humid, a fan will do less for increasing vaporization since the air is already saturated with moisture. Fans also only work as long as the air is cooler than you are, once the air is hotter than you, the fan warms instead of cooling. Since human body temperature is normally 98.6 F, once the temperature reaches 100 F fans do little and may even make you feel hotter. At temperatures above 100 F, using a fan is like using a fan on a car radiator to blow hot exhaust gas through the radiator instead of cool air, which will heat rather than cooling, increasing the fan speed will only increase the heating effect. This is why fans should not be relied on as your only means of keeping cool.

One of the very simple ways of staying cool that some people over look is to leave the oven off on hot days. Summer is not the best time for baking a turkey. Some times you may be able to cook in the microwave instead, which will generate a lot less heat. A trick my mother uses is to cook outside with a Nesco, which is an electric roaster oven that plugs into a regular outlet. Sort of like an oversized slow cooker, a Nesco lets my mother cook a ham for Sunday dinner with the family, without heating up the house. If you have a screened in porch, you could set up an electric hot plate and have an outdoor kitchen instead of overheating the house or overworking the air conditioner. Another appliance that can heat up the house is a dishwasher, especially models with electric drying elements. I have always wondered why dishwashers do not have exhaust vents, but they do not, so in hot weather you may want to consider hand washing and drying. Turning off unused items that generate heat like plasma TV's and other electronic devices and lights will also help. Switching from incandescent lights to fluorescent lights can keep you cooler as well as saving electricity since fluorescent lights generate far less heat than do incandescent lights.

There is another way of staying cool that works, but is really out there. The system consists of burying several hundred feet of pipe, 6 feet or more underground and using a fan or natural convection to pull in air through the pipes. The pipe chilled to ground temperature will cool the incoming air to nearly the same temperature. The problem is of course, that the cost of installing this system is large and the air coming out of the pipe can be rather musty and the pipes can be flooded by high ground water levels.

There is a rather simple air conditioner that is 80% cheaper to operate than conventional units; these wonder machines are called evaporative coolers. How they work is by using water to wet pads in front of a fan, the fan blows the air through the pads, which evaporates the water cooling the pad, which in turn cools the air. In direct evaporative cooling units, hot air is turned into cool moist air. While indirect units use a heat exchanger so that no moisture is added to the inside air. Pretty nifty, now for the downside. Evaporative coolers only work well in hot dry climates like in the southwestern United States and northern Mexico. The reason for this is that since an evaporative cooler works by evaporation, it can only lower the air temperature down to near the wet bulb temperature. The wet bulb temperature is the lowest temperature that can be reached by the cooling effect of evaporating water. Under dry air conditions, the wet bulb temperature is quite a bit lower than the air temperature, but as the humidity level rises, the web bulb temperature rises until at 100% humidity; it is equal to the air temperature. What this means is that evaporative cooling does not cool unless the air is dry. If you live in a hot desert, an evaporative cooler is for you, but if you have summer time humidity, forget it.

Now we come to air conditioners, which if you have properly insulated and weather stripped your home and shaded it, you will not need to run very much. I have a window air conditioner (12,000 BTU) that I use to cool our entire home (1000 sq ft), since the house needs little cooling to stay cool on hot days. If the other end of the house gets hot, I turn on the furnace blower to move the air around the house and I find that works quite well. The reason I went with a window air conditioner is that it would be quite expensive to have a central air system installed and with the restrictions on handling refrigerants, I would not be able to service it myself. While with the window unit, I could install it myself and if it breaks, I can replace it for less than the cost of having a central unit serviced. So far, I have used the window unit for 10 years and it still works fine. On the other hand, central units if installed right, are more efficient to operate and you do not have to have a big metal box sticking out of one of your windows that you have to lug in and out of the basement every year. But honestly, I find the window unit a hands down winner. If you need more than one air conditioner to cool your house, you probably should insulate and shade your house more. Before I increased the insulation on the house walls, I needed more than one window air conditioner and was looking at adding one in each bedroom for a total of four, but once I insulated, one was enough. I did find that having a window air conditioner in the bedroom can really keep you up at nights, so be sure to find a very quiet model if you plan on doing so. (The reviews on Amazon are handy for this)

I find with my house, that I can go most of the summer with no air conditioning. At first, I open the windows and as the weather warms, I close up the house in hot weather and ventilate at night with a fan. Then when it is too hot for that, I turn on the air conditioner. As a result, in some summers here in Wisconsin, I may only have the air on for less than a week out of the whole summer. Of course then there are summers where it is on for over a month.

A fellow I know told me how when he worked at a place that sold window air conditioners that they would take old "broken" units as trade ins, then they would clean the filter and coils and resell them as refurbished since a good cleaning was often all they needed. I remember one time staying at a inexpensive hotel with a window air conditioner that did not work. I pulled the filter that had enough lint on it that it looked like a blanket and cleaned it in the bathroom sink and the unit then worked great. So very often AC units are laboring away failing to cool properly while wasting as much as half their energy due to dirty air filters or a dirty coil. So keep your AC electric bills down by regularly cleaning the air filter and cleaning the coils every year or two as needed. (for how to clean coils see Pages 49-50)

It seems to me that you have been dozing off a bit in this chapter so I have decided to have a **HEAT EMERGENCY DRILL**. Don't panic, this is only a drill, but let's pretend that it is forecasted for the temperature to reach 115 F today and the power just went out, what do you do? With there being no electric power, my Father-in-law's trick of hanging out in the library isn't going to work, so what are you going to do, once you are done eating the melting ice cream from the freezer? The reason I ask is that you should have a plan. Now I would expect for some emergency cooling centers powered by generators to be set up, but I would also expect them to be over crowded, if they have them, and they may not. If there is no air conditioning, and no fans, which would not help in such heat any way, you are going to have to find another way of keeping cool. Ideally, you would be best off in a nice cool cave until the heat wave blows over. Like most people, I do not have a cave, but I do have a basement that thanks to some good insulation can stay cool in hot weather and I should be able to ride out the heat downstairs. Now many people do not have a basement, but what about a root cellar? You could build a root cellar and use it for storing vegetables, a storm shelter, a fallout shelter, and an emergency heat shelter. Lacking such underground retreats, a well insulated shaded house if buttoned up before the heat hits can stay cool for a while, hopefully until it cools off in the evening. Before it gets hot, close all the windows and doors and close all the curtains and turn off everything that gives off heat in the house in the early morning to trap and keep the cool morning air in the house. My experience has been that I can close the house up and ride out the first day of heat wave, but if it stays hot at night I will need the AC the second day. By having a good indoor thermometer and an outdoor one, you can monitor the difference and once the house is about as hot as it is outside, you can at least open the windows and enjoy whatever breeze there is. An old trick is to take a cold shower. Your town's water system should have it's own generators and should still be able to supply water in a power outage, if you have your own well, you will only have what you have in your pressure tank and once the pressure is bled down the water will stop so you will have to use it wisely. If it is extremely hot outside, the air will probably be dry, which means evaporative cooling methods should work quite well. Simple tricks like wetting your clothing with water can cool you down, and wet blankets or sheets can hung by or over open windows and doors to cool the air as it enters the house. If you have water pressure, a sprinkler can be placed on the roof and used to cool the roof by evaporation so that the house is far less heated by the sun heating the roof.

I will sound the all clear and end our little drill. It was a worst-case scenario but extreme hot weather has been known to cause blackouts as the power system is overloaded by everyone turning on their air conditioners. I find that it pays to have a back up plan, like in the drill above; it would have been handy to have a window air conditioner that could have been plugged into a gas generator. Of course, the trick in a power outage is to keep the generator from growing legs, since they are in such demand and loudly advertise their location when in use. A whisper quiet muffler would be a discreet option to have on a portable generator to reduce the risk of "disappearance".

I hope that I have made you think a bit about how to stay cool. Rather than just muddling through, you will do much better to think ahead and take steps now to insulate and shade your home, so in the future you will be cooler and need far less air conditioning. Which will save you plenty of money on air conditioning costs and maybe save your bacon from frying too.

Index